Hunting
SUPERBUCKS

Hunting
SUPERBUCKS

How to Find and Hunt Today's Trophy Mule and Whitetail Deer

Kathy Etling

The Lyons Press

Dedication

To all deer hunters everywhere
and especially to
Bob and Julie

Contents

Foreword

When *Hunting Superbucks* was originally published in 1989, it rode a wave of interest that would profoundly alter the hunting world. Whitetail fever was racing across America, infecting just about everyone with a sporting inclination. At the same time, more folks than ever headed for camps across the West in a quest for mule deer. Deer hunting was hot.

That enthusiasm, however, was not matched by an equal degree of know-how. Legions of newcomers sought help wherever it could be found while seasoned deer-camp veterans were hungry for answers that could turn their luck around. What was available in the sporting press at the time seemed only to whet the collective appetite for something greater. Into that void stepped *Superbucks,* a veritable epic of deer-hunting instruction unlike anything that had preceded it. From the first pages it was evident that the author, Kathy Etling, was not just another avid deer hunter who could spin a yarn, but was, in fact, a skilled researcher and journalist. It was a marked change in a genre that had previously offered mostly personal soapboxes ranging from useful mentoring to bald braggadocio.

Etling, meanwhile, demonstrated plenty of been-there, done-that expertise, but took her work to another level by integrating the insight of dozens of other authorities, from crack deer hunters to biologists to trophy club representatives, and others.

Furthermore, this book challenged deer hunters (even while capitalizing on a primary source of their passion) to focus solely on "superbucks"—the oldest, most elusive, and most impressive members of their race. No longer would it be enough simply to be the first among one's group to tag his or her buck. Etling made it clear that much more than random chance could govern who would take a rare, prized superbuck.

This updated and vastly expanded edition of *Hunting Superbucks* benefits from all the information about trophy hunting that has been amassed in the past dozen years. The fact that Kathy Etling has been able to freshen this seminal work proves once again that she is the consummate outdoor writer/reporter.

Those of us who have been fans of her frequent contributions to our favorite periodicals will take special joy from this work, which is unfettered by the inherent limitations of magazine articles. Here we find a writer with loads to share, the result of which is a living reference to study and consult with each coming season. Readers are lucky that Etling and The Lyons Press have undertaken renewal of what already was among the best of its kind. We will be better deer hunters for it.

John Zent
Editor, *American Hunter*
January 28, 2001

Preface

I must be honest: I'm addicted to deer hunting. I got into trouble when I was 19 years old, the first time I went afield in my native Missouri. In those days, any whitetail was fair game, and I was lucky enough to take a large doe my first time out. That doe was the beginning of a lifetime interest in the mule and whitetail deer.

Once I'd taken my fair share of does, my interest naturally turned to antlers. My first buck was a tiny seven point, but in my mind he was the Number 1-scoring deer in a new record book: my superbuck record book. That's how proud of those antlers I was. I was hooked!

From that season on, I tried to take a buck that was a little bit bigger each time I went hunting. By studying and learning from the hunting experiences I had—and from other, more experienced hunters—I figured I could gradually take bigger and better racks, maybe even someday a record-class trophy. The experiences I've had as I've bagged my 165-point whitetails and several 180-point mule deer have convinced me that hunting superbucks is an art and a science. And it can be learned. I've found there are people out there who really know what it takes to outsmart the deer we call "superbucks"—the bigger, harder-hunted, and smarter prime bucks that exist in almost every hunting area. Best of all, they're willing to talk with good, ambitious deer hunters about how they approach hunting for big bucks. These are the people I've asked to help you turn your quest for a superbuck into a reality. The advice from their lifetimes of big buck hunting is in your hands: *Hunting Superbucks.*

The fact is that nearly every deer hunter alive is a lot like me: each of us lives for the moment when we will walk up on a truly awesome buck we've just downed and think, "This one's in the book!" Whether that deer's rack actually makes the record book or not, the point is that superbuck hunting is a natural progression for a dedicated deer hunter. To the thrill of the hunt, you can add the hope of someday seeing your names in the *"Who's Who"* of deer hunting: the record books of the Pope and Young, Boone and Crockett, Buckmasters, and Safari Clubs, and the other state and regional record books.

The passion for big antlers is a true hunting impulse, and it takes lots of forms we can see on the hunting scene today. Clubs like the Mule Deer Foundation have been formed to represent deer hunters' interest in protecting quality deer hunting by dispensing information to its members and some portion of its revenues to deer research organizations. The researchers, in turn, are unravelling the mysteries of deer genetics, nutrition, and antler growth that will further good deer management.

This interest in trophy antlers has also created a network of big buck information sources. Magazines like *Deer and Deer Hunting, North American Whitetail,* and *Buckmasters* have evolved from the fascination with whitetail superbucks. Superbuck hunters like Dick Idol and Gene Wensel take to the lecture circuit. Hunters line up to buy or rent big buck hunting videos. Buck-o-ramas, the Buckmaster Classic, Whitetail Extravaganzas, and regional deer shows allow deer hunters to mingle with their peers, ogle the record book heads, and hear hunting experts expound on a bewildering variety of trophy topics.

Until now there has never been a book dedicated to the regular-season hunters who want to raise their sights from "get-your-deer"-style hunting to getting *the* deer—the big, smart prime buck in your own home hunting area. I figured the time was right for a book that spelled out for us the techniques and strategies the top deer hunters use. Here it is, as I've learned it myself, and in the super-bucks hunters' own words. They won't help you choose a bow or sight in your rifle or the other basics of our sport, but they will give you a glimpse of really *big* antlers in your favorite deer covers—guaranteed.

Interviewing these experts and researchers for this book was probably the most interesting indoor hunting experience I'll ever have. I firmly believe that my chances of taking a true superbuck have improved because of what they've told me, and I hope that when you finish the book you'll feel the same way.

Kathy Etling

Acknowledgments

Writing this book was a tremendous undertaking involving many different people from over the country. Their help was invaluable to me in many different ways. Without them, this book would never have become a reality.

First I would like to thank the late Clare Conley, who was editor-in-chief of *Outdoor Life* magazine. Clare bought my very first article, which really helped encourage me in my career as an outdoor writer.

Next, I'd like to thank all the deer researchers whose help and expert advice was so invaluable. Drs. Harry Jacobson, Larry Marchinton, Robert Brown, Richard Mackie, and Valerius Geist were always accessible and willing to help this non-biologist out.

The superbuck hunters who shared their hunting strategies with me, even though they had books in print at the same time, are certainly very special people in my book. Many thanks to Gene Wensel, Bob McGuire, Russell Hull, Kirt Darner, and Jay Gates.

I'd also like to thank Dick McCabe of the Wildlife Management Institute for all his welcome advice plus permission to reprint one of the illustrations contained in this book. And without the unbelievable amount of information I was able to gather from the two fantastic Institute books, *White-Tailed Deer, Ecology and Management* and *Mule and Black-Tailed Deer of North America,* my book would have taken much longer to complete and been much less informative.

Staff members of the various record-keeping organizations that were of special help include Hal Nesbitt of Fair Chase, Jack Reneau of the Boone and Crockett Club, Randy Byers and Kevin Hisey of the Pope and Young Club, and Russell Thornberry of the Buckmasters Trophy Record System.

I appreciate the interviews with many other hunting authorities as well: Gordon Blay, Gordon Whittington, Bob Zaiglin, Murry Burnham, Maury Jones, Jay Verzuh, Frank Hough, Bob Adamson, Lee Frudden, Ted Riggs, John Cole, Kelly Baird, Gorman Riley, Ernie Richardson, Stanley Potts, Jim Dougherty, Phil Kirkland, Alan Altizer, Jeff Brunk, and Bill Mundy each made my job easier.

Jim Straley was a big help in researching the chapter on mule deer migrations. And Dr. Jan Roth of Rimrock Taxidermy in Craig, Colorado, was a good source for the chapter on superbuck taxidermy. Jan's illustration of the caping procedure was also appreciated.

Jon Anderson was a great help in allowing me to hunt super muleys on what was once the Bolten Ranch in Wyoming. Now I hunt muleys in the same area thanks to Gene Carrico of Out West Safaris. And Dennis Smith, a retired game warden with the Wyoming Game and Fish Commission, really helped teach me about how a muley superbuck's mind works. Thanks as well to Benj Brown, Wyoming Game and Fish Warden, who has helped me out in many different ways and on many different occasions.

Colorado's Paul Gilbert sent me many interesting photographs of mule deer from which to choose.

And last but not least, I'd like to thank my editor on this book, Jay Cassell, for all the things that editors do, whatever they are!

Part 1

What Makes a Superbuck?

1

Antlers: How They Grow

I must have been very young when I first realized the strange, magical effect that antlers have on me. Whenever I saw a deer I'd pause to look a little closer, hoping to see antlers. Today, as a hunter, I still love to spot a deer sneaking silently along in the woods. And when that deer has antlers, it's the stuff my dreams are made of.

Hunters everywhere fall victim to the magical effect of antlers. We've named it "buck fever": that sudden, nervous failure to shoot straight—or shoot at all. It's never been called "*doe* fever." No, buck fever it is, and so it will remain until the end of time. And while most of us have taken does for one reason or another, the pride that we feel when we take a doe can't compare to the awe that one feels walking up on a downed buck. And if that buck just happens to be a superbuck—well, the emotions cannot adequately be described. As always, the things we hold most miraculous are those we can least explain.

Likewise, it's a paradox that many bucks escape the hunter *because* of their antlers. A mere glimpse of glistening white antlers through the grays and blacks of a hardwood forest sets many a heart to thumping within chests that are suddenly too small. Buck fever strikes! Your gun trembles; you can't seem to hold your sights steady on the target, much less pull the trigger. Your trophy walks away unscathed and antlers high. Even if you do manage to get off a miss, you've probably just taught the badly frightened buck another lesson, a lesson that will make him even tougher to take the next time around.

Ironically, the power of the antlers high atop the buck's skull seems to work its spell inside the *hunter's* head. I know. I've spent hours on my stand in the ultimate hunter's fantasy: I've imagined myself the deserving object of other hunters' envy as I brought my mythical record-book deer into the check station. In my daydream, other hunters crowd around, wanting to know how and where I got the monster of the county. I imagine reading news columns devoted to the incredible hunting skill that took the hulking grey monster with the oak-like beams. Tines like ivory daggers glisten in my mind. . . .

Yet when I finally see such a trophy, I freeze. *"My God, there he is,"* I gasp to myself as I try to steady my nerves. *"How should I get him mounted? Alert? Sneak pose? Turned left? Right?"* Right! By this time I'm so feverish that I couldn't hit the ground at my feet much less a trophy deer at 70 yards. There goes my record book entry over the ridge.

The various record book systems used to score antlers—Boone and Crockett, Pope and Young, Burkett, Safari Club, and the Buckmasters Trophy Record System—are in themselves tribute to the complex way we hunters think of antlers. There have been lots of terms coined over the years to try to describe antlers. "Typical" and "non-typical" racks; brow tines, drop tines, and all others; eyeguards, main beam, spread, mass—although they don't capture the magic of antlers, these words mean something very special to the hunter in pursuit of a trophy. Added up as official score, they can mean a record book buck and the trophy of a lifetime.

ANTLER GROWTH

But what do we hunters really know about antlers? To begin with, the buck fawn is actually programmed to develop antlers while still in his mother's uterus. This is when specialized tissues called pedicels begin to develop. Pedicels are the antlers' growth platforms on the skull. They're the link between the living bone of the animal's skull and the antler. While the antler is growing, nourishment in the form of blood is provided to the living tissue in two ways: from the capillary-rich outer skin or velvet (the only self-regenerating skin found among mammals); and through the core of the pedicel.

While they're in the velvet stage, antlers are the fastest form of bone growth known. A mature bull elk, for example, is capable of growing one inch of antler each and every day during the peak growing season. Growth like this can produce a rack of solid bone weighing well over 60 pounds in less than four months. A rack this big is equal in weight to an adult human male's entire skeleton.

So antlers develop as a lengthening of the buck's skull, and the completely hardened antler itself is similar to skeletal bone. But while they're growing antlers are composed of cartilage (the pliable tissue you can feel in your nose and ear) covered with fine-haired skin, the velvet.

Dr. Robert Brown of Mississippi State University says, "The outside of a growing antler is covered with velvet, a skin rich with veins and arteries which supplies blood to the antler . . . The pedicel also acts like a conduit that carries blood to the interior of the antler. If you could touch a velvet antler it would be quite warm because of all the blood. The velvet is also full of nerves and very sensitive to touch."

As antlers grow they gradually harden, from the inside out. Minerals like calcium and phosphorus are deposited to form a bony core.

By now everyone has read about how you can supplement deer's feed with minerals to help the animals grow larger antlers. But deer have evolved a way to get these minerals without help from humans.

"A deer can't possibly get all the minerals he needs for the development of his rack from his food," Dr. Brown said. "So each season a buck deer's body robs the minerals from its own skeleton, especially from the rib cage and sternum, to deposit them in its antlers. The stress to a buck's system is enormous since antlers grow at such a rapid rate.

"When a deer is growing antlers his ribs become brittle and can break fairly easily," Brown continued, "but wild deer take this in stride—and every year, too. Even if a deer breaks a bone while growing antlers the break will usually heal smoothly. And when antler growth is complete, the minerals are then restored to the temporarily depleted bones."

Up to this point, the pedicel has been a direct source of the blood needed by osteocytes, the true bone cells, in the growing antler. But once the message *"Stop growing!"* is given, the pedicel cuts off the blood supply and the antlers harden. This is the most intriguing part of the entire antler story: though the buck's skull is now *living* bone and the antler is now *dead* bone, the pedicel acts as a powerful connector, holding the living bone cells to the dead. Nowhere else in all of the animal kingdom does this kind of relationship exist. Normally, a living organism will do everything in its power to rid itself of dead tissue: not so with antlers.

Velvet itself has fascination for humankind. Bucks, stags, and bulls have long been associated with virility, and in many cultures dried antler velvet is still thought to be a cure for impotence or infertility. Even today there is a thriving market for antler velvet harvested from nearly every species of the deer family. All over the world venison and velvet farms are springing up to supply the demand that exists in China, the Far East, and the Soviet Union. Velvet is also used for other traditional medicines, primarily by women during the last trimester of pregnancy and while nursing. In the Soviet Union, velvet is still prescribed as a treatment for menopausal disorders.

Modern research science is also interested in the properties of velvet. Laboratory research on rats has also shown that velvet actually is effective as a blood vessel dilator and for stimulating red blood cell production. This might mean drugs for hypertension and anemic diseases could someday be derived from research on antler velvet.

SUPERBUCK ANTLERS

All bucks need three things to grow a set of trophy antlers: some time, good nutrition, and genetic potential. A buck usually comes into his prime at 4½ years of age. Barring sickness or injury, he'll maintain this prime condition for about three seasons, or up to age 6½. The next season generally starts a gradual decline in overall condition, including antler growth.

It's also true that deer grow trophy racks at 2½ and 3½ years of age if it's part of their genetic programming to do so. But generally speaking, a trophy of 2½ or 3½ years of age would just be more magnificent when he reached his prime a year or so later. On the other hand, superbucks won't develop in some heavily hunted areas simply because they don't live long enough to demonstrate their true antler potential.

Good nutrition is important to antler growth. Many trophy deer are taken from areas with low deer population densities, where food supplies are extraordinarily high in proportion to the numbers of deer.

But even a buck that spends 3½ years on the best range around won't grow a trophy rack if his genes aren't programmed to do so. It's good to remember that the genetic factor is the one element of a superbuck we can't see directly. A lowly spike buck may carry the genetic potential to eventually become a 14-pointer. A spike is often considered an 18-month-old deer—normal age for the first antler-bearing season, yet that deer could be younger than 15 months old. In my home state of Missouri, conservation officers have documented fawn births in late August and September, way past the normal birthing month of May. These late little fellows will be three or four months behind their class in every way, including antler development. Given time, good forage, and genes for big antler growth, that spike could actually become a record-book buck.

HOW ANTLERS DEVELOP

Now that we've determined what it takes to grow a trophy rack, let's see exactly how antler growth takes place.

Zbigniew Jaczewski, a Polish deer biologist, made an antler research breakthrough when he showed that the antler growth cycle was controlled by light. Jaczewski discovered that the deer's pineal gland transmits messages to other glands, based on the amount of light that passes through the eyes. As the days get longer and longer in March and April, more light signals the pineal—a pea-sized gland near the base of the brain—to release less and less of a hormone called melatonin into the deer's bloodstream. When the amount of melatonin in the deer's system is low enough, the pituitary gland—the master gland for growth—in turn releases the lutenizing hormone or "LH." LH is needed in turn to trigger production of testosterone, the male sex hormone, in the buck's testicles. And as the testosterone level rises in the buck's blood, the antlers start to grow.

Scientists have experimented with this chain of glands and secretions in an attempt to identify all the factors in antler development. For example, if the pineal gland is surgically removed, the buck may then grow his antlers during the winter and rub the velvet out in the spring—a complete reversal of the normal growth cycle.

If the pituitary gland is removed the deer will never develop antlers, even if artificially injected with testosterone. The pituitary performs so many functions that researchers still aren't able to isolate how it controls antler development with periodic releases of hormones.

If the testes are removed the antler cycle is irreparably altered. But how the antler cycle is altered depends on the age of the deer when it is castrated. A fawn that's castrated will never grow antlers. That's because pedicel development is a once-in-a-lifetime event. If this event is prevented from occurring by early castration, no antlers will ever develop.

When an adult buck is castrated he will grow velvet antlers during each growing season, but the velvet is never rubbed off and the antlers are never cast or shed. This is because the testes aren't the only glands that manufacture testosterone. And while a fawn needs the concentrated testosterone boost directly from the testes for pedicel development, an adult male deer will get enough testosterone to grow antlers each spring from the adrenal glands. However, the adrenals alone do not produce enough testosterone to create a *complete* antler growth cycle including shedding of velvet and antlers. A buck like this, with continuous springtime growth of velvet antlers, is called a "cactus" buck because of the weird shapes the antlers take.

Hypogonadism—undescended or undeveloped testicles—is another reason that bucks become cactus bucks. One area in Texas, the Central Mineral Region around Mason and Llano counties, has an unusually high ratio of deer with hypogonadism. Scientists suspect that certain forage plants growing on these granite soils cause this condition in deer by introducing high levels of minerals.

If a buck is castrated while he has hardened antlers, he'll lose his antlers within two weeks; then he'll grow cactus antlers the following spring.

Does can grow antlers too, if given shots of testosterone. A 24-point doe shot in Kentucky had undescended testicles in addition to normal female reproductive organs. The doe's undescended testicles supplied the testosterone that triggered antler development.

HOW LIGHT CONTROLS ANTLER GROWTH

Dr. Richard Goss, of Brown University in Providence, Rhode Island, researched how light patterns affect antler cycles. Goss knew North

American deer have definite antler cycles and that South American deer have antler cycles the exact reverse of ours. But at the equator, where day and night are always equal, bucks have no definite antler cycle. Some bucks keep their antlers for longer than a year; others shed them twice a year. But when these same bucks are relocated in the northern hemisphere, their antler cycles become identical to those of the native deer. So it seems reasonable that seasonal increases in the amount of daylight are the trigger for the antler cycle.

Dr. Goss kept study deer indoors where he could regulate light and record how different light patterns affected them. He discovered that he could compact the yearly cycle of increases and decreases in daylight into six months' time by putting two increments of daylight change into every day. In other words, he would include a month's worth of *change* in the amount of daylight in 15 days instead of the usual 30 days. When he did this, his study deer grew *two* complete sets of antlers each year. Sika deer bucks could grow *three* sets of antlers in a year in which the rate of daylight increases had been speeded up to make it appear as if three years had elapsed. These bucks still needed at least three to four months to grow a set of antlers, but then they "rub out" or rubbed the velvet off, and then shed the antlers immediately.

When Goss speeded up the artificial lighting to make a full year of increases appear to go by in two months, the deer grew no antlers at all. They simply couldn't keep up with the breakneck growth required. But Goss discovered that the following year, when it was spring outside, his study deer *on the inside* grew new antlers as though they, too, were outside. This was the first evidence supporting the theory that deer may have a biologic clock mechanism that lets them know when a year has passed, even if all other indicators are absent.

So light seems to be the only outside factor governing the antler cycle. Temperature, which may trigger the onset of rutting behavior, has no bearing whatsoever on antler growth or hardening. In combination with genes, food affects the size, but not the cycle, although undernourished bucks may shed their antlers early.

Research has developed many other interesting theories about deer and their antlers. Dr. Anthony Bubenik of Thornhill, Ontario, Canada, makes an analogy between the antler cycle and a human life cycle. He writes that a buck goes through three separate stages of sexual development every year of his life. When a buck casts his antlers early in the year, he loses all aggressive tendencies. During this period, the pedicels are healing. The buck's timid behavior parallels a human's infancy.

When the days begin to lengthen, a buck enters the antler growth stage, which might be considered an adolescence. This buck "puberty" really has two phases. The touch-sensitive phase, when he is extremely careful with his antlers, lasts about 75 percent of the antler growth period. The second, desensitizing phase occurs when the antlers "point," harden, and the velvet dies as the blood supply dries up. Now for the first time the buck will freely use his antlers to hit other objects, as in rub out behavior.

Finally, the velvet is completely shed and the new, hardened antlers show that the buck is ready to breed. The adolescence is over. Sexual maturity, the most important act of the buck's year, is about to begin.

FIGHTING

Until the buck rubs out his antlers, however, he doesn't act macho at all. His testosterone level is low and the female hormone, estrogen, is also present in his system. Dr. Bubenik explains: "During this time the buck's facial expressions are meek and doe-like. The males fight like females, standing on hind legs and flailing with forelegs at opponents' heads. I feel that it's at this time when dominance is decided, not later on when bucks have hardened antlers."

So, when deer start the rut they already know who the head honcho is. Perhaps they realize instinctively that their battles with pointed antlers could be dangerous. Bubenik feels battles with hardened antlers during the rut are more ritual than actual determination of rank.

Deer do use their antlers to fight with deadly intent for three reasons: first, when one buck wants another buck's doe, a rare event in a population where bucks are aware of their rank before the onset of the rut.

Second, a fight may result if a stranger wanders through the dominant deer's area. Fights like this won't last long: they end once status is determined.

The third cause of fights is when a young, inexperienced buck enters a prime male's mating area and disregards his threats and warnings. If the prime male is fit, this challenge can spell doom to the challenger. But after the rut, when dominant bucks are often exhausted from mating, an aggressive young buck may win out. An exhausted prime buck could be killed accidentally. If the younger buck wounds the dominant buck it makes the challenger even more bloodthirsty. He'll attack relentlessly, often killing the older buck in the process.

On the other hand, deer often spar, or engage in "play-fighting." Bubenik feels deer spar for one of two reasons: first, to learn necessary fighting skills for the future while determining the exact shape of their antlers. It's apparently very difficult for a buck to judge just how large his rack is until antler growth stabilizes during his prime years. Sparring or play-fighting is most common among deer that hang out in bachelor bands.

"Demonstration sparring," the second type, lets bucks test each other's rank to verify dominance. In other words, if a buck has any doubts about who's the boss after the foreleg flailing, this is the time to settle the matter once and for all.

Deer, like other competitors, try to fake each other out at times. Dr. Bubenik has watched whitetails, muleys, and elk use what he calls "antler deception strategy."

"In deception strategy the animal actually alters his antlers' shape by attacking vegetation and leaving moss, leaves or grass hanging on them instead of shaking it off. The buck purposely parades around with the extra matter on his antlers as if he knows it will intimidate other bucks by making his antlers look larger than they are. Deception strategy is practiced during long-lasting contests. When a buck resorts to deception strategy, the other male will give up and retreat. He'll be totally fooled by the deception."

So fighting is really the last stage of establishing dominance. Dr. Bubenik thinks bucks start soliciting for rank during the rut while they're still in velvet. He says, "They rub the pheromones from their velvet secretion on vegetation as a sort of pre-rut advertising campaign. They make sure that everyone else makes the connection by rubbing the velvet on their bodies and gently scratching it with their hooves so that they'll track their scent all over the countryside."

When deer shed their velvet, this means of scent communication is lost. Bubenik feels the deer improvise by coating their newly hardened antlers with pheromones from their urine, deposited either directly on the antlers, or on vegetation which they then rub with their antlers.

NON-TYPICAL ANTLERS

Non-typical antlers can be the result of genetics or of injuries, either to the antler itself or to the buck's body, particularly his legs. For example, if a buck injures his rear leg while still in velvet, the antler on the opposite side will be stunted.

Scientists think this is what happens: the deer injures his left rear leg. Since deer walk by raising and lowering legs on the diagonal, the right foreleg and injured hind leg support the body's weight half of the time. To compensate, the antler growth center slows down the *right* antler's development. This way less weight bears on the affected limb. If a front leg is injured, the antler on the same side will be smaller because it bears directly on the injured limb with each step.

If the antler suffers direct injury during growth it overdevelops. But even greater growth occurs the year following the injury: the antler appears to remember the injury for years to come. It's for this reason that the response is called "trophical memory." If the right antler is injured, only the right antler will develop excessively. This verifies the theory that each antler develops independently of the other. Antlers injured early in the growth cycle experience the most damage and result in the most spectacularly deformed antlers.

As the days grow shorter antlers start to harden. When the antlers are fully ossified—turned to bone—the velvet's blood supply dries up. Ossification proceeds throughout the final third of the velvet stage, beginning from the inside out. Once it's complete, the buck looks for trees where he can rub the velvet off. Some biologists believe the velvet actually dries out and falls off by itself. This stage is so synchronized to light patterns that it is a common occurrence for all the bucks in an area to shed their velvet within a three-week period.

A buck with hardened antlers is ready to fulfill his biological function by fathering the next crop of fawns, although not every buck gets the chance. In a well-balanced population most does are bred only by the prime males.

CASTING

The final portion of the antler cycle is called casting. Casting dates, unlike velvet shedding, are highly individualized and vary greatly. In one study it was found that an individual deer shed its antlers within a range of three months. However, under stable conditions from year to year, each individual buck sheds his antlers on a more precise schedule. That is, if buck number one casts his antlers on December 22nd, and buck number two casts his antlers on January 31st, evidence is great that each succeeding year they'll each cast their antlers on almost the same dates.

Mississippi State's Dr. Harry Jacobson said, "This possibly shows that whitetail bucks (on which this study was based) have a pre-programmed rhythm within their system which causes them to cast their antlers."

Dr. Brown sums it up when he says, "Casting is truly amazing. One day you can't knock a buck's antlers off, and the next day they may fall off. When the buck's testosterone level drops below the minimum needed to maintain a set of hardened antlers, the pedicel demineralizes. And that's when casting occurs."

After shedding in December or January, and perhaps even as late as March, the pedicel looks like an open sore for a short time, but soon scabs up and heals over. In a few months, they'll start the antler cycle over again.

No matter how much we learn about antlers, they'll always be one of nature's miracles. As long as hunters roam the forests and plains in search of bigger and better bucks, it's antlers that create the trophy dreams they seek.

2

How to Produce
a Superbuck

The big whitetail buck was tired. The rut was nearly over and his energy was spent. Every year it took more effort to maintain dominance and breed all the available does. And this year a hunter was hot on his trail. This man was using every trick in the book to reduce the buck to a year's supply of venison and a trophy of heroic proportions for his family room wall.

The buck knew about hunters. He'd been shot at earlier in his life, before he'd grown such spectacular antlers. Always he had come away from these encounters a little wiser and a whole lot warier. But this hunter was different.

The first hint of the man's presence in the buck's woods had come when the leaves changed from green to gold. The deer couldn't know that his tremendous rub trees had attracted the man's attention. Or that late one summer evening the hunter had watched as the huge buck stepped cautiously from a tangle of vines. From that moment on, the buck knew what it meant to be hunted.

Everything a whitetail buck requires was to be found within the deer's 600-acre home range: does, food, water, and cover. A small but growing deer population ensured that the buck did not have to travel great distances during the breeding season.

The big buck usually moved at night. During the day, he bedded down in dense thickets. And always, before making a move, he used his incredible nose to scent for man.

The days were very short now. Gun season had come and gone, and the buck sensed that it was only a matter of days before he'd be safe for another year. The hunter was still in the woods with a bow, and the big deer knew he couldn't drop his guard, even for an instant.

Even now the hunter searched the buck's range for the fat, round tracks. A breeze carried the hunter's scent to the buck's nose. Within thick briars, the buck lay still, his neck stretched out flat along the ground. His antlers were motionless in the fading light, when the whisper of the hunter's feet on fallen leaves reached his ears. The hunter stopped to look and listen closer than ten feet away from the whitetail's head. Heart pounding, the buck waited for darkness; then the hunter would leave.

Finally, hours later, the hunter sighed and trudged slowly away. The buck waited several minutes, and then moved out of the thicket. He went deep into the woods to another part of his range.

Storm clouds gathered, and the buck felt a vague discomfort in his chest as he walked; he moved faster, trying to find a place to rest without the hunter dogging his tracks.

Large raindrops pelted the deer's thick gray coat. Soon a downpour drenched the ground, erasing all signs of the buck's passing. The buck shivered, but kept plodding along until he reached a bluff, screened by a dense curtain of mountain laurel. Stopping behind the undergrowth, the buck wearily shook the water from his shoulders. He was so tired. Now he would rest: he sank to his knees and closed his eyes. The buck died that night in his sleep.

The hunter was baffled. He looked high and low for sign, but the buck had seemingly vanished. All the next year, he searched but found not even a track. The hunter was bitterly disappointed. Never before had he seen a rack to compare with that buck's. He guessed it would score at least 220 Boone and Crockett points, a new world record typical.

But the rack was gone by the next hunting season, chewed up by rodents where it lay. There was nothing left, nothing to indicate that one of the largest bucks ever had passed this way. A trophy was lost forever.

Sound incredible? It's true: this drama is taken from real life. Consider the number one non-typical whitetail, a monster buck that broke a record that had stood for 90 years—and broke it by 47⅞ points! Like the deer in my story, the great buck died of natural causes during the hunting season in St. Louis County, Missouri. The difference between the two is that the Missouri buck was found, so he reigns as the current world record.

On one hand, all superbucks are freaks: they survive as superbucks through a series of lucky breaks. Nonetheless, there are plenty of superbucks out there right now. In the past, the vacuum of solid information on giant whitetail bucks has been filled with the aura of mystery, the trace of legend that enhances big buck hunting tales.

But as you'll see in later chapters, a superbuck is still a deer in the end. Learning *why* a deer develops into a superbuck—what makes him tick—may help you locate, and eventually take, a trophy whitetail. Lately, more hunters than ever have been doing exactly that.

Of the top 50 places in the Boone and Crockett typical category (record book of 1999, 26 are occupied by bucks that were taken during the 1980s, and 1990s. Sixty percent of all large typical whitetails were killed fairly recently. In fact, 24 percent of the top 50 heads were taken during the 1990s.

The pattern is the same in the non-typical category: 22 of the bucks that qualified for the top 50 spots were taken in the 1980s, and early 1990s. This means 44 percent of the top 50 places were taken fairly recently. In fact, 12 percent of the top 50 non-typical heads were taken during the 1990s. Others haven't even been scored, because many people are unaware of the competition or don't care to enter it. There's always a catch-up period, and it's a sure bet that several more heads from the 1980s and 1990s will qualify for the top 50 in both categories. Big bucks *aren't* a thing of the legendary past. They're out there now for those hunters willing to get out and hunt them.

SUPERBUCK ANTLERS AND NUTRITION

There's superbuck potential in every state, but big-buck experts agree that there are certain areas in each state where no amount of management will ever produce a superbuck. Lack of good antler nutrients is the reason. Dr. James Kroll of Stephen F. Austin State University told me, "If you've got a place where the soil's poor, the nutrition needed for good antler growth is not available. Two areas that immediately come to mind are the extreme southeast portion of Georgia and the panhandle of Florida. A buck from either place is lucky to develop forked antlers. The superbuck hunter should take a good look at the soils in his state. He can call the local SCS [Soil Conservation Service] agent, who can help him with the various soil profiles. What he should be looking for is fertile soil that has enough calcium and phosphates for good antler growth. A good place to start is in an area that's produced good bucks in the past."

Eighteen to 26 percent of a deer's diet should be high-protein foods, especially during the antler-growing months of late spring and early summer. At this crucial time, agricultural products are excellent sources of protein. Soybeans, composed of nearly 25 percent available protein, alfalfa and clover are three crops that fit the bill nicely.

Naturally-occurring high-protein browse includes honeysuckle, greenbrier, and dewberry in the South, and pokeweed, jewel weed, aster rosettes, lespedeza, wild lettuce, and blackberry in more northerly ranges. Asters are the small sunflower-type blossoms seen in fallow fields during early summer. Take scouting trips at the height of the growing season and determine whether or not high-protein browse is available in a potential hunting area.

GROWING TIME

Good nutrition is only one of three basic requirements for fantastic antlers: age and genetics are the other two. Surprisingly, five of the last Boone and Crockett bucks Dr. Kroll has examined were only 3½ to 4½ years old. This is a bit lower than some earlier studies suggested for optimum antler growth. These bucks might have sported even better antlers later in life, but at 3½ to 4½ their headgear was good enough to make the book.

In some areas even that age is almost impossible for the average whitetail buck to reach. Recent studies conducted on bucks that weren't subjected to any hunting pressure at all indicate that a good portion of any age class dies of non-hunter related causes each year. So with or without hunting, only a very few bucks will live the full 3½ years or more required to fully develop the antlers for which their genes have been programmed.

To find a buck in this age bracket, look for an area that isn't heavily hunted. The areas that sustain the most pressure are usually the ones with the most deer. Concentrate on an area with a new or a building population of whitetails. Scout an almost inaccessible area. Those are places where the hunter has the best chance of taking a superbuck.

Another good place to check out is an area that looks like it has the nutrients to support a superbuck, but no hunting pressure. Dr. Harry Jacobson, a big-buck researcher formerly based at Mississippi State, knows of several tremendous bucks that he jokingly refers to as "fencerow deer," "backyard deer," or "city-limits deer." The hunters who shot these animals suspected the big bucks were to be found where no one else expected them to be, and hunted accordingly.

Dr. Jacobson told me, "Anyone who is serious about bagging a good buck must remember that whitetails are all very adaptable, and a superbuck is the most adaptable whitetail of all."

GENETICS

Genetics are actually least important. Both Dr. Kroll and Dr. Jacobson emphasized that, given a proper diet and the opportunity to live longer than 18 months, the overwhelming majority of bucks will eventually develop excellent antlers. They call this allowing the buck to develop to his "full genetic potential."

Jacobson and Kroll also feel that on some ranges does have been protected to the point of negative impact on this genetic pool. Up to 90 percent of 18-month-old bucks may be shot in a given area every year. That leaves very few to grow to superbuck age. The protected does expand to fill the available range, and the population gets severely out of balance. Soon too many deer are competing for too little food, with the result that there's not enough nutrition to go around. Stunted bodies and antlers are the end products. Managing the legal harvest of does to swing the pendulum back to a balanced sex ratio often works wonders in restoring a quality deer herd. Rather than having a big, unbalanced population of does, more range is available to nourish superbucks.

"EXPERIENCE"

It takes a series of lucky breaks for a deer to become a superbuck, and he learns from every one of them. Since the "bucks only" mentality endures in many areas, the bucks are shot at when they first develop antlers. Even a spike, most often a young buck born the preceding year, is fair game in many states. In no time, a buck—any buck—has made the connection between human scent and whizzing projectiles. After one or two near misses, the deer becomes cautious. He becomes warier and warier and soon limits his movements to avoid hunters. He becomes increasingly nocturnal, since there's little chance of running into a human in the woods at night. Jacobson and Kroll also believe that many big bucks feel safe moving around during the *middle* of the day.

"Deer are usually shot at early and late in the day," Dr. Kroll says, "and they adjust their activity to avoid hunters. That means that many darn good bucks move around in the middle of the day. A hunter who stays put all day long increases his chances of scoring on a superbuck. A hunter's chances for a big buck are best on opening day, and dwindle as the season wears on. Big bucks are extremely elusive. Even when they're not being hunted, they spend most of their time lying low. When a buck does decide to move, he knows where he's going and how he's going to get there. There's very little random travel involved in a big buck's life-style. It's like a zone defense in football when hunters enter the picture. A smart old buck can adjust his activity to completely avoid the hunters."

Dr. Jacobson added, "I think a superbuck is probably more sedentary than the average deer, and is therefore more likely to survive. The less a big buck moves, the less likely he'll be seen. But a lot of this superbuck mystique is created by the hunters themselves. You hear how smart, how elusive these critters are, and how ol' So and So shot at a giant buck the other day and the buck just took off and never stopped. First of all, very few hunters won't get flustered shooting at a big whitetail, so there are bound to be many stories about the trophy buck that got away. No mystery there.

"Second, because of a big buck's size, his sheer strength is amazing. When you shoot a yearling, he may run 100 yards before dropping. When you shoot a superbuck, an animal conditioned to survive, you're shooting at a superior specimen. He's likely to react very differently when shot. He may hide right away, or he may run a heck of a lot farther than you'd ever figure he could. He might even run uphill—he just might have the strength—and if a buck does that, some hunters won't even bother to check it out, because they can't believe they hit the deer. This is how a lot of giant bucks get away and how the mystique develops. Those bucks may die out there and never be found. Always be sure you follow up any shot at a super-buck. He may be lying dead just over the next ridge."

Adding to the mystique of the whitetail superbuck is the fact that the top non-typical buck was picked up, not shot, as was another of the top five Boone and Crockett non-typicals. Still another big non-typical recently came to light, also found dead. No autopsy was done on any of these deer. How many superbucks die of natural causes and are never found?

Dr. Kroll and Dr. Jacobson think there are quite a few, and for good reasons. "Once the bucks establish dominance during the summer, they have to stay on top," said Kroll. "Dominance isn't de-cided in the fall, with head butting and fighting. It's decided earlier, while the antlers are still in velvet. Two bucks stand up on their hind legs and flail away at each other with their forefeet. This is how the pecking order is determined. The top male, or alpha buck, must maintain that dominance or lose his position."

"A dominant buck has a rough go of it," added Jacobson. "He may be so busy asserting his dominance that he'll run himself into the ground. During the rut, he expends more calories and uses up fat reserves by breeding does and running off other bucks. Superbucks usually don't feed or forage enough to build up new reserves. When winter arrives, they're at a low ebb and survival becomes even harder. And when a dominant buck shows any sign of weakness no matter how trivial, the subordinate bucks will jump all over him. They jump him, push him around, and even gore him if they can. They gang up on him and do anything to edge him out of his domi-nant position. The cause of the buck loss that results from this kind of activity is called 'post-rut mortality' and is probably the reason why so many superdeer just seem to disappear."

Add to this the fact that during winter a buck is apparently pro-grammed to lower his nutritional input. Bucks consume less while does and fawns eat whatever is available. Possibly this is nature's way of ensuring that the next generation will survive. For whatever reason, this failure to eat properly undoubtedly also contributes to the stresses a buck must endure in order to survive another year.

A superbuck's magnificence lies in the eyes of the beholder. And any buck large enough to qualify for Boone and Crockett with 170 typical or 195 non-typical points is unquestionably a superbuck. There are many beautiful bucks with fine, impressive antlers that don't qualify for Boone and Crockett. A buck that qualifies for Pope and Young, although it has to score only 125 points, is still a wonderful trophy simply because a greater amount of skill is usually needed to bag a buck with a bow.

Even when taken with a gun, a buck scoring over 130 points is a real trophy. My husband killed one buck that scored 133, a far cry from the minimum Boone and Crockett score, but everyone is *still* impressed when they see that rack.

Superbucks *are* alive and well and could be just about anywhere. Hunters who long to match wits with one stand a good chance of doing so. A superbuck can be yours!

3

The New
Superbuck Genetics

Scenario: dawn was just breaking when the hunter noticed movement behind a sprawling mesquite bush. He froze. Moments later, a gigantic whitetail buck stepped out in the open. He raised his gun and fired once. The buck stumbled and ran only 25 yards before collapsing in a heap. The hunter walked over to the trophy and checked it for signs of life. When he found none, he started to field-dress the animal. But first he used his knife to sever the buck's testicles from the body. Then he took a small container out of his daypack and placed the testicles inside. Packed in a chemical solution, they would survive the ride to a major southwestern university. Here, they would be quick-frozen for future use in experimental research dedicated to the development of a line of "Superbucks."

Scenario: there were 20 does captured and bred to Rex II last year, but only Doe Number 14 had produced a fantastic-looking yearling buck. The ranch foreman watched as a tranquilizer dart found its mark deep within Doe Number 14's flank. Several burly cowboys carried her now-limp body into a nearby quonset hut where a veterinarian was waiting. Doe Number 14 had earlier been injected with a drug to make her superovulate, or produce a large quantity of eggs at once. Now, she had been stripped of these eggs, much like a spawning salmon in a hatchery. These eggs would now be inseminated in a small glass dish in the laboratory. The semen was from Rex II, the buck with the largest rack on the ranch. Within days, these fertilized eggs could be separated, with 90 percent accuracy, into buck and doe embryos. The doe embryos would be discarded. The buck embryos would be implanted in surrogate doe mothers. Six months from now, a crop of potential superbucks would fill the enclosure outside. Genetically, they would all be full brothers.

Bio-engineering a superbuck may sound unbelievable but it really isn't. Persons in search of the new superbuck are now doing, or will be doing, all of these things in the near future: the deer science of tomorrow is here now. One of the few questions left is not *if* man has the scientific knowledge to breed trophy deer, but *how long* it will take. And how long after that will anyone with the price be able to drive to an enclosure and shoot a buck bigger than anything on the pages of Boone and Crockett's *Records of North American Big Game.*

In fact, the first scenario is a reality right now. A container like the one described has already been designed. All that remains is to equip hunters who have been properly trained to use them. The second scenario is also feasible using methods currently practiced in cattle production. In fact, some embryo transplants have already been accomplished, and successful superovulation of does has also been accomplished in experiments. Live fawns have been produced using each method, too.

The economic value of superbucks is creating a market for trophies themselves. Prices in excess of $100,000 have been quoted for recordbook racks. That raises another question: should the buying and selling of deer racks even be legal? Or should hunters be above all that?

In any case, the demand for trophy deer has created lots of efforts to understand how to increase the supply of superbucks. Most big buck research currently is being conducted in the South. In Texas, for example, universities are involved in several different facets of deer research. Corporations provide funding for the research, and individual ranchers and managers are interested in improving the quality of deer on their land. Each represents a different segment of the hunting fraternity, but all are keenly interested in the phenomenon that is the whitetail superbuck.

Of all popular game animals hunted, the whitetail is the most elusive, yet still the most attainable trophy for the ordinary person. The chance of shooting one belongs to everyone, regardless of wealth or social status. For that reason, a whitetail big enough to make the book can't be bought yet—at least not on the hoof.

The good news is there's a lot being done in the quest for the superbuck, including several types of research that are of interest to the ordinary hunter who longs for a chance at an outstanding buck.

Texas A&M University in College Station, Texas, is one of these research schools. Their research ranges from habitat management to some of the most daring deer studies being done. Dr. Dwayne Kraemer of Texas A&M was instrumental in the design of the container mentioned at the beginning of this chapter. And researchers at the university have already succeeded in artificially inseminating whitetail does with frozen semen. Superovulation techniques are still being developed although early attempts resulted in failure. Surrogate mothers are being considered so that research scientists won't have to wait six years, for example, for one doe to produce six full-brother bucks. Genetic traits can be compared simultaneously when surrogates are used to carry fawns from one set of genetic parents.

Dr. Kraemer emphasized that, while superbuck configuration interests many people right now, big antlers are not the only thing that concerns researchers at the university.

"Superior antlers are important," Kraemer said, "but we're also looking for those deer that are best able to utilize their food, or that are the most adaptable to their surroundings. It's highly improbable that an outstanding set of antlers can be developed with consistency without any consideration being given to other factors.

"For example, if someone was to breed a line of deer too intensively—in order to concentrate a superantler gene—the result would be a severely inbred animal. With inbreeding comes the chance that birth defects may result, including reproductive problems. What good would super antlers be if the utility to pass them on to future generations was impaired?

"Right now, the management and the hunting of whitetail deer is a big industry in Texas," he continued. "People are going to get involved in superbuck breeding whether or not they have guidelines to follow. We're interested in supporting this with education—especially in the reproductive area. It's going to happen. We want to be sure that some thought accompanies any action taken. This will benefit hunting everywhere."

Dr. Kraemer is quick to point out that Texas A&M isn't interested only in big buck research, although that goal is high on their list. Researchers at the institution have a loftier goal in mind, even as they pursue the superbuck. They are interested in replicating the traits of superior animals to improve the quality of the breed in general. They are also trying to perfect procedures whereby surrogate mothers of non-endangered animals may be made to propagate endangered species.

Dr. Jack Inglis, a professor of wildlife management at Texas A&M, is also concerned with superbuck development. He approaches it, though, from the standpoint of habitat, not simply genetics.

"There's really no good way to manipulate genetics," he stated. "What if, after all this research has been done, the deer are back out on the range and a hunter shoots a scrawny-looking buck with an inferior rack because he thinks it's obviously poor stock. Maybe that was *the* superbuck and, because of a severe drought, he wasn't up to his potential. That's what habitat management is all about. Make the most of what you've got. You can probably make it produce good quality animals with a little work."

Dr. James Kroll, a professor of forestry at Stephen F. Austin State University, explained why some ranches' big buck programs fail to produce outstanding trophies.

"You must understand the basics of population genetics for effective trophy management. Let's say you have 1,000 people and you measure all of their index fingers. The majority would have normal-length fingers while some would have long fingers and others would have short ones. If we wanted only people with the longest index fingers, we'd have to remove every person from the breeding group with fingers shorter than a certain length. But what if we removed both those people with the longest and the shortest index fingers? The *average* would be favored. And that's what a lot of managers are doing down here with their trophy programs: shooting trophies [long fingers] and spikes [short fingers]." So in effect, hunters and managers help ensure the survival of "grade" or average-sized bucks.

"A good trophy management program must be under the control of a single individual who makes the decision whether each buck lives or dies," Dr. Kroll continued. "Many ranches don't want one person to have that kind of authority and so their programs suffer."

Texas is especially vulnerable to private big-buck management programs because such a large amount of land is privately owned and can be effectively fenced to contain the deer. Dr. Kroll explained more problems that can occur with such operations.

"It's sort of sad but, right now, some game farms are involved in 'hit-or-miss' superbuck programs. They buy or corral a big buck and turn him loose with their does. And that's where it stops. No one researches the does' backgrounds, and a doe contributes as much or more than a buck to a deer's traits. While bucks contribute points and shape, we believe does contribute mass and spread. And no one knows what kind of stock a buck like this comes from. Maybe he won't pass on his antlers. Maybe he *can't* pass on his antlers.

"These breeders overlook the traits that make a big whitetail so superior. Things such as cunning, daring, and a sense of survival are ignored in the search for bigger racks.

"Currently, many ranches are involved in superbuck development programs," Dr. Kroll said. "That's where the big money is, in offering fee hunting for the chance at a trophy . . . The only thing holding many of them back is the high cost involved. For example, one such program released a bunch of 'bred' bucks and later discovered that 50 percent had died. That doubled the cost for every survivor."

Perhaps breeding superbucks isn't economically wise, and Dr. Kroll posed an even more thought-provoking question: "A long time ago, there lived a relative of our whitetail that is known today as the Irish elk. What made this deer so unique was his incredible antlers—up to 12 feet in spread and 90 pounds in weight—all on a five-pound skull. Why did they develop these outsize antlers? No one knows. But it's believed that the size of these antlers contributed to the eventual extinction of the Irish elk. Could we be moving in the same direction with our beloved whitetail? It's a question worth pondering.

"Some breeders are losing sight of why so many people hunt," he added. "Bred whitetails hold no meaning for most people and they hold no meaning for me. Someday, you may be able to walk into a place, pay the price, and walk out with a Boone and Crockett caliber buck. But a wild trophy will always make my heart beat a little faster just by being the incredibly unique animal that he is, a chance combination of those qualities that make him so special coming together in nature to produce a trophy worthy of the name. No amount of dollars can buy what's put together like that."

Dr. Harry Jacobson, who was recently involved in genetic research at Mississippi State University, is probably the pioneer of big buck research. Jacobson and his team were the very first to extract semen from a dead buck, perfect a freezing technique that would preserve vital semen, and then successfully inseminate a doe. He worked with captive, known-line deer, looking for the reasons that they develop the types of antlers that they do.

Jacobson bred 16 different offspring from one trophy non-typical buck whose semen was extracted soon after he was killed. This semen was then frozen and used to inseminate several does. "Of six three-year-old sons of this buck, one of them grew antlers very similar to those of his father. But the true test of a buck's ability to pass on his antler traits will not be known until his son or sons are at least four years of age.

"One of the two-year-old sons of this particular buck grew a rack that had a 21-inch inside spread and 13 points. As researchers, it was plain to us that this buck's mother had carried excellent genes in addition to those that had been handed down by the buck's father."

On the population genetics of wild deer, Jacobson had this to say: "There are places in this country where there's room for genetic improvement in the population of wild whitetails, but they're probably few and far between. Many places have tried harvesting spikes in an attempt to upgrade their herd. But what if the spike gene was inherited from the mother? How would you go about eliminating those does carrying the spike-antler genetic code and not the ones with the heavyrack code potential? Almost impossible. What you'd have to do is cull the does severely while you're eliminating spikes so that the remaining does would almost certainly have been fathered by a fork-antlered or better buck. But a program like this is time consuming, and it takes years before you can see results.

"I've known landowners who just couldn't wait to get their hands on one of those big Michigan bucks to release as breeding stock to upgrade their herds, but they don't consider the risks involved. First, natural selection chooses animals suited to their environment. Big body size plus a dark color absorb sunlight and conserve heat for northern deer. Small body size and light coloration do just the opposite: they help dissipate heat in desert surroundings. Selective resistance to local disease is also a factor. A manager could still lose if his imported superbuck was a poor breeder. Some of my captive deer, the ones with the most outstanding antlers, are not the dominant animals. Other inferior animals do the bulk of the breeding.

"Don't misunderstand—genetics *are* important," Jacobson continued, "but they should be the very last step in a management program. More important is maintaining proper herd densities, desirable age and sex structure, and improving habitat. While genetic improvements for livestock have been accomplished through artificial insemination and other programs, it's a completely different game with wildlife. Domestic animal breeders can control all facets of their programs—including the selective removal of individuals with undesirable traits. This isn't feasible in the wild.

"We've progressed to a point where a few people have a little knowledge about whitetail genetics," he added. "But a little knowledge can be a dangerous thing."

Two ranchers who obviously agree with Jacobson are the men who run the H.B. Zachry Ranch in south Texas and the Y.O. Ranch, perhaps the most famous of all Texas spreads. They both use escape-proof fencing, but they also practice sound management principles for livestock and wildlife and adhere to a strict harvest schedule—one that takes both antlered and antlerless deer. Both also enjoy excellent success as producers of quality whitetail deer.

As Al Brothers, manager of the H.B. Zachry Ranch, said of those managers who are looking for instant solutions, "It's kind of like a cattle breeder who buys an expensive bull that's supposed to produce calves with more weight at weaning time—but then gives no thought to what that calf is going to eat. Some whitetail breeders are skipping the basics of good nutrition and trying to get right to the end result. It just can't be done."

Another ranch manager who is well attuned to what's happening today in superbuck circles is Bob Zaiglin of the Harrison Ranches in south Texas. Zaiglin, a certified wildlife biologist and noted big buck expert, is responsible for watching over and developing both the habitat and management techniques that successfully produced the first managed-area Boone and Crockett trophy, a 174⅜ buck that was taken by Steve Vaughn, president of administration for *North American Whitetail Magazine.* The Harrison Ranches are managed without the use of any escape-proof fencing, so all deer taken there are eligible for inclusion in the Boone and Crockett record book if they meet minimum qualifying scores and are otherwise taken in a legal manner.

The Boone and Crockett Club is watching all of these happenings with more than a casual interest. Hal Nesbitt, former administrative director of the club, said, "I think research is far enough along to make genetically engineered superbucks possible sometime soon. The prospect is daunting. What current administrators and directors of the club will do when genetically engineered bucks become reality is anybody's guess. More to the point, what will they be *able* to do? DNA swabs may become part of the entry process, and a genetic engineer adept at deciphering the information contained therein soon may be added to the Boone and Crockett staff."

Boone and Crockett already has taken steps to eliminate those deer not "naturally" bred by revising the Fair Chase Statement. The definition of "unfair chase" has been expanded to include "hunting game confined by artificial barriers, including escape-proof fencing, or hunting game transplanted solely for the purpose of commercial shooting."

As Nesbitt noted, "Escape-proof fencing is perceived as unfair even in the largest enclosures because a buck still may be trapped in a corner. And if he is, he will be unable to utilize his escape mechanism. That's why air-spotting and landing nearby are also illegal. There's little chance for an animal to escape."

What keeps hunters honest? Besides the fact that most game farm managers are not yet at the point where many are currently breeding Boone and Crockett-caliber bucks, not much. A notarized statement signed by the hunter and attesting to the fair chase must be submitted with any contending entry to the record book. Only that statement and a valid *state* hunting license are used to authenticate entries.

What about the future, when genetic-engineered bucks *are* possible? Nesbitt, who was interviewed when still a Boone and Crockett official, said, "At that point, I think we'll just have to consider a separate category for those type of bucks. But for the present, our system seems to be working just fine."

It's up to us as hunters to never lose our sense of the wonder of a superbuck in the wild. We should remember that although hunting at a ranch that selectively breeds its whitetails within escape-proof fencing may be a unique experience, it should never detract from the thrill of going after a result of a random mating between a buck and a doe: A wild superdeer that could be in your woodlot or mine right now.

Part 2

Whitetail Superbucks

4

Description of the Whitetail Superbuck

Scientifically, a whitetail superbuck belongs to family Cervidae, a family that includes all deer from the tiny tusked Asian musk deer to the huge Alaskan moose. Whitetail deer, along with their close kin the mule deer, are further classified in subfamily Odocoileinae, genus *Odocoileus.* Add the species name, *virginianus,* and to the taxonomists, those classifiers of plants and animals, you have described quite accurately the animal we call the whitetail.

For hunters, more familiar names are also more valuable clues to deer behavior. Whitetails (and muleys) are both herbivores and ruminants. The term herbivore means that they consume only vegetable matter. Ruminant refers to one compartment of the deer's four-chambered stomach, the rumen, which allows deer to store food temporarily and regurgitate it as a cud of predigested food. So a deer can grab a quick bite to eat in the open where it's vulnerable to predation and then escape to cover. There it will regurgitate the cud, or bolus, and chew it more thoroughly at its leisure.

All herbivores are basically prey animals. They evolved certain of their physical characteristics for one purpose only: escape from predators. Modern deer like whitetails come complete with well-developed escape mechanisms. Deer are long-legged, swift, and graceful so they can run like the wind. They have large, cupped ears shaped to catch the slightest sound. These ears rotate in all directions and are rarely still for any length of time. Deer have an unbelievably keen sense of smell. They are quite capable of smelling their primary predator, man, up to one quarter mile away under good conditions. Finally, they have good eyesight: peripheral vision so good that they can almost see behind them, combined with excellent binocular vision to the front.

While deers' eyes may not be ideally constructed for color and shape differentiation, they are still able to detect the slightest movements. Until very recently deer were thought to be colorblind, able to see the world only in shades of black, white, and gray. Scientists aren't so certain any more: bucks have been known to consciously bed down in cover that's similar to the coloration of their coat, possibly as a camouflage device.

Mule deer and whitetails share most of these characteristics. But the mule deer—although very closely related to the whitetail—is a relative newcomer to North America, having arrived only half a million years ago. By comparison, the whitetail arrived here from Asia 2.6 million years ago, well before its cousins the moose, caribou, and elk.

Whitetail superbucks differ from mule deer superbucks in several significant respects. Shape of antlers is one of them. A typical whitetail rack curves forward like a crown with single tines originating from the main beam. A mule deer's antlers grow up and out, with a typical four-point western count muley having two separate sets of forks (four points) that originate from both the left and the right main beam.

The next difference is that the brow tines of a whitetail superbuck are long while those of a mule deer are generally short or non-existent.

A whitetail's ears measure about one half the length of its head, while a muley's will usually measure three quarters of the length of the head.

The metatarsal glands, located on the outside of the hind legs, are the basis for another difference between the two deer. The whitetail's measure less than 1.65 inches in length, while a muley's usually measure at least 2.75 inches.

A whitetail's tail is brown on top and is fringed with white. A mule deer's is generally white on top with a black tip. It is the white hair on the underside of the tail that we see when the whitetail raises his "flag" to signal fright. The mule deer seldom uses his tail for this signal.

Finally, the whitetail's preorbital glands (tear ducts) are shallow while the mule deer's are deep.

Add to that the fact that even though agricultural area whitetails can get mighty fat, western muleys are generally larger, both in body weight and height. A mule deer superbuck will generally have a much blacker face as well.

For all their similarities, it's easy to identify the two species if you know what to look for. The exception is in areas where whitetail deer range overlaps mule deer range and hybridization has occurred.

Overall, throughout North and South America there are 30 subspecies of whitetail deer. Seventeen of them are located in the lower 48 states. Two of these are the tiny Key deer that inhabits the Florida Keys, and the southwestern Coues (pronounced "cows") deer that calls the desert southwest home.

ANTLERS

The dominant physical characteristic that all whitetail superbucks possess is their set of stately antlers. Antlers are not horns. Horn is made of a protein called keratin, a material almost identical to your fingernails. Horns are usually a permanent structure on the animal's head. Antlers are true bone that is grown and shed each and every year of a buck's life. Antlers not only serve as weapons, they also advertise the animal's sexual status and social rank. Though a mature buck's antlers are primarily a defensive weapon, they can also be turned into awesome offensive weapons if the occasion warrants.

PELAGE

When still a fawn, a superbuck has a dappled coat of small white spots on a reddish-brown background. This particular pattern is a superlative example of nature's own camouflage, as it blends in well with either sunshine or shade. A fawn doesn't lose its baby coat and spots until the molt occurs in late August to early September.

A whitetail superbuck will sport a thin, .04 to .18-inch deep reddish-brown coat during the warm months of spring and summer. During the molt, the summer coat disappears and in its place grows a heavier and darker, gray winter coat that varies from .2 to 1.1 inches in depth. This coat is remarkable for both its temperature-regulating properties and its ability to act as camouflage. It's no accident that the summer coat is a lighter color than the winter coat: light hair reflects the sun and keeps the animal cool during summer. Conversely, dark hair in winter absorbs the sun and helps keep the animal warm.

The whitetail's deeper winter coat traps more insulating air—because it's composed of an outer layer of long guard hairs stacked over a short underfur layer. This coat insulates so well that snow can pile up on the animal without melting from radiated body heat. If you were able to shave the winter coat off of a northern superbuck, the hair would weigh almost three pounds.

Sometimes hunters claim they've seen big white bucks with superracks, and bucks like this really exist. Very rarely are these white deer true pink-eyed albinos. Most often they are white deer that have brown eyes. In Illinois, it's illegal to shoot one of these whitetails. Even more rare are true melanistic deer, a phenomenon in which the deer's coat is totally black.

A whitetail superbuck's coat, while primarily reddish brown or gray depending on the season, also consists of quite a bit of white hair. His belly, underchin, and the area in front of the neck are all white. In addition, deer often have white around both eyes and muzzle. This facial white is not a true indicator of a buck's age since young bucks often are marked with plenty of facial white.

GLANDS AND SCENTS

For all the research that has been done on the whitetail deer, the animal's many glandular secretions are still not very well understood. There are five sets of external glands that serve as methods of communicating chemically with other deer. These glands give off pheromones, chemical signals that tell a deer's neighbors who he is and what he's up to. The five different glands include tarsals, metatarsals, interdigital, preorbital, and sudoriferous. The tarsals are located under tufts of hair on the inner surface of the hind legs. Metatarsal glands can be found on the outer surface of the hind legs. Look for the interdigital glands up between the cleft in the animal's feet. Preorbital glands are located at the inside corners of the deer's eyes. And finally sudoriferous glands are located in the spongy tissue of a buck's forehead.

In addition to this group of pheromones, deer also use urine as a means of communicating chemically. A whitetail doe indicates her sexual status and readiness through her urine. Bucks will also anoint velvet-covered antlers with urine. This is also thought to be an advertisement of rank and dominance.

However, whitetails apparently rely very little on pheromones to warn each other of danger. They much prefer using the flagged tail, the snort, or the foot-stomp as signals. The snort and the foot-stomp are the two sounds that deer make that are most familiar to hunters. But deer are also surprisingly vocal. They can grunt, bleat, and wheeze, either alone or in combination, to make a variety of vocalizations that mean many different things. These sounds will be covered in a later chapter.

A whitetail has three gaits: the walk, trot, and gallop. When a big buck trots he holds both head and tail up and wags the tail from side to side. When galloping, a whitetail takes several long strides between each high bound and can attain speeds up to 36 mph. And when need be, a superbuck is entirely capable of slithering on his stomach like a snake in order to make good his escape. Don't always look for a big buck to turn tail and run. Superbucks get that way because they also have nerves of steel. They like cover, any kind of cover no matter how small, and they know how to use it. They are probably more liable to stay put and wait you out than they are to run.

Superbucks—or any adult deer, for that matter—can jump a seven-foot vertical fence from a standing start, or an eight-foot fence from a running start. A buck's feet can withstand tremendous shock from those delicate-looking legs. These feet are really toes that end in hard hooves made of keratin, a protein manufactured by the body and similar to both our fingernails and the horns that other families of hooved animals grow.

The feet are quite tiny when a buck is first born, measuring about three quarters of an inch long. But when he achieves superbuck status, those same feet will often measure over three inches in length. A big deer track will often be nearly oval in shape. In soft ground or mud, two vestigial toes are also present, the dew claws.

Generally speaking, the largest-bodied whitetails come from the north, either from states like Minnesota, Wisconsin, or Maine, or Canadian provinces like Saskatchewan. Big northwoods superbucks often stand 40 inches high at the shoulder, although rare instances of bucks measuring 45 inches high have been recorded. Southern superbucks usually measure between 32 and 36 inches at the shoulder, quite a significant difference from their big northern cousins.

Any whitetail with a live weight of over 400 pounds is an exceptionally large animal, but large body weight doesn't always mean a spectacular rack. The heaviest whitetail ever recorded was killed in Minnesota and weighed 402 pounds field-dressed. Estimates placed the deer's live weight at 511 pounds. The heaviest New York buck ever documented weighed 291 pounds field-dressed and was estimated at 388 pounds on the hoof. Again, larger body size is an adaptation that makes it easier for a buck to survive cruel northern winters.

The farther south you travel, the smaller whitetails get. In 1980, the average field-dressed weight of a buck from the South Texas Plains region was 112 pounds. Deer from this region are generally the largest whitetails in Texas.

The length of a whitetail buck from the tip of his nose to the end of his tail will also vary north to south. Some of the very biggest whitetails in the northern United States and southern Canada have measured 95 inches, or just under 8 feet, from the tip of their nose to the end of their tail. In Texas this measurement drops to 72 inches (6 feet), and in the desert southwest it's only 60 inches (5 feet).

These great size differences can also make it difficult to pick out a truly big deer if you usually hunt in one area of the country and then switch to another. Up north, a huge body size will dwarf spectacular antlers, while in the deep south a deer's smaller body size will make average antlers look immense. So when judging a possible trophy in the field, be sure to keep an absolute measure for antlers in mind.

During the rut and late winter, bucks purposely restrict their food intake. This is thought to be an adaptation that helps the pregnant does and fawns survive through harsh weather conditions. Bucks are so conditioned to limit their rations that even when given extra feed they refuse to eat any more. When this behavior is added to the rigors of the rut it's easy to see why bucks will often lose from 20 to 30 percent of their body weight during this time. It's no wonder that bucks have a shorter lifespan than does. Even in areas with absolutely no hunting allowed, it's not uncommon for 20 percent of bucks *of each age class* to die during a year. The physical stresses of the rut and post-rut are simply too much for many animals to bear. And once the does are bred, the bucks are expendable.

A superbuck's large antlers are important for successful courtship, but large body size may be more essential for establishing dominance. That's because a real dominance fight, while rare, is often a shoving, pushing match that depends on brute force for its outcome.

A superbuck is in his prime from 4½ years of age until it's 7½ years old. Occasionally, studies have shown that there may be a resurgence of antler quality after age seven and a half, but that's not really considered to be the norm. He's old when he's 10 years of age. Often, an old deer will be a loner, a hermit with poor antlers which may very well be deformed because of advanced age and hormonal deficiencies. He may not actually choose to keep to himself, either. In nature's cruel way, old bucks eventually wind up outcasts.

5

The Crowning Glory: Antlers of a Whitetail Superbuck

Trophy hunters sometimes have to shoulder a bad rap: that they hunt for the finest specimens, leaving only inferior bucks to propagate the species. Well, anyone who has *tried* to consistently scout, pattern and hunt the master eluder that is the whitetail buck knows how ridiculous *that* claim is. The fact is that even areas in which almost all the *18-month old* bucks are killed each year don't develop a genetics problem. According to recent studies, an overwhelming majority of whitetail bucks living today have the genetic potential to develop into very good bucks, and many would develop into superbucks *if they were allowed to live longer.*

Eighteen-month old bucks can breed and sire other potential trophy bucks, even though they themselves still sport spike or forked antlers. So even though these bucks might not live long enough to become superbucks themselves, the genes to sire superbucks are passed on. Trophy hunters don't upset the genetic applecart. In fact, by concentrating on mature specimens, trophy hunters help an area's buck-to-doe ratio and ensure that more of a population's young bucks will one day assume real superbuck status.

In one word, *antlers* are the reason that people become trophy-hunting enthusiasts. And a whitetail's antlers are uniquely his, characterized by two heavy main beams that curve forward from thick bases, more or less on a parallel plane with his ears. Often the tips of these main beams close up in front, crown-like, nearly touching each other. Other racks remain wide open, main beam points ending as they point to the front. From these main beams sprout other lesser points or tines. A trophy whitetail's brow tines—the tines closest to the base of each antler—are usually long, sometimes measuring ten inches and more. Anywhere from two to five additional tines or points will usually grow off of each side of a big buck's main beams. Ordinarily, these will be single points that do not fork. The ends of the main beams, which count as points, are actually measured as part of the main beam itself. So a trophy whitetail will most often have from four to seven points on each antler.

"Typical" bucks are those with either no or very few abnormal points. "Non-typical" bucks have many abnormal points. The rack of a typical buck will score highest when it is evenly matched right side to left. Some bucks are scored both ways, as a typical and as a non-typical. Because it takes a higher score—195—to make Boone and Crockett as a non-typical, often a non-typical that doesn't have excessive deductions will score enough—170 points—to make the all-time records book as a typical.

SPREAD

A big typical whitetail buck's inside spread may approach 30 inches, but this kind of spread is rare. A super whitetail's inside spread is more likely to measure between 18 inches and 24 inches. In some cases, heads with inside spreads less than 15 inches have made the record book.

To determine what kind of antlers it takes to make a superbuck of Boone and Crockett caliber, I held a quick consultation with the record book. The inside spreads for typical heads vary from 14⅜ inches (only four inside spreads in the 11th edition of the record book measure less than 15 inches) to a remarkable 32-inch inside spread for a rack that currently ranks 25th in the world and which was picked up in 1991 in Comanche County, Kansas. Rather amazingly, one huge rack, which ranks number 10, sports an inside spread of just 15⅝ inches and scores 201. A super whitetail's spread is most likely to measure between 18 and 24 inches. The second largest typical rack in the world, one that had been the reigning champion for over twenty years, belongs to the Jordan buck and has only a 20⅛-inch spread. It's this head's incredible mass and near-perfect symmetry that kept challengers at bay until 1993, when Milo Hansen's great buck was finally able to outscore it to gain top spot in the record book.

MASS

Mass is important, especially mass well-represented throughout the rack as heavy tines and thickness extending to the tips of the main beams. A quick look at the Boone and Crockett record book shows that most racks that qualify have circumferential measurements (around the outside of the main beam) of between 4½ and 5½ inches at the smallest point between the base (or burr) of the antler and the brow tine. Of course, a rack that has extraordinary mass all the way to the tips will rapidly add circumference scores, compared to main beams that gradually decrease in circumference from the base to the tips. A heavily palmated rack that is even in its mass on both antlers may even make up for shorter tine lengths.

TINES

Most experts consider tine length more critical than mass when evaluating antlers. When you consider that a buck with a six-inch G-2 tine on each side (the first point after the brow tine) scores twelve fewer points than one with 12-inch G-2 tines—*just on this measurement*—you begin to understand why so much emphasis is placed on tine length.

If you truly want a superbuck for the Boone and Crockett record book, try to refrain from pulling the trigger on an eight-pointer. Although some are listed in the 9th edition, the highest ranked eight-point is tied for 343rd place with a net score of 175⅞ points. A ten-point rack will almost always have a better chance to qualify. The two extra tines usually add a minimum of five or six points to the score, which can be the difference between making the book or not.

So besides mass and spread, the hunter who is looking at an eight- or ten-pointer—and that's most of the big deer we see in the woods—should look carefully at the length of the tines. A buck may not have width, or many points, or even spectacular mass—but if his antlers have evenly matched tines 10 to 12 inches or longer, the head will probably come close to or exceed the minimum record book score.

Six- and seven-point racks with fairly short tines have qualified, too, but these are difficult racks to judge on the hoof. It would be very hard to pass one of these deer up, however, and if many shorter points are coupled with significant mass in long main beams, the buck could actually make the grade.

Antlers may be snow-white, ivory, or stained dark brown. The color of a buck's antlers is a good indication of what type of rub tree he prefers. Those stained the darkest are the result of rubbing interaction on high tannic acid tree species such as pine or cedar. Rubbing on oaks, hickories, and sagebrush will make a buck's antlers lighter.

NON-TYPICAL ANTLERS

Not all whitetails fall into the typical category just described. Non-typical whitetails have been known to grow up to 11½ pounds of antler mass on top of their heads. A cluster of bone like this can take any of a number of different shapes. Drop tines or tines that grow downward rather than up, multiple tines, forked antlers, side or "cheater" points (so called because they can extend greatest outside spread measurement), even gross palmation have all been recorded.

Some incredibly complex non-typical whitetail antlers have proven to be a real challenge to the scorers.

Basically, there are five record-keeping organizations dedicated to the task of tallying and logging for posterity the scores that your trophy attains. These organizations all recognize animal, score, hunter, owner, and state taken, and some include even more detailed information. First and foremost is the Boone and Crockett Club of Missoula, Montana, the country's oldest record-keeping organization dedicated to game animals. Boone and Crockett was founded by Theodore Roosevelt together with a group of his friends back in 1887, named for two great pioneer hunters, Davy Crockett and Daniel Boone. Dedicated solely to records of North American big game, the Boone and Crockett Club adopted the current scoring system back in 1950. While it's often accused of being unfair to antlers that lack symmetry or balance, Boone and Crockett is still the standard by which every other system is measured. To have *fairly* taken an animal that makes the book is no small accomplishment. And an animal that has grown the rack that makes the book is a buck to be cherished.

THE BOONE AND CROCKETT SYSTEM

The Boone and Crockett Club first formally recognized outstanding trophies in 1932. There were only a few trophies that made that very first list. The first competition for outstanding trophies was held by the club in 1947. This was the first time that a series of measurements were used to rank trophies by a score. In 1950 the system was refined still further and the scoring system as we basically know it today was the result. Animals that qualified as record book heads, including whitetail deer, were listed in the 1952 record book, the very first edition based on the comprehensive scoring system.

When the system was first developed, Boone and Crockett's minimum scores were much lower. In 1950 the minimum score for a typical whitetail was 140 points after a 60-day drying period; today it's 170. In 1950 the minimum score for a whitetail with a non-typical rack was 160. Today it's 195. Even with these relatively high minimums, quite a few bucks qualify each year.

"The fact that minimums have been raised so much is a testimony to the wonderful job that wildlife managers have done around the country," said W. Harold Nesbitt, former executive director of Boone and Crockett. "It's a tribute to modern game management techniques."

A deer with a few abnormal points can still be scored as a typical by Boone and Crockett, but the overall length of these points will be deducted from the rack's gross score (the raw total before deductions). This yields the "net" score. To be counted, a point must measure at least one inch in length and its length must exceed its width at one inch or more of length. As stated earlier, trophies with many abnormal points are scored as non-typicals. And it's in the scoring of non-typicals that both Boone and Crockett and Pope and Young really come under fire.

The category "non-typical" means just that, a rack that by its very appearance is truly different. Points may come off the main beams in any direction. Some non-typical racks are magnificent and yet very strange-looking. To try to counteract some of this strangeness the Boone and Crockett system looks for symmetry even in the non-typical category. This means that a non-typical could be judged as a basic four-pointer even if it has 45 scorable points like Ohio's Hole-In-The-Horn Buck. In fact, had this buck been scored as a basic five pointer as it originally was, rather than as a four pointer, it would now be the number one ranked non-typical in the world. The judging of this buck was unanimous, however, in crediting it with basic four-points-to-a-side symmetry.

Non-typicals that are off balance, say with lots of antler growth on the left beam and average growth on the right, are out of luck under Boone and Crockett. Even if the buck had grown a tremendous amount of antler material on one side, it's highly unlikely that he will rank anywhere in the book. Symmetry and balance count in the overall aesthetics of a set of antlers, at least by most humans' standards of beauty. But a system like this doesn't give credit to antler mass grown by a particular animal during the course of a single season.

Pope and Young judges non-typical antlers in a slightly different manner. In order to be considered as an entry to the Bowhunting Record Book, a non-typical whitetail must have at least 15 inches of non-typical points; otherwise it will be scored as a typical.

Another problem arises under both the Boone and Crockett and Pope and Young systems regarding inside spread. If the inside spread exceeds the length of the longer main beam, only the length of the longer main beam will be added to the score. So a wide inside spread doesn't gain you a thing. However, it doesn't count as a deduction anymore, either, ever since both record-keeping organizations changed their scoring techniques in the late 1980s.

The actual score sheets used by Boone and Crockett measurers when scoring a trophy are reproduced in these pages. By reading through the directions you can get a good idea of just what must be done in order to score a whitetail buck.

POPE AND YOUNG CLUB SYSTEM

As you have probably already gathered, the Pope and Young Club of Chatfield, Minnesota, scores almost exactly the same way as the Boone and Crockett Club.

Founded in 1961, the Pope and Young Club is named for noted archers and conservationists, Arthur H. Young and Dr. Saxton Temple Pope. All animals recorded in the Pope and Young record book have been taken through the use of archery equipment only. So bucks may qualify for both Boone and Crockett, which recognizes all legally-taken trophies, and Pope and Young *if* acquired by an archer. However, legal animals taken through the use of firearms are eligible only for listing in Boone and Crockett.

Some notable changes were recently made to Pope and Young's Fair Chase Ethic. These changes took effect several years after *Hunting Superbucks: How to Find and Hunt Today's Trophy Mule and Whitetail Deer* was first published. With so much electronic gadgetry finding its way onto the hunting and bowhunting marketplace, Pope and Young officials ruled that any animal taken "by the use of electronic devices for attracting, locating, or pursuing game or guiding the hunter to such game, or by the use of a bow or arrow to which any electronic device is attached" will not be permitted entry into the record book. In addition, "a bow shall be defined as a longbow, recurve bow or compound bow that is hand-held and hand-drawn, and that has no mechanical device to enable the hunter to lock the bow at full or partial draw. . . . A let-off of sixty-five (65) percent, using the A.M.O. standard method of measurement, is the maximum allowed."

Since killing any deer with bow and arrow is undeniably more difficult, minimum scores are correspondingly lower. For a typical whitetail, the current minimum is 125 points. A non-typical must score 155 points. In my opinion, any buck taken with a bow is a trophy.

SAFARI CLUB INTERNATIONAL

Safari Club International, located in Tucson, Arizona, is yet another record-keeping organization. As noted in a previous chapter, there are 17 different subspecies of whitetail recognized in the United States, and 30 subspecies recognized in North America. Safari Club, unlike Boone and Crockett, takes this into consideration when judging racks for their record book. Safari Club's position is that it's unfair to compare Florida whitetails with those from Minnesota, so they have established six different categories plus one for Coues Deer (Coues deer is also a separate class in Boone and Crockett and Pope and Young) to recognize superior specimens from a number of regions. These categories don't represent pure separation between any subspecies and don't pretend to—some degree of overlap will always exist. But they do attempt to take regional differences and some limited subspecies differentiation into account. Only four of these categories are concerned with whitetails from the United States, Canada and Mexico: (1) Northwestern: whitetails taken in North Dakota,

South Dakota, Wyoming, Idaho, Montana, Washington, Oregon, northern Nevada, northern Utah, and northern California. A typical minimum score of 125 points and a non-typical minimum of 131 will be required. (2) Northeastern: whitetails taken in the northeastern United States bounded on the west by Missouri, Iowa, and Minnesota, and on the south by Illinois, Ohio, Pennsylvania, and Maryland. Also includes Canadian whitetails from Ontario east. Typical minimum of 125 points. A non-typical minimum of 131 points is required. (3) Southeastern: whitetails taken in Arkansas, Louisiana, Kentucky, West Virginia, Tennessee, North Carolina, South Carolina, Alabama, Mississippi, Georgia, and Florida including all offshore islands. Minimum score for typical racks is 110 points; for non-typical racks it's 116 points. (4) Texas: whitetails from Texas, Oklahoma, Kansas, Nebraska, eastern Colorado, eastern New Mexico, and parts of northern Mexico. Minimum scores of 125 typical and 131 non-typical will apply. There is also a category for whitetails taken in other areas of Mexico.

Safari Club International's scoring system is also somewhat different from that of Boone and Crockett. A valid point must be at least 1 inch long. Roughly, points are accumulated by adding the total length of main beam, lengths of all typical points except tip of main beam (which was already included in length of main beam), plus the circumference of the burr at the base of each antler as well as the circumferential main beam measurement taken midway between each tine. Any typical point may be counted. To be designated typical, a point must grow upward from the main beam and not from the burr. A Safari Club restriction, which was only recently added to their scorekeeping system for both whitetail and mule deer racks, indicates that to be scored as a non-typical the sum of the total time length must equal 5 percent or greater of the rack's typical score. There are no deductions for any lack of symmetry.

BURKETT SYSTEM

The fourth system is the Burkett System, founded by Dr. Joseph W. Burkett. Scorers, termed tropaeologists, aim for an accurate score that's based only on the actual mass of a set of antlers. The Burkett System gives the trophy full credit for all lengths and circumferences. There are no deductions. Outside spread is measured but is used only as a tie-breaker.

As in Safari Club International's system, Burkett recognizes variations between different subspecies of whitetails. But Burkett goes even farther, recognizing all 30 subspecies as classifications. The most common classifications used include whitetails from these regions: Mexico, south Texas, north Texas, the Gulf Coast, Carmen Mountain, Virginia, Kansas, Dakota, northern, northwestern, and

Coues. By breaking it down like this, Burkett makes it easier for hunters in all areas of the country to take a record-class buck.

A rack may qualify for Burkett even while in the velvet, an important consideration for early season mule deer hunters. After measurements are taken, two percent of the score is subtracted to account for the antlers' increased size.

The Burkett System also deals with more methods of collection. Rather than lumping all racks in one total category, Burkett breaks them down into modern arm, primitive arm, archery, handgun, and incidental acquisition. Competition is confined to your peer group.

BUCKMASTER WHITETAIL TROPHY RECORDS

Finally, there is the Buckmaster Trophy Record scoring system developed by Buckmaster's editor, Russell Thornberry. Once known as the Alberta Trophy method of scoring, BTR provides an excellent way of assessing the actual score of any deer—whitetail, mule deer, or hybrid. This method does it without penalizing the rack for lack of balance or symmetry. The only criterion for inclusion in the BTR record book is that of a minimum score. The BTR does not believe that deer should be penalized in any way for the antlers they grow since they have no choice in the matter.

The BTR preserves many of the refinements of the *Alberta Trophy Deer Record Book,* and response to the new system has been overwhelmingly positive. Hunters seem to have grown weary of having outstanding antler racks score lower due to the presence of a few abnormal or atypical points. Within a few years of its inception, the BTR book contained almost 5,000 entries.

Here is how the BTR works. There are four classifications of antlers: perfect, typical, semi-irregular, and irregular. A perfect rack is one in which every typical point on one main beam has a matching typical point on the opposite main beam. There must be no more than one percent of irregular inches of antler in the total score.

A typical rack under the BTR system would be one where the total inches of irregular points would not exceed 5.5 percent of its total score. A 9-point typical rack, for example, with five points on one side and four on the other, would be classified as typical. The extra point would be considered "irregular" growth in this instance.

A semi-irregular rack would garner between 5.6 percent to 10 percent of its total score from irregular points.

An irregular rack would be one in which the total inches of irregular points exceed ten percent of its total score.

The BTR system further breaks down its scoring system to reflect the method of harvest. There are categories for hunters who use centerfire rifle, shotgun, blackpowder, centerfire pistol, compound bow, recurve bow, longbow, crossbow, pick up their trophies, or simply find outstanding shed antlers. With this system, there truly is something for everyone.

With all these record-book options available, it may be easier than you thought to take a qualifying animal. But always remember, a superbuck record really exists in the mind of its beholder. A hunter who matches wits all season long with a buck that scores 115 Boone and Crockett points should feel no shame in finally taking that trophy—if he can. Small bucks can be incredibly wily. And in areas with little hunting pressure superbucks can be much easier to take as well. So it's important for you to decide for yourself what will make *you* happy when it comes to antlers, considering what kind of heads it's *possible* to take in your hunting area. *Don't* set yourself up for continual failure. Make your goals realistic, including perhaps working your way up to trophy buck status over the seasons. The point I'm trying to make is that it's the *quality* of the experience that matters. Trophies are wonderful, but don't limit yourself to only bucks that will score 200 Boone and Crockett points. Remember, it's the sum of the *experiences* that will make you the type of hunter who will be able to capitalize on that once-in-a-lifetime chance that is the true whitetail superbuck.

When you do pull that trigger or loose the arrow that finds its mark, don't forget that a small buck should be treated as respectfully in death as a larger one. Take a moment after each and every kill to reflect on the animal that was, and what his life meant. Pause to listen to nature, for by taking a life *you've* assumed a greater responsibility. Clean off excessive blood from both the deer and yourself. If possible, arrange the carcass in your truck or car so that exit wounds aren't apparent. Cut off the animal's tongue if it's hanging out of its mouth. Take a moment to pat down the buck's hair so it isn't all scruffed up. European hunters customarily put a small green twig in the deer's mouth as a symbolic gesture that signifies the animal's last meal. It shows a respectful hunting spirit we might consider imitating.

Don't tie your trophy on your bumper or roof rack unless absolutely necessary. And if you must, please cover it with a tarp. For while some of the people you meet may be hunters, most won't be. We must respect everyone's feelings, but more importantly, we must generate respectability for our sport. Bleeding carcasses draped where they might offend aren't macho, they're tacky. Even I'm offended, and I love to hunt. When we denigrate the dignity of the animal, we denigrate ourselves and our sport. Remember, when we die they don't hang us on the fenders of the hearse.

6

The Life Cycle of a Whitetail Superbuck

It is early morning in mid-June in one of the Midwestern states. The drone of a farmer's tractor can be heard well inside the large tract of woods that abuts several agricultural fields. It's threshing time and the farmer is busy harvesting his wheat.

Inside the woods, several whitetail does are feeding along unconcernedly. They nip bits and pieces of succulent new plants, pausing to concentrate on those they like the best. Right now, the oldest doe has just uncovered some choice poison ivy to nibble on. The sunlight bounces off of the animals' red summer coats and distinctly rounded bellies and sides.

For no apparent reason, the oldest doe walks away from the other does. When they try to follow her, she gives them a hard look, then advances aggressively towards them. When they still appear to want to follow, she flails at them with her forelegs. That makes them change their minds. The oldest does are usually ranked the highest within the whitetail hierarchy. But all does seek seclusion in the weeks before they give birth.

Two weeks pass. The isolated doe is feeding when she feels a distinct twinge of pain. It's time to give birth. She walks until she comes to a small, sheltered glade. By now, the contractions that herald birth are getting closer together. She knows what they mean; she's raised fawns during several seasons already. In fact, the younger does she left earlier in the month are her fawns from the two previous years.

She turns around several times to help flatten the glade grass that grows thickly in the few spots with fairly deep soil. Then she lies down in the shade of a shortleaf pine. In less than 30 minutes, the doe is cleaning two brand new fawns, one a doe and the other a buck. She licks them all over, starting at their noses, to clean fluid and tissue from their nasal passages.

The doe baby lies nestled close to her mother, content with the attention she's getting. The baby buck, however, is already trying to stand. And within 15 minutes he succeeds, standing splay-legged and somewhat wobbly, but standing all the same. By this time, the mother has consumed all of the afterbirth. She's even eaten all the vegetation that was soiled during the birthing process. She is destroying all evidence of the fawns' birth so that predators will be unable to scent them. Now, her babies need nourishment. She stands up.

The buck fawn knows something good must be nearby, but he doesn't know what as he nuzzles his dam all over. She stands patiently until finally he hits paydirt when his nose strikes her udder. The baby doe is also up and she, too, finds the milk supply. Both babies nurse contentedly and somewhat noisily as the doe continues to lick their spotted coats clean. The buck is a big baby. He weighs just over eight pounds. His sister weighs about six pounds.

Now the babies are tired so they both collapse in the tall grass. The mother knows instinctively that she is going to need much nourishment in the coming days, so she moves away, feeding as she goes. The summer sun warms the fawns as they drowse the afternoon away. But by early evening, Buck is hungry again. He gets to his feet and is waiting when his mother enters the small clearing. With a bleat of delight, he runs to her and aggressively thrusts his nose under her rear leg. The little doe is much more sedate as she slowly walks up to start suckling.

Even now, there is a difference in the two. The buck fawn is already larger and much more aggressive and adventurous. His dam doesn't know it, but he's already explored the perimeter of the glade while his sister watched from her bed.

This time when the siblings are finished nursing, they each walk to a different bedding location. Buck leaves the glade and finds a nook between two large boulders. His sister returns to the glade, to a spot quite near the one she was bedded in before.

As the doe leaves, she notices a coyote out teaching her young how to hunt. Immediately nervous, the doe stamps her forefeet and snorts several times. The two young deer hear the doe and are puzzled. The baby doe shrinks back down, head close to the ground while young Buck moves farther back between the two rocks. The coyotes take off in the opposite direction and the doe relaxes. When they are no longer in sight, she slowly feeds away.

As the coyotes slink off, the pups begin a game of chase. They run through the woods, yipping and yelping. Within minutes they've covered a large circle that ends up right in the glade where the baby doe is almost asleep. When a pup almost runs her down, she jumps to her feet, frightened.

Mother coyote doesn't even hesitate as she follows her pups into the clearing. The young fawn means two things to her: an easy meal and yet another way to teach her babies how to hunt and survive. She's on the baby doe in a flash, breaking her neck with her powerful jaws. Her pups think it's just another game until they taste the tender meat and realize that it's dinner as well.

Off between the boulders, the buck fawn hears the snarls and yelps and tries to squiggle even farther out of sight. He's too young to know what's going on, but those noises are frightening. Sleep doesn't come easily, but he's young and eventually he forgets the scary sounds and dozes off.

Before it's completely dawn the mother doe returns. Her fawn is waiting and runs to her, bleating happily. The doe lets him nurse then looks about for her young daughter who is nowhere in sight. Anxious now, the doe moves off, grunting as she goes and leaving poor Buck to fend for himself. Confused, the little buck trails behind his mother as she looks for his sister. When she finds the scattered bones still covered with fawn hair, she knows what happened. Buck steps forward and he, too, sniffs the bones that are drenched with coyote scent. Forevermore, the smell of coyotes will make him extremely wary. The doe turns around. There's a baby to raise.

A month has elapsed: it's late July and the heat is intense. A drought has caught the countryside in its grip and many plants are rapidly fading. Buck now weighs 25 pounds. He's not nursing nearly as much. In fact, he forages for some foods on his own. One day instead of leaving Buck after he nursed, the doe encourages him to follow along. This he does, in high spirits at being able to accompany his mother to wherever it is that she disappears each day.

For several days the two of them wander the hills and fields of the doe's home range. The area that they cover isn't large, just under 80 acres. The buck has met several other deer, but they never stay with them long. One particular group looked quite strange with weird things sprouting out of their heads. His mother ignored them and he followed obediently, even though he was most curious about this group of strange-looking deer. The fawn didn't realize it, but in place on top of his own head were the pedicels from which his own antlers were already beginning to bud. Although still skin-covered nubbins, his "buttons" are already very much a part of him.

In no time at all, the small buck had memorized every trail and creek, every gap in the barbed-wire fence in the entire 80 acres. He's growing up but even so, he occasionally gets so wound up that he gallops about his mother, bucking and kicking the whole time. When he finally returns to her side, the fawn collapses in a tired heap, panting mightily.

By early September, Buck weighs over 60 pounds. One day the fawn and his mother watch as another deer walks right up to them. The two adults stand and sniff each other. Behind the new deer is a fawn. In minutes, the older doe accepts the younger doe. She recognizes her as one of her daughters from two seasons past. Now the four deer will travel together. The two fawns play together but only rarely. They are getting too old for that.

As the leaves begin to turn, Buck notices that the weather is getting cooler. He's already lost his spots and a thick gray winter coat is almost completely grown. He spends nearly all of his waking hours foraging now, as do the other deer in the group. He nurses very infrequently, mainly when he's been frightened or startled. By now, there are seven deer traveling together. Another daughter, this one with twins, has also joined up.

The deer are in peak condition as winter approaches. Often, in the evening, they crawl under the fence and go into the farmer's fields. The tender winter wheat is quite succulent and waste corn and soybeans litter the ground in nearby fields. The deer don't have to travel far to get all their nutritional requirements met.

When November arrives, Buck can tell that his mother is nervous. He doesn't understand it, but the hours that they're keeping are completely different from the lazy days of just a couple of weeks ago. Before, the doe would feed intermittently, mostly during the day. At night, they might feed for an hour or two before bedding back down. Now the doe is up almost all night as she wanders over her home range. She is very interested in several large, dark, smelly places on the ground and pays little attention to her fawn when she comes upon one of them.

Finally, the weather turns much colder. There's snow in the air and the wind is blowing from the north. The doe is now spending all her time around one line of scrapes in particular. Her time is near and she's signalled it by urinating in one of the scrapes. Soon, a buck comes trotting through the forest right for the scrape. Buck has seen bucks before but this one takes an immediate interest in his mother. Grunting, the big buck charges at the doe and she takes off in the other direction. The fawn tries to follow, but not only can't he keep up, it looks like his mother doesn't want him to. Not only that, the buck charged at him, tossing his antlers in a threatening manner when he got too close. Dejected, the young buck stayed near the spot where he'd last seen his mother.

Although it seemed forever to the fawn, his mother was back in less than 48 hours. Bleating—something he hardly ever did anymore—he rushed to her side. Now, she was like before, the model of serenity as she fed slowly through the woods. But one day, she stopped cold. Buck stopped, too, sniffing the wind like his mother was doing. It smelled strange and somewhat awful.

That's when he heard his mother snort louder than he'd ever heard her snort before. And she kept on snorting as she ran away. Later on, Buck was at the edge of the woods when he saw a strange animal walking towards the road. The animal walked on its hind two legs and had something shiny in its hand. Buck sniffed the air and there was that smell again. So like an obedient little deer, this time it was he who ran snorting deeper into the forest, the doe following quickly on his heels.

By January the weather had turned downright nasty. A heavy snow was followed by extremely bitter cold. A crust formed over the top of the snow so that the deer could no longer paw through to get to the black acorns that were scattered over the forest floor. They reverted totally to browsing, although the little deer preferred grain and nuts. Nights were harsh and days were little better. Sometimes all the deer could do was search for food all day and part of the night. The doe was getting very thin. And Buck was losing weight as well. But just when it seemed like winter would never end, it did.

The days began turning warmer and the trees and bushes began greening up. Buck and his mother stuffed themselves on the tender young shoots. The doe also seemed to be gaining a lot of weight. One day, when spring was well entrenched, she left the young buck who was by now almost as big as she was. When she did, she did not want him to follow. It took her some time, but when first she kicked him and then followed it up by flailing at him with her forelegs, she finally succeeded in making her point. She obviously did not want her son to follow her.

If Buck was dejected the day the big buck chased his mother, he was sorely distressed now. He didn't need the doe. He'd given up nursing long before. But she was his mother, the only security he'd ever known. And he would be lost without her.

But he must keep up his strength, so he fed as usual, looking for the doe whenever he spotted other deer. But as the weeks wore on, it became clear that she'd left him forever. One day, Buck was feeding along the edge of the cornfield when he noticed a bunch of bucks. By now he realized that the things growing on their heads were antlers. And because he had recently banged his head into a tree trunk and been rewarded by a stinging pain, he suspected that antlers were growing on his head as well.

Tentatively, Buck walked up to the group of older bucks. They watched him approach with some interest, then immediately went back to searching for food. When they crawled between the strands of barbed wire and headed for the forest, Buck followed. They were now in a different area than he'd ever been with his mother. He was sure that adventure was lurking just around the corner.

That summer, the bucks tolerated Buck's presence. And by August, the young buck was acquainted with much larger portions of the world. He had even crossed a road although the bright lights, noisy engines, and slippery pavement had him close to panic before he managed to escape behind his newfound buddies. He was feeling quite mature by the time he met up with his mother once again.

The doe wasn't alone. Behind her followed twin buck fawns. Buck came running over and sniffed his mother all over. She was not impressed, even though she recognized him. He tried to sniff the babies as well, but the doe chased him off. Hurt for the last time, he stood forlornly and watched his family leave. Slowly he returned to his buck buddies.

In another couple of weeks there was yet another change with which to cope. His antlers had developed into a small eight-point rack with a ten-inch spread. The rack was very good for a yearling (18-month-old) deer, but something strange was happening. His antlers were itching something awful. And some of his other buck friends were looking quite silly with shredded stuff hanging off of their antlers.

If Buck was upset when his mother left, he was really confused when the bucks gradually left, leaving him all alone, not sure of what to do. Just when he was feeling pretty grown up, his friends had deserted him. And now when he saw them they were often hitting at trees and bushes with their antlers or fighting with each other.

One day, another yearling came out of the woods and approached Buck. The two deer circled each other warily, sniffing. Buck remembered the other buck from the days just recently past. But now they both had hardened antlers and a sparring match was inevitable.

By now Buck weighed 120 pounds, quite hefty for an 18-month deer. He outweighed the other yearling by 15 pounds, plus his antlers were quite a bit more substantial. So when the sparring began, Buck had a distinct advantage. After close to 30 minutes of intermittent shoving and chasing, it was clear that Buck was the top deer—at least between the two of them. Buck knew it and felt very good about it. And that evening, he started rubbing his antlers on some small saplings just because it felt so good.

Within a few weeks it was clear that every buck in the woods enjoyed rubbing on saplings. Stripped-down trunks stood out in stark relief against the autumn landscape. Buck would watch the larger bucks in awe as they moved about the forest. Now scrapes were appearing and the musky scent of buck lay heavily about. But Buck was feeling a bit of the wanderlust. He knew he wasn't wanted in his mother's home range. And the spot where he was now hanging out really wasn't his choice at all; it belonged to several bigger bucks who had no use for him either. The only reasonable alternative was to find a spot of his own.

Now, Buck loved farm crops. So he took off along the edges of the fields, following from one cropfield to another. He crossed pastures and woodlots and even waded through several creeks. One night he came close to a farm house that was all dark and deserted. Pausing, he looked the situation over before he decided it would be safe to enter the yard in order to get to a big stretch of forest on the other side. As soon as he leaped the picket fence, however, he was set upon by a number of howling dogs. Scared witless, he jumped back out, the dogs still barking and yapping. He learned another lesson, this one about getting too close to buildings.

Finally, Buck came to a spot that he just knew was ideal. There were very few rub trees so he automatically knew there wouldn't be many other bucks. There were crops planted at the corner of a big forest. A creek ran through the woods, and all along one side a forest fire had recently burned. Buck didn't know it then, but this burn would turn into an ideal bit of escape cover. Well pleased with himself, Buck celebrated by hooking a couple of select trees. He even made a few small scrapes.

This was how he was occupied when he looked up and saw her. It was a young doe and she was looking at him. Lonely, and not quite knowing why, the buck suddenly had the urge to approach the doe. But as he headed in her direction, she bolted. It became a game then, as she ran and he chased after her. It wasn't until he felt the strafe of something hard along his haunch that he realized he wasn't quite alone in this endeavor. Out of the corner of his eye, he could see a huge buck that was running right on his heels, goring him as he went.

Buck screeched to a halt and turned to greet the older buck. The older buck wasn't in a friendly mood. Rolling his eyes and laying back his ears, the big buck advanced. Buck wasn't concerned yet. But when he saw the old buck raise the hackles along his back and neck, lower his head and then walk stiff-legged right for him, the younger buck decided to clear out and fast. The old buck took a swipe at him for good measure as Buck dashed by. The swipe was good, and Buck was rewarded with a stinging gash in his rear end. Whipped and desolate, the young buck made his way to the highest point in the forest, a spot where he could watch in three directions while, quite literally, he could lick his wounds.

Buck was a young deer, and full of curiosity. It was a brand new world out there awaiting his exploration and he was wasting time. Well before dawn, the buck was up and trotting through the woods, nose to the ground, smelling all the new, delicious scents. He'd gone just about a mile when he came to a screeching halt. *Man!* That old, disgusting smell. It was getting light by now so Buck stood shock still while he tried to figure out where the man was. Funny, the smell stopped right here.

He heard rustling in the tree over his head but disregarded it. Where could the man be, he thought to himself. Just then, a flash of fire shot down at him from over his head and a searing pain pierced his neck. Without even thinking, the buck turned tail and ran. Another shot rang out, and this one hit him in his back hoof. Another pang of pain lent wings to his feet. Now he was running flat out, straight through the thickest brush he could find. He ran until he came to another wall of man scent. Putting on the brakes, he stood completely still.

This time, the man scent wasn't as strong. And while the adrenaline was rushing through his body he realized that there was another scent mixed in with it—the odor of a doe. Sniffing now, the young buck stepped out of the thick undergrowth. And that's when another burst of gunfire blazed at his chest. Luckily, these shots weren't very close although they did splinter some branches over his head. Lesson learned. The buck stayed in the thick cover until darkness covered the woods. And while he did, he spent a lot of time licking his foot and his rump where the big buck had gored him. He couldn't reach his neck although it burned quite a bit. He didn't know it, but the bullet had taken a large strip of hair right off, hair that wouldn't grow back. The scar would brand him forever. Men would be talking about the big buck with the scar on his neck.

Buck lived out the remainder of that year in an uneventful manner. When February came, he lost his antlers. One moment they were still on top of his head, and the next moment they'd fallen right off, both of them at once. Buck wasn't very hungry that fall and winter; but by spring he was ravenous. And by summer he was getting very fat.

His antlers were growing at a rapid rate as well. Although still an eight-pointer, Buck's spread this year was going to be at least 16 inches. His brow tines were four inches long, and the remainder of his tines were from six to ten inches in length. His rack was fairly massive for a two-year old. During the summer, dominance was decided. And while Buck wasn't top buck, at least he wasn't bottom buck, either. In fact, because of his size, he was top buck of both the three-year olds and the two-year olds. Things were definitely looking up.

At the end of summer, he knew what to expect. When his velvet shriveled up and fell off, he started looking for rub trees. He thrashed them all soundly, building up the muscles in his heavy gray neck. And when the older bucks started scraping, he made his own line of scrapes along the outside edge of the soybean field where he liked to feed in the evening.

It was right at these scrapes where Buck was loitering one October evening. An older doe had moved seductively close to his scrapes before she turned and headed into the field to search out leftover beans. Buck was just about to follow when he heard grunting. Warily, he turned as one of the biggest bucks in the forest rushed into the field behind the doe. Although it was pitch black, Buck could hear the buck as he chased after the doe. Buck started to follow, but a blinding light caught him full in the face. He stopped and the light settled on the big buck.

"*Crack!*" A rifle shot punctuated the night. The big buck charged blindly right at Buck, who stepped out of the way. Then the doe rushed by. Buck started to dash back into the woods but he nearly fell on a huge lump that hadn't been there before. He stopped and sniffed. It was the big buck.

Buck stood there until he heard voices moving in his direction. He ran a short distance away, and then waited. "Boy, he's a beauty," said one of them men as he shined a light on the big buck's carcass.

"Keep it down, will you?" the other man replied. "I don't want everyone in the county to hear us."

"Don't worry, no one will," the first man said.

But then pandemonium broke loose. Although the poachers didn't know it, a game warden had been watching this very field. And now he came upon the scene. "You're under arrest," the warden said. "And thanks for leading me right to the evidence."

It was all too much for Buck, who turned and fled as fast as he could. By now, he didn't think he could be surprised anymore, he figured he'd seen everything.

But the very next day he discovered something new. For the first time, man-scent was in Buck's woods before November. Buck didn't know what to make of it until he watched from cover as a man climbed up high into a tree with a large stick and several smaller sticks with feathers on the end. Buck knew enough to avoid that tree from then on, or at least sneak up on it and look before venturing by it.

With the big buck dead, some does weren't getting bred as quickly as they normally would have. So Buck was quite surprised one morning as he checked his scrape line to find a doe waiting close by. Warily, he snuffled out into his scrape, sniffing at the intriguing mix of scents. He smelled himself and wonder of wonders, another female scent. The doe had signalled her readiness. And there was no other buck in the neighborhood. Buck took off after her.

She led him on a merry chase around his entire home range before she finally consented to stand. Instinctively, Buck knew what to do. In moments, he'd planted the seed of his first progeny within the doe. It was the beginning of a dynasty.

Buck had several other brief flirtations with does that autumn. One of them almost succeeded in getting him killed. And once he'd sped out of sight, the hunter responsible couldn't wait to tell his buddies about the handsome eight-pointer with the big scar that he'd almost nailed. For Buck's part, he decided things were getting too hot in the woods. He skulked into the old burn and came out only at night. He avoided open fields after dark like the plague. He was not only getting older, he was getting oh-so-much wiser.

That winter was one to remember. Cold and snow were so widespread and so severe that some deer died. Buck once again had little appetite for food, and lived off the fat reserves he had built up the preceding spring and summer. When February came, Buck didn't lose his antlers until close to the end of the month when one fell off one day and the remaining one the following day. By the time of spring green-up, he'd lost almost 30 percent of his body weight. His big body was almost gaunt looking.

Once buds started appearing on the trees, Buck couldn't get enough to eat. He gained back all the weight he had lost and then some. His antlers began to grow when he molted out his winter coat to exchange it for a coat of summer red. Bucks that had survived both the deer season and the brutal winter moved back onto their summer range. Buck was 3½ years old now and the second largest buck in the group. Not only that, he was also the second most dominant buck in the group once all the posturing and foot-flailing was complete.

He was a different buck now. Gone were his adolescent ways. He was regal in every sense of the word. His antlers were branching high above his head in a magnificent ten-point rack. At 3½ years his inside spread was 22 inches wide, quite respectable. The antler bases were becoming gnarled and knobby. And Buck himself was getting more heavily muscled all the time. The scar still stood out on his neck, a vivid reminder of his close brush with death. Now his face was not only filling out, it was also becoming whiter around his eyes and muzzle.

In the evenings, the farmer would watch his cropfields through binoculars. He was a deer hunter in addition to being a farmer. He began to recognize the big ten-point with the scar, and while he wasn't yet the largest buck around, he was by far the most symmetrical. Soon, the farmer longed to be the one to hang the beautiful animal on his family room wall after the coming season. But Buck had no intentions of ever letting anyone hang him on any wall. Life was good, particularly when there were no hunters in the woods. And by now, the idea of man was never far from Buck's mind.

Buck grew even larger as autumn drew near. But before he even had the urge to start rubbing, he noticed that the troubling scent of man was back in his woods. Always cautious, he became even more so. He confined all of his daytime activity to the old burn where brush grew thick and high. His bedding spots were in the same area atop a knoll that looked towards the cropfields. The prevailing wind blew right to his bedding locations, and through either scent or sight, he was able to scrutinize three directions at once. The creek formed the final side. And while Buck didn't realize it, the stream was deep enough to deter anyone from sneaking up on him that way. Through a combination of instinct and luck, Buck had chosen an almost impregnable fortress for his home range.

Once he smelled man odor, however, he gave up many of his former habits. No longer did he linger in the bean fields in the evening. And once the rut drew near, he would only move out of his thicket well after dark to rub and scrape.

The farmer was puzzled. Although he'd been trekking about, planning his hunting tactics, and therefore was the source of the scent, he had no reason to believe that Buck would abandon his schedule simply because he'd been doing a little scouting. In any case, the man soon located a spot where two heavy deer trails came together. Old rub trees nearby indicated that bucks, too, favored the area. So he brought two climbing stands into the woods to hang in different trees. That way he would be able to hunt no matter from which direction the wind blew.

He hunted the entire bow season, and gun season as well, but he never saw the big buck. There was much speculation as to whether the buck had been killed somewhere else. But after doing a quick phone check with neighbors and conservation agents, the farmer decided that Buck was probably just hiding out somewhere. Or so he hoped.

At 4½ years of age, Buck was becoming a legend. His rack would now measure 24 inches in inside spread. The beams were exceedingly heavy, and all his tines were very long. And even though the buck had still not quite reached his prime, he would already make the Boone and Crockett record book. There was no deer now that could seriously challenge him for dominance in the forest. When he fed with the other bucks, he was not only dominant, he was also the leader.

Shaking his head, the farmer watched as Buck strutted his stuff in the soybean field. By now, neighbors would visit just to get a look at the big typical. But as soon as the farmer headed into the woods, Buck took to the brush.

On the final day of the bow season, the farmer was out at dawn as usual. He had nothing to lose, so once more, he was walking over the entire wooded area that Buck called home. Buck, of course, would leave after dark to visit surrounding drainages to breed does. If he couldn't make it back to his brushy home before dawn, he'd hole up in cover wherever he could find it until it was nighttime once more.

Once, he spent the entire day in a brushpile 10 yards from a county road. Cars and trucks sped by all day. It made him pretty jittery, but he kept his head flat on the ground behind a fallen tree and no one was the wiser.

At dawn on the last day of bow season, Buck was hot-footing back to the old burn. His guard was down somewhat as he topped a small ridge. It was still too dark to see or shoot, so the farmer only knew that something big was headed his way. He stood completely still to try to discover what it was.

Call it a sixth sense, but Buck knew something was wrong. He stopped and sniffed the air. All he could detect was a faint odor of skunk. But that in itself was suspicious since the smell of skunk was often to be found where hunters had been sitting during the day. Without moving an inch, the buck waited. And so did the farmer.

Slowly, the sky lightened and the farmer could make out the tremendous buck 30 yards away, out in the open. Still, moving ever so slightly, he tried to nock an arrow.

Buck stood like a statue except for his ears which were twitching back and forth. He could hear something that wasn't natural but what was it? Twisting his torso around, the farmer drew the string back. But it was a cold morning and the limbs of the compound creaked a little. In a flash the buck leaped back over the ridge. The arrow flew but fell short. Even as the farmer rushed over the ridge, Buck was already stampeding down a small gully, his golden rack bouncing quickly out of sight.

Sighing, the farmer picked up his arrow and headed back to the house. He knew the deer would not return anymore this day. But before he had gone very far, an idea hit him. He backtracked to where he had shot at the buck and started looking around. Soon he found a light yet distinct trail, with several big hoofprints heading uphill. The farmer followed, and when he reached the top he had to fight his way through the brush. But when he saw a big scrape and nearby a large bed—nearly six-feet in diameter—he knew he had hit paydirt. Smiling to himself, he headed back home. Next year he'd be ready.

The farmer thought about the big buck often. And sure enough, Buck's rack was even larger than it had been the year before. At age 5½, it would score over 200 Boone and Crockett points and might even give the Jordan buck a run for its money.

This year, the farmer changed his tactics. When summer ended, he stayed out of the woods completely. And he made his hunters go to a different patch of forest to hunt that fall. So Buck wasn't disturbed at all.

But far from being lulled into a false sense of security, every nerve in the big buck's body was on full alert. He still went out into the fields to feed in the evening, but now he seemed to know that it was the farmer that was his adversary. He would stare at the house for long minutes each evening before taking nervous bites of the ripe bean plants. The farmer even commented to his wife, "It looks like the old boy knows what I'm up to."

Under ordinary circumstances, Buck would maintain the rack that he had at 5½ years of age for possibly two or three more years. Then, little by little, its quality would start to slip. His teeth would be wearing down and so he would also slowly lose weight and vigor. A whitetail buck is old by the age of ten. And many, many bucks die for reasons completely unrelated to hunters—and almost unknown to biologists—well before the age of 5½. So Buck was already a rarity, a mature whitetail buck, a real survivor. And because of the way he was programmed, Buck intended to remain a survivor.

So on opening morning of rifle season, when the farmer knew he would have his best chance to take the big deer, he was seated on the stump of an old burned pine tree, about 100 yards from the area with all of the big beds. The farmer had taken a chance. He'd gotten to his stand at 4:30 A.M., when he was reasonably sure that the big buck would still be out prowling. Now he sat shivering in the darkness, peering intently towards the big beds.

As the sky began to turn gray, the farmer heard the sound of swift walking moving up the hill towards him. He got his rifle up on his knees and struggled to see through the thick brush.

Buck was wary. He'd walk quickly for a while and then stop, sniffing. *Something was wrong, but what?* There *had* been more cars on the road this morning, but still, he didn't smell any man-scent. *So what was it?* He stretched out his neck and sniffed the ground. *Nothing.* So he moved off towards his bed, slower now, nose to the earth.

The farmer could now see movement, the tips of big antlers moving slowly through the brush. There was an opening that the buck should step into shortly. Sighting down the barrel, the farmer put his finger on the trigger and waited.

Moving slowly across the brushy thicket the buck was just about to step out. He paused just as the farmer took off the safety with a metallic *click*. Now he twisted his head towards the sound and stopped completely. What was that?

For long minutes it was checkmate. The deer was so close to home, so close to safety. Dare he take a chance?

Would the buck step into the opening, the farmer thought to himself?

The tension was palpable: who would win this round?

7

Whitetail
Superbuck
Behavior

Fifty years ago the total deer population for all of North America was less than 400,000 animals. Populations had steadily plummeted from estimated highs of 35 million deer around the year 1500. Of course, no one really knows for sure exactly how many deer lived back then, but as the continent was settled, deer were overharvested—there were no closed seasons in many cases. Habitat was destroyed as land was cleared for farms and cities.

Not until the first game and fish agencies began to experiment with basic wildlife management principles in the early part of the twentieth century did whitetail numbers begin to stabilize. Eventually, the animals rebounded until today close to 55 million whitetail deer inhabit North America.

Since 30 different subspecies of whitetail deer inhabit the North American continent, hunters often wonder if they're after the same deer in Montana that they're pursuing in Pennsylvania. Basically any whitetail is a whitetail, in terms of its basic, intrinsic ability to learn survival lessons quickly. But Dr. Richard Mackie of Montana State University said that not only do whitetails differ morphologically from region to region (slight skeletal differences, for example), but there are also behavioral differences.

Mackie explained, "While the gross behavior of all whitetails is roughly the same, differences certainly exist in such behaviors as manner of movement or the way different animals flee to escape predators. These differences have developed in whitetails from various regions because they inhabit such broadly different habitats and environments. The differences that do occur reflect adaptations to these environments so you get animals of somewhat different sizes and shapes plus variable behaviors.

"For example, in a brushy midwestern forest a disturbed whitetail buck will dive for cover and stay there until he feels it's safe to come out again. But a whitetail buck that lives on the western tallgrass prairie may flee like a forest-dweller—only out across the open plain because that's where *he* feels safe. Different habitats require that the whitetails that live there use strategies and behaviors specifically adapted to these habitat types."

All species of whitetails are survival-oriented. Those that are rarely hunted may not appear wary, but when put to the test they'd soon be just as cunning as their hard-hunted kin. Of all these survival-oriented animals it goes without saying that the canniest, craftiest, and wiliest of the bunch are those that are hunted the hardest and prized the most: the superbucks.

Occasionally, a big superbuck may survive and grow to an astonishing size through pure luck. But it's far more likely that a buck in his first year of life will be initiated by fire: *gun*fire—or at least the sound of gunfire during hunting season. If the buck isn't the actual target, chances are that his mother or another animal in his company is. If any of the animals are hit, or are killed, it's a lesson that the youngster won't soon forget.

The following fall, when the buck becomes a yearling (actually he's about 18 months of age), he'll be sporting hardened antlers. That really makes him fair game for most hunters. If he hasn't been shot at before, he'll be shot at now, especially since an 18-month-old buck is moving all the time in search of his own territory. This roving makes him very susceptible to hunting pressure. If the yearling lives through his first season, during which it's estimated that over 90 percent of all bucks perish, then he's well on his way to the age needed for super antlers.

A deer learns in much the same way that human beings learn, at least during the early stages of our lives: he imitates his mother. He investigates sights, sounds, and smells, and reacts accordingly. If his mother reacts with fear to human scent, then her fawn will also behave in a fearful manner. It's very possible that human scent itself isn't repulsive to whitetail deer, but the bad memories associated with it are, and that this reaction is passed on from animal to animal. You only have to observe game park deer to realize this is true. Where people are allowed to handfeed whitetails, you won't hear snorting or see white flags bounding away. The deer have been conditioned to accept the presence of people. In many cases, they seem to look forward to seeing them.

We hunters identify a deer by the way he looks. But behaviorists, a specialized kind of animal scientist, also identify him by the way he acts under different circumstances. They classify some behavior as innate or inbred: the animal was born knowing how to act. A buck's rut behavior and breeding is an example of innate behavior. But other behavior is learned from watching and imitating its mother or other deer. Behavioral scientists argue about where to draw the line between learned and innate behaviors. Deer behaviors that interest us as hunters are those that make the superbuck an unequaled master of evasion, and some of them do seem to be learned.

Deer *do* learn from their experiences and from watching other deer. They also learn from watching us. And after years of watching deer react in various tight situations, I personally believe that deer can think—not as well or in the same way as people do, perhaps, but well enough to escape *most* of us *most* of the time. Deer biologist Dr. Larry Marchinton, who recently retired from the University of Georgia School of Forest Resources, agrees: "I personally believe that humans and deer use the same basic 'thought' processes," he said, "but with one important difference: man has developed his rational behavior to a much greater degree." That rational advantage is the only area where hunters can compensate for the superbuck's advantage in superior hearing, smell, and sight. We can apply it to the whitetail's innate behaviors, and then fit in the superbuck's learned tricks of survival.

RANGES

A whitetail's innate behavior includes patterns of movements since these patterns are often adaptations it's made in order to survive. Deer "movements" must also include such patterns as home range size and shape.

A deer's home range must supply the essentials of life—food, water, and cover—yet be small enough so that the animal feels safe within it. On the average, a whitetail's home range is smaller than that of any of the other North American deer species. But remember that home ranges vary in size from one individual deer to another and from one region of the country to another.

Northern deer, for instance, generally inhabit a larger home range than southern deer. Studies done in Wisconsin estimate that the average deer there has a 440-acre home range. Compare that with the 210 acres of the average Florida and Alabama deer. One reason northern deer range farther is that year-round forage is generally harder to come by in the north country forests.

Deer living in plains areas—or any open area—often have larger home ranges than deer in heavily timbered or brushy areas. According to a study in Minnesota, deer in thick conifer forests averaged 5.1 miles from one end of their range to the other; deer on the Minnesota prairie averaged 9.6 miles. Again, forage is undoubtedly a determining factor: there is generally more food and more cover to choose from in areas of heavy brush and timber.

As a rule, bucks have larger home ranges than does, probably because does are "homebodies" in the deer world, since they must raise the young. For example, in a Missouri study the mean range size for does was 400 acres, but more than 900 acres for bucks. And bucks may expand their range during the rut: one buck in Georgia more than doubled his home range from 228 to 603 acres each fall.

Although migrations between ranges are thought of as mule deer behavior, whitetails exhibit migratory behavior, too, under special circumstances. In many states, especially those with extreme seasonal weather fluctuations, whitetails travel between summer and winter ranges. Migrations have been observed as far south as Missouri and northwest Georgia. If a migration pattern appears in your area, this piece of the hunting puzzle may complete the range picture.

YARDING

"Yarding," the tendency of deer to hole up in sheltered areas during the winter, is a behavior associated with cold temperatures. Deep snow contributes to the whitetail's yarding tendencies. The yarding instinct is a basic one: it's a survival tactic designed to conserve energy by minimizing body heat loss. Scientists suspect that in the past yarding also helped reduce wolf predation since it concentrates animals in herds. It probably still serves this purpose in deer states that have a healthy wolf population, like Minnesota.

As might be expected, whitetails move the most during the rut and the least during late spring when succulent food sources can be found everywhere. Late spring is also when the fawns are born: it's no accident that birthing occurs when does won't have to travel far to replenish vital milk supplies.

Totally nocturnal whitetails are undoubtedly reacting to unwanted human presence. A deer needs only a few unpleasant encounters to convince it to limit its daytime movements when man is around. But where deer are undisturbed, they apparently feel no qualms about moving freely during daylight hours.

WEATHER INFLUENCES

Various studies conducted around the country reflect the great variety of behavior observed in different deer populations during all sorts of weather. Most researchers agree that deer are most likely to be active when the relative humidity is low.

Yet in many locales even a steady rain doesn't deter the animals from moving. Cloud cover itself is a big "if": some researchers feel it limits deer movements, while others disagree.

When winds begin to rustle the leaves, deer get edgy. By the time winds are gusting in great bursts—strong enough to fly a kite—many deer's nerves seem to reach a warning zone, and they'll bed down, *unless* the rut is on. Even if deer bed, though, the animals will remain at high alert: standing, occasionally shifting positions, eyes, nose, and ears keen to the threat of danger.

Temperature is also a factor in deer activity and its effects depend on the overall climate where the deer live. If the weather is unseasonably warm during hunting season, activity will generally increase as the temperature drops. A deer that's already grown its heavy winter coat won't be out moving if he's going to be uncomfortable. This is true even in southern climates where deer are better adapted to warmer weather.

Likewise, in colder weather activity increases as the temperature rises. After a bitter-cold night or a temperature-decimating storm, deer forsake the beds where they've been conserving their body heat to soak up the sunshine on south-facing or east-facing slopes.

The combined interaction of all factors—temperature, wind, humidity, precipitation, and cloud cover—affects deer activity more than any single component. Deer adjust their activity to suit their comfort level no matter what time of year it may be. As a hunter it's your job to try to predict what they'll be doing at any given time. Some hunters have managed to raise their success quotient by keeping detailed diaries and journals and logging all the variables, such as temperature, wind direction and speed, relative humidity, whether it's raining or not, etc. Later on, they tie in daily deer sightings to this information, hoping to determine a pattern that applies to the area where they hunt.

SOCIAL BEHAVIORS

Other innate superbuck behavior is tied into the fact that whitetails are highly social animals. Does form doe groups, usually consisting of a mother and young from one or more years. Does won't usually tolerate other unrelated adult does.

Bucks—even superbucks—however, are usually more social than does. It's quite common for two to five bucks to form groups and move together all year long *except* during the rut, a time when complete independence is the rule. When the bucks are running together, however, they don't form permanent group attachments. Membership in these buck groups is constantly changing.

Each deer, buck or doe, strives to either maintain or improve its own unique position within its group or social hierarchy. As any animal matures, its rank may change. High-ranking animals dominate subordinates. And while dominants have been known on occasion to drive subordinates from the group forever, they're usually content if subordinates act submissively and just move away.

Subordinate deer not only avoid physical contact with dominant animals, they also shun direct eye contact. You'll never see one deer looking directly at another one unless trouble is brewing. Eye aversion is a gesture typical of subordinate behavior. In fact, even when deer are bedded, members of the group face in the same direction or away from each other but *never* toward one another. When passing, a dominant deer will lay its ears back and give the subordinate a "hard look." There's no doubt in anyone's mind that the dominant deer expects the subordinate to be submissive. Mutual grooming, when two or more deer lick each other, is one of the few frequently-seen whitetail interactions.

As a rule, social rank is based on size or age. Larger bucks usually dominate those smaller than themselves. For does, however, age is a better indicator of rank than size or weight. And while the gender groups usually don't interact, on those rare occasions when they do, adult bucks usually dominate does.

BEHAVIOR DURING THE RUT

Behavior associated with the three- or four-month period of the rut begins when bucks start sparring and ends when all breeding is concluded. Although sparring *looks* like the activity that determines dominance levels, it is probably merely symbolic. Many biologists and behaviorists think that dominance order is decided many months earlier, while antlers are still in velvet. At that time, foot flailing bouts determine the bucks' ultimate rank for the year. Bucks rear up on their hind legs and flail at each other with their forefeet, much as does do. By the time antler season does arrive, bucks with antlers already know where they stand in the hierarchy and can afford to play-act. They are learning fighting skills that may serve them later on rare occasions when true dominance fights with hardened antlers occur. True dominance fights are usually short-lived bouts of intense shoving and neck-twisting, seldom lasting longer than 30 seconds.

Courtship or doe-chasing usually starts between four to six weeks after bucks begin sparring. Once the bachelor buck groups break up for the season, the mature bucks strive out on their own.

The prime bucks begin trailing does half-heartedly at first. Does act quite coy, letting the bucks trail them but never letting them get very close. Early in the season, a buck loses interest in *trailing* a doe very quickly as she will often run off to keep him at a distance. Later on that's not the case. The closer to a doe's estrus cycle—the 24-to-36 hour period when she's willing to stand so that a buck may mate with her—the closer she'll let the buck get. As the buck trails the doe, she'll urinate periodically. The buck will sniff the doe's urine and perform "Flehmen" or lip-curl behavior, thought to help him determine how close to estrus the doe is.

While a dominant buck is tending a doe, his behavior is very defensive. Lower-ranked bucks are quickly threatened if they get too close. When a mature buck is rankled by a subordinate's presence he'll raise the hair on his back and neck, walk stiff-legged, or lower his antlers and hook them at his adversary. A wise subordinate animal would do well to get out of the dominant buck's way.

Two other important types of buck behavior involve rubs and scrapes. Interpreting these signs correctly is so critical to a superbuck hunter's success that they are treated in two later chapters.

LEARNED BEHAVIORS

Many hunters have heard stories of a deer escaping from an encounter with man by crawling on its belly. How about the deer that runs away keeping a large tree between itself and the hunter the whole time? Or the deer that gets away by running in a gully, or through a culvert, or by wading down a stream to throw hounds off its trail? So many deer have been reported using these techniques that it seems unlikely they all discovered them independently during encounters with hunters. In order to learn all these tricks, a buck would have to have a close encounter with man every day of the hunting season each and every year.

I hunt along the edge of a wildlife refuge where the deer are never hunted. I noticed these "unhunted" deer use the very same tactics on me. Where did they learn them? In some rudimentary way they've figured out our weaknesses and use this "logic" to beat hunters at their own game. That's why when many superbucks are finally taken, they're killed by hunters who were doing something the deer did not expect—sometimes unintentionally. You'll read about some of them in Part 3. For now, remember there are actually *two* ways to trip up a smart superbuck: first, learn everything you can about your buck's behavior and beat him that way; or second, do something "wrong"—hunting at the "wrong" time or in the "wrong" cover—and beat him by doing the unexpected.

I prefer the first strategy simply because hunters who blunder into a big buck start out at the *end* of the superbuck success equation. They're probably never going to duplicate the feat as long as they live because they won't have to learn all the factors in the equation. But if you learn the innate behaviors of deer, then add observations *from your hunting area* about what makes a big buck tick—you just might get to the point where you consistently get good deer. You're thinking like a superbuck! And who knows, one day that discipline just might bring you the kind of wall-hanger that will really light up your life—and you can say you outwitted a superbuck at his own game.

8

Favorite Whitetail
Superbuck Forage

Crack! The sound knifed through the silence of the December woods. It was the final day of Missouri's last split firearms deer season. I'd been hunting feverishly for a buck, so I turned with renewed hope towards the sound's source. As I watched, a thick, gray body moved slowly down the ravine that cut across the hillside in front of me. Cedars growing along the top of the cut helped obscure the animal from view.

Finally, I glimpsed heavy antlers. Not only was it a buck, it was quite possibly *the* buck, one of Boone and Crockett caliber. And apparently, *the* buck was in no hurry. He traveled as if in slow motion, head to the ground, stopping occasionally. But why? At last I figured it out: the big bruiser was scrounging for acorns and savoring every bite.

I'd like to report that my well-placed shot connected, but that wasn't the case. There was a shot, all right, but it missed completely. This was near the beginning of my deer hunting career, and buck fever still had me firmly in its grasp. I'm over the buck fever now, but I've never seen a rack anywhere near as good as this one since.

What fascinated me most about this buck was that unlike any other whitetail buck that I've glimpsed during the firearms season, this one was clearly foraging. While other, lesser bucks spend days with noses to the ground in hot pursuit of does or interesting scents, old Methuselah was calmly enjoying a snack.

Whitetails are infinitely adaptable creatures. One of the manifestations of this adaptability is in the tremendous variety of vegetation they'll eagerly include in their diet. Right there is the place to start hunting your superbuck; learn the basics of whitetail nutrition. It will help you understand more about the animal and help make you a better hunter at the same time. For as they take part in the never-ending search for forage, deer become vulnerable. Even if bucks rarely feed during the rut, the does do. And where the does are hanging out, that's where the bucks will be.

The food that a whitetail consumes must furnish him with the essential nutrients that enable him to grow as a fawn and live and reproduce as an adult. It must also be of sufficient quality and quantity so that bucks can grow the massive antlers that we all regard so fondly.

BASIC DEER NUTRITION

There are six classes of nutrients contained in food: water, protein, fats, carbohydrates, vitamins and minerals. When an animal consumes food, it must be digested—broken down into those six nutrients—before it can be utilized.

These nutrients are the same ones required by humans in different percentages. Deer seem to do well on a high-energy, high-protein (at least 16 percent) diet with sufficient amounts of two minerals, calcium and phosphorous.

Deer can survive on a diet containing as little as 8 percent protein even though this is considered starvation rations. Even at a level of 12 percent protein, however, only a few trophies will be produced. For optimum trophy buck production, researchers recommend a protein content of 18 to 22 percent in the forage the animals eat.

An overbrowsed range may spell the virtual end of quality deer hunting in that area, even if the population doesn't actually starve to death. Poorly fed does often experience a fawn mortality rate of up to 93 percent, compared to the 7 percent mortality rate of well-fed does. The long-range importance of maintaining a habitat with a good selection of protein-rich plants becomes apparent.

A deer, like us, needs energy to live. Energy is a property of protein, fats, and carbohydrates, measured in calories. When a deer eats the correct number of calories per day, its weight will remain constant. The food energy it takes in will be expended in basic body functions like breathing and the production of body heat. If it eats fewer calories than it needs, the deer's body will break down its own store of fat and ultimately its own muscle tissue for the fuel to carry on body functions. In this case, the animal loses weight. On the other hand, if the deer takes in more calories than it needs for body functions, the excess is stored as body fat.

A deer's digestive system is quite unique. Deer are called "ruminants" after the major portion of their four-part stomach, the rumen. Ruminants can digest food which humans can't—like woody browse—because microbes in the rumen can break these foods down for digestion. The rumen holds difficult-to-digest foods for several days while the microbes do their work. More easily digested foods can pass through within a few hours.

The rumen system is made to order for an animal that must eat, then often flee from predators. Once the deer is safe again, it can regurgitate its cud or "bolus" and chew it at its leisure.

Contrary to popular opinion, deer aren't exclusively browsers. Often, deer will resort to browse only because the area has been overgrazed. If woody stems are all that's left, woody stems are what deer eat. Given a choice, however, deer will alternate between grazing and browsing.

While deer will eat just about anything, whitetails still have favorite foods, what deer biologists call "ice-cream plants." And as long as a portion of their range provides these ice-cream plants, resident deer nibble at them, often until they kill them.

Whitetails enjoy eating plants that people also enjoy—enjoy looking at, that is. Maybe the prettiest things are also the tastiest. When I planted tulips, hyacinths, roses, white pines, and apple trees on our farm, the deer were glad I did. They promptly ate them all. My apple trees still live, although they're browsed back so high that they look ridiculous. My ancient lilac bush blooms and leafs out only over a height of four feet, the height at which whitetails will ordinarily give up.

Researchers have categorized the types of foods that whitetails eat. There are grasses, sedges, fruits, nuts, forbs, mushrooms, and browse—portions of shrubs and trees. Deer have also been known to eat dead leaves, bark, soil, and even their own droppings under extreme conditions.

Of course deer foods vary tremendously depending on the area of the country. Deer scientists have found enough coherent topographic features and vegetation types to divide the North American whitetail's range into 18 separate regions. Even that's probably not enough: within each of these regions exist other, less well-defined forage areas with even more diversity.

Whitetails inhabit the tallgrass prairies of the plains states, the Rocky Mountains all the way up to altitudes near 14,000 feet and even portions of British Columbia and Mexico. The huge variety of forage available to whitetails is truly mind-boggling. Still, some deer foods crop up more often than others, especially in agricultural areas. Legumes like clover, lespedeza, alfalfa, and cowpeas are all high in protein content. Deer might then move on to grasses like bluegrass, brome, rye, and orchardgrass. Deer go for row crops as well. Soybeans, corn, and sorghum are all on deer's "ice cream" list. So are wheat and oats. With or without encouragement, deer will leap fences to sample most varieties of garden vegetables as well; strawberries are a particular favorite. No fruit orchard is safe; deer love apples, cherries, plums, and pears, often risking their necks to get at them.

Deer like foods that occur in their habitat naturally, too. Wild mast, either fruit or nut, is one such preference. Acorns—white or red—are both eagerly eaten. White oaks are capable of bearing acorns every year if weather conditions are right, and these acorns have less tannic acid than red oak acorns so they're probably sweeter. One thing is certain: if deer discover a ripe white oak they will promptly abandon other food sources until every acorn is gone. There's another reason for acorn-gobbling as well. White oak acorns will quickly sprout or rot once they've been rained on. The deer seem to realize that they'd better get white oak acorns while the getting is good.

Red or black oaks don't bear acorns every year, since it takes two years for these nuts to mature. While a red oak acorn may be a little less palatable, it is hardy mast indeed. These sturdy acorns lie on the forest floor all fall and winter without sprouting. When the white oak acorns are long gone, red oak acorns will still be providing needed winter nourishment for deer and other forest creatures.

A favored soft mast that grows in many different parts of the country is the common persimmon. Persimmon trees are either male or female and only the female bear fruit. Persimmons ripen in late summer and some trees are still bearing fruit in December. It's common to hear stories of deer waiting eagerly beneath persimmon branches for more fruit to fall or flailing with their front feet to knock more off the branches.

Another excellent whitetail food source are the varieties of wild grape. Grapes are easily distinguished by their ropy-looking, twisted vines. The grapes themselves are often small and insubstantial looking, nothing like the commercially grown grapes you see at the supermarket. Deer love grapes dearly, fruit and leaves both.

Other sources of deer delight are the various wild berries. Deer love wild strawberries, raspberries, blackberries, and dewberries. Deer can be found nibbling on them from first greenup, when stalks and new growth are most tender, right through late autumn when the plants finally lose their leaves. They also eat the flowers and later make gluttons of themselves on the fruit. Berries are a good argument for clearcuts, since when a forest canopy is opened, berries often take over until mature trees shade them out again. They are an excellent deer food.

Other preferred foods that grow in many different areas of the country include honeysuckle, white pine, black cherry, blueberry, greenbrier, flowering dogwood, trumpetcreeper, poison ivy, sassafras, coral berry, redcedar, serviceberry, red maple, and several kinds of sumac—fragrant, dwarf, and smooth. Of course, the time of year when they are favored may vary from region to region.

In New England, pin cherry and red maple are eagerly sought after. According to a study by Scott Williamson of the New Hampshire Fish and Game Department and David Hirth of the University of Vermont, deer don't use these foods in the same proportions as they are found. That is, if the ratio of trees is 60 percent sugar maple to 20 percent red maple, deer don't eat more sugar maple just because it's easier to find. Red maple is an ice-cream species, so deer eat more of it even though it's less common.

In the southern Appalachian Mountains, Dick Harlow of Clemson University in Clemson, South Carolina, has made a career out of studying deer and their forage. According to Harlow, deer like mushrooms and often eat dry leaves, especially in winter. Dry leaves favored by the animals include those of oaks, mountain laurel, honeysuckle, and galax. "If a deer resorts to eating rhododendron leaves, that means there just isn't anything else around to eat," he observed.

Whitetails will also eat the pods of honeylocust or black locust trees. These dark brown pods are eight to ten inches long, and contain a number of round seeds. Whitetails devour the pods when they fall from the trees in autumn.

Farther south, tropical species enter the deer diet. Harlow was a pioneer in identifying what deer like, and here's what he has to say. "I found 193 different deer food choices in Florida alone. Dwarf palmetto, supplejack (rattan), deciduous holly, swamp cyrilla, redbay, yaupon, and sweetbay are all important food."

Up in the northwoods, beechnuts are eagerly sought by deer. During the spring, deer seek out aspen root suckers and the fiddleheads of bracken fern.

In the Midwest, deer devour asters (apparently an important food for midwest trophy deer production), goldenrod, pussy's toes, and tick trefoil (also called beggar's lice), a legume with a high protein content.

Out West, deer can eat snowberry, chokecherry, willow, and bearberry in the more northern latitudes. Some sagebrush and rabbitbrush enter the diet as we move through the high plains states. And farther south deer in portions of Texas eat panhandle grape, western soapberry, cottonwood, and sunflowers.

Bob Zaiglin, noted big buck hunter and wildlife manager for the Harrison Ranches of south Texas, has also studied deer forage extensively. "Deer down here love catclaw," he commented. "Catclaw's a very good deer food that maintains a high protein content all year long. Granjano is a brush species that's also a good protein source. In the winter, deer forage extensively for prickly pear, a high-energy food. Pear flats sometimes look almost white from the bites taken out of the plants by deer."

Of course, since whitetails are undisturbed by hunting pressure nine months of every year, it's during those months that they set the patterns they will follow as hunting season opens. So the first week of hunting is probably the prime time to capitalize on deer browse knowledge. Later on, forage patterns—especially the buck's patterns—will change with hunting pressure and the changes in available forage.

Hunters are one up on nearly anyone else who admires nature. Unlike most people, hunters are often out *in* nature as observers. A dedicated hunter spends time afield during seasons other than autumn, keeping an eye out for deer sign. That hunter is learning woodsmanship, the inimitable art of piecing together all the parts of the puzzle that we call deer hunting. How can he or she help but become a better deer hunter in the process? The hunter and woodsman appreciates even more the intricate world in which humans and whitetails live.

9

Where to Find Whitetail Superbucks

As whitetail hunters we've come a long way in a short time. A technique as basic as scrape hunting was virtually unknown back in the 1960s. The art of calling deer came into its own during the mid-1980s. Not only do we have a lot of new knowledge, and new techniques to capitalize on that knowledge, today there are a lot of deer available to hunters everywhere. Record numbers of animals can now be found in nearly every state, and seasons are more liberal than they've been at any time during the past 50 years. This information is good news for those hunters who like to get a deer every season, but it's bad news as well, especially for those hunters looking for a superbuck.

When whitetail populations soar, the numbers of superbucks in an area usually decline. The best superbuck hunting can most often be found in an area with a deer population that's still building. Once a population has peaked, range quality begins to decline. That means there are fewer high-grade nutrients available to bucks for antler growth. Areas with high deer populations also invite lots of hunting pressure and increased license quotas. That means more small bucks are culled from the herd, leaving fewer to develop to superbuck size. Poachers, too, are attracted to areas with lots of deer. And they reduce the numbers of bucks in an area as well by indiscriminate illegal harvest.

There's still a silver lining: paradoxically, more big bucks are being killed now than ever before. Maybe it's just *because* there are more whitetail hunters hunting larger numbers of whitetails than ever before. Whitetails are being managed intensively by state game and fish agencies in nearly every area in their range. Most states manage for quantity; a few have areas that are managed for quality. In some states, such as Texas, private ranches hire professional wildlife biologists to ensure that their whitetail deer attain good growth. Whatever the reason, record numbers of record book heads are being taken. According to statistics cited in Boone and Crockett's *Records of North American Big Game* (11th edition), which was published in 1999, 39 or almost 46 percent of the top 85 places in the listing for typical whitetail racks and 27 or a little less than 32 percent of the top 85 places occupied by non-typical racks were harvested from 1985 until 1999.

Whitetail deer researchers are nearly unanimous in the opinion that every state has the potential to produce big bucks. The only reservations that were expressed were for small, isolated areas of Florida, Georgia, and Texas. The fact is, a big buck could be living near your home *or* your hunting area right this very minute. Let's examine the various factors that make a particular area within a state or province a good trophy producer.

In this and in earlier chapters I discussed the importance of hunting areas with low deer densities and low hunter pressure. Good genetic breeding stock is another important consideration, as is the presence of fertile soil that produces nutrient-rich forage.

One clue to look for in the quest for a trophy buck is whether or not the deer in your hunting area are whitetails native to the state. While nearly every state's native herd has the potential to produce trophy bucks, deer that have been stocked into an area from a big buck state may produce offspring with larger antlers.

Dr. Larry Marchinton, Dr. Karl Miller, their colleagues from the University of Georgia together with writer and big buck hunter Duncan Dobie studied four adjacent southeastern states—Alabama, Georgia, Florida, and South Carolina—to determine whether genetics and/or environment were factors in the production of trophy antlers.

Wildlife biologists already knew that the largest-bodied and biggest-antlered deer were usually produced in the north. But no one really knew whether or not a transplanted Wisconsin buck, for example, would pass along his large antlers to later generations of home-grown Georgia bucks. Dr. Marchinton's study showed that, while large antlers are produced from stockings, heredity by itself is not enough to ensure the development of large antlers. Good soil and habitat are also required. Of the four states studied, Georgia had more than three times as many big bucks as runner-up Alabama. All of Georgia's record-class bucks have come from two regions—the Southern Piedmont and Southern Coastal Plain—and an unbelievable *83 percent* of these were taken close to major river systems.

River bottoms are important to good big buck production—another consideration for the trophy hunter. Fertile riparian soil grows heavy cover so bucks can escape, plus it produces a better quality browse. Fertile soil is so important to super antler growth that these researchers concluded that a lack of it is undoubtedly the reason why Florida has produced only one record-class buck, even though some Wisconsin deer were stocked there, too.

Now on to the various states and provinces. To help you determine just where most of the big bucks are coming from, I've analyzed the 1,292 listings in the Boone and Crockett Club's *Records of North American Whitetail Deer* (9th edition), plus the top 508 listings of both typical and non-typical racks in the Pope and Young Club's *Bowhunting Big Game Records of North America*. I've determined where each of the top 1,800 animals in North America were taken. Since kill sites are usually reported by county, by doing a lot of tallying I was able to come up with the top-producing counties in each state. With a little bit of detective work on your own part, it should be fairly easy to determine whether or not these counties contain any good riverbottom areas to hunt. When public hunting land is widely available in these counties it will be noted; other state and county public hunting areas may be available as well. So if you see some place that looks like a hotspot, continue your search with the local game and fish department.

Remember, no big buck is worth a trespassing violation. Many of the top big buck areas are going to be on or near private land because intensive agriculture often contributes a lot to an area's big buck production. Asking permission is one thing; flagrantly disobeying the law is another. To take a big buck illegally is like cheating at solitaire—the only one you're cheating is yourself.

By the way, if some states seem under-represented in the record books, it's quite possible that some people don't feel the need to register their big bucks with a record-keeping organization. For example, while Maine has quite a few Boone and Crockett entries, no Maine deer qualifies within the parameters I've set for the Pope and Young listings. Either residents of Maine don't archery hunt, or they don't list the big animals they're taking. It's hard to believe that there aren't some whopper bucks being taken in Maine with a bow. Of course, there are pockets of bowhunting ardor throughout the country as well as other areas where there are very few bowhunters. Tradition plays a part in whether an area's residents become archers or remain riflemen and women.

Certain states and provinces produce the majority of the truly monstrous bucks, but today other states little-known for their trophy buck potential are coming on strong. Here are the listings based on my analysis of the 9th edition of Boone and Crockett's record book. More recent editions contain almost 32,000 entries, far more than can be easily tabulated without a special computer program. Adding to the problem, officials at Boone and Crockett do not compile statistics on record book racks sorted by state and county of harvest. I have, however, made special note of some of the more spectacular trophies that have been taken in recent years.

UNITED STATES

Alabama. One of Alabama's top-scoring Boone and Crockett record typical bucks scored 182 7/8 points and was taken in Hale County. One of the state's largest non-typical bucks was taken in Sumter County and scored 230 7/8 points. At the time of this analysis, eleven trophy bucks had been taken from ten different counties. Only one county produced more than one big buck, and that was Sumter. The most recent trophies were taken in 1980, one in Lee and one in Opelika Counties. Part of the Talladega National Forest is located in Hale County. Alabama is an up-and-coming trophy state. Look for more big bucks to be entered into the record books from this sleeper state in the future.

Arkansas. Arkansas' leading counties are Desha with six trophy bucks; Arkansas with five; Chicot with three, and Pope with two. The Boone and Crockett record non-typical which scored 206 1/8 points was picked up in 1959. Most of Arkansas' records are old kills. Coincidentally, Desha and Chicot counties border the Mississippi River and Pope County lies next to the Arkansas River. Portions of the Ozark National Forest lie within Pope County's borders.

Colorado. Colorado is coming on strong. The top-scoring typical head racks up 186 3/8 points and was taken in Adams County in 1996. The top-scoring Colorado non-typical roared into the book in 1992 with a score of 258 2/8 points. It now is tied with two other heads at number 26 in the world. As expected, big whitetails are popping up all over the eastern plains with concentrations along the state's fertile river and creek bottoms.

Connecticut. Connecticut garnered its largest typical buck in 1993 with the harvest in Litchfield County of a 179 4/8 ten-pointer. This buck dovetails nicely with the former Connecticut record, a 1984 pick-up that scored 177 2/8, as well as a buck taken in 1987 that scored 176 2/8. Both these latter bucks also were taken in Litchfield County, which seems to be the place to go for big bucks in Connecticut.

Georgia. Top producing Georgia counties include Newton, Jasper, Macon, and Dooley. Georgia is a real comer, however, with Troup, Carroll, Heard, Tift, Harris, Wheeler, Dooley, and Wilkinson counties all producing Boone and Crockett record book heads during the last decade.

Idaho. Many of this state's top scoring whitetail racks come from Nez Perce, Bonner, and Kootenai counties. Whitetails inhabit the panhandle section of Idaho and public hunting may be found in the

Kaniksu National Forest in Bonner County and in Coeur D'Alene National Forest in Kootenai County.

Illinois. Illinois farm country contributes more than its share of big bucks to the record books. Amazingly enough, these bucks are spread fairly evenly across the entire state and many of them were taken in the 1980s. One of the top ranking counties is Peoria County with both the number one typical in the state scoring 204⅛ points (it's also the world record Pope and Young buck) and the number one non-typical state head scoring 267⅞ points—plus several other record heads. Other top counties include Canton, Pope, Jo Daviess, Mercer, Perry, Adams, Hancock, Quincy, Lake, Vermillion, Will, Lawrence, Fulton, Macoupin, Winnebago, Jefferson, LaSalle, McDonough, Cook, Sangamon, Edgar, and Tazewell. Illinois' so-called "Golden Triangle" country, which lies nestled between the Mississippi and Illinois Rivers, has been relinquishing many giant whitetail racks, most of them from hunting outfitters in Pike County. One of the best of the Pike County bunch is Carter's Hunting Lodge. Areas that consistently produce big bucks are, like Carter's, generally privately owned. The state does own and manage some public hunting land.

Indiana. Indiana is well represented in the record books. The current top Boone and Crockett typical garnered 195⅛ points in 1990 after being killed in Parke County. The runner-up typical scored 194⅜ points in 1983 after being harvested in Vigo County by two young boys. The Indiana state record typical came from Fulton County. This immense rack scored 248⅛ and was taken in 1990.

Iowa. Iowa is corn country and that kind of terrain is home sweet home to monster bucks. Iowa has a wealth of great trophies on the books, including a remarkable 15 of the top 83 places currently awarded to Boone and Crockett typical racks, as well as eight of the top 83 places for non-typical racks. No matter how you look at it, many fantastic scoring racks are coming from one of our smaller Midwest states. Counties to look out for include Wapello, Monroe, Johnson, Warren, Iowa, Monoma, Cherokee, Union, Clinton, Linn, Jones, Clayton, Dubuque, Cedar, Harrison, Worth, Lyon, Boone, Des Moines, Clay, Lee, Fayette, Van Buren, Marion, Keokuk, and Lucas. What's more, a few years back, Iowa revised its game laws so that non-residents are now able to apply for a permit to hunt deer in the state. That's a big improvement, since non-residents not so long ago were unable to hunt Iowa deer, period. Iowa has little federal land but there is a significant amount of state and county land. Contact the county government located in the seat of government of each county, or contact the Iowa Department of Natural Resources in Des Moines.

Kansas. Kansas continues to go places with whitetail deer: right into the record book hall of fame. In fact, I wouldn't be surprised to see the next world record head come from Kansas. This state is growing heads that simply have to be seen to be believed. Several hundred record book heads are now listed for Kansas, with more qualifying every day. Recently, the following top-ranked bucks have been taken in the state: a monstrous 197⅞ typical picked up in 1991 in Comanche County; a 194⅞ typical taken in Leavenworth County in 1985; a number of great non-typical heads, such as the 280⅞ taken in 1987 in Shawnee County, a 253 taken in 1994 in Miami County, a 250⅞ picked up in 1988 in Washington County and a 246⅞ taken in 1992 in Anderson County. Any of those counties would present a good bet to the big buck hunter. Others include Chase, Lyon, McPherson, Butler, Sumner, Riley, Barber, Jefferson, Republic, Greenwood, Marion, Cowley, Gray, Waubausee, Clay, Doniphan, Douglas, and Coffey. Many of the top Kansas state record book bucks were taken in the 1990s. Expect even more during the new millennium. Non-residents must apply for a permit to hunt deer in Kansas.

Kentucky. Kentucky is another sleeper state, one producing many more big bucks than it has in years past. A surprising number of the big bucks in Boone and Crockett and Pope and Young have been taken during the 1990s, including a 1995 pick-up from Barren County that scores a remarkable 238⅞. Top counties include Gallatin, Todd, Trigg, Scott, Lewis, Hardin, Pulaski, Union, and Meade. Part of the Daniel Boone National Forest lies within Pulaski County, and Land Between the Lakes is accessible via Trigg County.

Louisiana. Louisiana, land of bayous and waterfowl, is also home to many nice-sized whitetail bucks. Marshland and farmland contribute equal amounts to Louisiana's ability to grow 'em big. Although few of Louisiana's bucks qualify for the top typical listings in Boone and Crockett, in 1994 Tensas Parish yielded a buck that scored 281⅞ as a non-typical. Top parishes where buster buck genetics are likely to be found include Bossier, Tensas, St. Landry, and Claiborne. Concordia, in particular, has a good track record for producing big racks. Part of the Kisatchie National Forest lies in Claiborne County.

Maine. Maine has long been noted for its superlative whitetail hunting. Bodies and antlers are both bragging-sized in Maine bucks.

What's more, a good number of Maine's record book bucks have been taken in recent years. One of the finest was a 238% head harvested in 1996 in Piscataquis County. Record buck-producing counties include Waldo, Aroostook, Hancock, Penobscot, Knox, Somerset, Washington, and Maine. Most Maine hunting is done on private ground, although many of the state's paper companies allow fee hunting on their holdings.

Maryland. Maryland has a number of Boone and Crockett and Pope and Young heads listed in the record books, although not as many as those states with a wealth of giant bucks, such as Illinois, Iowa, Kansas, and Minnesota. Neither are Maryland's bucks noted for breaking into the top echelons of the big buck ranks. Nevertheless, hunters can take respectable trophies in this eastern seaboard state. Top counties include Dorchester, Queen Anne, Ann Arundel, and Talbot. The most recently taken high-scoring trophy came from Talbot County in 1994 and scored 183%. Maryland's public hunting lands are owned or leased by the state Wildlife Administration, Forest and Park Service, Tawes State Office Building, Annapolis, MD 21401.

Michigan. Michigan sits on the northern tier of states, but unlike her superstar neighbors, Wisconsin and Minnesota, contributes only an average number of heads to the record books. Michigan is also more populous than the other states, one reason why fewer top trophies have been taken here. Regardless, the 1990s were good to Michigan big buck hunters. One Jackson County hunter in 1996 bagged a 198 typical, while another harvested a 193% typical in 1986. Top counties to scout include Iron, Van Buren, Baraga, Alger, Charlevoix, Allegan, Shiawassee, and Branch. Portions of the Iron Range State Forest and Baraga State Forest may be hunted in Iron County; part of the Baraga State Forest is located in Baraga County; the Hiawatha National Forest is in Alger County; portions of the Hardwood State Forest and Mackinaw State Forest may be found in Charlevoix County; and the Allegan State Forest is in Allegan County.

Minnesota. Bring out the big guns for record-book heavyweight Minnesota. Big bucks abound in Minnesota, land of a thousand lakes and even more alder swamps, places where bucks can escape to grow big! An unbelievable number of record bucks have come from Minnesota. Top bets for record bucks (with available public lands following each top-producing county in parentheses) include St. Louis County (Superior National Forest, Kabetogama State Forest, Lake Jeanette State Forest, Burntside State Forest, Bear Island State Forest, Cloquet Valley State Forest, Sturgeon River State Forest, Whiteface River State Forest, and Fond du Lac State Forest); Winona County (part of the Richard J. Dorer Memorial State Forest); Itasca (portions of the George Washington State Forest and Bowstring State Forest); Beltrami County (Buena Vista State Forest, Black Duck State Forest, Red Lake State Forest) and Olmstead County (Richard J. Dorer Memorial State Forest); Fillmore (Dorer Memorial State Forest); Marshall, Otter Tail, Aitkin (Hill River State Forest, Savanna State Forest, Solana State Forest), Houston (Dorer Memorial State Forest), and Koochiching (Pine Island State Forest and Koochiching State Forest); Meeker, Hubbard, Lincoln, Douglas, Murray, Dodge, and Chippewa; Norman, Anoka, Rice, Freeborn, Sherburne, Pine, Clay, Pope, Becker, and Faribault; Pennington, Minnesota, Roseau, Martin, Redwood, Murray, Traverse, Lyon, Wabasha, Stearns, Kandiyohi, Blue Earth, Mower, Todd, Grant, Cook, Chisago, Renville, Swift, and Goodhue. Nearly all of Cook County consists of public land including portions of the Superior National Forest, Pat Bayle State Forest, and Grand Portage State Forest. Minnesota remains a great bet for millennium trophy hunters since giant bucks continue to be harvested there at an astounding rate. Included in this number are a 197% typical taken in 1986 in Wright County, a 195% typical taken in 1995 from Anoka County, and a 245% non-typical taken in 1990 in Kittson County.

Mississippi. Top counties for Mississippi big bucks include Wilkinson, Adams, Winston, and Bolivar. A remarkable non-typical head that scored 295% was taken in Winston County in 1995. This buck ranks number three in Boone and Crockett's all-time records book. Part of the Homochito National Forest is located in both Wilkinson County and Adams County.

Missouri. Home of the world-record non-typical, a tremendous buck that scores 333% points, Missouri also has quite a collection of lesser trophies. There are many additional typical and non-typicals listed in Boone and Crockett as well. One notable addition that's yet to be included on those hallowed pages was taken in 1999 by a St. Louis County bowhunter. This huge typical scored 191% points. Its St. Louis County harvest locale underscores the importance of urban and suburban areas throughout the country as potential big buck incubators. Most big Missouri bucks are either taken in such areas or tend to hail from those counties lying north of the Missouri River in prairie-agricultural terrain. Some of the best counties include St. Louis, Clay, Jackson (all urban and suburban counties), plus agricultural hotspots such as Scotland (Indian Hills Conservation Area), Warren (Mark Twain National Forest), Atchison (Brickyard Hill Conservation Area), Shelby (Hunnewell Conservation Area), St. Charles (Busch Conservation Area, Howell Island Conservation

Area, Weldon Spring Conservation Area), Chariton, Jackson (Reed Conservation Area), and Christian (Busiek Conservation Area).

Montana. Montana's got plenty of big whitetails in all the major record books. Top counties include Flathead (Flathead National Forest), Missoula (Lolo National Forest), Sanders (Lolo National Forest), Fergus (Lewis and Clark National Forest), Rosebud, Teton (Lewis and Clark National Forest), and Madison (Deerlodge National Forest, Beaverhead National Forest, and Bitterroot National Forest). Surprisingly, only one big Montana whitetail has cracked the uppermost echelons of the Boone and Crockett record book during recent years. That buck was a 188% typical taken in 1992 in perennial favorite Flathead County, the same place and year a 229% non-typical was also harvested.

Nebraska. Like most heavily farmed states, lots of big bucks called, and still call, Nebraska home. Look for big bucks in counties like Keya Paha, Pawnee, Harlan, Hall, Knox, Furnas, Boyd, Antelope, and Saunders. The most recent Nebraska boomer buck to qualify for the Boone and Crockett rankings is a 233% non-typical taken in 1986 in Custer County. Hall County must be considered the state's top big buck producer.

New Jersey. New Jersey, although hunted heavily, has few entries in the record books. Why this should be so is anyone's guess. The state's soils are capable of producing top heads, according to biologists.

New York. Within the Adirondack wilds, New York bucks have a good chance to get away from it all. Big bucks are still being taken in our second most populous state. One typical scoring 179% was taken in 1995 in St. Lawrence County and another scoring 178% was taken in 1993 from Monroe County. In 1992, a 225% non-typical was taken from St. Lawrence County as well, sending all eyes skittering in this northern county's direction. Other top counties include Cattaraugus, Clinton (Adirondack Park), Allegany, Livingston, Essex, and Steuben. If you can obtain permission—and where it's legal—bowhunting New York's suburban counties such as Westchester and Suffolk could very well pay off in huge buck dividends.

North Dakota. North Dakota is sparsely populated, yet a good number of its whitetails continue to make it into the record books. The state is situated on the northern tier of the grain belt, so excellent forage is available for the state's deer herd. Counties to watch include McLean, Pierce, McKenzie, Emmons, Burleigh, Slope, and Morton. A 195% typical was taken in 1994 in Pierce County.

Ohio. Ohio, one of our most populous states, is also contributing more than her fair share to the whitetail record books. Big bucks literally live among people in many of the state's subdivisions and rural areas. Quite a number of trophy animals have been taken in the 1990s, too. A typical scoring 186⅞ was taken in 1990 in Logan County, while a 262⅛ non-typical was harvested in Ross County in 1995. Best bets for big bucks include Muskingum County (Blue Rock State Forest) and Licking and Tuscarawas Counties. Don't neglect Logan, Ross (part of Tar Hollow State Forest and all of Scioto Trail State Forest), Vinton (portions of Tar Hollow State Forest, Richland Furnace State Forest, and Zaleski State Forest), Coshocton, Richland, Washington (portions of Wayne National Forest), Geauga, Delaware, Huron, Greene, Mahoning, Preble, and Belmont.

Oklahoma. Oklahoma doesn't have a lot of record-book bucks listed, but it can claim at least three huge non-typical bucks killed in the latter part of the 1980s and the 1990s. A buck scoring 225⅛ was taken in 1987 in Dewey County, while in 1993 a 223⅜ non-typical was taken in Comanche County. Rounding out this triumvirate is a 219⅛ non-typical taken in 1996 in Pontotoc County.

Oregon. Oregon continues to be poorly represented in the latest editions of the record books. Not enough big buck data exists for a comprehensive county-by-county analysis.

Pennsylvania. Pennsylvania is surely one of the hardest-hunted states in the Union, yet it still produces some good heads, although none of them scores high enough to attain the highest tiers of the record books. Pennsylvania publishes its own big game record book and that source has in the past indicated that Bradford (parts of Tioga State Forest), Westmoreland (Forbes State Forest), Clarion, McKean (Allegheny National Forest), Allegheny, Montgomery, and Erie are all top producing counties. Allegheny and Montgomery counties have both produced numerous big heads in recent years, so you might want to start your search there.

South Carolina. South Carolina isn't producing very many heads worthy of inclusion in the record books.

South Dakota. Although quite a few South Dakota whitetails qualify for the record books, few have been taken recently. One of the exceptions is a 182⅝ typical taken in Jones County in 1989. Perhaps this shouldn't be surprising. South Dakota has been ravaged by harsh, deer-killing winters a number of times during the past decade. Top counties are Lyman, Kingsbury, Day, Perkins, Brown, Yankton, and Jones.

Tennessee. The largest recent record book buck taken in Tennessee was a 208% non-typical from Van Buren County in 1994. Although at times past it has appeared as though this state is coming on strong for big bucks, entries haven't been as numerous as they probably should be, considering Tennessee borders Kentucky, where plenty of big bucks have been recently taken. Good Tennessee counties in which to start your search are Decatur and Hawkins.

Texas. Texas does everything in a big way, and its bucks are no exception. In a state with a deer population guesstimated to be from five to six million animals, there are plenty of representative animals in the pages of the Boone and Crockett record book. The highest-scoring recently taken typical head is a 190% typical from Shackelford County. The best recent non-typical is a 224% taken by a woman hunter in La Salle County in 1992. Overall, the top counties include Webb, Dimmit, Frio, LaSalle, Maverick, McMullen, Jim Hogg, Zavala, Duval, Kenedy, Starr, Kleberg, Zapata, and Cottula. As ranchers improve their management techniques and fine-tune their management programs, more Texas bucks should qualify for the Boone and Crockett record book in the next decade.

Virginia. The top-scoring Virginia Boone and Crockett non-typical was taken in 1992 in Warren County and scored 257⅝, so big bucks are still inhabiting the green hills of this state. Good trophy counties are Augusta, Warren, and Shenandoah. The George Washington National Forest is located in Augusta County.

Washington. The state of Washington has more non-typicals qualifying for Boone and Crockett than typicals. Included in this number is a 223% non-typical taken in 1992 in Stevens County. Most whitetail hunting is done in the far eastern portion of the state. Stevens must be considered the top county, while other good bets include Spokane, Whitman, and Okanogan. Public hunting land in Stevens County includes portions of the Kaniksu National Forest and the Colville National Forest. Okanogan National Forest is open to hunters wanting to hunt in Okanogan County.

West Virginia. Look to Wetzel and Wyoming counties first in West Virginia.

Wisconsin. Wisconsin contributes more than its share of big bucks to the record books. Wisconsin's top-scoring typical is also the second best typical whitetail ever taken, the legendary Jordan buck taken back in 1914 in Burnett County. The largest recent Boone and Crockett typical scored 185 and was taken in 1995 in Crawford County, where another big 188% typical came from in 1986. Then there's the 187⅞ taken in Langlade County in 1994. A 232 non-typical was taken in Barron County in 1988, while a 223⅜ was taken in Iron County in 1994. Top Wisconsin counties overall include Buffalo, Bayfield (Chequamegon National Forest), Marinette, Rusk (Flambeau River State Forest), Price (Flambeau River State Forest, Chequamegon National Forest), Vilas (Northern Highlands State Forest and Nicollet National Forest), Dane and Waukesha (Kettle Moraine State Forest South), Sawyer County (Chequamegon National Forest and Flambeau River State Forest), Burnett (Knowles State Forest), Menominee, Ashland (Chequamegon National Forest), Oneida (Northern Highlands State Forest), Florence (Nicollet National Forest), Dodge, Waushara, Saulk, Pepin, Lafayette, Langlade, Richland, Hayward, Jefferson, Oconto, Lincoln, Winnebago, and Trempealeau.

Wyoming. Good things are coming from Wyoming. The eastern plains are producing great bucks, and quite a few have been finding their ways into the record book. The best trophy hunting seems to be in Crook County, where public hunting is allowed in the Black Hills National Forest.

CANADA

Canada would be another option for those of us willing to endure all for a mega-whitetail. With their cold winters, deer up there grow on the average to a much larger body size than southern deer, and with this increased body mass comes larger antlers as well.

According to Russell Thornberry, once a noted big buck guide and expert from Canada and now the editor of *Buckmasters* magazine, if every head taken in Canada large enough to qualify for Boone and Crockett were listed it would literally rewrite the record book. "Interest in publicizing record book heads in an organization based in America is low among Canadian hunters," Thornberry said. "Saskatchewan alone has its own record book with thousands of entries. Inclusion of all these bucks in the Boone and Crockett would increase the number of entries currently listed by who knows how many."

Now here are each of the provinces and the numbers of Boone and Crockett typical and non-typical heads that they've produced—plus where to go for your best shot at a big Canadian whitetail:

Alberta. Russell Thornberry recommends that hunters concentrate their efforts on the major river valleys of the central agricultural region. Most of Alberta's big whitetail bucks have been taken within an imaginary rectangle that extends from Edmonton east to Cold Lake on the Saskatchewan border, then south to Empress and then west to Cochrane, which lies about 20 miles west of Calgary. Finish the rectangle by extending the side back to Edmonton.

British Columbia. The best big bucks spots in British Columbia include the Fort St. John region as well as along the Peace River drainage.

Manitoba. Look for big bucks along the central western border with Saskatchewan, particularly in the Duck Mountain region and along the Swan River drainage.

New Brunswick. The eastern Canadian province with the most record-book entries is New Brunswick with 17. The largest New Brunswick typical buck scored 175% and was taken in Kings County in 1973. The province's largest non-typical scored 249% and was taken in 1946. New Brunswick hotspots include Kings County with three entries, two of them occurring in the 1980s.

Topography makes any predication of where you might go to score on a big whitetail extremely difficult. Ideal conditions for superior antler growth exist any place where government forest butts up to agricultural development.

Nova Scotia. Nova Scotia has 10 total entries, including a monster 193% typical taken in Antigonish County in 1987. The largest non-typical taken in this province is a 233⅛ buck harvested in 1987 near Condon Lakes. No area in the province is represented in the record books more than one time. Again, look for forest butting up to agricultural operations for your best chance of big antlers.

Ontario. There are quite a few Pope & Young entries from Ontario, including a typical taken in 1984 that scores 170. This buck, which was killed in Puslinch Township, is not entered in the Boone and Crockett record book, where you'll find just three Ontario entries in the non-typical category and none in the typical category. Two of these three came from Rainy River, one in 1930 and the other in 1969. The most recent Boone and Crockett entry was taken in 1988 from Rideau River and scored 208% points as a non-typical. The only places with more than one record book entry are Puslinch Township and Wellington County.

Quebec. In a check of both the Pope & Young and Boone and Crockett record books for whitetailed deer, I found just two listings for Quebec. The first was for a 172⅝ typical killed in 1996 in Acton-Vale. The other was a non-typical Boone and Crockett buck taken in 1959 from Argenteuil County.

Saskatchewan. The reigning world-record typical, the Milo Hanson Buck, was taken near Biggar, not far from the Red Feather Indian Reserve. Hanson's great buck scores 213⅝ and significantly overshadows the once-champion Jordan Buck at 206⅛. Lots of tremendous deer call Saskatchewan home, but those in the northern part of the province are extremely difficult to hunt. A quick flip-through of the record book pages reveals that big bucks are coming from everywhere in Saskatchewan these days.

MEXICO

Mexico is coming on strong with a number of top heads making the most recent edition of the record book. There are places to head for if you can tolerate the presence of a state-appointed guide and are willing to pay the price required. Nuevo Leon seems to be the top-producing place right now, although some good bucks are coming from Coahuila.

In conclusion, I talked to Gordon Whittington, editor of *North American Whitetail Magazine,* a deer hunting expert with his fingers on the pulse of the whitetail hunting world, to find out where he feels the next world-record head will be taken. "In all honesty, I believe that another world record may be alive and kicking right now somewhere in Canada," he said. "But I also believe that the next record might just as easily come from Kansas, Missouri, or Illinois. Wisconsin and Minnesota are also good bets. For non-typical bucks, my money would have to include Ohio."

There is my part: a listing of top buck spots plus the opinion of one of the top analysts of big buck success trends. Now all you have to do is provide the legwork to bag a big one legally and it could be *your* name that's listed in the next edition of the record book.

10

Interpreting Whitetail Superbuck Sign

Every creature leaves some evidence of its existence behind after it dies: fur that was shed, or an abandoned shell, or bones. Modern man leaves more evidence of his existence than any creature: homes, cars, garbage, and the pollution in the air all testify to human activity. Whitetails, too, leave signs of their passing on this earth, but these are gentler, transient indicators. Whitetail sign consists of shed antlers, tracks, rub trees, beds, scrapes, and droppings. These small evidences of a deer's existence are clues that can be pieced together to present a picture of his daily movements. By interpreting whitetail sign correctly, we increase our chances of becoming consistently successful big buck hunters.

RUBBING

Whitetail sign often gives us clues to his behavior, and why he acts the way he does. Rub trees, for example, become visible in late summer and early autumn at about the same time as a deer starts to shed the velvet from his antlers. Scientists used to think that bucks rubbed antlers against trees to remove itching velvet. But since velvet dries up and drops off anyway, even without rubbing, there must be other reasons for deer to rub trees.

When a buck rubs away the bark on a sapling's trunk, he creates a signpost that advertises his presence in an area. Forehead glands allow the buck to spread his own individual scent on the rub. When a buck makes a rub on a sturdy tree, it also helps develop his neck and chest muscles. His swollen neck may give a doe a distinct sexual message about a buck's dominance level. A muscular-looking neck along with his antlers may also help a buck dominate or threaten other bucks.

Bucks rub as they move, so rubs are also directional signs for hunters. By looking carefully at a rub or a series of rubs, a hunter can determine which way the buck was headed. Line up the bare rubbed side of each tree; that's the side that was facing the forward surface of the buck's antlers, so that's the direction he was traveling.

SCRAPING

Another sign of whitetail activity is the scrape. A scrape area can be as small as a teacup or as large as a ten foot circle. A scrape may appear dank and musky, or dried out. While bucks make most scrapes, does also make scrapes on occasion. Whether the urge to scrape comes from internal signals from the buck's hormone system or external signals from the doe, no one yet knows.

If you're searching for scrapes, be sure to sniff the air occasionally. An active scrape can often be smelled—even by a hunter—before it's actually seen. The direction of travel of the scrape-maker can also often be determined, especially early in the season. Look to see in which direction footprints in the scrape are headed or in which direction debris from the scrape was scattered. A buck seldom turns around on a scrape, so the debris will be on the side *opposite* his direction of travel.

Scrapes do tend to occur in the same locations from year to year. By keeping a topographical map marked up with the locations of current rubs, scrapes, and trails, it's often possible to piece the parts of your superbuck puzzle together from the comfort of your home.

LICKING BRANCHES

Certain scrapes—those under licking branches—are tended all year. Licking branches are gathering places for deer. It's known that bucks and does alike lick and rub on given branches. It's been speculated that what they're doing is depositing identifying pheromones contained in the saliva to let other deer know they've been there. Studies still underway seem to lend quite a bit of credence to this theory, although all the data isn't in yet.

BEDS

Beds are another type of sign that is important to the serious whitetail hunter. The size of a particular bed, together with the presence or absence of other beds nearby, can help an astute woodsman determine whether it belongs to a buck or a doe. Superbucks are usually much larger than does, so they leave large beds. During autumn, superbucks are usually loners unless trailing an estrous doe during the rut, so look for larger, *single* beds. Does, on the other hand, often congregate in doe family groups except during estrus. Smaller beds nearby could indicate the young of the year.

Even the pattern of urination in a bed can provide a clue to the sex of its occupant. A doe will rise and urinate towards the edge of her bed. A buck will urinate inside the bed itself, towards the center. A light snow can help decipher this critical whitetail clue, since it shows urination patterns more clearly.

Bucks prefer bedding on high spots or thickets that are fairly hard to approach. Often, the prevailing wind will be blowing towards the bedding area. The bed's higher elevation allows the buck to watch the other directions. And it's not unusual for one or more sides of the bedding area to abut natural obstacles such as deep creeks or bluffs. Bucks will also bed near the top on the leeward slope of ridges where scent pools after blowing across the summit.

The hunters with the best success records prefer to hunt close to bedding areas but not in them. It's best to avoid disturbing a deer's bedding pattern since they're useful sign.

TRACKS

Tracks are another excellent indicator that a superbuck's nearby. Some big bucks have hooves close to three inches long and nearly circular in shape. When Alan Altizer took the current Tennessee state archery record, a buster buck that scored 173 Boone and Crockett points, he reported that the buck had been leaving tracks that were the size of a small cow's. Some other trophy bucks, however, have small feet in relation to their size.

Many hunters who have long studied deer tracks are convinced that while the largest tracks don't always belong to bucks, it is possible to distinguish buck tracks from doe tracks. Josef Brunner, a hunter and naturalist who lived in Wyoming at the turn of the century, determined whether a track belonged to a buck or a doe by drawing a line down the center of a set of tracks, front to back. The average left and right buck tracks, he felt, were spaced farther from this center line than were doe tracks. Another indicator, he felt, is that the toes of a buck's tracks would point farther outward. Brunner also observed that bucks were less likely to place the rear hoofprint right over the front hoofprint, as a doe would. Instead, a buck places his rear hoof somewhat back of the front hoofprint. And according to Brunner, a buck's track will show more pronounced drag marks, especially during the rut and winter.

Another well-known deer hunter from the Catskill Mountains of New York, Larry Koller, agreed with some of Brunner's observations. Koller believed that older bucks show a tendency to walk with their front hooves wider apart than does and yearling bucks. He also agreed that mature bucks "toe-out" with their front hooves.

Finally, a hint from Merritt Compton of Trumansburg, New York. Compton follows buck trails until they pass between trees growing on each side of the trail. By looking carefully, he's often able to determine how wide a buck's rack is by where the antlers have knocked bark off the inside of each tree.

Analyzing sign can be time consuming, but it's undoubtedly one of the major ways that hunters finally apprehend the superbucks of their dreams. The following chapters will go into greater detail on the intricacies of interpreting whitetail superbuck sign.

11

Hunting Superbuck Scrapes

It was already late November in eastern Tennessee when Luke Fuller decided to do a little extra scouting. Fuller was after a big buck he knew lived nearby. Trouble was, this particular trophy was going to be one tough nut to crack since the buck was almost completely nocturnal.

The whitetail he was after was a huge one, however, and Fuller was determined. Moments after entering a thick tangle of brush, he discovered a big scrape—one that measured more than five feet across.

Fuller's buck had made one mistake: that scrape. Two days later, when Fuller returned to hunt the scrape area, the buck made a second, fatal mistake.

It was nearly 8:00 A.M. and Fuller was waiting on stand, wondering if he'd see the buck at all. Then the big deer trotted quickly through the thicket and toward the scrape. Fuller could hardly believe his eyes. He had less than five seconds to get the buck in his 3 × 9 Redfield scope. Holding his breath, he squeezed the trigger of his .270 Winchester Model 70 Featherweight. The 130 grain Remington Core-Lokt bullet struck home. The buck was his!

And what a buck it was: 30 total points and a Boone and Crockett score of 223⅝ made Fuller's deer the current Tennessee state record non-typical. A new state non-typical champion has been green-scored and should knock Fuller's buck from first place in 2001.

Fuller got his trophy buck because he was able to capitalize on what he knew about scrapes. In his case, the big non-typical buck played right into his hands. Many hunters fervently believe in hunting scrapes, but there are even more for whom scrape hunting just doesn't pan out. One thing is certain: if the big buck you're after makes scrapes, identifying them could put you on the road to super-buck success.

What is this phenomenon called the whitetail scrape? Can any scrape ever be hunted with a reasonable expectation of success? More important, how do they fit into the overall scheme of things for the serious superbuck hunter?

A scrape is an area of ground that has been cleaned or pawed out of the dirt by a whitetail deer, usually right before, during, or after the rut. A scrape may be as small as a few inches across or as large as 6 to 10 feet in diameter. But remember: the size of a scrape in most cases usually has no correlation to the size of the deer that made it.

THE LICKING BRANCH

Apparently, an overhanging limb is important when a buck chooses to make a scrape. In one Georgia study, an overhanging limb was associated with 86 percent of the scrapes, usually hanging between four and seven feet above it. This limb is often easy to pick out because it's been mutilated by antler raking or chewing. Experts theorize that this marking is a whitetail ritual associated with scrape behavior. As the deer rubs his head on the overhanging limb, the sudoriferous glands on his forehead and the preorbital glands above his eyes secrete pheromones to give the limb his own unique scent "signature."

If this limb is chewed or licked by more than one deer, the scrape could be a buck hunter's mother lode—a licking branch. A licking branch is visited all year by many different deer and always develops into a primary scrape—a great place for a big buck hunter to hunt. Licking branches are like a Club Med for deer—a great place to see and be seen.

Even if the deer aren't literally seen by other deer, as they lick on the branch they deposit salivary pheromones that tell every other deer in the area that they were there. All licking branch locations become scrapes, but *not* all scrapes have licking branches above them.

Alan Altizer of Blountville, Tennessee, is one scrape hunter who has scored big by adding licking branches to his hunting repertoire. Altizer took the former Tennessee archery state record typical buck near an old scrape that he located before the season.

"It just so happened that the old scrape developed into a fresh *new* scrape," Altizer said. "Part of the reason was because it was also a licking branch location. I hadn't even heard of licking branches back then. But since I killed my 173-point Boone and Crockett buck near one, I've really started to look for them."

According to Bob McGuire, noted whitetail hunter and outdoorsman, licking branch behavior is quite different from pure scraping activity even though some aspects are similar. For one thing, when a dominant buck is at his scrape, he *will not tolerate* the presence of a subordinate in or near that scrape. His behavior becomes agonistic, the deer researcher's term for combative and threatening behavior.

However, bucks will tolerate the presence of subordinates at licking branches *before* the rut. During the summer, older does may actually dominate even the highest-ranking bucks at the licking branch. Through the year, each deer's behavior at the licking branch continually updates other deer on its relative status within the herd's social structure.

"There is a lot of body language at the licking branch," McGuire said. "The hierarchy is obvious. You can watch the dominant buck threaten a subordinate or give him a hard look, but he will tolerate the lesser buck's *presence* as long as it's not during the rut. The lower-ranking animals respond to such threats with a submissive, sway-backed posture. Whitetails are social animals, and bucks like to hang out together during the spring and summer. And the focus of their activity? The licking branch.

"The important thing about licking branches is that you can look for and find activity during hunting's off season," McGuire continued. "Best of all, the highest concentration of activity is before scraping begins.

"Hunters can now take matters into their own hands," McGuire explained, "by careful, all season scouting for licking branch locations."

Alan Altizer added, "The year after I got my 173-point Boone and Crockett buck I looked for any branches that showed signs of nibbling and licking and had bare spots beneath them that weren't necessarily scrapes—just beaten ground where lots of deer hooves had kept anything from growing."

Altizer did his homework well. The year after he took his big trophy, he connected on two more good archery bucks.

THE SCRAPE

Licking branches are important, but since more is known about scrapes, they remain a crucial piece of the buck puzzle. An active scrape is kept scrupulously clean of litter. Early in the season, the deer that made it may or may not urinate in it. Rub-urination—behavior in which a buck urinates over his hocks into a scrape—becomes more common as the peak of the rut approaches. The act of pawing and urinating together at an already established scrape is called "freshening" the scrape.

The old chicken–and–egg riddle can be applied to scrapes, too. Although scrapes are made as a dominance display geared toward other bucks, they are also used for meeting does. It really isn't known whether a buck randomly makes a scrape that attracts a doe or whether before the rut—even before she enters estrus—a doe's unique pheromones actually stimulate a buck to scrape. What is known is that very often old scrapes develop into new scrapes each hunting season.

Alan Altizer makes good use of that fact. Right after hunting season *ends,* he scouts for scrapes or scrape lines. "I know from experience that the scrapes still being tended will have the biggest bucks the following year," he said. "I've located many of my best bucks like this.

"I've discovered that bucks tend their scrapes until around March 1st—at least in Tennessee," Altizer added. "Don't forget to look for shed antlers around old scrapes, either. It's a great spot to find them and a good way to help you estimate what size the buck will be during the coming hunting season."

Another scrape myth every hunter has heard: a scrape is usually embellished with the hoofprint of the buck that made it. Studies at the University of Georgia by Terry Kile and Dr. Larry Marchinton discovered that only about *a third* of all scrapes have distinct tracks visible in them. Of these, most of the tracks were small and tentatively identified as belonging to does.

What about the theory that all bucks scrape? Or that *only* bucks scrape? Wrong again, apparently, on both counts.

Once more, researchers at the University of Georgia are at the forefront of research in the deer woods. Drs. Karl Miller and Larry Marchinton and their associates studied ten groups of penned deer over a four-year period. Both bucks and does were included, and the deer ranged from one year old to 8½ years old. These deer populations were manipulated so that every year each group was made up of different animals. So over four years, 40 different groupings of animals were studied. Researchers could study how a deer behaved with many different companions, in many different social or dominance structures.

"Three-and-a-half-year-old bucks dominant within their groups produced nearly all the scrapes," Marchinton said. "We manipulated these groups so that in several cases the dominant buck was young—1½ or 2½ years old. But even as dominants these youngsters didn't scrape. After these young bucks matured, several of them did scrape as dominants."

What this experiment means is that the scrapes we find when afield are probably made by deer 3½ years old and older, assuming the buck–to–doe ratio is within normal limits (about one buck to four does in a hunting area). The "trigger" for scrape behavior is the buck's testosterone (the male hormone) level. A 3½-year-old buck has a higher testosterone level than a younger buck, and this is the reason he starts to make scrapes.

Scrapes serve two purposes: they are an aggressive display directed at other males; and they are a means of communication between buck and doe. It's possible that since scrapes are made mainly by dominant males within a balanced population, estrous females hang around them looking for the best mate.

Now let's back up and look at this information on scrapes once more with the buck–to–doe ratio in mind. There are some populations that are hunted so hard that virtually *no* bucks reach 3½ years of age. Young-buck populations occur in states where the emphasis is on *quantity* of deer killed, not the overall quality of deer. In these instances, immature bucks may scrape, but less than a mature dominant buck. Immature bucks are certainly capable of breeding—and often do if the dominant buck leaves an estrous doe untended, perhaps to run another buck away.

That's not the only factor affecting how many scrapes we see in the woods. Dr. Harry Jacobson of the University of Mississippi has this to say about which animals make scrapes: "I have one big dominant buck in my deer pens that has *never* made a scrape in his life. And as a big buck hunter myself, I wouldn't doubt that there are other dominants in the wild so survival-oriented that they don't even venture out to breed, much less scrape."

Don't forget that in areas where there are many does eager to be bred, there is no need for a buck to scrape. Dominance doesn't have to be established since there are so few bucks to challenge the dominant. With does everywhere the bucks don't have the time or the energy to lay down a scrape line. So a lack of scrapes may not mean there are *no* bucks at all, simply that proportionately there may not be many bucks.

As the buck-to-doe ratio approaches 1 : 1, the number of scrapes in an area will increase. If there are *several* mature 3½-year-old bucks competing for the does in one area, there will be even more scrapes, and perhaps the opportunity to take a real mossyhorns.

If all this isn't confusing enough, what about *does* that scrape? Does in the wild have been observed to make scrapes by researchers and hunters alike. One doe watched as a six-point buck scraped, and then made an identical scrape as if responding to his action.

To summarize, in a well-balanced deer population scrapes will be made almost exclusively by the dominant buck. Since the dominant buck is also probably going to be the biggest buck in the forest, knowing how to interpret the scrapes that are found is essential.

If evidence of scraping is absent from an area it can mean several things: (1) there are no deer at all; (2) there are only a few bucks that are run ragged servicing many does; and (3) although there is a dominant buck, he's so survival-oriented he doesn't scrape at all.

If that mature buck won't scrape, be prepared for the toughest hunting of your life because the chances are that this buck won't ever show you where to look for him in the woods.

TYPES OF SCRAPES

There are different kinds of scrapes: knowing where and when to look for each is important.

Scrape-making parallels breeding activity very neatly. Over much of North America both scraping and breeding peak in mid-November—but not simultaneously. Scraping actually peaks *before* breeding: once the does are receptive to mating, the bucks neglect and focus their attention on breeding.

Remember, every scrape you discover is part of *one particular buck's* complex living pattern. Even though individual deer maintain their own separate and distinct behavior, all bucks behave in at least a few predictable ways.

The most predictable one is that scrapes are usually found in areas with little understory vegetation. Bucks like to make obvious scrapes. *But an exception to this rule may often be made for trophy bucks.* As Alan Altizer says, "The big racks have had just about everything tried on them. They often adapt by making their favorite scrapes in thick, heavy cover."

Look for other scrapes along game trails, old roads, or in small openings. As you do, pay close attention to the lay of the land, available forage, and cover. All are important to the whitetail buck and the kinds of scrapes he makes.

Remember, even a superbuck will make different kinds of scrapes if he's seldom disturbed. This is why many big buck experts are successful at taking trophies year after year: they ferret out undisturbed areas to hunt there. Some hunters walk miles to get to a remote location while others pay for leases even in the Midwest and East. Still others gladly do farmers' chores all year long for permission to hunt an undisturbed deer population. A spot like this is where they will be able to take the easiest super-trophies, and good scrapes are one advantage.

BOUNDARY SCRAPES

A boundary scrape is an early season scrape that can be found along the edges of a buck's territory or range. Boundary scrapes are often the first scrapes made—five to six weeks before the peak of the rut. Look for them along fields, fence rows, or waterways. Boundary scrapes are often laid down near the perimeter of a favorite late summer or early autumn feeding area, such as an alfalfa or soybean field.

Hunting boundary scrapes might be productive during the early season, but as food preferences shift, so does all deer activity, including scrapes. And as hunting pressure increases, deer lie lower. If does abandon an area, or if the buck doesn't have to travel along a particular route to get to the does, boundary scrapes may be abandoned. Don't waste valuable hunting time in an unproductive scrape location. As the deer shift feeding and travel patterns, you should too.

TRAIL SCRAPES

Scope out the trails that connect favored feeding areas. As acorns ripen and crops are harvested, again, these trails may be abandoned. Then look for the most productive hunting along trails laid down in some kind of cover.

A buck's trail will often parallel the trail used by the area's does, but that doesn't mean bucks *won't* use the does' trail. Look for scrapes along both types of trail.

Be careful not to overlook scrapes. Trail scrapes and boundary scrapes aren't very large: often smaller than a dinner plate. But trail scrapes can be extremely productive if area does are still using the trail. Stay alert to what the deer in your area are feeding on—and how they are traveling to get to the feed.

TRAVEL LANE SCRAPES

One type of scrape that every dedicated superbuck hunter should be familiar with is the travel lane scrape. These scrapes are usually made by the biggest, smartest bucks in the woods. They can usually be found in the thickest cover between prime bedding locations and breeding areas. You won't see many deer near a scrape like this but the bucks you do see will be good ones.

The best time to hunt a scrape like this is early in the morning, well before the buck heads in to bed down. It's likelier you'll ambush a big buck in a hurry to get back to the safety of his bedding ground than one just off of his bed, fresh and alert. A deer on his bed may have heard you approach his position. Always remember that the buck may have alternate routes and it may be a long time—if ever— before you're on the right route at the right time.

Look for perimeter scrapes right inside a wood line late in the season. Bucks often check these scrapes during the afternoon. Perimeter scrapes, like all scrapes, aren't as productive once hunting pressure gains momentum.

BREEDING SCRAPES

Find a spot with a good concentration of does. Find where the does bed, travel, and feed—and you'll also find breeding or "primary" scrapes. Breeding scrapes are the biggest scrapes a deer makes. Right before the rut peaks, they are scrupulously tended by the buck responsible. Once a doe urinates in the scrape to indicate her readiness, the buck takes out after her and never leaves her side unless forced off by a more dominant buck—until the time he breeds with her.

It's at this time that a buck is most likely to make dumb mistakes. But it's also the time that scrape hunting can really turn sour. The buck may come back to the scrape *only* after he's bred the doe, and then he may return *only* to the scrape that has produced the most does for him. Since bucks have been known to make more than 200 scrapes during the breeding season, just what are the chances that you'll be perched in a stand overlooking just the right scrape? Well, as high as one in 200, worse odds than you'd get at the average thoroughbred racetrack.

A better strategy is to hunt an area well downwind of a scrape line or several fresh scrapes. Be sure this location has a good field of view of the area you expect the buck to appear. When the buck moves in to scent-check his scrapes, he approaches from downwind: try to plan it so that he winds up *between* his scrape and your position.

Consider two alternate stand sites for each scrape or scrape line location. That way day-to-day wind shifts won't undermine your scrape hunting strategy.

Be sure to travel as quietly to your stand as possible. Bucks often hang in an area of many scrapes waiting for approaching does, especially prior to the rut's peak. If they're in the vicinity they'll investigate any suspicious noises from well downwind. If they get your scent you'll never even know they were nearby.

When you're hunting a big, dominant buck, clear as little brush for shooting lanes or stand construction as is practical. Big bucks are more liable to notice changes in their home range. And since they prefer to travel in thick brush, a sudden clearing will send up warning signals.

Another point to consider: think about subtly marking a quiet travel route to your stands well before the season. The markers could be something as simple as a series of broken branches or minute pieces of fluorescent or bright ribbon.

Never use a flashlight on the way into your stand; rely on night vision, which is usually remarkably good. The idea is not to give the buck any indication that there's a hunter in the woods.

For hunting scrape lines, treestands provide better visibility for the hunter and less chance of being scented by the deer. Since they are positioned well off the ground—most experts indicate a minimum height of 12 feet to be effective—they allow a hunter more freedom of movement than a ground stand.

On the other hand, ground stands or blinds are extremely easy to slip into and leave. They are also much quieter than many portable treestands. A well thought-out ground blind will easily blend your silhouette in with the rest of the terrain. Avoid skylining yourself along a ridgetop at all costs: even the slightest movement is readily detected against a light background.

When hunting from your stand or blind, move to shoot when the animal's eyes are hidden from view. This is most important when after mossyhorn whitetails. These bucks have seen nearly every trick that man has up his sleeve. To outwit them you have to outmaneuver them and never let them catch you in a mistake. One mistake when after a super big buck and you just might not get the chance to make another. He'll be gone—for good.

Scouting for scrapes before, during, and after deer season increases the enjoyment of searching for the superbucks. Just remember that there's no animal in the woods more aware of what's going on around it than your quarry. Think and plan accordingly!

For example, remember that the best way to check out a scrape is from a distance, with a good pair of binoculars. Nothing can put a big buck down faster than a good whiff of human odor.

Finally, for another scrape-hunting angle that might help you succeed in the whitetail woods, I've turned to Ernie Richardson of Shelbyville, Illinois, who probably originated the mock-scrape concept. Richardson has been using mock scrapes successfully for many years and has spent a lot of time perfecting the techniques required to take big bucks consistently. Since a mock scrape appeals both to a deer's sense of smell and its sight, exceptional care must be taken when preparing one.

"First thing, right before the rut, I make several small scrapes right in the deer trails in my area," Richardson explained. "I make these small scrapes by clearing away the leaves down to bare earth so I can determine just how many deer are using the area, and also to discover the size of their tracks. If there's a real trophy around, I'll know it right away.

"Once I've figured out where the hot spots are, I make like a deer," he continued. "I run a phony trail using real deer urine *away* from these hot spots—always off of the main runs. The urine I use is either buck urine or doe-in-estrus, although I've found that doe-in-estrus is better during the peak of the rut. At other times, though, one urine is as good as the other. Dribble the urine from a plastic container as you walk, just like a deer would dribble urine as it walks through the woods. The whole point is to duplicate what real deer do out in the woods.

"But remember, your fake trail must join up with a real trail at some point. It won't do any good to have a deer trail of your own making just running somewhere in the woods where you think a buck should be. The buck will be out there on a real trail, and will discover your mock trail, and come to investigate.

"Now comes the scrape-making part," Richardson said. "I wear plastic or rubber gloves that have also been scented with deer urine to make the actual mock scrape. I paw out my scrapes good and deep and at least two square feet. And I dribble whatever urine I'm using as a scent marker in each scrape when I'm through.

"I sweeten my mock scrapes with deer droppings that I've collected using my gloves and a plastic bag. And often, I won't begin to hunt until one of my friends has bagged a deer. Once he does, I collect the tarsal glands off of it and use them for my scrapes, too. It doesn't matter whether these glands are from a buck or a doe.

"I tie a rope about 18 inches long to each gland and beat them into the scrape. Then when I'm on my way to my stand, I tie the rope to my rubber boots (because rubber is more scent-free than leather) and let the glands bounce along behind me.

"In the past, I've made some mistakes," Richardson admitted. "And one of the worst has been to bring my scent trail right to my stand. I've missed a good buck because he came right to me, looking for the doe as he came. It was impossible for me to draw my bow without him seeing me.

"Now, I go past my tree stand and hide those glands where a doe might actually be bedding. I fool Mr. Buck into heading that way while making sure that as he goes, he'll be in position for me to make a good shot with my bow," Richardson added.

Richardson has another reason for digging out those mock scrapes good and deep. "I personally believe that the smell of overturned earth is as good a cover-up *and* attractant as there is for hunting the whitetail deer," he said.

"So I firmly feel that you can't make your mock scrape too big. You have three attractions going for you: the sex scents of whatever deer urine you're using, the curiosity value of both the tarsal glands and deer droppings you place in the scrape, and the smell of the earth itself," he concluded.

Choose your scrape-hunting stand well, hunt it wisely, and—with a little luck—a superbuck might be yours!

12

Hunting Superbuck Rubs

Myles Keller, Gorman Riley, and Greg Miller are each incredibly successful whitetail deer hunters. Keller, who lives in Claremont, Minnesota, listed 33 different bucks in the most recent Pope and Young record book. One of Keller's bucks also qualifies for the Boone and Crockett record book with a score of 175⅜. This buck, a tremendous eight-pointer, was, for a time, the Wisconsin state archery record.

Gorman Riley, of Pine Mountain Valley, Georgia, has also broken the Boone and Crockett barrier with a buck that scores 170⅝ points. Riley hunts with both bow and gun, and he gets many of his deer the hard way: by stalking.

Greg Miller, of Bloomer, Wisconsin, is another whitetail hunter dedicated to being the best hunter he can be. He hunts the deep woods of northwestern Wisconsin—an area of very low deer densities—and yet he consistently scores on big, heavy-racked and high-scoring bucks.

Why are these three whitetail hunters so successful? What secret do they share besides their incredible perseverance? The answer is that each of them relies heavily on their knowledge of the whitetail rub.

Deer rubs have always been obvious in the whitetail woods. Most hunters discount them entirely, because they appear to be random behavior. "They just show you where a deer has been, not where a deer is going to be," goes one old saying. But Keller, Riley, and Miller say this isn't the case at all. Rubs are very significant to them.

"A serious hunter should pay attention to rubs," said Keller. "They tell you a lot more than just the fact that there's a buck in the area. For instance, the more rubs in one particular spot that you can find, the closer you probably are to a buck's home area.

"What's even more important is that I feel that the very first rubs—the ones you find in late September—regardless of their size, are made by the older, dominant bucks," he continued. "Later on, as the rut progresses into November, there is undoubtedly some correlation between the size of the rub and the size of the deer, but this isn't true when rubbing begins each year. *The first rubs that you find—even if they're small—probably belong to the deer that you'd like to hang on your wall at home.*

"Back in 1984 I had a lot of trouble pinning down one particular big buck," Keller said. "I knew where he was probably hanging out, in some really dense cover, but that was all I could determine. The very next fall, I was out there in the same area as soon as this buck began to rub. When I found the first few rubs, I was able to figure out how he was traveling through the area. I set up my stand accordingly and killed that deer soon afterwards."

"I feel that very large rubs are probably a big buck's primary signposts," explained Gorman Riley. "You'll often find them on trees like a pine that look bright or white underneath once the bark's been rubbed off. This makes them fairly obvious even from a distance. When I find a rub on a tree that's 4 inches in diameter or larger, I believe that there's a good chance that it's been made by a good-sized buck. Rubs made specifically as signposts are often made on the same trees year after year. And it's not unusual to find these signpost rubs along streams.

"You can tell quite a bit from the way a deer rubs a tree," he added. "If the bark's really been stripped off, both close to the ground and high up on the trunk, it shows that the buck was really feeling aggressive. And the dominant buck is usually the most aggressive buck in the woods. One rub like this doesn't mean much by itself, but when you find a bunch of them together, you'd better start hunting there as soon as you can."

Riley feels that groups of rubs and rub lines are both important, but he also likes to find active scrapes nearby. "Look for rubs *and* scrapes in combination," he said, "not just one or the other."

And when Riley says bunch of rubs, he means bunch. "When I got my first Boone and Crockett buck back in 1983, I'd found more than 100 rubs in a one-acre area," he said.

Riley doesn't hunt right in an area with lots of rubbing activity. He prefers instead to locate the heaviest cover near a concentration of rubs and hunt there instead. "When I hunt dense cover I can rarely see farther than 30 or 40 yards," he said. "If you can see any farther than this, a big deer won't feel safe. And if he doesn't feel safe, he probably won't be moving when you can see him anyway."

Greg Miller has spent thousands of hours in the woods just analyzing whitetail rubs. Miller probably knows more about deer and their rubbing behavior than any non-scientist in the country. He spends incredible amounts of time playing rub line detective, trying to unravel a specific buck's travel pattern. What's more, he succeeds.

"If you pay attention to detail you *can* pattern individual bucks," Miller explained. "Often a buck will leave a characteristic gouge or scratch on a tree when he's rubbing on it. That gouge or scratch will be repeated every time he rubs a tree if it comes from a tine that's growing at a funny angle. An excessive amount of shredded bark can mean the buck has a lot of rough burrs on the bases of his antlers. Scratches above the main rub, or even on another nearby tree, can indicate tines of exceptional length.

"Bucks will also usually have a favorite type of tree that they like to rub on. Often they'll prefer a certain size of tree as well . . . I've identified one deer's circular travel route because he prefers pines that are as big around as my thigh or bigger. We call him the '3-pound coffee can buck' since that's about the size of his rubs. We've never seen him, but we sure can pick out his rubs."

Miller says that deer often rub trees the exact same way each time, indicating direction of travel. "The side of a tree that's rubbed shows you where he's headed," he said. He also has discovered the same thing as Gorman Riley—that bucks will rub on the same trees from year to year. "They'll even start using another buck's rub line if the first buck gets killed," Miller added. "They're sort of like big bass. Catch one out of a spot, go back later and there will probably be another big bass in the same spot. Likewise, if conditions are ideal, another deer will also be attracted to a really good area."

By finding rub lines and revisiting them after the season ends, Miller is able to determine what kind of bucks are left for the next year. "A big buck's rub line will very definitely show you where he'll be hanging out during the pre-rut period," Miller explained.

Rub lines do exactly what the term suggests, said Miller. They go from one point to another, usually in a fairly linear pattern. And while you will often be able to start at a rub and see the next rub, in some cases this isn't possible. "Two years ago, when I'd found some Boone and Crockett class sheds on one particular rub line, I'd sometimes have to go 200 yards before finding the next rub," Miller said.

Anyone lucky enough to find a rub line that two or more bucks are using has a real treat in store. Miller says this happens all the time. But practice makes perfect, and with practice, you'll be able to tell that more than one animal is using the trail.

"Rub lines usually originate near bedding areas. More rubs occur along buck runways, and then terminate near water, food sources, or doe areas," Miller said. "Clusters of rubs gave me a lot of trouble at first. I couldn't figure out why the buck made so many rubs in one little area that I call the 'staging area.' Eventually I figured it out. The staging area is always very close to the bedding area. The buck gets up, stretches, and makes a rub. Since he beds in about the same spot each day, he'll make a new rub nearby each day. It doesn't take long until there are a bunch of rubs in one location."

Miller can't emphasize enough the virtue of patience when hunting a good buck that you've patterned from rubs. "You've got one chance for a big buck—that's it," he said. "If he even suspects that you're there, he'll change his habits. It's tempting to put your stand near where you know he's bedded and take the chance that the wind won't blow erratically. Don't do it. Wait and be sure of the wind. That's probably the single most important factor in big buck hunting success."

Since Miller likes to get as close as he can to staging or bedding areas without disturbing the buck, it's imperative that he get in there as early as possible and stay until almost dark. "The bigger the buck, the more likely that he'll to be more nocturnal," he explained. "So, in many cases, you're going to have your best opportunity for a shot as he's returning to bed at dawn, or when he's first going out at dusk. In any case, rub lines produce best when they're hunted before the peak of the rut. Once the peak hits, everything becomes unpredictable."

Miller agrees with Keller and Riley that the size of rub is directly proportional to the size of buck. "I've picked up 50 different shed antlers on rub lines over the past three years," he said. "Some of them are incredibly huge. And I've found it to be true, big bucks are usually rubbing on big trees."

As time goes on, more scientific studies have addressed buck rub behavior. Much of what the scientists have discovered supports what these deer hunters have said. The researchers have uncovered additional information on rubs as well.

First, rubs are visual and olfactory signposts that bucks make for other deer. Rub trees are selected because they are easily seen (white and bright under the bark), and because they have a distinctive smell—cedars, black cherries, and pines are often chosen because they are all aromatic. The deer's forehead sudoriferous glands, which become active in autumn, contribute a buck's own "signature" scent to the rub on a tree.

Because bucks apparently make their rubs deliberately noticeable, they might be weak territorial markers. Bucks' rubs also become more obvious—more bark is exposed—as the peak of the rut approaches. And rubs will occur in the very same areas year after year.

These rubs may also actually help promote estrus in does. Studies performed on domestic sheep indicate that the presence of priming pheromones from rams is effective in making ewes ovulate. Consequently, it's been hypothesized that rubs, along with scrapes, are a source of priming pheromones that might stimulate the doe into starting her estrous cycle. The priming pheromones at work here would be the glandular secretions from the forehead glands plus any urinary deposits the buck might leave at scrape sites.

Another study indicated that more rubs appear when there are more bucks 2½ years of age and older in that area. Most rubs *are* located along deer trails, logging roads, and in drainages along streams. When food is hard to get, it appears the number of rubs in an area decreases. Ultimately, foraging becomes more important than rubbing. So when the number of rubs in an area drops off dramatically, don't assume that there are fewer deer. It could be that there is less food.

It has also been discovered that a buck makes anywhere from 69 to 538 rubs in a year with an average of about 300 rubs per buck, or 2½ rubs per day for a period of four months.

Yearling bucks are less aggressive, display less courtship behavior, and demonstrate less scent-marking behavior (scraping and rubbing) than older bucks. These young, 18-month-old bucks make few rubs during the pre-rut period even when no prime-age bucks are around to dominate them.

Bucks that do rub their antlers during the pre-rut period are indicating dominance. As Myles Keller noted, the first rubs to be found probably are from the big, dominant bucks, and the prime-age bucks keep rubbing throughout the entire autumn.

Rubs do let you know where a buck has *been*, so they just might help you figure out where that buck will be again. What's the rub? One of the very best big buck indicators there is; one that will help your whitetail hunting success, year after year.

13

Whitetail Superbuck Travel Patterns

I looked at my watch and smiled to myself. It was after 10:00 A.M. Time for the action to start. Oh, I knew that other hunters sometimes questioned my tactics. But it didn't matter. *If they only knew what I knew. . . .*

All thoughts fled when I heard the quick rustling in the leaves behind me. Either one of our horses had escaped their pasture, or there was a big animal heading my way. I turned quickly, getting up to my knees as I did.

My breath started coming quicker. I forced myself to think about anything but a trophy. The crunching got louder, and then I saw him: a big buck topped the ridge and started on a diagonal for the bottom of the hollow. He was moving rapidly. I could see the sunlight glistening on his gray back and ivory antlers as I raised my rifle and set my elbow tight against the sling.

Thump, thump—could the deer hear my heart? I eased the safety off—and sure enough, he must have heard the thumping. At least it seemed he did! The deer tensed, stopped, and peered right at me. But no clear shot presented itself. I felt my knees begin to wobble.

If I connected on this one it would be the best whitetail I'd ever gotten. Quickly, I forced myself to think about other things. The surest way to miss a deer is to be mentally hanging him on the den wall.

Nose up, the big eight-pointer warily sniffed the cold November air. Long minutes later, he took one hesitant step that put him right in line with a stovepipe-sized opening that cut through the undergrowth. I knew it was going to be my only chance and I took it.

The blast of the rifle echoed off the hill in front of me as the buck leaped forward. A good hit! I watched as the big deer gathered momentum that carried him down, down to the bottom of the hill. He was dead on his feet and collapsed as soon as he hit level ground.

I had gotten my buck—the biggest of my hunting life to date—at 10:00 A.M. But everyone knows that big bucks are nocturnal: they bed all day and only move early and late. That's what I thought, too. And it's often true, particularly during the post-rut period after the deer have been spooked by hunter activity. My determination to become a deer hunter—and a *good* one—made me change my thinking about bucks. And when I changed my thinking, like many other big buck hunters, I changed my luck.

When I first started deer hunting I was as green as they come. I spent long hours with every other deer hunter I knew. I hung on every word, sopping up deer lore like a dry sponge. My husband and I haunted the farmer on whose land we hunted, begging him to share with us just one more pearl of his deer hunting wisdom.

Eventually, what we learned began to fit a pattern: hunt early, hunt late, shoot straight, and most important of all, be in the right place at the right time. If I had been successful, even moderately so, from the very first, I'm sure I'd be following those rules today. Thank goodness I wasn't! For deer hunters, failure is the best teacher of all. And I was a real failure. But I was a *persistent* failure: I never gave up. True, I got a big doe my very first time afield and I basked in the glory of success. But it only whetted my appetite; I was determined to bring home the venison once again—only this time a cut that sported antlers. But it would be many years before I bagged my second whitetail.

During the next few seasons I simply *never* came in from the field, and I learned a lot because of that stubborn kind of hunting. Other hunters socialized at brunches back at the farmhouse while I froze in thickets and on tree stands. I hunted during a storm that encased my rifle barrel in a thick coating of ice and froze my eyelashes together. I almost gave up. At high noon I was rewarded: I saw a cluster of deer moving away, looking nervously over their backs—but why were they moving this time of day?

Later, I found out that another hunter had decided to come back out and give hunting another try. He had entered the woods not far from my stand, and the deer moved into sight. That simple observation started me re-thinking about deer patterns. Over the years I began to formulate my own theory of how deer really behaved in response to hunter movements. While it's true that deer *do* move early and late, *I always see the most deer between the hours of 9:00 A.M. and 1:00 P.M.* I think it really hit home on one hunt in the early seventies.

It was 10:30 on an extremely cold day. The wind was still. Bob and I had just met at his stand. I'd been walking all morning, but Bob had been sitting stock still for hours. He decided he needed to move about to work up some body heat. So as he abandoned the stand, I settled back to do some serious stand hunting.

He'd no sooner climbed down the steps when I heard an animal moving swiftly toward us. The stand was situated at the neck of a small hollow and faced a gentle slope. About halfway up the slope was a large cedar glade. Stately evergreens stood guard at the edge of the hardwoods; I could only catch glimpses of the buck's brown coat as it flashed in and out of the trees. Even at this distance I could see the antlers plainly: they were magnificent.

"Buck," I called to Bob. The deer was making so much noise that he wasn't likely to hear anything. Bob paused and listened. I knew he'd seen the deer when he hunkered down and got into a steady shooting position. Moments later one shot rang out from the .270 Winchester and the buck took off. It took us hours to find the buck, but it was worth the effort. He was a fine eight-pointer that scored nearly 133 Boone and Crockett points. And Bob took him during midday.

Before this hunt I'd spent a lot of the midday hours walking about. Like many other hunters—Bob included—I'd get cold and feel the need to stretch my bones after five or six hours. Looking back I realize that I usually saw deer as I wandered through the woods. At the time I thought I'd jumped the deer; now I'm not so sure. I think it's time to discard the myth that deer don't move in the middle of the day. The simple fact of the matter is that most deer move period-ically all day long—whether or not they are disturbed. *Many super big bucks will pick and choose times to move during the day as well, especially in response to hunter pressure.*

To help prove my point, let's consider the scenario in which a deer is undisturbed. Deer are cud-chewers: they like nothing better than to eat for a while, swallow the wad of food that's formed, and then move to a nice cozy place to lie down and chew their cuds.

Deer also move about at midday to find favorite foods. If there is a good stand of white oaks where ripe acorns litter the ground below, there's a good bet for ambushing a midday deer. Very few does or young bucks can resist these sweet-tasting morsels. And if does are there, bucks may be close by—big, dominant bucks *if it's during the peak of the rut.*

I sat watching the woods in front of my stand, wishing for a deer. It was 10:00 A.M. before a lone doe fed into view along the acorn-littered forest floor. One shot put her down in her tracks. I field dressed her and then climbed back up to my stand to wait for my husband.

It had become a tradition for him to visit me at lunchtime. While I have the patience of Job, Bob likes to get out and move around. Stand hunting works much better for me; my reflexes aren't as fast as his. I like being sure of my shot before firing.

An hour passed; then an hour and a half. And then I noticed movement in the undergrowth through which my doe had traveled. I watched as a deer materialized, nose to the ground. He was a mon-ster, and he was out and about at high noon. Where was Bob?

Just then I heard him. He was moving quickly down the hill be-hind me, not a care in the world. I looked around and saw him wave at me. I motioned for him to stop.

He crouched down and looked hard at the woods in front of us. But that old buck hadn't gotten to be a mossyhorns by being dumb. He froze. There we waited, all three of us, Bob, the buck, and me. Who would break first?

"What do you see," Bob hissed at me.

"Buck, a big one," I hissed back.

"Where?" he said. "I can't make him out."

"Right at the edge of that clearing—near those scrub sumac bushes." I indicated the spot with my finger.

Still the buck held tight.

"I'm coming down to you," Bob whispered as he walked half crouching for the final ten yards. "I can't see anything from here."

With that the buck exploded. He swapped ends and snaked away faster than you could imagine.

"Damn," Bob muttered. And we both were participants in the writ-ing of another chapter on buck behavior—the one that teaches that it's no fluke that trophy bucks move in midday.

Dr. James C. Kroll, of Stephen F. Austin State University in Texas, has a theory on why deer—big bucks in particular—move about dur-ing midday.

"Deer are usually shot at early and late in the day," Kroll says, "and they adjust their activity to *avoid* hunters. And while this does mean that they may become more nocturnal—there shouldn't be *any* hunters in the woods at night—it also means that they will move around in the middle of the day, too. A hunter who stays put *all* day long increases his chances of scoring on a superbuck."

Why is this so? Think about it. Early in the morning an army of hunters is on the march. Many whitetails are jumped as hunters slog through swamps and trudge up hills. Alarms sound in the whitetail brain. Something is afoot. Those deer that can hide out by bedding down do so as quickly as possible. The deer that weren't alarmed are the ones most likely to get shot—along with those frightened enough to run helter-skelter into the sights of a waiting rifleman.

Even on opening day, the action has died down by 8:00 A.M. John Q. Hunter looks at his watch, feels his stomach growl, and realizes that he's beginning to get cold. He remembers the hot thermos of coffee and the lunch he left back in the trunk. Oh, and while he's at it he might as well visit ol' Harry on the next ridge. He's just posi-tive he heard Harry shoot and maybe he could help him drag his deer out.

So John Q. gets up and lumbers away. He's been sitting in a cone of scent that's been cascading all across the valley. Soon the scent dissipates, the woods noises return to normal, and the big whitetail buck that's bedded a scant 200 yards away in a bramble thicket gets up.

The same scenario is taking place in deer woods all over the country. Deer learn to move during midmorning hours *because* hunters are moving then. The deer have patterned *hunters!* They know John Q. is not likely to stay out all day, so they sit tight and wait for him to leave.

That's not all. Simply by moving, many hunters kick deer out of hiding spots and straight to those hunters still waiting. The hours between 8:00 and 10:00 A.M. are when the best deer drive occurs— and it's one that's not even organized.

Find a good travel lane—one that hunters use—and figure out where the deer will run when kicked out by the marching troops. Situate your stand downwind of where the deer will likely run—and get ready for action.

One of my friends told me a story from opening day in New York's Adirondack Mountains. It was opening day madness: hunters were everywhere. My friend sat high atop a rock outcrop watching them leave their vehicles, walk into the woods, meet, talk, and then walk out to their cars again. By noon he was discouraged—no, *disgusted* was more like it.

Then he noticed several hunters meeting right under the rock he was perched on. He watched as they sat down and drank a can of soda together, laughed, smoked, and cut up. When they left, my friend was finally ready to pack it in. The other hunters hadn't been gone for more than ten minutes when something else caught his attention.

When he managed to focus on the movement, he couldn't believe his eyes. There, beneath the rock he'd been sitting on, *right where the hunters had been sitting,* walked a ten-point trophy buck. The unconcerned deer sauntered over to the empty soda can and began sniffing around. He never knew what hit him. The time? *Twelve o'clock noon.*

That buck was conditioned to hunter behavior—he wasn't even afraid of the hunters' scent that must have pervaded the area. He was used to hunters fraternizing, then *leaving*—and he knew from past experience that the woods were safe during the middle of the day.

Dr. Kroll has performed extensive radiotelemetry studies that show big bucks *know* where permanent hunting stands are located. Not only that, they also seem to be able to tell when they are occupied!

"It's downright humorous to radio-track bucks during hunting season," Kroll said, "and watch as they move quietly through safe zones and travel corridors. And when do they travel? Mainly at midday during the hunting season. So, that's one of the best times to hunt. Most of the Boone and Crockett bucks I know about were killed right around 10:00 A.M.. I take a backpack ladder stand in with me before daylight and stay on it all day long. If I've picked a bad place, I don't move; I just use the time to plan my next hunt."

Stanley Potts of Clinton, Illinois, is another big buck expert with three huge bucks to prove it. He is extremely skilled with both shotgun and bow, and knows his quarry intimately. And he *loves* to hunt during midday.

"I've just never killed a big buck in the morning," Potts said. "I've killed more bucks during the hours from ten to three than any other time. Even my monstrous 195⅝ typical was killed at 3:30 in the afternoon. And that's contrary to everything you ever read."

When I asked Potts why he thinks midday is the prime time for bucks, he replied, "They just aren't as suspicious then. Especially during the *peak* of the rut. Those big old dominant bucks can't help themselves. They are out and about chasing does—and probably every one of them has had a run-in with a hunter before light, or right at nightfall. They're conditioned to be extraordinarily wary then.

"You don't want a whitetail to be any warier than he already is. They're wary enough to begin with. I like to do the unexpected because that's how I trip them up. Like two years ago when I got a big eight-point with my bow. This buck scored 140 Pope and Young points and I got him by double-tricking him. I was hunting at noon *and* I was hunting in a rainstorm—both things hunters don't usually do.

"I watched him trail a doe for a quarter of a mile. He came right at me across an old soybean field, twitching his tail all the way. The wind was blowing and the rain was slashing. It was cold and wet and miserable but I got my deer."

Another of Potts' big bucks scored 160 points and it, too, was killed when most other hunters were warming up back at their trucks or grabbing a little shut-eye. Potts took that one with his shotgun at one in the afternoon.

Always keep in mind that as you adapt your hunting times and methods to reap big buck rewards, those same bucks will once again adapt their behavior in order to survive. After a couple of years of hunting during midday in the same spots, mix it up a bit: scout out another area in order to trip up a midday buck there. The odds will be that the midday bucks in your former neck of the woods might be nearly totally nocturnal by now.

While buster bucks may be up and about at varying times during each and every day, just how and where do they move?

According to studies by Dr. Kroll, travel patterns for big bucks follow a seasonal schedule. "During the pre-breeding period most bucks are predictable, even the big, dominant ones. They use travel corridors to move back and forth from bedding locations to preferred feeding areas. Travel corridors are protected areas leading from one focal point to another within the buck's home range—from a favored source of feed, to water, to cover, for example."

The ideal deer travel corridors are areas along habitat edges, along creek drainages, in heavy brush abutting clearcuts, and in thickets bordering agricultural fields. Bucks use travel corridors in all of these places but put a special emphasis on ones located along creek drainages and extremely heavy edge habitat.

A big buck's pre-rut behavior is as predictable as any behavior that the buck is likely to exhibit all year long. As the rut progresses, however, the buck's behavior changes dramatically. During this time, he eats very little; he's restless and erratic. It's incredibly difficult to discern any type of pattern in his movements. He travels at random as he moves from one sanctuary to another, looking for more does to breed. Consequently, tracking him down becomes largely a matter of chance—and that chance is based on what you can piece together about his travel patterns.

Dr. Kroll feels that dominant bucks often have several "core areas" within their home range—places they frequent most often. These core areas may change with the season—it's not unusual for a buck to have spring, summer, fall, and winter core areas. Even these seasonal core areas may be fragmented by the buck into several different autumn core areas, for example. All these core areas make big bucks hard to pattern, so be certain that the core areas you identify are the ones *currently* in use.

Kroll believes that within each core area exists yet another favored buck hideout, the "sanctuary." "A sanctuary is simply a place where a big buck can hide and be virtually unapproachable by hunters," Kroll stated. "To identify a probable buck sanctuary simply ask yourself where *you* would hide if you wanted to completely escape detection on the piece of land you're hunting. It's amazing how accurate a method this is for determining where the bucks will be holed up."

Kroll also believes that an ideal sanctuary will be chock full of thick, dense cover and have some late winter foods that the buck can eat to recover at least a portion of his strength.

"Hunters should always be analyzing every detail of their hunting area each and every minute that they're afield," Kroll emphasized. "How many of them know that does prefer the more open areas like fields and mature forests with little understory while bucks thrive on thick, protective understory that literally makes it difficult to move. That's why 'buck range' is often the least accessible portion of a particular area. Bucks will be hiding out in immature forest, swamps, briar patches, anything that makes it hard on a hunter. One thousand acres of forest is not necessarily 1,000 acres of deer habitat. And it's certainly not 1,000 acres of buck habitat."

The really big buck can throw another curve at the hunter, namely its ability to cover large areas. Studies have documented that, as bucks get older, the size of their home ranges will nearly always get larger. Plus, once the rut is in full swing, many mature bucks will often travel great distances—*even completely out of their traditional home ranges*—to search out doe groups to breed.

The best way to take such a buck is to pattern his behavior as accurately as possible. Then lie in wait well downwind of a favored travel corridor during the pre-rut period, when buck movements are still predictable. This may mean that the only way for a crack at the truly big buck in your area that you know about will be with a bow, since archery seasons are usually the only legal method of hunting the pre-rut period.

Never place a stand right *on* the travel corridor. Tales of the trophy deer that hangs back to watch his intended path for many minutes abound at the cabin dinner table. Bucks like these watch for a give-away movement before they enter the trail. The buck may not know that it's an impatient hunter, but as a survival-oriented animal he can't afford to risk his precious hide on anything out of the ordinary. So the deer turns away to find another travel route.

If the rut arrives, however, and you're still buckless, remember that even at the peak of the rut bucks prefer to follow major topographical features such as ridges, shelves, or drainage systems as they travel from one doe group to another. When the rut is in full swing, superbuck hunting becomes a game of percentages: Will the buck make a mistake and possibly get in a travel rut *during* the rut? And will the hunter be properly positioned in order to take advantage of the mistake?

Another good way to put the odds in your favor is to stake out a saddle or swag connecting two hollows. Carefully cover *any* type of depression that could possibly hide a buck from view as he travels about.

Then comes the most difficult time to hunt any superbuck: the post-rut period. If a mature buck survives until most breeding behavior is waning, then he's wiser and warier than ever before. He's had additional and *vivid* experiences to add to his survival-oriented behavior. Most mature bucks are *totally* nocturnal by the post-rut period. And what's worse, a few extraordinarily cautious individuals will *stay* nocturnal from this point on. So the question is, how can you connect on these survivors?

One of the ways that Dr. Kroll recommends is the silent drive. "This works best from mid-morning to mid-afternoon," he said. "Once possible prime buck sanctuaries or bedding areas have been identified, look at the lay of the land. Apply your knowledge of probable escape routes and place the standers there.

"Check wind direction and plan the drive accordingly. You don't have to be noisy to move a big buck out of an area. When bucks move they'll usually flee *into* the wind and very often downhill."

Big buck travel patterns are important: you aren't going to connect unless you can locate the deer. And you can't locate the deer if you make all of your plans from the comfort of your home. Anything worth having is worth working for, and when you make a whitetail superbuck your goal, your work is certainly cut out for you. Luckily, a knowledge of trophy whitetail travel patterns will help make your job easier.

14

The Hunter's Edge for Superbucks

It was a gray, sullen day. The wind was gusting in brutal blasts and the chill cut straight through to the bone. These weather conditions should have made this day a washout for whitetail hunting.

I had a different theory in mind. All autumn long I had been lured to a tangled patch of cover on this particular farm by abundant deer sign. The cover was a whitetail paradise of brambles and briars nestled between a river-bottom field and a ridgetop corn field that had long since been picked. I shivered in my ground stand nearby, but my hopes were high.

Would the deer be moving anywhere in the cutting wind? Only time would tell. The heavy scudding clouds began to add to my woes: great white flakes began drifting out of the sky to coat the ground. I sat and waited some more. Soon my patience was rewarded. I could see movement through the thicket in front of me. I watched expectantly as a big doe picked her way daintily through the newly fallen snow.

Then I saw him. Close on her trail walked the biggest buck I'd ever seen in my life. His antlers were high, wide, and massive and had at least ten points, maybe more. A "book" buck for sure!

I eased off the safety and waited for the big deer to step into the opening I'd selected. As he did, I squeezed off a shot from my 30.06 Springfield sporterized rifle.

The deer dropped; it looked as if he was hit hard. I crawled under the barbed wire fence that wove its way through the small section of edge habitat and walked closer, admiring the handsome antlers.

When I was less than five feet away, the huge buck staggered to his feet. I was astounded! I immediately got a case of Superbuck Fever. It was only my third deer season and I wasn't prepared for the sight of my wall-hanger jumping up when he was supposed to be dead! Unfortunately, the buck escaped and I couldn't even get off another shot. There was no blood; and the snow should have shown some if the deer had been hit solidly. Bob and I later theorized that my shot had been deflected by a vagrant bit of brush and only hit the buck in the antler, momentarily stunning him. The shot was enough to put him down but not enough to keep him down for good.

I had nightmares for several years over "the one that got away." But the real lesson of that day turned out to be the one that has paid off more than once: hunt the edge for superbucks! Hunting conditions that day couldn't have been worse, yet I had nearly gotten a superbuck in the middle of the day. The next year Bob capitalized on what I'd learned. He took a buck that scored close to 140 Boone and Crockett points, a true superbuck for southern Missouri. He did it hunting a similar location. We call the spots where these big deer like to hang out "the hunters' edge."

EDGE: WHAT IT IS

An edge is a place where two or more habitat types come together. The scientific name is "ecotone." Edge is even better when *more* than two kinds of habitat converge in one place. Look at a topographic map: many times, abrupt changes in landforms are where ecotones can be found.

For example, if a pine forest abuts an oak woodlot, the boundary where they meet is edge. And where a corn field stretches alongside a drainage ditch choked with sassafras and persimmons, that's edge, too. Another kind of edge is where fertile creekbottom merges with wooded slopes.

Deer like crop fields, grasslands, legume strips, hardwoods for mast, old clearcuts for browse—any grouping of diverse plants. The more mixed up the habitat, the better. And more deer will use it, too. Individual ranges often overlap, and the best edge may be included in the territory of many different deer. Draw an imaginary line around a cornfield. If that line is all choked with cover, that's a good example of edge.

All deer have home ranges sometimes less than 200 acres in size. Superbucks are no exception: in fact, these big, secretive deer will often concentrate their activities within a core area of 40 acres or less that shifts only slightly as the year progresses.

A core area is a place where all of a deer's living requirements can be met within one small area. Here a deer can eat, bed, and possibly water without drawing attention to itself. But as the seasons change, and food sources shift, core areas may also shift. So within a deer's home range, there may exist several different core areas that vary with the time of year. Summer may find a superbuck in a blackberry briar patch, feeding on tender shoots in June and on ripening berries in July. September may find the same buck in a thicket of post oaks near a favored white oak stand. As darkness falls, the big bruiser will travel along the perimeter of his core area, lapping up the sweet white oak acorns. Later that winter, the buck might move into a field of standing corn, where cover and food are abundant.

It's important to remember that core areas aren't chosen for food alone. To a superbuck, security is more important than food. Edge, particularly thick, tangled edge represents the ultimate in security. Predators, especially the human variety, find it difficult to move about in cover like this without making a lot of noise.

Edge also provides shelter from the elements. An animal can slip into one cover type to feed and then back into another for protection. The right kind of edge satisfies all of a superbuck's requirements.

Edge also provides a buck with an excellent spot for concentrated rubbing and scraping activities. Edge plants often include preferred rub trees, especially fragrant pine, cedar, and sassafras.

An area with many rubs is known as a "dominance area" and a superbuck may have several dominance areas within his home range. A buck may move from one dominance area to another, looking for a willing doe, or he may stick closely to one favored dominance area. In any case, edge is a great spot to start the search for your superbuck, especially if it's included in a dominance area.

I discovered just how great several years ago: I noticed that a buck had really ripped the edge apart along the border of a small bottom field. There were rubs and scrapes everywhere—mainly where a little hollow merged into the field. A spring branch ran on the other side of the bottom. Brush-choked fencerows completed the picture. I picked a ground stand downwind from the buck spot and waited.

All day I watched does escape through the edge. But I wanted a buck, the bigger the better. Around 3:00 P.M. some hunters up the hollow decided to drive it. I wasn't prepared when a fine eight-point buck leaped from his bed in the edge *not 20 yards from where I was sitting*—that's how tight a big buck will hold. I shot but missed as he stampeded across the meadow and leaped the fence.

Since then, I've come to realize how vital edge is to all deer and particularly to a big buck. I've also figured out how to scout it and how to hunt it, and many other big buck hunters are successful because they concentrate their efforts on edge.

One hunter in particular comes to mind. Gary LaRose hunts on a farm neighboring ours in Ste. Genevieve County, Missouri. He has had fantastic luck hunting edge. But is it really all luck?

Gary started his hunting career like many of us—with lots of well-meaning advice but no guarantee that any of it would work. As the youngest hunter in deer camp he took a lot of ribbing that made him determined to become the best deer hunter he could be.

His turning point as a hunter came in the late 1970s. It was the last day of gun season; it was cold, miserable, and rainy. The other hunters headed for home and they suggested that Gary do the same. But Gary remembered a brushy corner where the farm bordered a county road. Traffic traveled the road all day long, but this spot looked good to Gary because it was chock full of cover.

With the wind and rain blowing steadily in his face, Gary eased through the undergrowth. Within minutes a doe jumped up. And then a heavy-beamed ten-point scrambled close behind her. Gary made his chance count. He tumbled the buck with one shot from his open-sighted 30.06. The buck scored 140 Boone and Crockett points, a superbuck anyone would be proud of.

Since then, Gary's perfected his edge-hunting technique. A large powerline cuts through the farm where he hunts—made to order for an edge hunter. So that's where he concentrates his efforts. If the air is still, he finds a good spot to stand. If it's windy or rainy and he can stalk stealthily through the brush, he opts for that. But he gets results. His string of successes includes two really fine bucks killed right on that powerline—one a massive 13-pointer and another that scored 153, not bad for an Ozark whitetail.

SCOUTING AND HUNTING THE EDGE

Each of these hunting methods illustrates a unique feature of edge hunting.

I had a chance at a tremendous buck because I was willing to gamble on a whitetail quirk that's become more apparent the more I hunt: deer leave their beds to forage through edge during high, gusty winds. Some hunters actually prefer these days for stalking, since both hunter *and* deer are handicapped by noisy woods.

Under these conditions, superbucks will often be out, but in the densest cover. In many cases these big bucks don't associate vile, nasty weather with hunters.

A hunter doesn't have to be as silent in bad weather since the gusting wind camouflages his approach. On the other hand, a deer won't make any noise either as it approaches the hunter. Deer will be extremely nervous when it's windy, and a superbuck—*the* ultimate of all deer—will be more nervous yet. A hunter must stay alert, looking for the tell-tale sign that spells "deer."

Always walk or quarter into the wind. Keep the sun at your back whenever possible so it shines into the deer's eyes, making him unsure of what he's seeing. You must confuse as many of the superbuck's senses as possible.

Don't expect to see an entire deer in broken cover like edge. Instead, try to find the white of a throat patch or the glint of sun off an antler. Bend over occasionally to look for deer legs among the saplings. Watch for the flicker of an ear or a tail. Even a shiny black nose can be the clue you're searching for.

Stand hunting the edge is also a very productive method. A few years ago I killed one of my best bucks, a fine eight-point that hangs on my family room wall today, by hunting a portion of edge that served as a travel lane instead of as a core area. I found a strip of heavy cover connecting two distinct ecotones, a pine ridgetop and a hollow of hardwoods. A dense growth of understory snaked its way between the two habitat types. It helped that the understory traced the route of a slight saddle over the ridge. On opening day I sat downwind from the tangle and waited. Shots rang out from all directions, but nothing spooked through the thicket. By evening, I hadn't seen a thing.

The second day I returned to the same spot and took my nine-year-old daughter with me. As daylight dawned cold and clear we only heard a few shots, then a last one about 8:45 A.M. But five minutes later, the sound of trotting hooves came from within the overgrown mess in front of us. My daughter couldn't help it. She jumped up, and the buck came to a sudden halt. In any case, all I could see was the high, white, sweeping antlers—but no shot presented itself. Finally, after many long moments, the animal moved just a bit into an opening. I shot, and the buck barreled out of the cover and careened down the slope where he dropped over dead.

Locate your stand where you can watch field edges and nearby deer trails. If you can locate your stand downwind from a major trail, so much the better. When possible, have two or more stands, each oriented to a different approach. That way no matter which way the wind is coming from, you'll have a spot to set up in.

Because of the very nature of edge, it's sometimes hard to find good trees to build stands in or climb. Sometimes a ground stand is the only alternative. Hay or straw bales, strategically placed well before the season, work well. Camouflage cloth clipped onto brush with clothespins is also good. Anything that breaks up your outline, such as a blowdown or old stump, will work in your favor. Try to use material native to the area whenever possible.

Remember, to be successful don't hunt out of one stand all of the time. A superbuck will be on to you in a flash. The trick is to make the buck slip up.

Gary LaRose discovered one of the most productive edge hunting methods when he bagged his first edge buck. Drizzle, heavy mist or fog obscures a deer's vision and interferes with his sense of smell. Since dampness muffles the sound of brush, a hunter can be much quieter than normal. Deer don't seem to sense their disadvantage during wet weather; rather, they seem to let down their guard—perhaps because they rarely encounter humans during inclement conditions. Whitetails will often browse in edge for long periods during or after a light snowfall, for example.

So scout the edge in your area all year long. In the winter look for browse lines—places where deer have been nibbling on favored plants. Ordinarily, a deer will only nip the tender ends. If the winter is extremely hard, they eat much larger browse branches, up to a pencil's thickness.

After a snowfall, trails show up better than usual. These may change before the next hunting season, but potential patterns can be discovered now. Also keep an eye out for old rubs and scrapes; they have a habit of reappearing in the same area year after year. An old scrape kept open after hunting season ends means that the buck that made it will be that much bigger the next year.

Summer is a good time to scout for bucks. They're less wary while growing their antlers. Watch for them in early evening while they feed in fields, entering them from favored edge patches. Focus on these when you begin your serious scouting in early fall.

Summer's also a good time to inspect the acorn crop. Edge bordering a group of fertile white oaks is utilized most. If the mast crop is poor, edge increases its potential as a good place to score as the season progresses and deer must move farther to find food.

When fall's in the air, look for rubs and scrapes. Edge becomes alive at dusk and dawn. Territorial scrapes are often found around natural perimeters—like fencerows or the grown up edges of fields—both excellent edge types.

Once the season's under way, redouble your edge-hunting efforts. Once whitetails have been disturbed, they look for any secluded pockets where they can hide out for the rest of the season. Lots of edge looks too small to hold a deer: looks can be deceiving.

Last, but not least, be flexible. If you do your homework and come up with a fantastic bit of edge that should hold your superbuck, that's great. But if you still haven't seen your deer a week into the season, quit hunting! Devote *another* day to scouting. Chances are, the buck hasn't abandoned the area. Instead, he's probably moved his core area a short distance away; or, he's changed his travel times or pattern. Adapt, as he has, and the trophy may soon be yours.

There are many ways to scout and hunt the edge for superbucks. And each one can show you that hunting the edge gives *you* the edge—the hunters' edge, that is.

15

The Importance of Stands

The vast majority of whitetail deer, including the elusive super-bucks, are taken by hunting from stands. Those hunters who pay the most attention to their stands are generally those who are most often rewarded by the sight of a monarch whitetail slowly ambling into their sights.

The process of choosing a stand can be as simple as plopping down at the base of a big oak tree or as involved as the hunter wants to make it. Of course every year some big deer are taken by sheer luck, but the hunters who consistently return with thick sets of wall-hanging antlers are those who take some time with stand placement.

It wasn't too long ago when "stand" meant literally that. A spot on the ground where the hunter stood until a deer happened by. In the 1950s some bright hunter realized that deer rarely looked *up*—above their own eye level. So, by climbing a tree and hunting from on high, surprise would be on the hunter's side. Soon hunters realized how well this trick worked, and they *all* began climbing trees. Before long, deer sensed that danger didn't always come from ground level. They began looking up.

The fact that deer do look up doesn't cancel all the benefits of hunting from a tree. And there are also decided advantages for those hunters who choose to hunt from the ground.

To better consider the criteria for successful stand placement, first we must consider the habits of our quarry. There are three general periods of buck activity: the pre-breeding period, the breeding or rut period, and the post-rut period. Buck behavior is most predictable during the pre-breeding period. So this is the time when it's easiest to trip up Mr. Superbuck. At this pre-rut time, a buck follows fairly set patterns, using travel corridors to move from bedding areas to feeding areas and back again. Look for the first rubs and you won't be far off the travel corridors deer use to move from bedding areas to feeding areas and back again. A heavy trail usually means that a doe group is using it; light signs of use identify it as a buck corridor.

Once the rut begins, most bucks simply can't be counted on to behave in any predictable manner, as they move from hot doe to hot doe. Unfortunately, the buck you've patterned all year may simply get up and get out of the area. A dominant, breeding buck may travel from doe group to doe group, breeding them as they come into estrus. This is good news for the buck, but it could be bad news for a hunter who's sitting tight in a tree stand that *can't* be relocated.

The one exception is when that hunter is after the rare, big, mature buck that lets the other bucks do the breeding. A buck like this will stick to a schedule of pre-breeding activity, feeding and bedding all season. Unfortunately, a buck like this usually lets the other bucks do the breeding because he's been scared, and badly. Survival instinct takes over. Often this buck is completely nocturnal.

Another thing to consider is the fact that, in unbalanced populations of whitetails where does far outnumber the bucks, it is impossible for all does to be bred during each estrous cycle. So every month, does come into heat again, and bucks continue to chase them. A hunter's chances of randomly waylaying any buck increase, but the chances of consciously bagging one particular trophy buck decrease.

That's because by the time the rut has progressed to what we ordinarily call the post-rut period, the trophy bucks in the area have learned a lot of lessons about how to avoid hunters. If the ratio of bucks to does was unbalanced to begin with, perhaps due to bucks-only hunting, then those few bucks have learned even faster, since all the hunting pressure is on them. So the best time to trip up a trophy in this population is actually in the beginning of the season, before they've been wised up by other hunters. As the superbuck becomes more sure he's in danger, he will probably react in one of two different ways: by becoming more nocturnal and by sticking closer to home—or both.

Even in an area where there's a fairly balanced whitetail population, the bucks still alive after the rut are cautious. They won't move without a good reason. Sometimes that reason is food, especially if a primary food like acorns failed or was in short supply during the pre-rut period. The buck's energy reserves will be low and he must venture forth to feed.

If food is plentiful close to a buck's core area, however, or if food was plentiful during the pre-breeding season, don't count on seeing the buck at all, even though he will probably return to his core area on his pre-breeding home range. He'll lay low.

Now that we've reviewed the very basics of buck movement, how and where do we place our stands? First, although treehouses look very sturdy and comfortable, think long and hard before building one. Most of them require lugging lots of lumber, nails and tools back into the woods. For what? Hammering nails into trees may cause them to die within a year or two. The treehouse has to be checked several times a year, and there's no way to be absolutely sure that a tree is still safe.

Every year hunters are seriously injured and even killed when juryrigged treehouse steps and homemade tree stands give way and crash to the ground. This type of stand isn't even allowed on most public hunting ground. Any type of permanent device in a tree is usually forbidden: tree-steps or tree stands nailed in any way to a tree are outlawed. Some states refuse to allow hunters to use tree stands at all, and many national forests won't let you permanently mount climbing stands if screw-in steps are used. Screw-in steps could allow the tree to become infested with disease-causing insects. Many farmers and landowners frown on them as well.

Many big buck hunters instinctively believe that a superbuck will notice *anything* permanent in his neck of the woods. The noise and hoopla that accompany the building of a permanent stand won't escape the detection of the big buck in the neighborhood. Very likely, the buck will alter his travel patterns to avoid the stand, so that hunter won't see him no matter how carefully he's patterned his movements.

The climbing tree stand is far better and infinitely more mobile. Although a climbing stand can still require extra care, in its favor is the fact that hunting strategy can be altered to fit the stage of the rut. During the pre-breeding period, travel corridors near the bedding area can be covered. Later on, breeding scrapes, doe travel corridors, or trail convergences can be watched. Finally, during the post-rut period, a two-man drive may bust that buck out of his core area and right past a stander in a nearby tree.

Climbing tree stands can be relocated as often as the wind direction changes in the fall, and when the weather is changing, that can be often. Care should be taken to scout alternate stand sites for every eventuality. Fumbling about in the woods while it's still dark, trying to find a new stand location because the wind is blowing from some strange direction—well that's one of the best ways to let a big buck know that something's afoot!

Another consideration when purchasing a climbing stand is noise. Many of them make a lot of racket both when they're being used to climb a tree, or while a hunter is standing on one. Groans, moans, and creaks can often give a hunter away at a crucial moment after hours of waiting for that special buck.

Archers should also be aware that some designs limit their ability to draw their bow easily and unobtrusively. Every hunter who uses a climbing tree stand should also use safety straps to tie themselves to the tree.

Dr. David Hirth of the University of Vermont collected data on whitetails in south Texas that indicated practically no deer noticed a stationary observer on top of a ten meter (33 feet) high platform, but it isn't necessary to climb *that* high. First, while this study shows that if a hunter *doesn't* move, the deer won't see him, most of the time the hunter *has* to move. It's knowing *when* to move, and *how* to move that's important.

Second, when a hunter is too high in a tree, the extreme angle of the shot could mean he's aiming at a smaller target and there's less chance for a killing shot, either with a gun or with a bow.

Many hunters feel very high stands help keep scent from reaching the ground in concentrated doses. But according to research by Dr. James Kroll, any stand 12-feet high or higher will work reasonably well for hunters who are scent-conscious.

When you're picking a stand location, remember: big bucks are super-sensitive to any changes on their home ranges and they may avoid an area where there's been any unusual activity—especially if that activity is accompanied by a liberal dose of human scent. When you're up against a superbuck, you can't be too careful.

It's far better to have only a few good shooting lanes and to take advantage of those. Surrounding branches not only conceal your presence, they also help obscure your movements.

Never place a stand right over a travel corridor or breeding scrape. It's far better to be a minimum of 30 yards from where you think the buck will be if you're gun hunting, and at least 20 yards if you're bow hunting. And *never* cross the buck's trail when you're going to your stand. In fact, don't ever let your scent carry to where you *think* the buck might be bedded, even if it means walking a good distance out of your way to or from your stand.

Ground stands *do* work for big bucks, but you must reason your choice of stand carefully. So here are a few considerations for successful ground stands.

Of course, ground stands are extraordinarily maneuverable, in some circumstances even more so than a portable tree stand.

If you wish to change your position, all you'll usually have to do is walk to a better vantage point.

Next, few things are more available than a ground stand. Ground stands are everywhere you look. The more cut up the territory you hunt, the better. Ground stands are ideally suited to hills and hollows. For example, the spot where I took my largest buck (and saw two others even bigger) was atop a rock that overlooked a narrow hollow. It was part luck and part planning, but when I sat on the rock I'd chosen, the prevailing wind blew into my face. That meant that the area I was watching was completely free of my scent most of the time.

When the wind blew from behind me, all I had to do was cross the hollow and sit on a narrow rock ledge on the other side. I could still view the bottom where the deer liked to prowl, and once more the wind was blowing my scent away from the scene. To duplicate this maneuver from a tree stand would either mean moving the stand to another tree or having more than one tree stand in an area. Moving a tree stand often means *noise;* having more than one stand in each favored hunting location quickly becomes expensive.

Other examples of good ground stand locations include saddles in ridges, on top of bluffs, and at a spot where you can cover a natural bottleneck. You can also sit with your back up against a large tree, much like a turkey hunter does. The tree will break up your outline and, by moving periodically around its base, you can stay shaded if the weather is warm or stay in the sun if it's cold. By using an easily carried hot seat or cushion, you can conserve body heat that would quickly be lost in a tree stand.

Ground stands are less of a hassle than even portable, climbing tree stands. The days of hauling the stand to your hunting area on your back, sweating all the way, are over forever. Hunting from a ground stand means noiseless, trouble-free hunting. No climbing up in the dark, praying that your edge cuts deeply enough into the tree so that you don't wind up flat on the forest floor. No more dropping wing nuts into the leaves at the base of your tree, never to be found again. No more hand climbers and safety straps. No more moments of terror when the wind whips the forest into a frenzy of waving limbs.

"On windy days I'd much rather hunt on the ground," said the late Ben Lee, who lived in Coffeyville, Alabama, a noted whitetail hunter. "It can be hard to shoot accurately under the best of conditions. With the wind blowing the tree back and forth, it can really get tricky, especially with a bow.

"The wind helps in one other respect as well," Lee added. "When you're on the ground, it will help obscure any movement a hunter might make. An alert whitetail won't notice a hunter nearly as easily if there's a wind to camouflage his movement."

"Another point is that when you're on the ground, it's an easier shot. When I hunt in a tree in any of the southern states it's often from an elevation of around 25 feet," Lee said. "The extreme angle can make any shot on a whitetail difficult, but especially any bow shot."

When you hunt from a ground blind or stand, you can take advantage of some of nature's own covering scents. I clear large areas around my stand down to bare earth to keep fallen leaves from crunching beneath me as I shift to check the terrain. The newly exposed earth itself gives off a fresh scent. As stated before, Ernie Richardson of Shelbyville, Illinois, swears that the smell of fresh earth acts like a scent magnet.

"Whenever a farmer plows up a field, you can bet that it will be full of deer tracks the next morning," Richardson said.

I sometimes crush twigs and leaves of aromatic vegetation such as cedar, pine, sassafras, and fragrant sumac. This is nature's own method of masking your human scent while hunting on the ground.

Ground stands are ideal for those who pattern their hunting tactics around doe movement, as during the actual breeding season. Does hang much tighter within their core area than bucks do, but they're by no means static animals. When white oak acorns ripen and fall, the does won't be far away. Later, they'll be hanging near the persimmons. Knowing how to hunt from a ground stand ensures you can move with the deer. Choose a ground blind *without* a completely clear field of view between the food source and you. Keep some vegetation between you and the whitetail so you won't be noticed as readily. Your movements are easier to detect on the ground, but this is one way to make them less obvious.

A ground stand on a ridge that separates a south-facing ridge slope from a north-facing slope has its own advantages. Hunt the south-facing slope on chilly mornings as deer move back in to bed down. South-facing slopes are preferred browsing spots for late autumn whitetails, especially in the more northern latitudes. North-facing slopes pan out when the days grow unseasonably warm or when you're hunting farther south. Deer use the shade available on north-facing slopes to escape the heat. Knowledge of *where* the deer are likely to be is an essential part of locating your ground blind.

One of the most respected whitetail authorities I know, Bob Zaiglin, is another believer in ground stands. In 1985, Zaiglin took a big deer that grossed over 170 Boone and Crockett points. "Whenever you use an elevated stand you can run into backlighting problems," he noted. "If you're spotlighted against the sky, it can draw a deer's attention right to you.

"Another thing for any archer to consider is camouflage," Zaiglin continued. "Very few patterns at present are designed to blend in with the sky. Hunt on the ground and take your pick of desert, hardwood forest, swamp and many other patterns that will help the hunter blend right into his surroundings.

"Blaze orange can also stand out whether or not you're in an elevated stand. But down on the ground it is possible to remain hidden. Surrounding foliage can be used to help obscure the giveaway glare of hunter orange. This can help cut down on the number of times an alert whitetail will pick you out from your surroundings." For an added precaution, blaze orange ribbons tied to foliage around your blind will alert nearby hunters to your presence without alerting the deer.

Other important ground blind points according to Zaiglin include the fact that even though a natural topographic feature may not be available for use as a ground stand, it's easy to construct your own using native materials. "I just take bits of brush or small saplings and stack them together in a semi-circle," he said. "Another method I've used is to wrap camo material around nearby brush and then get behind it. Doing this means that there's no distinct shape such as a square or oval that will give you away. And building a blind like this doesn't take any time at all," Zaiglin added.

Mobility counts in Texas, too. "Late in the season, when bucks are running the does, is when mobility is most important," he said. "You have to get out there *with* the deer. I can almost guarantee that if you see a buck chasing a hot doe in a particular spot, if you hunt right there for the next three days, you'll see him again. We've taken some good bucks by capitalizing on this bit of knowledge."

The territory Zaiglin hunts can be as thick as the devil: "When you hunt in really heavy brush," he said, "elevated stands are out. To get the biggest bucks it's better to look *under* the brush rather than over the top of it. Big bucks will sneak around in the thickest stuff they can. Your best bet is to be on the same level as they are."

Zaiglin is also noted as an excellent antler rattler and deer caller. "My style of antler rattling is well-suited to the ground," he explained. "One of the things that I've really found works is to rattle the antlers together in the regular way and then pound them into the ground, as though two bucks are pawing at the earth with their hooves. There's no way to do this when you're up in a tree.

"I alternate calling on the grunt tube with rattling the antlers together and then pounding them on the ground," Zaiglin continued. "If my movements are concealed by the blind, any curious buck will ease in closer and closer, trying to get a better look. That's when he'll become vulnerable."

Sometimes rattling or calling from a tree stand will focus a deer's attention upwards. I've occasionally had deer come in looking up into my tree for the source of the sound. Even if you remain motionless, the deer know something is wrong. Not only won't you get a shot, you're unlikely to lure that particular deer into that location again, at least for another year.

Through planning it's possible to mix up your hunting styles to take advantage of the terrain and vegetation in your area. Both elevated stands and ground stands work for big bucks. It's knowing when to use the tree stand and when to sit on the ground that's going to make the difference. In other words, the hunter must be just as flexible and just as adaptable as his quarry when he's up against a superbuck.

16

Stalking the Whitetail Superbuck

You're a hunter. You're one with your surroundings. The wind sighs softly as you ease forward, footsteps blending into the sounds of the pine forest. A bird flits by without noticing your alien presence.

A large, fresh scrape looms into view. All senses alert, you pause. The big whitetail buck that made it could be close by. Your fingers tighten on the string of your bow but you force yourself to relax. Beneath your feet, you're conscious of each pebble, each leaf, each twig that shifts without breaking. You aren't an alien at all; you *belong* here.

Suddenly, a movement catches on the periphery of your vision. You freeze. A large, heavy-racked buck is moving methodically towards you; you avert your eyes to keep him from feeling the heat of your gaze.

The buck stops and you take a chance. You open your eyes just as he angles down the hill. He's not looking your way now, so you get ready. As he passes within fifteen yards you pivot, crouch, pull and release, all in one fluid motion. The arrow springs forward to pierce the buck's hide. He leaps forward, stumbles and falls.

He's a dandy and you're celebrating already, as excited as a kid who's just killed his first deer. You're the ultimate deer hunter, a stillhunter and stalker, the outdoorsman who hopes to succeed on the deer's level.

All over deer country there's renewed interest in the challenge of stalking. Stillhunting hearkens us back to the days of the frontier, when hunter and hunted went one on one. Just as some hunters prefer recurve bows to compounds, there are those hunters who, whenever conditions are right, prefer stillhunting over stands. And some of them have been quite successful stalking the incredibly challenging whitetail superbuck.

Let's examine the very different methods of four successful still-hunters—one from the pineywoods of Georgia, one from Colorado's windswept plains, one from the Michigan northwoods, and one from the scrub-oak cutover forests of Alabama. Their techniques may help you to devise a plan that might work on the superbuck you're pursuing.

GORMAN RILEY

Gorman Riley is a master stalker with both bow and gun. Riley offers more insights into what it takes to stalk a whitetail superbuck successfully than perhaps any other hunter today. Riley took his first deer when he was ten years old. Since that time he's taken a Boone and Crockett buck that scored 170⅝ points and a non-typical that scored 187, as well as many other bucks that score between 140 and 160 points, plus, as he says, "a slew that score in the 120s and 130s.

"I believe that stalking will work anywhere," he said. "But to be successful, first you must do a little preliminary work. To begin with, try to pinpoint by sight, if possible, the buck that you're after before the season even starts. Once you know you're on the trail of a big buck, it will help keep your interest up and encourage you to hold out a little longer. If you aren't able to sight him, then look for big buck sign: large scrapes, big tracks, rubs six-inches in diameter and over.

"When sizing up an area to stalk you must determine how to approach it without spooking the deer," Riley continued. "The hardest areas to approach are those that: one, have wide open areas to cross where deer can see you coming; two, are secure behind a physical obstacle such as a large, deep creek; three, consist of thickets so dense that briars literally tear your clothes off; or, four, have a prevailing wind that consistently blows against your approach.

"I try to plan my stalk so that I'm slipping through the prime portion of an area at first light," he said. "When stalking, you must hunt hard from the moment you step out of your car. You can't let your attention slide for even an instant. Once you're in your area, hunt where you've found the most sign. Maybe you'll get lucky and kill that buck. If you don't, the buck is probably nocturnal. If so, he'll usually be bedded nearby, out of sight, in a thick, brushy area. This area may only have lightly-used trails leading into and out of it."

Riley is a firm believer in scent. "I'll use a deer musk early in the season," he said. "But later on, I'll use two types—deer musk and doe-in-heat, since deer are supposedly capable of smelling and identifying two separate scents at once."

Unlike many big buck hunters, Riley isn't afraid of using scent on his person. "Usually, I use doe-in-heat on the toes of my boots," Riley explained. "But if I've been having trouble with a buck that's been consistently catching my scent, then I'll put some on my knees, the points of my shoulders, and on the brim of my hat. It really helps. I'm not saying that deer can't scent the man-smell anymore. What I am saying is that I believe that when they smell man *and* deer at the same time it confuses them, slows them down a little, and often that's all the time I need."

For downright difficult bucks Riley will resort to sprinkling baking soda on his shoes and shirts to try to absorb any lingering human-odors or household smells. There's more to stalking than just reading sign and keeping the wind in your favor, Riley said.

"First, once you manage to get in an area without spooking the deer it's important to work very slowly through the woods, moving from one obstacle to another. For example, if I'm hunting in fairly open woods I move from one large tree to another. Then I wait awhile before moving again. Whenever possible I follow breaks in cover. This means that I move just inside the edge of a pine thicket so I'm able to look out into adjoining hardwood bottoms where cover's not so plentiful. The deer will be found right along these edges, where the hardwoods come up against the pines, so I should be in an excellent position to score.

"I always try to step on bare ground, rocks, or logs that haven't rotted yet," he continued. "To feel the ground with my foot *before* I put my weight on it, I prefer wearing camouflage, high-top tennis shoes with a soft, pliable sole. Often, I'll wade in shallow creek channels or hunt down in creek beds, looking out.

"Remember the part of a deer you see first as he's moving through the underbrush are his legs, the white lining of his tail, and the white rings around his eyes. The same is true when a deer is looking at you. Your legs will really stand out unless you camouflage them. Black boots will stand out just like white ones will. Few things in the woods are black. Use either camouflage footwear or brown or gray boots that blend in with bare ground or tree bark.

"Often I'll just get a feeling about a spot. When that happens, I'll either sit down in a gully with just my head poking out or lie down next to a log with my head propped up so I can still see. Or, I might just stop and lean against a tree. I don't know how many times I've done this and then had a good buck wander by. Often, if I'd taken just three more steps the deer would have seen me.

"When I'm stalking I try to plan a route that will let me walk slowly and carefully with the wind in my favor so that I'll eventually end up back at my vehicle. When you first start stillhunting, no matter how slow you think you're travelling, you're probably *still* not moving slowly enough," Riley added.

Riley says that stillhunters have one distinct advantage from standhunters. "If you stalk along trails you'll come into contact with a lot more whitetail travel lanes than you would from a stand," he stated. "So your chances of intercepting a good buck are much better. You'll see more deer, but if you're not moving slowly enough all you may see is their tails."

Riley's tricks use the terrain to his advantage. "Instead of walking along the top of a ridge, skylighted so that animals on either side can see me, I prefer getting just below the crest of a ridge where I can just see over and stalking silently along like that," he said. "I just slip along, occasionally poking my head over the crest. That way I can see most of what's going on down the other side. This is how a turkey scopes out the woods, just looking over without exposing himself. Of course, you must be very alert to animals on the same side of the ridge on which you're stalking."

Riley usually grows a beard during hunting season since it helps to break up the telltale white of his face. "I pull my hat brim way down, too," he added. "And I always wear soft, quiet clothes, something made of 100 percent cotton. If I have to wear a heavy coat that may be noisy, I wear cotton *over* it. You'd be surprised at just how quiet you can be even when working through the densest cover."

Riley has had some unbelievable stalking experiences. "One of them in particular points out just how much you can get away with if you're stalking slow and moving into the wind," he said. "I'd been slipping through the heart of one particular area where I suspected a big buck had been working. I really pay attention to all the critters in the forest, and this day everything in the world seemed to be active and feeding. I knew that if the birds were feeding and chirping like they were that day, that the buck I was after was probably feeding, too.

"I had been slipping slowly through the woods, but when this thought came to me—I just froze right where I was. I stayed there for a long time, eyes straining, trying to see all around me. Finally, in some dense brush about 50 yards ahead of me I could make out what appeared to be a huge deer's body. I really started looking then, and eventually could see the white line of his tail off to the right and his white eye rings to the left. By straining a little more, I could then see large antler bases starting right above the eyes.

"I waited there a good fifteen minutes without moving and barely breathing," Riley continued. "The buck was skittish. He'd seen me ease into the area but he hadn't gotten my scent. Plus, he hadn't seen me move for so long that by this time he wasn't sure what he'd seen. Finally, he ran 20 feet into the brush, turned and started coming up the trail towards me. As he did, I caught a glimpse of rear tines better than ten inches long, a spread at least 17 inches wide, and a rack that I was sure would score over 140 points. He was moving quickly along the trail, often through areas less than a foot wide. As he got near my position, he did a head bob. When he moved his head down, I threw my rifle up. And as he bobbed his head back up, I fired."

Riley tries always to stalk with gun or bow cradled in his arms, ready to lift, aim and fire. If his arm gets tired, he'll sling his Browning 7mm/08 lever-action rifle over his left shoulder. "I'm left-handed," he said, "and I've discovered if you walk with the gun slung behind you it can be easily accessed for a quick shot. Put your left hand (if you're left-handed) on the sling, the thumb right where the strap goes over the shoulder. Put your other hand on the lower portion of the rifle right where the sling attaches to the gun. By practicing, you'll be able to get your gun quickly into the ready position."

Riley uses a Redfield 3 × 9 Leupold Vari-X III scope. "It's invaluable for picking out holes in the brush," he commented. "And sometimes, even when you're stalking, a 300 yard shot will present itself. I prefer to be prepared."

Riley also uses a camouflage gun chap to help his gun blend into the surroundings and cut down on noise at the same time.

Gorman Riley is a good shot, and he has quick reflexes. "I hope I don't sound like I'm bragging," he said, "but I try my best to kill a big buck the very first time I see him. I might not get the opportunity again. As soon as I first catch sight of him, I drop into shooting position and try to make the shot *if it's possible.* This often means shooting on the spur of the moment. I use my scope to pick out a shot, even one that threads through the brush. I don't advise this for everyone; you have to be confident."

But Riley isn't overconfident. "I almost never take a shot at a buck running through the brush," he said. "I'll let him go and hope I find him later. Nothing is worth wounding an animal."

Riley prefers stalking in rainy weather. "Rain eliminates the sound problem," he said. "Deer just can't hear you as well." But he doesn't like windy weather at all. "In my experience, animals don't like to move in a wind. A wind nullifies a deer's nose, its best defense. And wind eliminates *your* hearing, a stalker's greatest weapon.

"Hearing is the most important factor a big buck stalker can call into play. You're usually moving very, very slowly anyway. Then each time you pause, you must learn to listen. I listen as hard as I can in every single direction. I cup my hand so that it's shaped like a deer's and place it behind my ears to help funnel in any sounds. You'll be surprised how much better you'll be able to hear noises in the woods. In no time at all you'll be able to distinguish between the sounds that birds, squirrels, or deer make."

Riley pays attention to every animal in the woods for a couple of other good reasons. First, if he's not able to move nearly noiselessly, he'll adopt the noise pattern of some other animal. "Say you're hunting through some newly-fallen leaves," Riley explained, "where it's impossible to take a step without making them crunch underfoot. What you should do in a case like this is imitate the way a squirrel hops along as he moves from tree to tree. A squirrel makes an erratic noise, nothing at all like the steady rhythm of a walking man. It's more of a quick *'chook, chook, chook!'* pause, *'chook, chook,'* long

hen you pause, look and listen. Then mix the pattern up
t."

, by listening to how animals in the vicinity are behaving,
Riley's often able to tell if a buck is nearby. If so, he can often get
ready to shoot before he even sees the animal.

"Squirrels will let you know if there's a buck in the neighborhood,"
he explained. "If you hear a squirrel just slowly complaining with no
letup, watch out. Either a deer or a man is approaching. For some
reason, squirrels don't like bucks very much. Maybe it's the antlers,
but they usually raise more cain whenever they see a buck. I've often
been able to track a buck's progress through the woods just by listening to the squirrels along the way."

To summarize what this master stalker has to say about hunting
whitetail superbucks remember these points: (1) always be as silent
as possible; (2) move with the wind in your face; (3) move short distances at an extremely slow pace; (4) always scan the area around
you with both your eyes and your ears; and (5) if you can't be silent,
then imitate the natural forest sounds.

LEE KLINE

Lee Kline, an archer from Loveland, Colorado, offered this refine-
ment. "I pre-scout a locale looking for 'transient areas'—travel lanes
between feeding and bedding grounds. One example is a long ridge
that leads from good feed, such as a cornfield, to a bedding area.

"Stillhunting requires a lot of concentration. Nervous energy is
high because you never know where an animal will be. You're in a
state of suspense, moving just fast enough to keep from standing
still.

"When I do move, I look around carefully. New angles open up
completely new vistas. I like to stillhunt crosswind or into the wind
and not necessarily in a straight line.

"I literally scour the shadows with my binoculars for details. I've
often spotted deer extremely close to me that were completely unaware of my presence," Kline added. "Talk about a thrill!

"Once when I was stillhunting for whitetails in some sawgrass I
thought I saw antlers in a distant clump of trees. Then again, it
could be branches, too, I reasoned. When I was about 80 yards
away, I thought I saw movement.

"I hoped that I was on to something but the closer I got, the less it
looked like a deer. After an hour I'd almost forgotten the 'antlers.' A
crosswind was blowing from my right to my left as I eased on past
the spot where I'd seen the antlers. To tell the truth, I'd forgotten all
about them since I'd spotted a whitetail doe and was concentrating
on her.

"I was ten yards past the spot when all hell broke loose behind me," Kline said. "I turned around just in time to see a humongous mule deer buck still in velvet come tearing out of there. He must have just gotten a whiff of my scent.

"He came bucking out of there like a bronco, cottonwood branches hanging off his antlers. That buck was in the 180 to 190 Pope and Young class, a real monster. I had to stop and laugh because he would have been mine—I did everything right—and yet I stalked right past him.

"This incident taught me the value of patience; now I never give up on an animal until I can absolutely confirm that it *isn't* a deer. And it proved to me that when you're stillhunting, you can't let time dictate to you," Kline emphasized. "I'd always longed to stillhunt up on a real trophy and when I finally did it, I blew it. Now, if I have to stand in one spot for 15 minutes glassing a willow patch to determine whether I'm seeing sticks or antlers, I do it. You can't think about time when you're stillhunting. You must make time stand still. The longer you can afford to stand and scour shadows with your binoculars the better off you'll be. Patience pays off when you're trying to see into shadows. As the sun moves shadows shift and change. Suddenly you're able to see clearly what you only thought you could see before."

Kline also says that sunlight changes the reflective character of your equipment and clothing. "A stray reflection will blow your cover quicker than anything. That's why I try to hunt from within the shadows. It's tough to do, but it works.

"I also watch openings and try not to walk across them. Whenever possible, I hunt around them. Occasionally you have to cross them. Sometimes I dart across small openings, the theory being get across as quickly as possible; other times I'll creep across large openings hoping I'm moving so slow I won't be spotted. I do what feels right to me at the moment."

Kline also likes to hunt when it's damp or even during a light rain when sound is muffled and slow movement isn't as apparent. He likes early mornings best, with evenings a close second because that's when he's had his best luck spotting game. But he will still-hunt all day long, since he realizes some animals are up and about while others remain bedded. He'll also stillhunt when it's dry if there's a good, stiff wind to hide the sounds of his passage.

PAUL KERBY

Paul Kerby of Kingsley, Michigan, stillhunts himself and also guides hunters. "A lot of hunters want to try it," he said, "but not everyone can handle it. You have to be in tune with your environment. It's almost a combat-type situation: one false move could blow everything. The key is to know your area and to travel light."

Like Kline, Kerby uses a recurve bow because it's quiet and light. When using a firearm his choice of weapon is a Winchester Model 100 automatic or a Remington Model 660 bolt action rifle: both small, easily handled guns.

"Heavy, awkward boots and coats are out. So are binoculars and big hunting knives, because you have to travel quietly. Scoot across nonproductive areas, but slow down if you know deer could be nearby. And always look the edges of woods over carefully. You're looking for something not right, something that shouldn't be there, that horizontal line in a landscape of verticals.

"One time I was all set to stand hunt over an alfalfa patch. But I knew it was going to be tough since the wind was swirling in all directions.

"So I started stillhunting instead," Kerby explained. "I came to a little gully and followed it down towards a small valley. As I eased up a little knoll I paused to look the area over and it's a good thing I did. Three bucks were moving off a hill 50 yards away. They came to within 16 yards of me, but only two of them left. I took a good eight-pointer.

"I like the idea of stillhunting because you're doing something, you're not waiting for the deer to come to you. You're going into the cover where he's holed up.

"One technique that works in hardwood forests is to walk over a hill or knoll so that just your head clears the top. Start picking things out—deadfalls, brushpiles—scan it all. If there is a deer that you don't see, he'll often bolt when you start moving again," Kerby added, "and that might be the chance you need."

BILLY MACOY

Here's a completely different method of stillhunting—but one no less exciting—from Billy Macoy, a top-notch deer hunter from Lineville, Alabama.

Macoy's taken many record-class whitetails, from the scrub oak cutovers that dot the Alabama landscape. After about two years, these areas grow up thick with brush. Macoy's discovered that deer love to hole up in spots like these.

"When hunting clearcuts I always walk with the sun at my back," Macoy said, "so the deer aren't sure what it is they're looking at. And I *want* the wind to blow my scent in front of me. I don't care about being quiet, either. I want those bucks to know someone is there.

"After walking for several hundred yards, I stop dead still. Then I watch and wait for 10 or 15 minutes. If there's a buck in the area pretty soon he won't be able to stand it. He'll jump up or ease up to see what's going on. That's when you can nail him as he's standing there looking around."

Macoy also uses a slingshot to shoot pebbles into the thick tangles of blackberry and honeysuckle that grow wild in the bottom of hollows. After shooting, he watches and waits.

"Deer hold tight in these cutovers," Macoy added. "But make no mistake about it, they're probably in there. Two years ago I was hunting near Selma when some dogs ran a buck right through a clearcut where I was standing. I shot and thought I'd missed but decided to investigate anyway.

"I walked to where I'd last seen the buck—and where the dogs had just run through—and another buck jumped up 15 yards away. I shot him and he dropped. As I walked over to look at him, yet *another* buck jumped up and ran off. I hurried back for my hunting buddies and we wound up jumping three more bucks out of this one 100-acre clearcut.

"I jump the best bucks in cutovers before the rut ever starts," he said, "especially if there's been a cold snap. Bucks will search out east-facing slopes where the sun can warm them in the early morning.

"And if you jump a good buck and he gets away be sure to go back to the same spot a day or two later. Eight times out of ten, the buck will return and bed within 100 yards of the exact same spot," Macoy stated.

Four hunters, four different methods of stillhunting and stalking. Any one of them will work if terrain, vegetation, and circumstances permit. Choose one or choose elements of several. Stillhunting one–on–one for superbucks, as these hunters agree, is the ultimate hunting pursuit!

17

Scents for Whitetail Superbucks

Almost an hour had passed since I had seen the doe. She had appeared silently on the crest of the ridge behind me, before turning and easing back out of sight. I kept that doe in mind while I scanned the woods beneath my stand. Occasionally, I'd check the ridge, hoping to see a buck. Eventually, I began to give up hope. When a buck finally did appear, I nearly missed seeing him at all.

He was there one minute and gone the next. All I saw was a glimpse of antlers backlit against the sky—and then nothing. The wind picked up while I weighed my options. One, I could sit there and continue watching the forest floor and perhaps another buck would wander by. Two, I could go back to the house for lunch. Or three, I could chase after the buck that I had glimpsed moments before.

Several factors swayed my decision to go after him. For starters, the buck wasn't spooked. I was fairly sure he hadn't seen me. And he appeared to be on the doe's trail so his attention was probably elsewhere. But the compelling factor in my urge to follow that buck was to test a theory: I'd just run my hunting clothes through the automatic washer with an assortment of weeds and leaves and I smelled like the woods themselves. I was eager to see if I could trick that buck with my new "natural" odor.

As I topped the ridge, it suddenly occurred to me that the woodsy scent would need to work perfectly since the wind was blowing from my direction towards the buck. I paused as the first inklings of doubt crept into my mind; but then that same wind helped firm my resolve. I'd found that it was easier to walk up on a whitetail under windy conditions than at any other time.

I checked my rifle and started after the deer. I hadn't walked far before a slight movement caught my eye. I halted and discovered I was a mere 40 yards from the buck. The wind was at my back, blowing scent right to his nose. The deer whipped his head around and looked at me. Long moments passed as we stared at each other through a network of branches. At any minute I expected him to turn tail and run, snorting all the way.

But he finally put his head back to the ground and moved off. Unbelievable? I thought so too, as I eased up closer and connected on a 35-yard shot.

Later, as I stood admiring the eight-point, I wished I'd washed my clothes with leaves every one of the years I've been deer hunting. I'd gotten my buck and I'd done it in a fairly unorthodox way. While this buck was by no means a superbuck, his nose was probably no less sensitive than the average whitetail's. So washing my clothes along with natural foliage *would* obscure my scent in the nose of a bigger trophy animal.

Superbuck hunters are competitors, and competition for trophy animals breeds invention. Nowhere else is this competitive urge more evident than in the development of deer scents. Myriad scent products are hawked in sporting goods stores, catalogues, and hunting magazines. Lures, masking scents, chlorophyll tablets, body washes, instructional cassettes, books—you name it and someone is selling it. Add to this theories of the pre-hunt vegetarians and the do-it-yourself techniques of hunters like me who wash their clothes with leaves—well the confusion mounts. What *is* the truth about deer scents? How do you decide whether to use lures, masks, or *no* scent? What about a combination?

There is no right decision—at least not one that's right for everyone all the time. Only experimenting can determine what works for you. But there is basic information about scents that will help you decide where to start.

Pheromones are hormone-like chemicals produced and released by deer and other living creatures (including, to a lesser extent, humans) so that they can communicate with each other. While deer do communicate by visual displays and sounds, smell is far and away the sense they rely on most. By emitting a particular faint odor, a deer tells other deer how it's feeling, how it's going to act and why. The sense of smell was probably the first form of animal communication and is of primary importance in the deer's survival and propagation.

Kairomones are a type of pheromone, which give only the *receiver*—in this case deer—an advance warning. When we're around other humans, we're almost unaware of the subtle scent pheromones we each emit. But that same subtle scent that may attract us to one another will almost certainly send a deer fleeing. Our pheromones act as a deer *kairomone*—a warning—so they are a distinct disadvantage to the hunter.

A person who isn't clean, or perspires profusely, reeks with kairomones. These kairomones are the result of various natural biological functions, such as respiration and perspiration in a human. For example, when we perspire some glandular and hormonal secretions are carried via sweat and out through the pores to the surface of the skin. Over two quarts of moisture are expired through the pores of our skin each day—more if we're active—and this moisture is chock full of kairomones.

Some dedicated hunters make great efforts to control their kairomones. They eliminate meat, highly spiced food, and strongly flavored foods such as broccoli, cauliflower, and onions from the diet for a minimum of seven days to significantly reduce body odor. Meat is eliminated because there is a definite relationship between meat consumption and the type of odor emanating from the body afterwards. Animals that pose a threat to deer are all either meat eaters or omnivorous (meat and vegetation eaters). Mountain lions, coyotes, wolves, dogs, bobcats, bears, and man all fall into the same category to a deer: *danger.* The sensitive nose of a deer will warn him when any of these meat-eating animals are detected. If meat is eliminated, the telltale smell will gradually fade and eventually disappear. Smokers should give up smoking for as long as they can stand it as well.

Even without giving up meat, it's possible to counteract human odor to some degree. First, it's important to be scrupulously clean. A bath and shampoo before hunting works wonders. Odors from home and work cling to the body and to the hair. Bathe with an unscented soap, like Shaklee's Basic H, or plain baking soda. I prefer baking soda because it's an active agent. It actually neutralizes the bacterial action that takes place on your skin for up to 12 hours, especially if you leave a thin baking soda film on the skin. I even rinse my hair with a baking soda wash to retard oil production. Hair oil, produced by the sebaceous glands in the scalp, is loaded with kairomones.

Commercially prepared body washes are available, but you can get the same results much less expensively with baking soda. If you can't take a full bath before you head into the woods, a sponge bath is better than nothing.

Dale Forgette of Walker's Lures in Locust Grove, Georgia recommends using Tucks in the backwoods during freezing weather when it's difficult to bathe. These are individual unscented pads that retard bacterial action on the skin. They can be bought in any drugstore in containers of 50.

Don't smoke, wear aftershave or use scented deodorant. Don't brush your teeth with commercial toothpaste or use mouthwash. Baking soda doesn't taste good, but it's a great toothpaste when combined with hydrogen peroxide and it serves well as mouthwash with plain water.

Nearly every good whitetail hunter I know is a fanatic about clean clothing. The consensus seems to be this: wash clothes often and use baking soda or an unscented laundry detergent like Arm & Hammer or Tide Unscented. It isn't as important for the outer layer of clothing to be washed or changed every day *if it's not exposed to home and auto odors.* It is important for the clothing next to the skin to be fresh.

Some cautious hunters hang their washed clothes in an old barn, others keep them outside in the rain and sunshine, and still others seal them in plastic garbage bags. The objective is the same: to keep them away from possible unnatural scent contaminants such as gasoline, food odors, or smoke.

Finally, hair and beards are a real problem since they act like wicks for odor. I've found that one way to really keep oily hair smell under control is by not wearing a hat on the way to my stand so that perspiration evaporates instantly. Once I'm there, I wear a one gallon plastic bag over my hair, being sure to tuck all stray strands under the bag but keeping my ears out. Then I put a stocking cap over the bag. I may not look good but I know it works.

SCENT-ADSORPTION

Scent-adsorbing clothing, such as that patented by Scent-Lok, as well as W.L. Gore's Supprescent series of odor-reducing garments, really work. Of course, the wise hunter will continue to take every other precaution, including donning clothing away from any suspicious odors, taking clothing off immediately upon returning to vehicle or cabin at night, and storing the clothing in a scent-proof bag or container after the day's hunt.

Sniff clothing often to see if your nose is able to pick up even a whiff of a scent that isn't supposed to be there. Watch nearby deer. By observing their responses, you will be able to tell when clothing needs to be recharged (in a hot dryer for at least 45 minutes for Scent-Lok).

Scent-adsorbing clothing has made a world of difference during the past several years in the lives of most big buck hunters I know. It's expensive, but it works!

MASKS

Before our deer season a few years ago I decided to try a homemade, natural mask scent. I picked leaves and branches indigenous to my stand area—things like pine boughs, cedar limbs, and aromatic sumac. I tied them all together in a pillow slip and, after washing my clothes in baking soda, I washed them once more in plain water and my sack of weeds. My clothes smelled great.

Then I tied the clothes in a plastic sack and waited until opening morning. I had to walk more than a mile to my stand so I wore another set of clothes until I was about 200 yards from my stand. Then I changed in the woods and tied the sweaty clothes in another plastic bag. It sounds weird, but it's one effective way to mask the kairomones your skin produces.

Masks, whether they are homemade or bottled, have one purpose: to hide or conceal human scent. The best way to do this is to make your scent blend with others in your surroundings. No matter how clean you are, and how well your mask works, there will always be some residue of human odor available to the whitetail's supersensitive nose. The idea is to minimize your scent.

Bob McGuire, a whitetail deer authority who's taken many dandy bucks, says, "It's hard to decide how a deer is going to respond to scent out in the woods. There's just no practical way to control all the other variables like wind, the presence of other humans, and the behavior of other deer. Cover scents must be neutral—locally abundant but not overly desirable to deer. That's their purpose—to mask your presence as much as possible since I feel that it's *impossible* to totally cover human scent. However, it is possible to *confuse* the deer to the point that he doesn't know where you are or when you passed through."

Bob's *locally* abundant point is significant. One masking agent used by many hunters is red fox urine. Think about it—how many red foxes have you seen in the woods? Sure, they're nocturnal, and it might work if there isn't much hunting pressure. But if twenty hunters hike through an area and ten of them are tracking red fox urine on their boots and half of them aren't clean themselves, it won't take Mr. Buck very long to figure out what's up: red fox scent equals man.

Bob McGuire himself uses red fox urine but he employs it as a scent tactic on the way to his stand. He carries a small atomizer filled with red fox urine. If he jumps a deer enroute he immediately sprays the urine on the ground, and then walks quickly into the wind. The deer will normally circle downwind. When he does he'll pick up a basic fox smell, a scent condition that is more natural than fox urine tracked all over the woods.

I'd suggest the same tactic with another traditional mask: skunk scent. Skunk essence is an allomone—a chemical signal which gives the sender an advantage. Skunk scent is probably the best known example of an allomone in nature. No predator will attack a skunk because of its scent defense unless it's starving and survival is at stake.

"If a skunk is upset, chances are he's been upset by the exact same enemies that would do harm to a whitetail," Dale Forgette said. "Those enemies are coyotes, dogs, and humans. So why in the world would a smart, old buck hang around where danger is lurking? His survival depends on *avoiding* danger. In test after test I've proven that skunk essence acts as a *negative* lure since a whitetail buck will investigate from afar until he discovers just what it was that annoyed that skunk. And you certainly don't want a wary old buck investigating your presence in any way. Because if he does, he'll soon find out that it's you smelling like a scared skunk. I feel so strongly about this that I've dropped skunk essence completely from my line of scents and lures."

However, other hunters who have experienced more than their share of big-buck success use skunk scent and swear by it. Gene Wensel, a noted bowhunter and trophy buck expert from Bloomfield, Iowa, uses an oil-based skunk mask before mid-October. "I feel the best skunk mask is oil-based, not water or alcohol based," he said. "Because of the oil, the mask won't weaken or wash off as easily and doesn't freeze."

OTHER METHODS

Many hunters wear rubber boots to further nullify human scent. Scent can't escape rubber. Rubber-bottomed pacs are better than all-leather, but pacs allow scent to escape through the leather uppers.

One hunter who's had phenomenal success while wearing leather boots is Stan Christiansen of Hudson, Kansas. Stan is the first man to shoot five Boone and Crockett bucks with a bow, one of which has not been officially scored.

Stan is a farmer and he discovered that by wearing cow manure–encrusted boots to his stand he really confused deer. Stan hunts farm ground, so the bucks accepted the smell as entirely natural and they let down their guard.

There are many other products that mask human odor: apple, acorn, and other food scents, to name a few. Notice that I call these masks and not lures. Most expert deer hunters I know simply don't believe that it is possible to lure hungry deer in with food scents. Autumn is the time when food in the woods is most abundant. A deer would have to be starving to be lured in by food smells at this time of the year.

Finally, another mask that many big buck experts believe really works is a spray product named Scent Shield manufactured by Robinson Laboratories of Minneapolis, Minnesota. Judy Anderson of Robinson Laboratories explains how Scent Shield works. "When you spray Scent Shield lightly on any type of surface that absorbs odor, something like leather or fabric, the chemicals in the spray actually eliminate the odor-causing gas molecules," she stated. It will even cancel out the smell of tobacco smoke on clothing. "Spraying it on your skin won't work, however, since skin isn't absorbent like fabric is," she stated.

LURES

A deer is a social animal, especially during the rut. The buck is interested in what is going on in his neck of the woods all year round. Since deer communicate mainly through odors, pheromones are the key to luring superbucks.

Each deer has its own distinctive smell, its signature so to speak. One source of a deer's scent is the skin glands. (These are classified as preputial, anal, metacarpal, metatarsal, tarsal, sebaceous, and Harderian glands.) There are interdigital glands, located between the hooves and two newly discovered glands, the nasal and the pineal, of which the exact functions remains largely unknown. All these glands produce odors for marking territories, determining social status, and to encourage reproduction. These glands aren't the only source of a deer's scent. Other odors come from body fluids such as seminal fluid, urine, and vaginal discharges, plus the odors from deer droppings. Scents are of primary importance to a whitetail and it shows in the great diversity of scenting mechanisms at work in his body.

Now, along comes the hunter. The whitetail has a keen ability to detect human odor. This same great sense of smell can also be an asset to the hunter. It becomes an asset when hunters appeal to the deer's social and reproductive urges in its own language: pheromones.

There are two basic pheromonal scents that appeal to deer: matrix scents and doe-in-estrus scent. Matrix is a combination, or should be a combination, containing both buck and doe urine. According to Dale Forgette it should contain no estrous urine whatsoever; in fact it should contain no sex-related scents at all.

"Matrix should attract deer—both bucks and does—because of a whitetail's naturally curious nature," Forgette said. "Whitetails are very inquisitive in unpressured situations. A good matrix lure can be used any time of year *because* it contains no sexual scent that would be unnatural early in the hunting season.

"A matrix brings deer in because they normally establish breeding dominance well before the breeding season. When a buck smells the urine that's contained within the matrix he comes in to investigate to see who just moved into the neighborhood, who's the new kid on the block. The buck is responding to an unfamiliar scent: the pheromones, or identifying scent signature of a given animal contained in the lure."

One scent that acts like a lure is that of the interdigital glands, the glands found between the split of the hooves in the foot of the deer. These glands secrete a natural mixture of chemicals that are deposited on the ground as the deer goes about its daily travels. Although the odor will persist for some time—up to several hours—the natural smell changes somewhat as the hours roll by. As evaporation of the scent takes place, deer are able to distinguish an old trail from a fresh one.

Research by Dr. Larry Marchinton at the University of Georgia revealed the actual chemical composition of this interdigital gland scent. It is made up of six short-chain fatty acids that can be synthesized in a laboratory. Bob McGuire immediately set out to do just that. At the time of Dr. Marchinton's discovery commercial production of the synthetic scent was not profitable, but within three years McGuire and his staff—with the help of several outside consultants—were able to synthesize the interdigital gland discharge economically.

McGuire's team used technologies from the food industry so that his synthetic interdigital scent maintains its freshness. When it is finally deposited on the ground by the hunter, the original "just-passed by" smell is intact.

McGuire admits that it's not possible for a synthetic mixture to surpass a fresh, natural scent. "Hunters can collect fresh scents from their own harvested animals," he explained. "The interdigital glands do not spoil quickly and may be skinned out and frozen or preserved for later use. Be sure to wear plastic or rubber gloves when you attempt this so you don't contaminate the glands with human scent. Once the glands are removed, they can be stored in either ethylene glycol or glycerin until they're ready to use them."

McGuire warns against collecting other scent glands, however. "Other glands are both difficult to retrieve and extremely difficult to maintain in a fresh state," he stated. "And it's extremely important for hunters not to mix glandular discharges from different deer."

Some trophy hunters do remove the tarsal glands from the back legs of deer. You'll find the tarsal glands on the inside of the rear legs even with the hocks. Once they've done this, they either freeze them to use later or use them immediately.

Ernie Richardson of Havana, Illinois, has taken several big bucks through the use of tarsal glands scent. Richardson may take the glands to a primary breeding scrape where he pummels them into the bare ground while wearing scent-free gloves. This new scent will infuriate the scrape's dominant buck. Another use for these glands is to help in the establishment of a hunter's mock scrape, which has the same results.

Ideally, interdigital gland scent should be used for ground trails. Another scent, perhaps urine, should be used for scent posts themselves. McGuire recommends pooling the urine on the ground in puddles rather than hanging or dripping it on brush or foliage at a deer's nose level.

Estrous lure should be used only during the active breeding cycle. Never use a sex scent until active breeding scrapes are obvious; to do so only warns big bucks to "Beware."

Once the does start the rut (both bucks and does have a rut), many experience estrus at the same time. Even superbucks are whipped into a breeding frenzy at that time of the year. Their normal caution deserts them to some extent, leaving them much more vulnerable to a hunter's carefully calculated plan. After matching wits with a superbuck through the year, it's somehow satisfying when you place sex scent along a buck's trail, watch as he appears and checks out the scent, and then exhibits the Flehmen response.

The Flehmen response is a lip-curling behavior. The buck actually breathes droplets of the scent into his nasal passages. While he determines whether or not the scent is worth further investigation, he curls his lip back and rolls his eyes. He stretches out his neck, and his antlers are laid back. He'll stand for long minutes, savoring the smells; I suppose he's almost in buck heaven.

Dr. Marchinton has his own hypothesis on the Flehmen response. Marchinton's team questions the idea that the buck is testing the doe's urine for an actual estrous cycle already in progress. They think it's entirely possible that the buck's lip-curl behavior is a test for those does *about* to come into heat. Bob McGuire was so enthralled with this aspect of Marchinton's research that he trademarked the name "Pro-Estrous" for a near-equivalent synthetic urine.

Sex scents such as urine are not usually used on your body, or even around your stand. Remember, they draw a buck's attention. He'll begin looking for the doe, sometimes after sneaking in from afar. You might not even hear him, but when he discovers you, he'll turn tail and be gone before you even suspect he's in the neighborhood.

The most universally accepted method of using a sexual attractant is to sprinkle it in an active scrape. Some hunters do hang scent pads in the general vicinity to keep the scent wafting in the thermals during the day. If you use a pad, one is enough—don't overdo it. The scrape should be upwind from your stand and a shooting lane should be selected in advance. And while estrous doe urine, including McGuire's synthetic urine, is the safest, most conventional route to take, there are alternatives.

Through experimentation, McGuire has also discovered that other urines can work just like estrous doe urine, and that includes—unbelievable as it may sound—human male urine. He's not sure why it works, but he knows that it does, especially when deposited in a buck's scrape.

McGuire feels that fresh urine of any type has an amazing attracting ability for whitetail bucks. McGuire says that there's no relation between an animal's body odor and the odor of its urine. He also says that he's never witnessed a bad response to human urine— even right after the bucks performed Flehmen response to it.

McGuire made his discovery when he was testing to prove that the scent of human urine was a repellent and he found just the opposite. This idea is just controversial enough that I'm not sure that I'd recommend it, especially since it takes so much effort to *mask* human odor. If you want to experiment, it's worth a try, but I don't think I'd try it on the superbuck you're after.

One of McGuire's other discoveries that *has* worked for other hunters is estrous cow urine. Both McGuire and Charlie Alsheimer of Bath, New York, an avid trophy whitetail hunter, have used estrous cow urine and with excellent results. They get it from dairy farmers and use it just like estrous doe urine.

Alsheimer feels that its sexual pheromones are just different enough from those of a doe to appeal both to a buck's sexual urges and to his curiosity. He's had tremendous success since he started to use it several years ago.

By minimizing human odor through cleanliness and masks and then appealing to the whitetail's social and sexual urges, it's possible to enter a new dimension of deer hunting.

18

Using Calls for Whitetail Superbucks

Deer calling isn't a new technique: what *is* new is that more and more hunters have recently discovered that it's an excellent way to attract and take superbucks like the former Kansas State record whitetail that Mike Rose took back in 1982.

Rose is from eastern Kansas, and he hit the jackpot on his first experiment with a bleat call. Rose was bowhunting. He blew once into the bleat call and watched in amazement as an unbelievable buck responded. The buck was a monster that ultimately scored 182 Boone and Crockett points and currently ranks 39th in the Pope and Young record book although it originally ranked 10th.

Rose and hunters like him have discovered a way to make deer hunting a more active sport. No longer does a hunter have to sit in his stand and wait for the deer to come to him. Calling makes it possible to take some command of the situation and try to lure deer—especially buster bucks—closer.

Deer were thought to be nearly non-vocal, despite the fact that elk and moose, well known for their vocalizations, belong to the same family. What's more, both of these cousins of the whitetail readily respond to calls. Nonetheless, very few hunters ever thought of going after whitetails armed with a call. There was an excellent reason for this reluctance: no one knew what kind of sound a whitetail made.

Enter Dr. Harry Jacobson, wildlife biologist and deer researcher from Mississippi State University. Jacobson, along with Larry Richardson, was one of the first researchers to study the whitetail acoustics extensively. "Deer are surprisingly vocal," Jacobson stated. "There's absolutely no reason why a whitetail buck wouldn't be just as susceptible to a call as other members of the deer family."

The research of Richardson and Jacobson identified seven different vocalized sounds from their tape recordings of captive deer. These were the bleat, distress call, nursing whine, grunt, alert snort, snort-wheeze, and aggressive snort.

While deer make all of these sounds, not all of them will call deer. That's simply because some of these calls, like the snort-wheeze, are alarm calls. Only three calls will actually drag in the object of our desire, the bona fide superbuck: the bleat, the grunt, and the aggressive snort.

BLEAT

Deer calling originated with northwest coastal tribes of Indians who used primitive bleat calls with great success on Sitka blacktail deer. These Indians were great observers of nature and soon made the connection that fawn deer bleat to get maternal care and nourishment. The bleat is a cohesive, social bonding sound. It says, "Come, I need you."

The bonus of the bleat call is that all adult females will respond, whether or not they are currently nursing fawns. And if you're successful in luring a doe close during the rut, there's a good chance that a buck will be following her.

Since the bleat is a cohesive call, does may also use it when looking for a buck. Although this exact sound—the bleat of a doe looking for a buck—was never documented in Jacobson's study, many deer hunters believe it calls deer. One of them is Mike Rose. "There's no doubt in my mind that my buck was really looking for whatever made the sound. He crept down the path to my stand with every sense alert."

"Spring is a good time to practice the bleat call," Jim Dougherty commented. Dougherty, a well-known archer with many fine whitetails to his credit, has been calling deer for years. He feels pre-season practice is the best way to hone your skills *without* alerting every buck in the neighborhood that something fishy is going on.

"In early spring the does are just dropping their fawns and cover is at a minimum," Dougherty said in explaining his unusual tactic. "When does feel their young are threatened, they'll run rough-shod right at humans with little regard for their own safety."

My husband, Bob, also called a tremendous buck across a stream during archery season a few years ago. And while he didn't get a chance for a shot, he's confident that the buck was responding to the call.

A bleat is a good call to use and to know about, but for many superbuck hunters the grunt is the finest call of all.

GRUNT

David Hale was waiting in his deer stand, bow in hand. It was early October and Hale was hunting Kentucky's Land Between the Lakes. Suddenly, he heard a sound behind him.

"I was concentrating on the hunting," he said, "listening for the sound of a deer walking through the leaves when I heard a very distinct grunting noise—sort of like a loud belching sound. I didn't know what it was; I sure wasn't prepared to see a tremendous buck rush under my stand, close on the heels of a doe.

"It was early for a buck to be running a doe," Hale continued. "And he was moving funny, all bowed up in the belly with his tail sticking straight out. But the strangest thing about the incident was the noise the old boy was making. Luckily, the grunting didn't keep me from killing the buck, which was the second largest ever taken with a bow in that part of Kentucky."

Hale thought about the strange grunting noise his buck had made. As time passed, he thought about it less. Eventually he joined up with Harold Knight to found Knight and Hale Game Calls of Cadiz, Kentucky, but it wasn't until 1984 that David Hale finally remembered the sound his big buck had made.

"I'd acquired a whitetail buck and doe which I kept in a pen," Hale explained. "I could lead the doe outside the pen to eat, but whenever I did the buck would run around grunting. I figured that the buck was worried that the doe wouldn't return. Something clicked in my head and I knew that if I could duplicate that sound I would really have something."

After two years of experimenting, Knight and Hale succeeded in developing a realistic grunt call. Formerly marketed by Keeper Bait Company as Deer Formula's EZ-Grunter, the call has been modified and is now called the Pro-Grunter. Knight and Hale also sell a model called E-Z Grunter Plus. This model can be used as a grunt call either by blowing through the call or by sucking air into the call. This inhale/exhale actually duplicates an ardent buck's breathing as he grunts. "Hyperventilation" is how David Hale describes it.

What exactly is a grunt call and when do you use it? To find the answer to that question I searched through the studies and discovered a comprehensive paper describing various types of grunts that deer make. Dr. Larry Marchinton and Tom Atkeson of the University of Georgia School of Forest Resources identified twelve different whitetail vocalizations in their study.

"We know that there are several different categories of grunt including the tending grunt," Marchinton said. "A buck hot on the trail of an estrous doe will very often use the tending grunt. If a hunter can imitate this sound, he might possibly fool other bucks into thinking an estrous doe is nearby."

That's just what Harold Knight did. "I spotted this buck when he was 200 yards away," Knight related. "I grunted and immediately the animal threw his head up to try and wind me. Although the wind was in his favor he didn't scent me—quite possibly because I'd set out some matrix lure.

"The buck stood there for a minute. Then he started walking towards me. What's unbelievable is that he never paused, just kept on coming all the way. I finally arrowed him at 22 steps. This wasn't a young buck either, but a nine-pointer with a 19-inch inside spread. I'm convinced that he was looking for a hot doe that was being tended by a grunting buck."

"That's only one of the reasons that a grunt call works," said David Hale. "I believe deer respond to a grunt for several reasons.

"First, the buck grunts because he's ready to breed," Hale explained. "Grunting keeps the buck on the doe's mind until she's ready, too. A tending grunt will lure both bucks and does in. Other bucks want a piece of the action. And does that are ready to breed will come because they're looking for a buck.

"Second, deer don't like to be separated. That's why my penned buck would grunt when I'd take the doe away. The grunt is like a lost call, sort of a 'Where are you?' "

Jacobson's study classified all grunts as being either dominant-subordinate or cohesive. Dominant-subordinate grunts are those used by the dominant deer when threatening or intimidating another. Typically, they are used to maintain status within the hierarchy.

Cohesive grunts are the social grunts. Does use a cohesive grunt to call to their fawns or other does. The tending grunt of a buck to a doe is also a cohesive grunt. And it is this class of grunts that most call manufacturers try to imitate.

A good grunt call won't sound like a motorboat or "ducky." You should be able to blow it so that the sound is slowed way down and a low, distinct clicking sound can be heard. The sound itself is very guttural—so guttural that Harold Knight wanted to name the call the Hog Call.

Hog Call would have been a good name. I met my husband one morning after bowhunting, and Bob swore that he thought one of our neighbor's pigs had escaped and was about to run under his tree stand.

"All I could hear was squealing and grunting," he said, "and then I could hear running in the leaves. Pretty soon, a buck darted past, nose to the ground and grunting like a pig."

That's when I began to listen harder. Since then I've heard many bucks grunting, especially when they're chasing does. The grunt is loud enough to be heard by a human a hundred yards away under still wind conditions. Of course a whitetail buck can hear it from an even greater distance, a fact that I learned when I took my biggest whitetail.

I was hunting on our Missouri farm. It was the second day of our firearms season but all I had seen were 14 does and two small bucks. I wanted a good buck, and I was determined to wait for one.

My stand is located along a power line lane. It's an excellent vantage point from which to observe the surrounding territory. Although it was cold and drizzly, the leaves on the forest floor were still crackly underfoot.

I could hear the deer well before I could see it, making its way up the hillside opposite my stand. Using my binoculars I discovered it was only a doe. In a couple of minutes, though, I could see a second deer following behind, nose to the ground and about 30 yards behind her.

It was a spike buck. I was disappointed, but I watched them walk away through my binoculars anyway. Then I got the bright notion of using the grunt call, but it was almost too late to do me any good.

I pulled the call out from under my jacket and blew into the tube, cupping my hand around the flexible end to direct the sound across to the opposite ridge. The spike and doe kept moving. But in a matter of seconds another, bigger deer came tearing off of the top of the hill like a bat out of hell.

I sat there in disbelief as this buck hit the spike's trail and pivoted after him. It was now or never as I threw up my 7mm Weatherby Magnum and found the big boy in my Burris scope. When I fired, he dropped and then he rolled right over a bluff. I stayed put with the scope still on the animal until I was sure that he'd stopped rolling.

The buck was a good ten-pointer with one long brow tine broken off from fighting. He'd dropped so fast because my shot had gone right through the neck. I wouldn't have taken him without using the grunt call. The grunt convinced the animal that the spike had dishonorable intentions towards his doe. It set old Romeo off into a frenzy, and he was on his way out to take care of the young upstart when my bullet cut short his plans.

Bob also took a big buck while archery hunting his first season afield with the grunt call. "My stand was located on a thicket on a rocky ridgetop," he said. "Nearby was a spot where bucks just loved to scrape. I hadn't had a chance to scout this autumn yet since we'd been hunting out West for several weeks.

"I'd been sitting there for several hours when I heard the unmistakable sounds of an animal on the deer trail that wound around the end of the ridge. I sat there listening as he followed the trail closer and closer to me. I was sure he'd come straight up the ridge. Instead, he stayed on the trail until he was almost out of hearing.

"That's when I realized I had nothing to lose so I made several short grunts," Bob explained. "The deer stopped at once. And when it started moving again it was coming right towards me. I got set and moments later I could see the deer pause at the scrape.

"He pawed at the ground, urinated in the scrape, and then licked the overhanging branch. All I could really see, however, were these tremendous antlers weaving in and out of the leaves. I didn't have a clear shot so I had to wait. Finally, as the buck started moving away, I was able to pick an opening in the branches and thread my arrow right through it."

Bob's buck had been all but lost. It had already worked its way well past his position, but the grunt call convinced him to come back to investigate. The big eight-pointer was probably freshening his scrape to reassert his dominance. He was checking the overhanging branch for the giveaway pheromones of a rival buck. In any case, Bob is positive that he bagged this buck because of the grunt call.

The grunt is such a subtle sound it might easily be missed. Many hunters might not notice the sound because just seeing a big buck makes them so excited they wouldn't hear *any* noise the deer might possibly make.

Any reasonable grunt would probably call in a dominant buck that was in a fighting mood. For simplicity's sake David Hale describes just two grunts that work best for him—the short grunt and the long grunt.

"I'd always recommend the short grunt unless you're able to see the deer and you can tell that he isn't paying any attention to you. I like to use the short grunt because it's the call my penned buck used.

"It's educational to watch deer while you're grunting at them," Hale continued. "They'll try to wind you, they'll stare and then drop their heads real fast to try to force you into moving. They'll often come in so fast that overblowing is a potential problem. Grunt too long and a deer will come in and stare right up your tree.

"To make a short grunt, blow five to ten times in ten seconds to a minute. The rhythm should be short, choppy, and sort of fast. This can be broken up into three grunts, pause, three grunts, pause, four grunts, or however it sounds best to you. If you can actually hear a deer grunt, so much the better since you'll have something to copy.

"The long grunt is slower and more drawn out than the short grunt," Hale added. "You don't need to make as many calls when you're making the long grunt."

Bob Zaiglin, wildlife biologist and ranch manager for the Harrison Ranches of south Texas, is another hunter convinced about the grunt for big bucks. Zaiglin manages the Harrison Ranches for trophy-class whitetails and he knows the tricks that are needed to take them, too. This past season he took a big buck himself that grossed 173⅛ Boone and Crockett points—and he took it while using a grunt call.

"I use the grunt call whenever I'm rattling late in the rut," Zaiglin said. "While I'm grunting and rattling I really tear at the brush with the antlers. Bucks and does both come in to the call.

"Once I was guiding a film producer while he shot video footage of whitetails responding to rattling. The only problem was that the bucks were being a bit uncooperative.

"So I began to grunt while rattling. While the producer taped I used this technique four different times *and it worked every time,*" Zaiglin emphasized. "The deer wouldn't gallop in, they wouldn't run you down. But they came in close enough that in every case a rifle-man would have had a shot.

"In two of the cases an archer could have shot," he said. "One of these bucks was a dandy twelve-pointer in the Boone and Crockett 160-point range and another would have scored in the 150s.

"I developed my call in 1985 but 1986 was the first year that I really used it. I wanted it especially for augmenting late season hunting, when rattling loses some of its effectiveness."

Gordon Eastman, the late video producer, was so impressed with Zaiglin's call that he manufactured and marketed it for Zaiglin under the name Zaiglin's Trophy Deer Call.

"For years I'd watched deer and listened to them grunt," Zaiglin explained. "I knew it meant something so I monkeyed with the call until I got the sound I liked. Mainly I grunt to add a little enticement to my rattling.

"Early in the season I don't make much of a commotion. I rattle just a little and grunt the same way. It doesn't take a lot to bring them in when every buck is waiting for breeding to begin.

"During the heat of the rut when deer are most active I rattle more and grunt less. And late in the rut when all the bucks are concentrated around the few does not yet bred I grunt more and rattle less," Zaiglin emphasized.

"My theory is this," Zaiglin said. "A buck comes to a grunt call looking for a hot doe. And the doe comes to the call hoping that she might literally get some of the smaller bucks away from her, particularly later in the season. She's hoping that there's a bigger buck there to chase the young ones away.

"A whitetail is quite simply the most curious animal there is, and this is why the grunt call works," Zaiglin stated. "What's more, even if it won't draw them in to you, it will often make them set themselves up for the shot. That's what happened with my big buck this year.

"I'd seen this buck the first time on Christmas Day. I knew he was good but I didn't really have much of an opportunity to look him over since he was running.

"The next day I rattled all morning. I had super success and rattled in ten bucks with the biggest being three or four young bucks that would have scored in the 130s. About midmorning I went back to where I saw the tremendous buck the day before. Sure enough, there he was again.

"He was hot after a doe, and I could see four very tall tines and could tell that the rack was quite heavy. The buck was moving about behind some brush so I started grunting in the hope that I could draw him out into the open.

"I wound up grunting for about ten minutes, really mixing up the calls," Zaiglin related. "I'd use two grunts, three grunts, four grunts, grunts of various lengths and combinations but always ending up with one long, drawn out grunt. I did this once a minute.

"The buck kept staring from about 150 yards out. Finally, curiosity got the best of him. He stepped out from behind the bush to see if he could identify the buck that was doing the grunting. That's when I let him have it with a shot from my .270 Winchester right through the shoulder."

Zaiglin's trophy had 25-inch main beams, 22⅝-inch inside spread, and huge 6½ and 8-inch brow tines—a superbuck in anybody's book.

A grunt used in conjunction with rattling is probably interpreted as a dominant vs. subordinate type grunt by other bucks. They feel that two bucks are squaring off to fight and the grunting is vocalization of their agonistic behavior. Another variation of this type of behavior is employed when using the aggressive snort call.

AGGRESSIVE SNORT

It's true that deer snort when frightened—that's called an alert snort. A deer will snort when he feels like fighting: the aggressive snort, the "I dare you" of a buck's world.

The aggressive snort consists of from two to six snorts made in quick succession. It occurs during or after a lunge between sparring bucks or while a buck is tearing up the turf while working over small trees.

During Dr. Jacobson's study, noticeably aggressive males could be provoked into lunging and using the aggressive snort by the researchers. And therein lies its value. It's hard for a red-blooded buck to pass up a challenge. Often, that buck is the dominant buck of an area and a trophy to boot.

Bill Harper, a past owner of Lohman Manufacturing, developed the snort call in the early seventies. Harper believes in the snort call, and his method for scoring on big whitetails incorporates many little tricks he's learned through the years.

First, he locates an active scrape. He gets to the scrape real early and digs up the earth with his heel. Then he sprays doe-in-heat scent right on the scrape and drips it randomly back downwind to his stand. He also applies the scent to bushes and trees.

When he reaches his stand, he douses a cotton wad with a few drops of skunk scent and puts it in a baby food jar or empty film canister, climbs into his stand, and waits for daylight. When it's light enough to see, he makes four or five snorts, maybe rattles a bit, and waits.

"The secret to calling in bucks with the snort call is to imagine what a rank old buck would be doing if he was challenging all comers to a brawl," Harper said. He doesn't always use antlers along with the snort call but thinks that sometimes the two together make powerful medicine—the kind big bucks just can't ignore.

A word of caution: even the best caller can't ignore the basics of good woodsmanship. Be quiet when going to your hunting area and be sure the wind is in your favor. Face in the direction you expect the deer to appear from and move slowly once he's within your sight. These calls will work wonders, but they can't do the impossible.

As David Hale said, "Calling is no miracle-worker. It can't turn a poor hunter into a great hunter overnight. The basics still have to be there. Calling is only an aid. And it's only as good as the hunter who's using it."

I agree wholeheartedly. Over the past two years of hunting I've only called in three bucks, but one of them was a mighty fine animal that I wouldn't have taken otherwise.

Calls—whether bleat, grunt, or snort—just might be the key to unlocking your trophy hunting luck. They are one more element to help you improve your big buck hunting success.

19

Rattling for Whitetail Superbucks

Like most whitetail hunters, I'd heard about "horn" rattling for bucks. A few years back, I actually rattled in my first whitetail—a big, heavy-horned eight-pointer. He came in stiff-legged, neck hackles standing straight up, just spoiling for a fight.

I didn't get that deer, but I did get a new form of buck ague: horn-rattling fever. I couldn't learn enough about rattling fast enough to suit me since it looked like the ideal way to bring in a giant buck. So, several years ago, I talked to a few friends and took what turned out to be a crash course in antler-rattling. These hunters were well-known for their ability to fool whitetails—*big* whitetails—with the sounds of mock whitetail battles.

Murry Burnham of Marble Falls, Texas, is an antler-rattling legend. At the time of the interview, he'd been luring in Texas bucks for more than 30 years.

Jim Dougherty of Tulsa, Oklahoma, had many years' experience. Dougherty, who ran an archery shop, hunted exclusively with a bow, and rattled in fine bucks all over the country.

Bob Zaiglin was not only a certified wildlife biologist with a Master's Degree, he also managed the Harrison Ranches of south Texas. While at work he observed whitetails nearly every day and was able to rattle them up both for himself and for the ranches' hunters under every condition imaginable.

And Stanley Potts of Springfield, Illinois, had also been rattling successfully for many years. At the time of our interview, his largest buck to date scored 195⅝ points.

This panel of experts was extremely informative—not only because of what they agreed on, but also for the ways in which they disagreed with each other. Common sense combined with creativity had helped each of them master a particular method that accounted for some of the best trophy bucks taken in the country. Here's how they did it:

When is the very best time to rattle in a buck?

Burnham: "Near the beginning of the rut. I've rattled successfully in south Texas as early as November. Bucks are ready to fight for does well before the does are in heat."

Zaiglin: "I rattle in south Texas, too, but I have my best success two weeks before and two weeks after Christmas—the peak of the rut down here."

Potts: "The week after the rut's peak—in Illinois around November 12th to 15th—is my favorite time. Once bucks have had a taste of rutting it's in their blood—they're boiling to come in."

Dougherty: "Right before the peak of the rut no matter where I'm hunting."

Describe your favorite rattling technique.

Dougherty: "I start out with some subtle clicking noises. Then I build the pace and volume to clacking the antlers together frantically. I usually rattle in heavy cover so that first soft series, which is quite audible to deer, is often enough. I rattle for three to four minutes with short intervals in between. If I really believe in the spot I'll wait five or ten minutes and run another series."

Zaiglin: "After things settle down around my stand, I pound the bases of the antlers into the ground to mimic the sound of running deer. Then I rake at nearby brush with the antlers to make more racket. After that I really clash the antlers together hard for 15 to 20 seconds. I stop, wait and then repeat the entire sequence in five minutes. After the *second* complete sequence I scrape small tree limbs and make additional noise *in between* the actual rattling sequences. Then I start *increasing* the amount of time between sequences until there's, say, 15 minutes between the fifth and sixth sets. I seldom stay in the same spot for more than 30 minutes."

Burnham: "My favorite technique is ideally suited for a tract of rolling country about a mile wide and three miles long—and if there's a gully running down the middle, that's great. Complete camouflage is a must. I travel in the bottom of the gully with the wind in my face while going from one rattling spot to the next. By doing this, bucks won't approach from downwind or get my scent.

I always sit in front of the cover, never behind it. Whenever I can I'll climb right into the middle of a clump of bushes. Then I can shake the bushes when I see a buck coming and hold the antlers so he can see them as I rattle. I rattle for 15 minutes or less at one location."

Potts: "I do 80 percent of my rattling from a tree stand. First, I crash the horns together real loud and grind them back and forth. Then I pull them apart and hit them together again but *without* that initial force. I quit after another minute and a half and wait silently for three or four minutes. If I haven't seen anything, I just grind the horns lightly in case a big buck has slipped in but is still out of sight. They like to come in and stop, look and listen. I'll wait for 45 minutes to an hour before rattling again. If it's not the peak of the rut I'll rattle again right before dark. So I average rattling about three times a day. If it is the peak of the rut I rattle all day every 45 minutes."

How about other rattling "tricks" that help you out where others fail?

Dougherty: "I've found that using a grunt call when rattling is often effective."

Burnham: "I'll carry dead sticks to my rattling site to knock the antlers against. And I like rattling in rocks where I can rake the rocks to make noise like two big bucks pushing each other around. And finally, I like my antlers to have bumpy bases to grind together for yet another sound."

Zaiglin: "Pounding the antlers into the ground like the sound deer make when they're running is something few people try. I've brought deer in simply by pounding the antlers into the ground *before* the horns were ever hit together."

Burnham: "I put doe-in-rut scent downwind from where I rattle and wear descented clothes. I depend on my cedar oil deer scent to cover my odor and have found that it also attracts deer."

Potts: "I put Tink's #69 buck lure in front of my stand in three different spots—wherever I think the deer will come from. It makes the difference for a bowhunter."

One of you—Stan—rattles mainly from tree stands. If hunting on the ground, how far do the rest of you move after a series of rattles?

Dougherty: "Depends on the country but usually about half a mile."

Zaiglin: "Between 150 and 200 yards."

Burnham: "In open country I move about a half mile; in hilly country less than that. Tall-timbered country should be rattled from every 300 yards."

Describe your personal favorite set of rattling antlers.

Dougherty: "Mine are an oddball pair with some palmation on the main beams which gives more hitting surface."

Potts: "I use a medium-sized ten-point rack."

Burnham: "My favorites are eight-pointers with 4½-inch bases and ten-inch tines."

Zaiglin: "I guess mine are really different from everybody else's. I use *two* right antlers so I can slam them together hard without hurting my hands."

Have you made any modifications to your rattling horns other than drilling holes for a cord?

Zaiglin: "I remove the brow tines, too, and cut all the points ½" shorter to make the ends blunt. I also grind down the bases so the burr is smooth to save my hands."

Burnham: "I saw the brow tines off but I *like* that rough burr. It gives a good, alternate sound to use on stubborn bucks."

Potts: "I really alter mine; I cut the brow tines off and the tips of all other points off. I like to make a rattling set out of antlers that still have the skull plate attached. I saw through the middle of the skull and sand and file the skull plate so it becomes a nice big knob to hold on to—so you *don't* have to grasp the antlers themselves."

Do you use "fresh" antlers each year?

Burnham: "I would if I could get them, but I've used my present ones for at least ten years."

Dougherty: "No."

| Potts: | "I've used mine for five years. I keep them in the house, never outside or even in the garage." |

How about synthetic antlers?

Burnham:	"I tried them once and broke them the second time I hit them together. I had to walk two miles to get my regular pair. But I think that problem has been corrected with the new synthetics."
Dougherty:	"You're right. I've clicked a couple of rocks together to get a buck's attention. And I've also rattled an arrow on my bow riser. A couple of times it's actually worked."
Burnham:	"One thing that's worked for me in a pinch is breaking dead sticks. Cedar or any kind of dry stick that makes a loud 'pop' when it's snapped is good."
Zaiglin:	"I'm pretty proud of some synthetics I designed based on my favorite set of real antlers. They're called Zaiglin's Rattlin' Horns."

How about soaking old antlers in water to restore the sound?

| Dougherty: | "If you keep your antlers out of the weather they shouldn't dry out and open up. If a pair's been in the weather for any length of time you probably can't restore them." |
| Burnham: | "Soaking old antlers will restore the good sound on a temporary basis but it's bad for them in the long run. It dries them out." |

What is the best time of day for rattling?

Burnham:	"There is no set rule. I rattle all day and have as much luck."
Potts:	"My best time is from mid-morning to mid-afternoon but I've rattled them in all day."
Dougherty:	"It can be effective all day. But I think morning is best, mid-morning is good. I haven't had much luck in the afternoon."
Zaiglin:	"My best time is early morning; second best is late evening; and worst is probably midday. I've rattled bucks in all day long, however."

What kind of weather conditions are ideal for rattling?

Burnham: "Give me cool or cold weather that's overcast with a light mist or drizzle."

Potts: "A little wind to muffle the sound is good so the buck can't pinpoint where the noise is coming from. I don't think bucks will come *real* far—they'll hear you but they won't come in."

Zaiglin: "A cold, crisp morning following a dry norther with little or no wind. But I like an overcast day with a light drizzle, too."

Dougherty: "Cool, still mornings with a light, steady breeze."

What kind of setup do you prefer when rattling?

Zaiglin: "Rattling alone is best. But when I'm guiding, the hunter or photographer sits next to me facing the opposite direction to spot bucks sneaking in from behind."

Dougherty: "Two hunters are best. The one that's going to shoot should be closer to where you think the deer will appear. A shooter on the ground off-line and concealed can get a shot at a buck whose attention is diverted to the rattler."

Burnham: "I pick my spot when I'm scouting, even down to which bush I'm going to rattle from. Starting on the downwind side of an area I'll rattle into the wind. Some bucks are smarter and won't charge in but will sneak in and *always* circle downwind. If I'm guiding, the hunter or photographer *must* be ready—the gun or camera can't be laid to one side. And bucks are easy to spook so timing is important. Be sure the buck's eyes are behind something when you make your move. The rattler should make plenty of noise to cover his companion's movements."

Can you ever over-rattle in an area?

Dougherty: "An area can be over-called with *any* calling form. If you rattle up a buck and spook him he's wise for a long time."

Zaiglin: "Definitely. Some trophies may be fooled only once, if ever."

"Have you ever rattled a buck in, had him run away, and then rattled him back again?"

Zaiglin: "Rattling up the same buck twice isn't uncommon. I've had them charge in and almost run me over before making a 180-degree turn and disappearing. But often when I clash the antlers together, they'll turn around and come right back in."

Burnham: "If I rattle more noisily after they run away, I've sometimes brought them back. And the snort call really helps bring them back."

What advice would you offer a hunter who's never rattled before?

Dougherty: "Read and learn as much as you can. There are excellent video and audio tape selections available."

Zaiglin: "Have confidence in the technique and keep on trying."

Burnham: "Know the area where you plan to rattle down to every tree, creek, thicket, trail and opening. You have to be confident, should never give up, and *don't* be afraid to make a lot of noise like two bucks in a big fight."

Potts: "Don't get discouraged. You might rattle 100 times and not see a thing but that 101st time might just bring in the giant buck of all time."

Burnham: "Some people give up too easily. They simply don't believe in the technique and call it quits. Don't come back to camp at mid-morning; stick with it. Rattling is a great way to add more excitement to your deer hunting."

Part 3

Whitetail Superbuck Hunters and the Stories Behind the Trophies

20

Gene Wensel

Gene Wensel is one of those lucky whitetail hunters who has nothing left to prove to anyone but himself. Wensel has confined himself to bowhunting only for whitetails for quite some time. He's done so just for the challenge.

"The way I look at it, when you're hunting with a gun, you can either *hunt* a buck or *shoot* a buck," he said. "There's a big difference. Don't get me wrong; I started out gunhunting. It's just that for me, hunting with a gun lost its challenge. To make the results worthwhile in my own eyes, I constantly impose additional self-limitations. To be a good bowhunter is a challenge. One that requires more physical effort plus closer involvement both with the animal and with the environment."

Even while limiting himself to hunting only with bow and arrow, Wensel's managed to take so many fine trophies that it seems unfair—unless you knew the kind of man and hunter Gene Wensel is. He is one hunter who knew what his dream was—to consistently take good bucks—and consequently set about making that dream a reality. Wensel has written several books, including *Hunting Rutting Whitetails* and *One Man's Whitetail,* that he sells from his home in Bloomfield, Iowa. These books should be required reading for anyone who wishes to become the high caliber of hunter that Gene is.

Even though he's taken many fine heads, at this stage of his hunting life—a stage he calls "maturity"—Wensel hesitates to reveal just how many of his deer qualify for either Boone and Crockett or Pope and Young. By reading his books, however, I have discovered that he's taken one buster 12×12 non-typical buck that scores 197⅝ points and another big 10×8 that scores 179. I've also managed to ferret out the fact that he's taken three others that score 138-plus, 140-plus, and 147-plus. At one point he admitted that several years ago he "had seven or eight that qualified for Pope and Young," a number that must have increased considerably during the intervening years.

"I'm not in any race," he added. "You must always remember that deer hunting is a sport and not a game. You only keep score in a game. And even while admitting that's where I once was coming from,

I like to think those days are behind me. Today, too many hunters are becoming too competitive in the race to become well-known."

Although Wensel concentrates solely on big bucks to maintain the challenge, he discourages young or beginning hunters from being too picky. "Everyone wants a trophy," he commented, "but no one starts out shooting one big buck after another. It takes time to get all your ducks in a row so that you can consistently n.ake the right decisions. One hunter from Rhode Island told me he's been hunting for many years and yet has never shot a deer—*any* deer. It's not that he hasn't seen any deer, it's that he won't shoot any because he's looking for a trophy. What makes him think he'll be *able* to shoot a big buck if one comes along? Buck fever does happen.

"Hunting trophies is something that a hunter usually grows into. My son Kenny has seen my trophies and is impressed with them. And maybe someday he'll make the same choice that I have, to pursue big bucks seriously. But his first time out last year when he'd just turned 12, he shot a doe. And let me tell you, I was with him, and when he did we were the two happiest guys in the world."

Wensel is inordinately successful at what he does. Why? "I swear, there's no big secret, no magic formula," he insisted. "If there was, believe me, someone would have sold it by now. At seminars, guys think I'm holding back. They're sure that there is some secret. But anyone could kill more big bucks if they start hunting with their brain and their heart, rather than with their feet. You have to use your intelligence to the utmost to outwit deer.

"And that doesn't necessarily mean that you have to learn to think like a deer," Wensel continued. "What it does mean is that you have to learn to think like a predator. Because that's what man is, the ultimate predator. Think of it like this: there are three types of predators. There are the canines like the coyotes and wolves; the felines like the big cats; and the raptors like the owls, hawks, and eagles. A hunter chooses to hunt like a canine predator when he picks out a style of hunting similar to the way a wolf hunts, say tracking or driving deer. He gets on a trail and stays there. Or several of them work in 'packs,' so to speak, such as when conducting a drive to force the animal to move and expose himself.

"Feline-type predators are those that stalk and slip noiselessly through the woods, waiting for their chance," he added. "And hunters imitate raptors when they are perched in their tree stands, watching and observing their quarry before making their move."

Another point that Wensel is quick to make is that he won't hunt where there aren't any undisturbed deer. "I've talked to guys who tell me how many hunters they're up against, say in Pennsylvania," he explained. "And they want me to tell them how to connect on a trophy buck. The first thing I tell them is to get out of where they're hunting and find some place where they can hunt undisturbed deer. They might have to drive farther. Or they might have to do some chores on a farm to get and keep permission to hunt. Or they might even have to do some hiking or get their feet wet in a swamp somewhere. But what I'm saying is that *the best way to bag a big buck is by hunting where the deer are undisturbed.* Hunters who are serious must sniff good areas out. Being able to consistently hunt undisturbed deer was a big factor in my decision to move from Vermont to Montana 18 years ago."

How does Wensel find the big bucks that he goes after? "Unlike some guys, I *never* ask other people if they've seen any big bucks. For one thing, everyone has a different definition of what a big buck looks like. I can't really afford to waste my time scouting for bucks that just won't meet my standards.

"Bars are good sources of information," Wensel confided. "You have to hang back and just listen. When someone gets a loose tongue, you can often discover where a big buck is located. However, you also have to remember that drunks not only talk a lot, they have also been known to lie or exaggerate as well."

Wensel admits that he finds most of his bucks himself while out scouting. "There's a time for scouting and a time for hunting," he said. "I look for sheds in the spring. Rubs and scrapes are also still evident then. It keeps you from messing up your area right before hunting season. August is a great time to try to locate bucks that are feeding in fields at dusk. I use a spotting scope or long range binoculars with a good twilight factor for this activity. If you're scoping an area from your vehicle, stay in the car with the windows rolled up, don't talk, move, smoke, or play the radio. And don't park close to where you expect the deer to come into the field. You'll be surprised at how close some big bucks will come to your vehicle. Don't point the front of your car towards the deer, either. If you park straight on, they seem to think the car is coming at them or something. In any case, they'll avoid coming closer.

"I get excited whenever I find deer tracks the size of a coffee cup," Wensel explained. "I automatically assume they're from a good-sized buck. But I've also seen some great trophies that only had medium-sized feet."

Wensel looks for big rubs when he's scouting, too. "Bigger rubs mean bigger bucks *up to a point.* One time I watched a buck that would gross maybe 125 making a rub on a 12-inch tree.

"I don't scout all year long any more, or even as much as I'd like to. At one point in my life, I spent all of my free time in the woods studying deer. I had no answers and plenty of questions. But now I can go into an area that I've hunted before yet haven't been in for a year, and if the deer are *undisturbed,* their movement patterns will be about the same as they were before.

"A disturbed deer is just harder to figure out," he continued. "You aren't watching normal deer actions when you're observing a disturbed deer. What you're seeing is *reactions*. And that makes them unpredictable.

"Early in the bow season is probably the best time to take a trophy buck because they're still undisturbed then. By the time gun season rolls around and deer hear all the car doors slamming and can see and scent all the hunters in the woods, they become an entirely different animal."

Although he is a firm believer in the value of scrape hunting, Wensel also feels that it is fairly difficult for many hunters to both read and interpret scrapes because of all the extraneous factors involved. These factors, alone or in combination, may determine just how viable scrape hunting in general, or even one scrape in particular, may be in your neighborhood.

Some of these factors include the health of the herd, the buck-to-doe ratio, the number of mature bucks in the herd in your area, the number of mature does, the age structure of both sexes, the time of year, the terrain, the wind, whether the deer are disturbed or undisturbed, and the weather.

However, Wensel is quick to say that, "Under the right conditions, there is no better place to hunt than at a scrape for a really big trophy whitetail."

If you're hunting in an area with an unbalanced buck-to-doe ratio, Wensel's advice is to find a spot where the balance is better—even if it means traveling to a different state. Suggestions on where to start the search in your own area for better balanced populations include scouting around refuges or no hunting areas. Also whenever possible look for hunting opportunities around limited access areas such as those around military bases, prison grounds, large estates, monasteries, etc. As Wensel says, "Competition between mature, undisturbed bucks for available does in a well-balanced population is the single biggest desirable factor for optimum scrape hunting and rattling success.

"Don't worry about what class of scrape you've found," Wensel emphasized. "Some guys spend an entire season looking for a primary scrape when one may not even exist anywhere in their hunting area. But if you find a fairly large scrape that's fresh, dark, damp, with an overhanging branch and a lot of fresh deer sign such as big tracks, rubs, droppings, in its vicinity, go ahead and hunt the thing."

While Wensel feels individual scrapes can be vitally important, he's also a great proponent of scrape lines. "I encourage most hunters to hunt a scrape line a lot sooner than I will to hunt one particular scrape," he said. "A single scrape may predict a buck's eventual return, but so will a line of scrapes. In addition, a *line* of scrapes will also give us direction of travel when he does return."

Wensel recommends hunting at or near active scrapes or scrape lines from the time they appear right through the peak of the rut if the buck to doe ratio is under 1:4 (one buck to every four does). If the ratio is from 1:5 to 1:8, he suggests concentrating on them until the peak of the rut and then forgetting about scrapes and concentrating on areas with lots of does. If the ratio is any higher, don't even worry about scrapes. Stick in areas with lots of does. To determine the buck to doe ratio in your hunting area, check with local game and fish officials.

"One of my very best big bucks tips is that I'm firmly convinced that any scrapes found during the month of September are *made only by mature bucks*," Wensel added.

Wensel also likes to do much of the preliminary scouting in a new hunting area from an airplane. That's right—an airplane. "The best time to fly an area is when there's snow on the ground and no leaves on the trees," he said. "Look for heavy trails in the snow. Look for structure or edge. Whitetails love structure. This could be the edge of a field, or a creek next to timber, or even softwoods next to hardwoods. Any type of structure is important. And look for small patches of heavy security cover. Look for water sources. Take your camera and take plenty of pictures. Keep the top of the lens pointed north as you take your photos so that you don't get confused. And always try to keep a landmark in the picture for reference later on when you're piecing together your clues.

"A lot of hunters think renting a plane is too expensive for whitetail scouting. But if you split the cost with a hunting partner, it's not too bad. You can cover a lot of territory in half an hour.

"Once I do fly an area, then I order aerial photos from the Soil Conservation Service (SCS) that's located in each county seat," Wensel said. "When you get the photo, cover it with a piece of plastic and mark it in several different colors. Use one color for trails, another for scrape areas, another for rub lines. Keep switching colors and mark bottlenecks, bedding areas, feeding areas, tree stand sites, swamps, water, buck sightings, direction of the prevailing wind, anything and everything that may be important.

"The first thing I look for is density of cover versus structure," Wensel emphasized. "Look for security cover in relation to structure. Soon you should be able to pick out patterns of deer movement or activity. Travel corridors should become evident.

"Remember, the biggest bucks will not use the main trails from about the first of October until about the 10th of November. Big bucks will travel parallel to the main trails. Stand sites close to bedding areas are hard to pinpoint since trails near bedding areas peter out.

"Once you've placed your tree stand, don't be afraid to move it," Wensel advised. "I've moved a stand site three or four times in a very small area simply because I've observed different patterns of buck movement over a period of time. If all else fails in your search for a travel corridor to hunt, then revert to hunting near scrape lines again.

"Whenever possible, I like to hunt as close to bedding areas as possible without getting in them," Wensel said. "A good way to find them is to go out and jump undisturbed deer at midday. Or, find a food source and then backtrack. Deer usually bed high and feed low in mountainous country. In hilly regions, pay attention to travel direction. When vertical trails turn horizontal on a mountainside, the bedding areas will be located somewhere up the slope."

As far as what time of day is best to be on stand, Wensel says that the hours just after dawn used to be his favorite time to be in the woods. "But over the past five to seven years, it's getting better in the evenings and worse in the early morning," he stated. "I think this change is a result of whitetails adapting to hunters who are out at the crack of dawn. Instead, now they move *before* daylight and they get where they want to be right at dawn. Then next time they move is after 9:00 A.M. Then, big bucks are up and about again at midday and then later on, about an hour before dark."

One final tip that Wensel offers is this: "Always be very careful with wind direction. If you're putting up a tree stand or walking through tall grass or brush on your way to a stand, always wear rubber hip boots to keep your scent from spreading on to ground foliage. And be sure to remember that there are morning stands and evening stands. Make sure you have enough portable stands so that you can hunt both types. The minimum number of stands that I feel you can get away with would be three.

"I myself have 30 to 40 portable stands although the most I have out at one time is probably 12. I padlock them to the trees to discourage thieves. I lubricate any squeaky moving parts with corn oil, sunflower seed oil, or some similar oil. Avoid petroleum distillates since they leave a residue of odor that deer may avoid.

"A piece of clean, odor-free carpet attached to the stand is another good idea," he continued. "It muffles the sounds of your moving. The height I prefer for my stands is right around 16 to 18 feet up in a tree."

Wensel doesn't only look for the biggest and the best bucks. "Many times I'll kill a buck that's taken a lot of hard work to pin down," he said. "Some come harder than others. Now I'm to the point that if a good deer comes by that looks like it's still growing, I'll let it go.

"Lots of people weigh success only by how many trophy deer they've got," Wensel concluded. "But overall, that's not fair to either hunter or deer. And many hunters, when faced with the dilemma of whether to shoot a forkey or a doe as they stand side by side, still shoot the buck. That's how the buck-to-doe ratios got lopsided to begin with. That's why big bucks are getting harder to find. And that's the attitude serious trophy hunters have got to reverse."

21

Russell Hull

Russell Hull's home state is Kansas, so it would be easy to make light of his whitetail hunting accomplishments. After all, *anyone* from bigbuck Kansas could become a superbuck hunter. But Hull is from Hill City in *western* Kansas, where pressure is heavy and habitat is restricted. Moreover, Hull doesn't believe in making it easy for himself: he's a bowhunter, period.

Hull works harder than any other two men for everything he's got. He owns and operates a wheat and milo farm, works the swing shift at a power plant, manages his own deer scent and game call business with several full-time employees, and does some outdoor writing on the side. He's a father, a husband, and on top of it all, he's managed to become one of the country's pre-eminent superbuck hunters the hard way—by bowhunting.

In 2000 his Kansas deer hunt ended without a deer. But that's the price you may have to pay when you set high goals for yourself like Russell Hull does.

"A hunter should set a minimum standard of quality for the buck he's looking for and then pursue that standard," Hull says. "Not all areas of the country are equal in their capacity to produce superbucks. But remember, you won't ever shoot a really big buck if you consistently use your license to take little ones. And once you pull the trigger or loose that arrow, you've made your decision until the next season."

Hull believes that bowhunting trophy whitetails satisfies a need in himself. "There's an awful good feeling in matching wits and woodsmanship against a wild animal on a one-to-one basis," he stated. "A hunted animal is so alert and cautious that it's simply incomprehensible to a non-hunter. A movement is liable to give a bowhunter away, especially at the close distances that are required to kill an animal with a bow and arrow. Little things like the noise an arrow makes as it's being drawn across the rest, or the faint odor of human scent on a swirling wind may be all that it takes to spook a deer that you've been after for months."

Hull has been bowhunting deer for 36 years. He started archery as a hobby seven years before that. "We didn't even have a deer season here in Kansas until 1965," he reminisced. "I hunted hard that first season even though I didn't know what I was doing. Even so, after six weeks I managed to kill a trophy buck, the first legal deer killed in our county. The buck scored 144 Pope and Young points, a great way to start out. But it took me ten years before I killed another Pope and Young-class buck."

Hull became a serious trophy hunter in 1977. At that point he decided he liked the challenge of going after big bucks well enough to devote all of his free time to hunting them. But being a successful big buck hunter requires a lot of time, starting soon after bow season stops. Hull's serious scouting begins in late winter, when he starts looking for the deer still alive after the end of all seasons. Cold weather and lack of hunting pressure means deer may start moving back out into the fields during daylight hours. Hull believes that seeing a trophy whitetail consistently is the first and most important step in hunting the animal. Once he finds a big deer, he begins searching the nearby landscape for old rubs and scrapes. Later, he walks his favorite areas looking for shed antlers. Then during turkey season he looks for both deer and old sign while he's out hunting. In July, he pulls out a spotting scope to scan the fields for possible trophies as they feed in crop fields.

"Judging a rack is a big part of the challenge of being a superbuck hunter," Hull commented. "While you're actually hunting, you may not have much time to make up your mind. Often, you can be wrong. When I'm looking at a rack I look for mass, long points, good inside spread—a big whitetail will have a 16-inch spread from eartip to eartip—and long main beams. I consider beam length very important since it can account for up to 33 percent of a rack's total score."

Hull also keeps a hunting diary. "I always record hunting dates, the time of day I was out, what I saw, wind direction, temperature, location, any food sources the deer were using, scrape activity, rubs, anything pertinent," he explained. "Over the years you'll be able to pick up a distinct pattern in where the deer should be and what they'll probably be doing during a given period."

One of the most important factors governing where Hull places his stands is the availability of a good entry trail *for the hunter.* "You have to be able to get in and out of a big buck's area without disturbing it with telltale scent or noise," he said.

"Many big bucks in this part of the country only travel the woods at night. They've learned to become almost completely nocturnal, except during the peak of the rut. They don't even bed in the timber, preferring instead to lie down out in the open where no one can easily approach them. It's hard to find them, too, when they're bedded out in a depression in a cropfield. But when they do start moving along the riverbottoms and creek bottoms during the frenzy of the rut, you have to be out in your stand as much as you're able."

Hull feels that the first or false rut, which occurs around mid-October in western Kansas, is a good time to catch a superbuck prowling about with his guard down. By that time most does are nearing the start of their estrous cycles, and a few older does may actually begin estrus. Enough scent is wafting around to start the bucks moving. "Most seasons have just started a few days before and the bucks don't usually realize that they're being hunted yet," he said. "Once a trophy knows he's being hunted, he's going to get that much harder to kill."

When rifle season is over, Hull moves his center of bowhunting activity to the thickest cover he can find, because he knows that's where the bucks are going to be, pushed there by all the pressure of gunhunters.

When it comes down to choosing a tree for his stand, Hull tries to pick one out that is large enough to conceal his outline. He never wants to stand out. To help minimize detection, he places his stand high in the tree—18 to 22 feet whenever possible—and to one side of the trail or scrape, never directly above it. By locating his stand off to the side, Hull ensures that he won't wind up on the buck's line of sight as the deer scopes out his trail from a distance. A particular stand site is used no more than two times in a row. Hull always tries to locate several good trees around each hotspot so that changes in wind direction won't mean he can't continue to hunt a promising area.

If Hull's going to concentrate on one scrape, it must have an overhanging branch that shows licking or gnawing activity, otherwise he won't hunt it. Hull feels that scrapes with marking branches above them get the most attention.

Hull prefers a portable stand that he designed himself, one with a folding seat. "If you aren't comfortable you won't stay out there," he said.

He carries this stand in and out with him every day. "Some people will steal a stand if they find one," he said. "And besides that, since other hunters know I'm after a good trophy they naturally want to know where I'm hunting. But after I've done all the legwork it takes to find a good buck, I don't necessarily *want* them to know. It's unfortunate, but these days there is too much unhealthy competition among hunters. No one respects the fact that you've spent a lot of time going after a particular buck; if they find out, they want to move right in on you."

Ground stands and stillhunting are two other options that Hull eagerly uses when conditions merit them. "When you're hunting as much open country as I do you soon learn to take the best advantage of any situation. I've taken good bucks using both tactics."

When he's stillhunting, wind, rain, snow, drought, fog, or heavy dew are all factors that determine how fast Hull is able to travel. Barometric pressure is particularly important to buck movements.

"I've found that while bucks move during a high, stable barometer, they'll move even better when the barometer is fluctuating," he noted. "It doesn't seem to matter whether the barometer is rising or falling, the bucks will be out and about."

Hull also likes to stalk when conditions are windy and wet, as long as wind isn't excessive. "When the wind's blowing, I head for heavy cover because that's where the big bucks will be hanging out," he stated. "Real windy conditions are bad for bowhunters; they affect your arrow flight too much."

Under extremely dry conditions something as innocuous as a branch cracking underfoot could give your location away. Dry conditions call for slower, more careful movements. "Take two steps and then wait," Hull advises. "Carry a walking stick to break up the steady rhythm of your two feet striking the ground. By hitting the stick to the ground at every step it's possible to change the cadence of your footfalls so they don't sound like a human's. Another trick I use is to call on a diaphragm turkey caller every now and then. It really throws deer off their guard. They assume that you're really a turkey moving through the brush."

Hull always moves with wind currents in mind. He hunts into the wind, following a line of travel he's planned out beforehand. He uses the surrounding terrain to help mask his movements by traveling in ditches and gullies and behind trees and deadfalls whenever possible. Hull never crosses openings until he takes a good long time to search the nearby timber for hidden deer.

"If you do see any deer, stay put," he advises. "It may not be alone. Take a while to carefully study the area before attempting to get any closer. And if you manage to get within the animal's critical 45-yard alert zone, really slow down the pace. Be especially careful about too much noise. And remember that any excessive movement—even ones made while the animal is looking away—just might be detected by the animal's extremely sensitive peripheral vision."

Hull stillhunts for another reason. "It's a great way to scout your way through the woods and see what's going on," he said. "But always use total camouflage, including fletching covers for the arrows."

Another Hull trick: he uses moleskin on his flipper rest and the side of his bow's sight window. It helps keep the bow quiet during very close shots that might otherwise spook deer.

Hull likes to hunt in rain whenever possible. Western Kansas is given to droughty spells, so bucks are more liable to be moving in a rainfall because it spells relief. In Hull's mind, being able to see tracks after a rainfall and so determine what kind of animals are in an area is a distinct advantage.

Hull manufactures and sells a pleasant-smelling scent he calls Cover-Up. "Animals seem downright curious about the scent," he said. "It's extremely effective where I hunt, and I hear the same thing from other hunters all over the country. I also bathe using a non-scented bar soap plus I use a deodorant crystal that's rubbed over your moist body to keep body bacteria from forming and multiplying. Keeping the body clean and odor free is very important when you're after a big whitetail. I also avoid the odors of scented soap, cologne, perfume, tobacco, oil, gasoline, or strong foods. I use a doe-in-estrus lure only rarely, during the peak of the rut. It's too easy to spook deer using sex lures when you shouldn't."

Although Hull has had success rattling, he feels that so many people are using the technique these days that deer don't respond as readily. "If you can find an area where there's not too much pressure or interference it's still a good tactic," he explained. "Every year I still manage to rattle or call in two or three bucks. But it's difficult to get big whitetails in this part of the country to respond. They're just too wary. Actually, I think it's easier to rattle in a mule deer than it is a whitetail."

Hull manufactures both a short-range and long-range grunt call plus a bleat call and snort call. "Calls are another tool. They're just effective enough to keep it interesting."

He took three of his bucks by using calls, however: two in 1985 and one in 1986. "I took a 154-point non-typical whitetail in Nebraska after the rifle season using a call," he said. "The others were both 140-class bucks."

The 154-point buck was particularly rewarding for Hull. "We'd had a snow so I started to scout out big tracks, looking for anything to try to determine if a big buck was in the area. Finally, I found some good tracks so I decided to locate my stand nearby. After I got up in it I realized that I still needed to trim some brush, so down I went, back on the ground. While I was trimming, some does came along, saw me, snorted, and ran away. Later on I watched as a big non-typical started moving down the trail behind me. I got my bow ready, but he stopped and left. I knew that he must have gotten the scent of the spooked does.

"I'd positioned my stand in a natural bottleneck of woods. The next time I hunted there temperatures were extremely cold. After about 10 minutes, I watched another bowhunter leave the woods, but I stayed, and this time everything worked to my advantage. I waited a while and then grunted; the buck came right on in. Later, I figured I'd gotten between the does on one end of the bottleneck and the buck on the other."

Hull has taken many big bucks but so far his biggest are two typicals that score 164 points and 157 points. Hull is one superbuck hunter that does it his way—the hard way—and still manages to always come out on top.

22

Bob McGuire

Bob McGuire of Johnson City, Tennessee, was an engineer by profession and then, for many years, devoted his life to sharing his knowledge of hunting with others. Always a keen observer of the outdoors, McGuire's hunting experience brought him to conclusions not readily apparent to 99 percent of the other whitetail hunters in the woods. And the more he discovered the more he wanted to learn, and then share that learning with others. McGuire started BHP Books, his hunting video production companies, and developed many hunting aids including his deer calls and scents.

McGuire has spent many days afield hunting mature whitetail bucks and many more at whitetail research facilities in Tennessee, Georgia, and other states. A portion of the profits from various McGuire enterprises ensures that funding continues on whitetail research projects at universities with which he's been affiliated.

Bob McGuire is something of an enigma as a hunter. He strives to discover the causes of seemingly insignificant deer behaviors—things that other hunters may have completely overlooked. In uncovering the reasons for these details, he's started unravelling the threads of quite a few whitetail mysteries, some of which have helped him take many good bucks. His knowledge of mature whitetail behavior could fill volumes. *Advanced Whitetail Hunting Techniques* is an outstanding compilation of McGuire's hunting anecdotes and observed whitetail behaviors and should be required reading for anyone longing for a big buck.

McGuire doesn't have to travel great distances to find areas with little hunter pressure. He feels that some of the best locations in the mid-south are to be found close to home in suburban areas with farmland nearby. To locate and pattern big bucks one of the first things he does is try to establish where in an area the animal is bedding. The popular belief is that big whitetails prefer bedding on the highest ground in an area; McGuire believes it's far easier to find a mature buck's bed in the *least traveled* area of his home range.

"I've often found big bucks bedded right in those thick, narrow hedgerows around Ohio farm fields," he said. "And I've seen bucks bed right down in the middle of empty pasture fields, too. I watched one real good buck, probably a five-year old, bed down three mornings in a row in the middle of one such field. The buck would walk right out to a small clump of brown grass and disappear. It actually looked as though he'd crawled in a hole."

McGuire also likes to hunt in areas that have been strip-mined. "Lots of hunters walk along the tops of the pits," he said. "But you have to be willing to crawl along the sides and down in the gunk where a big buck might be hiding. Always use a masking scent like red fox urine, something that will hide your scent as you approach. And you don't want any human scent lingering in the area to give you away after you leave. If you're lucky enough to discover a big buck's bed, don't get too close. That could be enough to make him change his habits."

McGuire, like so many other observers of trophy buck behavior, believes that a buck turns nocturnal in reaction to human pressure. Two ways to counteract this inclination are by rattling during the rut, and planning two-person sneak drives near the end of the season. "These drives work best when the hunters enter a buck's sanctuary from the downwind side," McGuire explained. Divide the next couple of hours into ten-minute segments. During the first ten minutes, one hunter may sneak around but the other must stay put. The second one stands immobile, watching for any buck movements and waiting for a shot. By alternating these ten-minute periods of sneaking and standing, it's possible to really cover a thick, brushy area where a big buck might be hiding."

Although McGuire continually tries to pattern trophy bucks, he's quick to admit that the animals' movements are governed by complex factors including lunar cycles, human pressure, amount and type of forage, and the advancing rut, any one of which could be enough to change a buck's routine. Like so many other dedicated hunters, he says he sees many deer out in foul weather during the rut, and a large percentage of these deer are mature bucks.

"I believe these bucks are anxious to freshen scrapes diluted by rain," he stated. "This works to a hunter's advantage in a couple of ways. First, deer's senses are dulled when it's nasty out. They rely less on scent and more on their eyesight. If you happen to see one freshen a scrape during the rain, get ready. There's an excellent chance that when the rain stops he'll return from the same direction in which he left to freshen his scrape again. This linear movement between scrapes during and after foul weather is one of the most predictable whitetail behaviors I've observed. The one drawback, especially for a bowhunter, is that if you do hit a deer, the blood trail will be harder to follow."

McGuire has hunted in three different habitat types: river bottoms, typical of plains hunting in Montana; deep woods, like those in Pennsylvania; and agricultural areas like those in the Midwest. Bucks from each habitat develop unique movement patterns.

"Always use topo maps before entering a potential hunting area," he advises. "An hour spent really looking over a topo map can be more productive than several hours spent running randomly through the woods. Look for good ways to get into your area, trying not to cross deer trails. Find waterways to wade in for a scent-free approach to ridge bases whenever possible. Remember that rub and scrape lines often run along ridges, especially along the prevailing upwind edges of ridges or hills where a deer can quickly catch suspicious scents. I've noticed that bucks rely much more on the wind in mature forests than they do in thickets or fields.

"If you want to hunt acorn forage sources, the best ones can be found on the southern and western slopes of hills. When you begin scouting in earnest, try to determine at about what elevation the best acorns are growing. Then set your stand up in a similar site on the hillside where you're planning to hunt. Deer will usually approach a hillside acorn source in the evening from either above or from downwind along the ridge.

"In agricultural areas, bucks become partial to circular routes. Their movements are almost entirely in one direction as they travel around their circuit. A circuit may cover several miles and include multiple bedding and feeding sites that the buck favors. Ag-area bucks usually travel at night and bed in spots where they're able to move with a nosewind to the next feeding area."

McGuire has patterned specific mature bucks whose circuits encompassed periods of from two to six days and lengths of up to seven miles. He advises hunters who plan to hunt agricultural area bucks to plan intercept points based on what they're able to determine about a buck's circuit. The best intercepts are those on trails the buck uses to leave early morning feeding areas.

"Hunters should remember that, even though a buck will usually travel his circuit or junket in one direction, any little thing could make him reverse directions and move the opposite way," McGuire cautioned. "Storm fronts, wind shifts, or hunting pressure are all enough to make him alter his pattern."

McGuire has had success using another agricultural area tactic on big bucks: hunting the standing corn. "Move into unharvested fields from downwind," he explained. "Then slowly move through the rows of corn only when the sounds of the wind rustling in the standing stalks disguise the sounds you make moving. Your object is to catch the buck bedded in the corn. As you get closer to the upwind end of the field, you'll see more deer. Once the corn is harvested, it has an unsettling effect on all the deer in an area as feeding, travel, and bedding are all affected. Be sure to hunt any recently harvested area as long as it coincides with the season."

McGuire has paid a lot of attention to wind and its effects on deer. One thing he's discovered is that he rarely sees deer on evenings with an easterly wind. "Mature bucks are survivors because they are so much more scent-sensitive than other bucks. Just a wind shift is usually enough to make them turn around and head back in a different direction."

Paradoxically, McGuire has reported seeing bucks with large racks traveling through open fields with a tailwind. "Apparently bucks are not averse to traveling any open area with a tailwind as long as they can see for a long way," he said. "And while deer may sometimes tolerate a tailwind as they travel to feeding or bedding grounds in the morning, they almost always move with a nosewind in the evening."

One of McGuire's best strategies involves backtracking a buck in the snow. "If you happen to jump a buck like this in an area with heavy, fresh estrous sign, put your stand up right there. He'll quickly return to take up where he left off, so interested in the rut that he throws caution to the wind. Anyway, most humans leave right away, so I carry a stand with me for just such an eventuality."

For those hunters who watch scrapes he has this advice. "If a buck comes in sneakily and nervous, it's probably a subordinate buck, worried that the dominant buck is somewhere near. If the first thing this buck does is inspect the overhanging limb, you can bet it's a subordinate. But if the buck goes directly to the scrape with his nose to the ground, you're probably looking at the dominant animal. But the dominant isn't always the buck with the best antlers. Super-buck hunters should remember that."

Although McGuire places great faith in an animal's ability to communicate through the use of scent, he's not so sure about the ability of most scent manufacturers to duplicate that scent exactly. For this reason, he won't use commercial interdigital scent or doe-in-estrus urine. "We've discovered that bucks perform the Flehmen lip-curl attempting to identify a doe's pro-estrus urine, not estrus urine," he explained. "Pro-estrus identifies the urine immediately prior to pre-estrus urine."

McGuire has already produced a commercial synthetic interdigital scent that has shown great promise and is hard at work on duplicating the pro-estrus urine as well. For trips to his stand, McGuire prefers to use red fox urine on both his rubber boots and on one glove that's used to deflect any branches obstructing his travel path.

Bob was one of the earliest hunters to recognize the advantages that deer calls could bring to the hunter. He's learned a lot more about the tactic. "If a buck is alone he'll respond better to the sound of a soft, tending grunt, occasionally used," he said. "If he's in the company of another deer, that's when you have to wear out your call, blowing it almost constantly for as long a time as you have to. I've called at bucks almost 250 yards away and had them come in. First, get their attention with a loud contact call. I make this—and all calls—with my mouth and it sounds almost like a cry. I've videoed so many deer that I've called to study their responses that I'm beginning to predict with a high degree of reliability whether or not I'll be able to call a particular animal in close enough to bowkill."

Some procedures must always be followed when attempting to call deer, McGuire warns. "Never move if a deer is facing towards you. Never call if he's looking towards you. Only call when he's either moving in another direction, hidden by brush, or looking away."

McGuire outlines many of these strategies in greater detail on his many deer hunting videos. By following them, hunters will not only become better deer hunters, their success rates on superbucks should also improve.

23

Bob Zaiglin

Bob Zaiglin has one of the dream jobs. He combines his background in wildlife biology with his love of deer and the outdoors to make a good living from doing what he likes best: studying big whitetails! As wildlife manager for the Harrison Ranches in Texas, Zaiglin is in the unique position of actually being able to manipulate the whitetail populations on 200,000 acres. He can do what the rest of us can only imagine: build his own superbuck population. In the process, he's learned a lot about what makes a superbuck tick and he's taken a bunch of big deer as well.

Zaiglin doesn't rely heavily on genetic research or some of the off-the-wall techniques employed by other Texas ranches to accomplish this task. He relies on tried and true methods such as working hard to improve the habitat so that it can not only support cattle, it can also grow big deer. By conducting doe hunts and culling a number of small bucks each year as well, he's been able to build the Harrison bucks into some of the biggest and best in the country. Several Harrison hunters have taken bucks that have grossed high enough to be included in the Boone and Crockett *Records Book of North American Big Game.* Even more bucks have just missed. Zaiglin himself has taken close to twenty bucks that score 150 points or better. One of them made the record book, and several came within a hair's breadth of making it.

How did one guy get so lucky? "I was born and raised in Pennsylvania where you couldn't hunt on your own until you were 16," Zaiglin said. "I just had an urge to hunt, even though no one else in my family did except my grandfather. When I was eleven, I'd tag along with my neighbor when he took his beagles out rabbit hunting after school. I went deer hunting with a shotgun and slugs for the first time when I was 13 and I was hooked on the sport. When I turned 15, my parents bought me a .300 Savage. And I got my first buck, a five-pointer, when I was 17." Zaiglin says that the thrill of that first buck is still his most exciting hunting experience ever.

Zaiglin's love of deer hunting expanded from that point onward. He began hunting in both Pennsylvania and West Virginia and took four bucks during the next three years. "It was quite an accomplishment to take *any* buck in the area that I was hunting during the mid-1960s," Zaiglin recalled. "With lots of hunters pursuing every buck in the woods, the averages were definitely against me."

Zaiglin went on to graduate from West Virginia University with a degree in wildlife biology. "Wildlife has been good to me," he said. "I'd already gotten so much enjoyment out of my days in the field that I wanted to be in a position to give something back to the resource. And I couldn't think of a better way than by learning as much as I could about wildlife so that I could eventually work *for* wildlife. I had some anxious moments, though. I thoroughly enjoyed hunting and I knew that most wildlife biologists were plenty busy during hunting season. My choice of careers might have eventually wound up limiting my hunting time in the field, but I felt it was a chance I'd have to take." Then he received a fellowship for graduate studies at the Caesar Kleberg Wildlife Research Institute at Texas A&I University in Kingsville, Texas. The Caesar Kleberg Institute was at the forefront of antler research studies in the United States.

During the time he was at A&I, Zaiglin had the opportunity of doing some of his graduate work while under the supervision of Al Brothers, who helped pioneer whitetail deer management programs on Texas ranches. Brothers, manager of the H.B. Zachry Co. Ranch, was one of the very first biologists to manipulate habitat in order to increase the antler size of the ranch's bucks.

When Zaiglin graduated in 1978 with a master's degree in range and wildlife science, he went to work with Dr. James Kroll at Stephen F. Austin State University, another noted big buck researcher. There, Zaiglin was in charge of telemetry and field research studies.

When the opportunity finally arose for him to go to work for Valley View Ranch in east Texas—to put to work all the management techniques and practices that he'd been studying for so long—he couldn't turn it down. During the five years he worked at Valley View he studied another technique as well: rattling horns for big whitetail bucks. To this day, rattling is his favorite way to hunt *el muy grande* buck.

Zaiglin really struck gold when he went to work for Dan Harrison II and Bruce Harrison in the type of job that all biologists dream of: wildlife manager of almost a quarter of a million west and south Texas acres. As a certified wildlife biologist with an extensive background in big buck management, Zaiglin's credentials impressed the Harrisons enough that he has been allowed wide latitude in managing these extensive ranch holdings and in developing increased hunting opportunities on them. During the first six years of putting his management theories into practice, Zaiglin noticed a significant improvement in the quality of the game at each location. Part of this was due to the generally good weather conditions existing for much of the time. Without sufficient rainfall, habitat deteriorates and the quality of a whitetail's rack can be severely affected. Other whitetail ranges don't reflect the immediate cause and effect relationship between weather and deer that's evident in Zaiglin's Texas bailiwick. And while there's no denying the indirect influence of rainfall on the Harrison's whitetail quality, it soon became obvious that the bucks were getting bigger for other reasons as well.

"Quite frankly, Boone and Crockett bucks don't fit the norm for whitetails," Zaiglin said. "They're actually freaks within a population. Even down here where we manage for large antlers under the best type of harvest constraints imaginable, you won't find a Boone and Crockett class buck behind every mesquite bush. We've got some, but just like anywhere else you have to work for them."

Zaiglin manipulates habitat in a variety of ways to ensure that the bucks have enough good quality forage to grow outstanding antlers. "We do a lot of roller chopping," he said. "That's using a bulldozer to pull four large rollers that chop the brush. When brush is cut back it allows undergrowth to sprout, creating lots of new, succulent forage. Another benefit of cutting back the brush is that it increases visibility so we're able to see the kinds of deer we're producing."

Zaiglin also plants food plots and does some prescribed burning to encourage palatable plants. Burning knocks back the vegetative overstory, letting in more light and permitting more forbs—ideal deer food—to grow. Tank pond construction and upkeep ensures a reliable water supply. When all these factors are combined with sufficient doe harvest, buck quality can improve dramatically, something that's already happened at the Piloncillo Ranch. Zaiglin is implementing the same kinds of changes at the Harrison's Sonora Ranch, and there should be a significant improvement in the quality of the deer there as well.

Zaiglin's personal management philosophy is this: manage so that the deer will do well even in bad times; that way, when optimum conditions exist deer quality is *excellent.*

"The climate in south Texas can be rough on deer and that's often reflected in low recruitment replenishment numbers," Zaiglin explained. "In 1983, for example, we had a fawn survival rate of between seven and 14 percent. In 1987 it skyrocketed to 65 percent and then dropped down to between 25 percent and 30 percent in 1988. We don't harvest predators on the ranches I manage as part of my management plan. I believe that mountain lions, bobcats, and coyotes all play a natural part in a deer herd's population dynamics by helping to regulate the population in places where I'm not able to achieve my population objectives. When you're looking at over 200,000 acres, there's no way that you can accurately determine what exactly is needed to best manipulate herd numbers. I let the predators help me out.

"During the course of a hunting season I see many, many bucks that I've never seen before. Many of them I rattle up. Hunters who don't think you can rattle up a big buck should think again. It's possible but it's by no means easy, even down here. Remember, to get a good set of antlers means that buck has had to survive for five or six years. Big bucks run the gauntlet of survival for that entire time. They get good at avoiding humans. They don't get big by being stupid, even where we can offer them a measure of security. When a buck tops 160 Boone and Crockett points, the odds are slim that anyone will ever see him. Even with very little hunting pressure, most bucks in this class become primarily nocturnal."

Zaiglin is a firm believer in rattling, but he warns anyone who is thinking of trying it to be extremely careful. "Every time you call in a little buck—the kind that's most likely to respond—you run the risk of educating him. He might see you or get your scent. If he does, he'll be warier in the future. And if he spooks, he's liable to warn off any bigger bucks lurking nearby, the ones letting the smaller bucks risk any possible danger."

Rattling works well on the Harrison Ranches because Zaiglin manages for a good buck–to–doe ratio, something around 1:2. But because of the high buck to doe ratio, scrape hunting is a complete bust. "We've got lots of bucks so we've got lots of scrapes," Zaiglin explained. "They're superabundant because there's so much competition for does. In other areas, a big buck's scrape can be his undoing. It lets the hunter know there's a big deer in the neighborhood. Down here, scrape hunting usually just won't work."

Zaiglin likes to make an analogy about rattling. "Rattling is to deer as an ambulance and sirens are to people. When you hear them you want to know what's going on. When deer hear the sounds of rattling they're curious. They want to know what's going on, too. So they come on in to see if they can find out."

Calling is another Zaiglin secret. "The grunt call will work by itself," he said. "Last year, using the call alone, I was able to attract and hold my biggest buck ever, the one that grossed 173⅝ points. This buck came in strictly out of curiosity. Calling works well alone, but when you combine it with rattling it can be downright deadly."

A superbuck's biggest failing occurs during the rut, Zaiglin believes, when he often will ignore caution to pursue a willing doe. "You have to spend as much time as you can in the woods during the rut," he advised. "The late rut is especially important. Big bucks are still difficult, but you just might trip one up at this time."

Zaiglin feels that coverup scents and sex scents probably work best on public land where there's lots of hunting pressure and you want to squelch any human odor. But he questions the ability of any of the scent producers to consistently produce a top quality doe-in-estrus urine.

He has several favorite methods of hunting the brush country. He'll walk or stalk along small ridges, or possibly consider a ground blind in an area that he feels holds a hot deer crossing. He prefers ground blinds because of the mobility factor: you can just get up and move without a lot of disturbance.

As for what type of hunting conditions work best, Zaiglin much prefers weather that turns cold after having been continually hot. If a misty rain is falling that's even better. "Overcast conditions are usually ideal," he said.

He doesn't like hunting hot days during a full moon although he has had some success hunting the midday period on days like this. Protracted telemetry studies on the Piloncillo Ranch confirm that mature bucks are much more active at midday during the rut.

A Texas ranch may just be your best bet to get a superbuck, but the ones like the Piloncillo don't come cheap—$6,500 for a five-day hunt. At that, the waiting list is so long that it's likely that most of the hunters on it will never have the opportunity to hunt the ranch. A far better chance exists for hunting the Sonora Ranch, which is building better buck quality. Here, for about $2,500 (the 2001 rate for three days), a hunter stands an excellent chance of harvesting a buck in the 130- to 140-point class. And within the next couple of years, it's quite probable that the bucks will average even larger, even though a 130-point buck is nothing to sneeze at.

Bob Zaiglin feels that he's the luckiest hunter in the world. Right now, he's taken lots of good bucks and helped others take them, too. He's probably the most successful wildlife biologist in Texas. He's in demand as a speaker and writer, and is a consulting biologist for a number of hunting magazines. Bob lives in Uvalde with his wife, Jan, another excellent whitetail hunter, and two daughters. Bob is living proof that you can have it all.

24

The Number One Typical Whitetail: the Hanson Buck

When the 1992 whitetail hunting season drew to a close, few in the hunting world would have predicted that it would be the last full year of the James Jordan buck's reign as undisputed ruler of its narrow universe, that of the Number One Typical Whitetail Trophy in the record books. Indeed, there were even some among the hunting cognoscenti who had dared to predict that the Jordan Buck was too large and too perfect to ever fall; that it would remain number one forever. That was not to be the case.

When Milo Hanson, a deer hunter from the farm country near Biggar, Saskatchewan, joined in a deer drive in November of 1993, it would prove to be the most important deer drive of his life. The area around Biggar is flush with rolling forests of poplar and stretches of open pastureland. Such terrain is made to order for deer drives and the hunters who know how best to conduct them. Hanson and his hunting partners had been driving this country for deer for many seasons. On this morning, the four men would be hunting land owned by Hanson.

Hanson was joined on that fateful morning of November 23 by one of his neighbors, John Yaroshko. Hanson and Yaroshko drove over to meet Rene Igini and Walter Meger with whom they had planned to hunt that day. As soon as the two had pulled up, Meger and Igini told them about a monster buck they'd watched enter a nearby willow run. What's more, they were told, the big buck had not come out of the thicket.

Fresh snow blanketed the surrounding forest and fields so tracking would be easy. Igini followed the buck's trail while the rest of the hunters took up positions around the willow patch. Hanson took a stand to the south of the willows. As luck would have it, the big buck bolted in his direction. As Hanson tells it, that was his first real look at the buck. "My heart was pumping," he said. "We shot, but missed it."

Igini continued his dogged pursuit of the buck. More than once, the tracks were lost when the big deer wandered into places where other deer had been feeding or hiding. All day long the four men stayed on the buck's track, pushing the animal from poplar patch to willow thicket and back again. They were just about to give up when the huge whitetail ran out of a stand of aspens and into a narrow neck of willows growing upon Hanson's land.

Three of the men posted themselves around the willows, while Igini walked the buck's tracks. The buck raced from cover and gave the standers a running, broadside shot from a distance of about 150 yards. Hanson and Igini fired several times apiece, but no bullet found its mark.

The buck had darted into the next run of willows. This time, though, when the buck ran out, it turned directly away from Hanson. He shot, and the buck sagged to its knees. "You got him!" Yaroshko yelled, in what would prove to be a somewhat premature statement.

The buck staggered to its feet and took off, heading for another patch of aspens. Hanson ran after it, racing up the hill to the last place where he'd seen the giant deer. When he reached the spot, he looked down the hill and saw the buck below him. The big deer was standing stock-still. Hanson raised his gun, aimed through his 4-power scope and fired a shot from his .308 Winchester Model 88 lever-action rifle. Down went the buck. But Hanson could still see its head and massive rack over a clump of willows. He fired again, putting the buck down for good.

The buck was declared the new Boone and Crockett Club World's Record in Dallas, Texas, at the 22nd Big Game Awards Program. In being so declared, the new world's record Hanson Buck scored 213⅝ and didn't just break the Jordan Buck's record of 206⅛ points—it shattered it. The buck that some said couldn't be beaten had been, and how!

"Shooting this buck gave me a feeling I will probably never experience again, even though I had no idea it would be declared the world record," Hanson said in an interview with Boone and Crockett Club officials. "I had never seen a bigger buck. The buck left me shaking."

The buck has left many other superbuck hunters shaking as well. Shaking in the dim hope that someday, we too might be blessed with even the merest glimpse of something approaching the splendor of that magnificent crown of antlers worn so proudly by the new world-champion Hanson Buck.

We may mourn the passing of the days when the Jordan Buck reigned supreme, but if this rack was to be usurped, at least it is to a worthy and perfect new champion. As the French so aptly put it: "The king is dead. Long live the king!"

25

The Number Two Typical Whitetail: the Jordan Buck

Even in deer hunting some things are truly stranger than fiction. Start with the chances that a buck—any buck—will someday achieve Boone and Crockett status. The odds are probably greater that someone will breed another super-racehorse like Secretariat. After all, there are a limited number of thoroughbreds being bred each year, and experts handpick the pairs to be bred for specific traits of the parents, like speed, endurance, and heart.

The trophy whitetail, on the other hand, is a chance concoction of one doe out of millions and one buck out of millions coming together to mate. No one has papers on either one of them. And yet, in a good percentage of the cases, there is an excellent chance that the off-spring, if male, will attain Boone and Crockett size—that is, if he lives long enough and gets the proper nutrition. Living long enough is a problem today: just look at how few bucks out of the millions born each year make it into Boone and Crockett.

What could be stranger than the story of the former all-time num-ber one typical whitetail buck, an animal that sprung from precisely this type of random mating? What could be stranger than the fact that this huge, almost perfect buck held on for years to its number one record book status *by only 1⅝ points?* Or the fact that the buck was killed almost 75 years ago and then lost by the hunter for 50 years? It's an incredibly strange story—but that is exactly what hap-pened.

Let's take a step back in time to the snowy dawn of November 20, 1914 when 22-year-old James Jordan and his friend Egus Davis set out on a quest for some venison. The two friends were hunting just south of Danbury, Wisconsin, along the Yellow River near a place where the Soo Line Railroad cut a swath through the river valley.

The two hunters traveled through the valley in a rented horse and wagon, keeping an eye out for deer the whole time. Shortly after dawn, Davis was rewarded when he settled his rifle bead on a lone doe and pulled the trigger. The deer dropped in its tracks, falling in a thick blanket of newly fallen snow. Davis, who had forgotten his knife, borrowed Jordan's to clean the doe. And since he now had his meat, Egus Davis was all for quitting on the spot and packing it in for the day.

But Jordan hadn't connected yet, and he was a stubborn hunter. So he decided to continue hunting while Davis made the trip back to his farm with the doe. Once Davis and the wagon were out of sight, Jordan began slipping quietly towards the river, keeping a sharp eye out for any new, tell-tale deer sign.

It wasn't long before Jordan came to a spot where several sets of fresh tracks cut across the snow. He looked, then looked again. One set of tracks was enormous. Jordan immediately imagined that they belonged to a tremendous buck and set off on the trail.

It was easy tracking in the snow. So easy that Jordan was unaware of how close he was getting to the point where the railroad tracks almost merged with the river. When Jordan finally did realize it, he paused, just as a train whistled from around the bend. The whistle startled the deer, and the big buck, along with three does, jumped up from their beds in a weedy thicket right in front of Jordan. The buck stood there majestically, poised against the snowy backdrop, as he listened to the train come hurtling around the curve. Jordan instinctively shouldered his gun and took aim at the neck of the biggest buck he'd ever seen. Slowly, he squeezed off a shot.

At the sound of the shot, the deer split up. The does went one way while the magnificent buck went another. Jordan fired at the buck until he'd emptied his magazine, but the buck took off as if unhit and literally disappeared from sight.

At that point, Jordan was shaking. He felt reasonably sure that at least one of his bullets had hit the big deer although there was no blood trail. And when he felt in his pockets, his positive feeling gradually became a sinking one in the pit of his stomach when he realized that he had only one shell left. Resolutely Jordan chambered the round and vowed to make it good, if kind, when he got the chance.

Jordan got on the buck's track and stuck to it like glue. The big buck was running flat out and at first he gave not one bit of evidence of Jordan's belief that he'd probably hit the buck with his very first shot. The buck's track snaked through the thick brush on an eventual intersect with the Yellow River. Jordan followed behind, looking hard for blood. He could barely believe his eyes when he finally saw what he was hoping he would. Blood! And although it wasn't much, it proved that his gut instinct had been right.

By dogging the buck's tracks, Jordan eventually caught sight of the big animal as it wove through the brush ahead of him. By now, there was no denying that the bullet was having an effect on the buck. He was slowing noticeably. Soon, Jordan was able to keep the buck in sight continuously, although he had no chance for a good, clean shot. But still, he stayed right behind the deer as the two of them got closer and closer to the shallow Yellow River.

Jordan was well aware that the gun he was using was on the light side for such a big whitetail. With only one shell left, he resolved to wait for the closest shot he could get. He stayed on the deer's trail, and, eventually, the stumbling animal came to the very edge of the river. Uncannily, they were now at a point only a couple of hundred yards from the Jordan farm where he and Davis had started out in such high spirits that very morning.

Now Jordan felt sure that the buck was on his last legs as he watched him falter at the edge of the current. But the buck surprised him once again by jumping into the river. As Jordan himself moved up to a spot on the edge of the river, he watched as the big deer stumbled out on the shore on the other side. By now, he could tell the buck was failing visibly. And although most of us would question Jordan's choice, he opted for a spine shot to bring the buck down clean and fast.

Luckily for him, as the gun cracked, the buck fell. Jordan's heart was in his throat as he quickly waded through the icy water, keeping an eye on his prize the whole time. He knew only too well of the possibility that the buck might once again take off, leaving him standing there with an empty gun. But this time, luck was with him. The buck was down for good, and Jordan could finally get a close-up look at the magnificent antlers and huge body. He wasn't disappointed. The rack was as perfect as one is likely to get with ten long, heavy points and massive main beams that were almost palmated where the tines sprouted upward. Estimates placed the deer's body weight at 400 pounds, truly a monarch worthy of the incredible set of antlers. The antlers themselves were rubbed to a golden-brown patina that gave off a warm glow amid the frozen landscape. To say that Jim Jordan was overwhelmed would be an understatement.

When Jordan attempted to field-dress the buck, he realized that he'd lent his knife to Egus Davis earlier that morning. The deer wouldn't spoil in the sub-freezing weather, so Jordan headed back to the farm to find Davis and tell him about his good fortune.

Davis couldn't wait to get back to see the buck based on Jordan's description. But as Jordan brought him back to the spot where he had left the deer, his feelings of elation suddenly turned cold and hollow. For the deer was no longer on the river bank. In fact, it wasn't in sight at all. Jordan was in a sweat. Where could it have gone? Quickly, he analyzed the situation and came to the realization that, just possibly, the buck had given one final, reflexive kick after he'd gone for Davis. And quite possibly, that kick might have catapulted him off the bank and into the swiftly-moving Yellow River.

Panicky now, Davis and Jordan ran downstream along the river's bank until they located the carcass. It was hanging over a rock about halfway across the stream. Jordan didn't even give it a second thought: he waded right out into the hip-deep water to lay claim to his prize once and for all. Or so he thought.

Jordan was, quite simply, the talk of the town. Sight-seers came from miles around to see his tremendous trophy. No one had ever seen a buck even remotely close to the buck that Jordan had taken that day in 1914. And even though Jordan was anything but rich, because the deer was so special, he decided to have it mounted.

George Van Castle, a taxidermist who lived in the nearby town of Webster, Wisconsin, offered to mount Jordan's buck for the sum of five dollars. So Jordan turned the unskinned head over to Van Castle, who promptly took it back to Webster. Thus began Jordan's second odyssey for the largest typical buck of all time.

It seems that Van Castle didn't stay in Webster for very long. When his wife died, he soon afterwards pulled up stakes and moved to Hinckley, Minnesota. When Jordan hadn't heard from Van Castle for several months, he took a trip to Webster to find the taxidermist. What he found instead was that Van Castle had moved to Hinckley. But Van Castle might as well have lived hundreds of miles away instead of the 25 miles it actually was. For in between Hinckley and Danbury was a deep, swift stretch of the St. Croix River, a stretch that had no bridge. By the time Jordan did get to Hinckley, he found out that Van Castle had moved again—to Florida this time. And for all anyone knew, he'd taken Jordan's spectacular buck with him.

No one knew it then, of course, but Jordan's mounted buck never made the trip to Florida. Van Castle had stored the mount in the attic of his old house in Hinckley where it gathered cobwebs and dust bunnies for the next 44 years. In yet another strange twist of fate, Jordan and his wife eventually moved to Hinckley where they operated a tavern for many years.

It was 1958 before the huge whitetail made his next appearance. This time the trophy turned up at a rummage sale in Sandstone, Minnesota. Bob Ludwig, a forest technician for the Minnesota Department of Natural Resources, was so impressed with the size of the decrepit mount's antlers that he bought them for three dollars. According to Ludwig, by this time the antlers were black with accumulated filth. The mount itself was altogether worthless with sawdust leaking out from innumerable openings in the moth-eaten deer hide.

In 1964 Ludwig read an article detailing the method used by the Boone and Crockett Club to score whitetail antlers. Intrigued, he decided to measure the big rack. Imagine his surprise when his preliminary measurements gave the antlers the score of 205 points, at that time a new world record. Ludwig didn't have a lot of faith in his figures, so he mailed his completed score sheet to an official scorer in St. Paul, Minnesota. The scorer, Bernie Fashingbauer, talked to Ludwig by telephone and although the two men decided to arrange a date to conclusively score the antlers, no firm date was set.

It was over a year later when Fashingbauer was hunting in the neighborhood and noticed Ludwig's name on a mailbox. He dropped in and scored the head at 206⅝ points, a new world's record. Later, in 1981, the head was sent to Pennsylvania and the score was changed to 206⅛ points when a math error was discovered.

But what had happened to Jordan? Unbelievably, Jordan was Ludwig's cousin. And after the rack was initially scored in 1964, Ludwig made a point of meeting with Jordan to show off the incredible set of antlers. Jordan didn't need a second look to come to the conclusion that the antlers weren't so mysterious after all. Indeed, they belonged to the buck that he had shot on that long-ago snowy morning of November 20, 1914.

Ludwig was unconvinced. For one thing, Jordan's buck had supposedly had a bullet hole through its rack. This buck didn't. All witnesses to the event were long since dead. The debate continued for years as Jordan tried to convince officials at Boone and Crockett that the buck was indeed his.

In the meantime, a trophy collector, Dr. Charles Arnold, purchased the incredible set of antlers from Ludwig for $1,500. But the controversy continued on whether the buck was from Wisconsin, like Jordan claimed, or from Minnesota, where the rack eventually had come to light. James Jordan never relented in his belief that the buck was his. Eventually, Fashingbauer, Arnold, and the Boone and Crockett Club itself uncovered enough evidence to convince a Boone and Crockett committee that Jordan had killed the magnificent number one typical trophy in Danbury, Wisconsin.

Jordan spent ten long years trying to convince everyone involved that the buck was his. He wasn't interested in money, only the recognition that came from taking such a spectacular animal. James Jordan died in October of 1978 at the age of 86. The buck was officially declared as the product of James Jordan's hunt by the Boone and Crockett Club in December of 1978. In one final, bizarre twist, James Jordan's buck did indeed elude him in the one place it mattered most, in the record book.

26

The Number Thirteen Typical Whitetail: the Brunk Buck

There are lots of exciting stories about top Boone and Crockett bucks, but the tale of Jeffrey Brunk's big typical is almost unsurpassed. Brunk, a 16-year old from Revere, Missouri, had already gained an enviable reputation as a top-notch whitetail hunter by the autumn of 1967. What's more, he did it in the space of three short years. He was allowed to use a gun for the first time when he was 14. Since that birthday, he'd managed to connect on both an archery deer and a firearms deer each season. In fact, during his very first firearms season, he managed to bag a big 12-point buck that eventually dressed out at 215 pounds. "That's probably the largest buck you'll ever see," said his proud father. His father was wrong. Three years later, he got his first glimpse of the big buck he nicknamed "the Phantom." And that was when he decided to try to claim the trophy as his own.

Revere is located right near the Iowa border in the extreme northeastern corner of the state. At the time, Brunk lived with his family on a 300-acre farm. His father raised pigs and grew corn, soybeans and other crops. Jeff was a typical farmboy who liked all types of hunting, but who was particularly crazy about deer hunting.

The Brunk farm lay smack dab in the middle of the Corn Belt, a place where bucks grow fat and sassy, given half the chance. Far from a habitat of row crops and pastures, this portion of the state is cut up with lots of woods and cedar thickets, places to which bragging-sized bucks could escape from the local hunters who took to the field each fall in the hope of putting some venison in the freezer.

It was only by the sheerest coincidence that young Jeff Brunk even became aware of the Phantom's existence. He was returning home from a day of quail hunting with some friends when three deer bolted from a wooded draw. First, two does took off and ran across an opening; they were followed by a much larger deer. Brunk initially thought he was watching a couple of fawns followed by their mother. But when the third deer skylined itself on the top of a large hill,

Brunk could pick out tremendous, pure white antlers. "He was by far the largest buck any of us had ever seen," Brunk said.

Archery season was in full swing, so Brunk and his friends hurried home, got their bows, and returned to the spot, full of enthusiasm. They'd seen the buck dart into a woodlot that was surrounded by open fields and they figured he must still be in there. Although they drove the area thoroughly, the buck managed to outmaneuver them. To this day, Brunk believes that the big buck was holding tight in the woods. "The big ones are like that," he said. "And this particular one was just too smart for us."

Even though the big buck was a trophy of staggering proportions, Brunk and his friends were the first hunters who had actually sighted him. And that's why he gave the animal the nickname "the Phantom." "His horns were so white and ghostly that the name just seemed to fit," Brunk commented. "To get as big as he was, he must have stayed pretty well-hidden during the day and come out only at night to feed. He slipped up when he let us see him."

Slip up he did. Young Brunk's pursuit of the buck became relentless. Although he didn't have much evidence to guide him, he started hunting for the deer. Unfortunately for Brunk, the Phantom evaded him for the rest of the year.

The year 1968 started out on the same discordant note. Archery deer season opened on October 1st, but by the time firearms season rolled around in mid-November, Brunk had still not seen the animal. He hadn't heard of anyone else seeing him either, so his hopes were high that the deer still roamed the countryside.

It was on the second or third day of gun season. Brunk jumped several does while stillhunting along the side of a deep hollow. "As I watched the does run off, the Phantom suddenly jumped up and ran after them," Brunk related. "At that time, all I had was an automatic shotgun with slugs. I shot twice but I knew it was hopeless . . . he was too far out for any shotgun. I felt sick."

The young hunter was thoroughly frustrated. When he arrived home that evening, he told his father that he had to have a deer rifle, and that he would buy one himself before the next deer season. On that note, he went to bed.

The Phantom seemed to have been swallowed up by a crack in the earth. Brunk couldn't turn up hide or hair of him the rest of the year. But the balance of the year was not spent in vain. "First, I knew his home range had to be much larger than I originally thought it was," he said. "I'd seen him twice. The two different locations were several miles apart. And since I still hadn't heard of anyone else spotting him, again I decided that he must be almost completely nocturnal."

The boy discovered other information about the big buck by relentlessly stalking through the neighboring hills. "Soon I could recognize his tracks," he commented. "And I finally began turning up big rubs and scrapes that I knew had to be his."

In 1969, things started looking up in Brunk's quest for the Phantom. His father, a hunter himself, understood completely what his son was going through. He knew how much the teenager wanted to bag the big buck. So for graduation, even though times were financially tight, he bought him a Browning automatic rifle in .30/06 caliber. Now Brunk had the range. But would he get the chance to use his new gun on the Phantom?

Jeff realized that his best chance for the big buck would come during the firearms season when the whitetail rut was in full swing in Missouri. So he killed a doe during archery season and resolved to concentrate on the Phantom once the gun season opened. He'd added even more information to his gradually expanding knowledge of the big buck's area. He'd located an area of dense clear thickets where he believed the Phantom bedded during the day.

Missouri's firearms deer season lasts only nine days. Traditionally, it starts on a Saturday. By the second Sunday—the last legal day of the firearms season—Brunk realized that it looked like the Phantom would win the battle of wits once more. By 9:00 A.M. Jeff had been stillhunting for several hours, his favorite whitetail tactic.

"I was hunting the lower portion of a hillside that was covered with cedar," he said. "I was moving very slowly, not making a sound, in an area where I'd found several of the Phantom's large scrapes. I knew he had to be in there somewhere.

"Even though I'd been stalking for a couple of hours, I'd only traveled a short distance up this one particular draw that cut up the hill. Suddenly, I saw him moving through the woods in front of me. At first, all I could see was that huge set of white antlers."

Immediately, Brunk dropped to one knee and raised his rifle. When the deer stepped into a small opening about 50 yards away, Brunk squeezed the trigger. "He turned and ran," Brunk remembered, "but I couldn't see any sign that I'd hit him. I looked for blood but with no luck. I still figured I must have hit him, so I took off in the same direction that he had run, towards an area with several draws filled with heavy cover. I figured if I'd wounded him he'd probably go there to hole up. I guessed right. He was in the very first draw. When I got close and he heard me, he barrelled out of there. But it was much too thick for me to shoot at him again.

"He disappeared over a rise and I could hear him run into the next draw. I listened and could tell that he stopped again. I figured he must be hit fairly hard to keep stopping like that. But since I still hadn't found any blood, I wasn't really sure. When I went down in the draw after him, he took off again. This time I managed to shoot twice."

Brunk finally found some blood even though he wasn't sure which shot had connected. "There were only a few drops, but at least I knew I'd hit him."

Brunk tracked the deer across a field and into some timber on the other side. By the time the boy reached the timber, however, the blood trail had all but disappeared. "I had to get on my hands and knees to try to find any trace of him," he said. "I tracked him for a long time, losing the trail several times along the way. Once I had to make a big circle to find another spot of blood, and when I did it was 300 yards away from the last spot I'd found.

"At this point, he started bleeding a little bit more. So I was able to keep after him as he climbed a ridge. As soon as I topped the ridge, I jumped him. And this time as he ran straight away from me I was able to shoot three more times. The third shot hit his femoral artery, and he really slowed down. I could tell that he stopped but I couldn't see to shoot."

At this point, Brunk tried to move into a better position. When he did, once more the buck took off running. Again, the boy fired and again he scored a hit, this time in a rear leg. "That last shot dragged him down to a walk. By this time I was feeling awful. I didn't want him to suffer but he just kept on going," Brunk recalled.

Finally, the Phantom stopped and turned broadside to Brunk at a distance of about 100 yards. "When I shot this time, he dropped in his tracks. I was relieved that at last I'd put him down for good." Unfortunately, the buck was down but not quite out. As he approached his trophy, the Phantom jumped up and once again attempted to run off. Brunk fired his final shot from only 20 yards out, and the deer that wouldn't die went down for good.

It had been over three hours since Brunk had fired his first shot. "I fired nine times and had only brought ten cartridges with me that morning," Brunk said. "My first shot had gone through one lung. That alone should have put him down sooner than it did. Of the nine shots I'd taken, I hit him seven times. Three of the shots had hit him right in the boiler room, but he just wouldn't give up."

Brunk knew the big 13-point Phantom buck was record book material. So after field-dressing him, he covered him up with brush and hurried home to get his family. "I felt both sad and happy," he said. "When you kill an animal like that, you can't help but feel some regret."

A green score of 185 Boone and Crockett points meant that the buck was quite probably a new state record. After the 60-day drying period, an official scorer gave the Phantom 197⅝ points, unquestionably the new state record. When the buck was officially measured by the Boone and Crockett records committee, he scored 199⅝ points and ranked number four in the book.

This closeup of the preorbital gland shows the secretions containing pheromones that deer use to leave messages on rubbing trees. Likewise, the rough-haired area visible on the forehead is packed with the sudoriferous glands that deer biologists theorize also secrete pheromones. *photo courtesy Jan Roth.*

Casting is the final stage of the antler cycle. Antlers aren't usually shed at the same time; note the raw pedicel in the process of healing over. A buck's behavior is keyed by the antler growth cycle; after casting the bucks are much less aggressive. *photo courtesy Duncan Dobie.*

A whitetail saying "I was here" with pheromones from his saliva; both does and bucks will "sign in." *photo courtesy Bob McGuire.*

The buck that tore up this pine meant business; note that he rubbed almost halfway through the tree's trunk. If you find a rub like this very early in the season, it's probably a prime buck's core area, and it's time to start scouting the area for a superbuck—fast, before hunting pressure changes his pattern. *photo by the author.*

Stan Potts looks at a superbuck-size rub: most often there's a relationship between the size of the rub and the deer's dominance status. Rubs can tell the hunter a lot more than just that there's a buck in the area, according to the superbuck hunters in Chapter 12. *photo courtesy Stan Potts.*

The salt in a buck's urine will keep snow and ice from sticking to a well-used scrape. Even after the season, it pays to scout for scrapes that are being maintained by the carry-over deer—next season's superbuck. *photo by the author.*

A licking branch is visited all year long by many individual deer—a sort of bulletin board for the area. In early autumn, it may develop into a primary scrape so it pays to scout for these branches early. *photo courtesy Duncan Dobie.*

Look for the licking branch right over an active scrape; it's usually mutilated from repeated antler-raking or chewing by deer depositing pheromones. *photo by the author.*

Proof that spike bucks aren't necessarily genetically inferior: they just need some time and good forage. This year-by-year collection of antlers from J. C. Brown's penned buck shows that by age 6½ the deer sported a respectable eight-point rack. *photo by the author.*

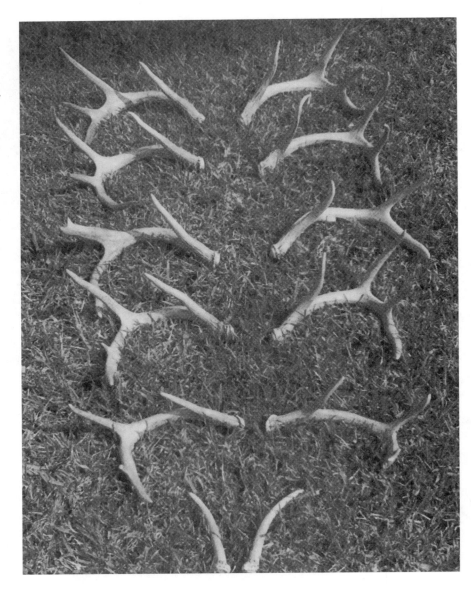

The ideal superbuck stalking scenario: dense cover and thick grass. Big bucks prefer to establish core areas in thick cover, which you can use to your stalking advantage. A skilled, patient stalker can use the cover to get close. *photo by the author.*

A ground stand position downwind from a thicket that may contain a superbuck gives this hunter the dual advantages of mobility and the ability to slip in and out of the hunting area undetected. *photo courtesy Bob Etling.*

A trail as obvious as this one is usually a doe family trail. Superbucks sometimes travel along a well-used trail at the peak of the rut; at other times they're more likely to travel parallel to it and downwind from the trail. *photo by the author.*

Good stand placement helped Harold Knight harvest this nice Kentucky whitetail. You can see "the hunters' edge" in the background, where the thicket breaks off suddenly into a cutover clearing. *photo courtesy of Harold Knight and David Hale.*

Rattle 'em up! Another record-class Texas buck falls to Bob Zaiglin's rattling horns. Zaiglin uses two right antlers so he can really slam them together. "I pound the bases of the antlers into the ground to mimic the sound of running deer. Then I rake at nearby brush with the antlers to make more racket. After that I really clash the antlers together hard for about 15 to 20 seconds. I stop, wait, and then repeat the entire sequence in five minutes." *photo courtesy Bob Zaiglin.*

Bob Zaiglin on his rattling stand. He repeats his rattling sequence as many as six times, with increasing intervals between sequences. But he says, "I seldom stay in one spot for more than fifteen minutes." Does it work? Zaiglin has taken eight bucks that scored over 150 Boone and Crockett points. *photo courtesy of Bob Zaiglin.*

Another superbuck from Bob Zaiglin's management area on the Harrison Ranches in Texas: look at that "cheater" tine on the right antler! *photo courtesy Bob Zaiglin.*

THE WHITETAIL HUNTERS

Murry Burnham is extra careful to use a scent in combination with rattling: "I put doe-in-rut scent downwind from where I rattle, and I wear de-scented clothes. I depend on my cedar oil deer scent to cover my odor and have found that it also attracts deer." *photo courtesy Murry Burnham.*

Gene Wensel, a Montana superbuck hunter, has a number of Pope and Young Club records—and some of them even qualify for Boone and Crockett listings! "Under the right conditions, there is no better place to hunt than at a scrape for a really big trophy whitetail," Gene says. *photo courtesy Gene Wensel.*

Kansas grows wheat, and wheat grows big bucks. Russell Hull harvests them both. Russell masks his stalking movements by imitating natural sounds. "Carry a walking stick to break up the steady rhythm of your two feet. Another trick I use is to call on a diaphragm turkey caller every now and then." For more stalking advice, see Chapter 21. *photo courtesy Russell Hull.*

Some hunters rely on rattling to bring in big bucks like this. Many contend that hunting out of the same tree stand more than three times is taboo because a big buck is smart enough to figure out that something isn't quite right. Stay too long in one tree stand and the resident superbuck may move his activity somewhere else. *photo courtesy Noel Feather.*

Where did Gary LaRose find these Missouri superbucks? On "the hunters' edge" powerline cuts, heavy cover connecting feeding areas to bedding covers—any place where two or more habitat types come together. *photo by the author.*

"Show Me" superbucks: Missouri hunter Jeff Brunk's trophy collection once included his Number Thirteen Boone and Crockett typical whitetail, "The Phantom." Jeff tells the story of his three-year quest for the superbuck in Chapter 26. *photo courtesy Jeff Brunk.*

Bob McGuire calls in Tennessee superbucks with his synthetic lures, calls, and rattling antlers. In Chapter 22, he observes that, "In agricultural areas bucks become partial to circular routes. A circuit may cover several miles and include multiple bedding and feeding sites that the buck favors." He advises hunters to set up intercept points based on the travel pattern. *photo courtesy Bob McGuire.*

Will the next World Record Typical come from Canada? Some big buck experts think it will. The Boone and Crockett entries from Canada suggest there's reason to look for a superbuck trophy where Russell Thornberry took this heavy whitetail in Alberta. Find out which counties and provinces are producing the most superbucks in Chapter 9. *photo courtesy Russell Thornberry.*

Ernie Richardson shows you how to fool a superbuck with mock scrapes in Chapter 11. *photo courtesy Ernie Richardson.*

Oklahoma is OK for superbucks, and Jim Dougherty has made an art of calling whitetails to his bow. "I start out with some clacking noises. Then I build the pace and volume to clacking the antlers together frantically. I rattle for three or four minutes with short intervals in between." *photo courtesy Jim Dougherty.*

This Tennessee superbuck made the mistake of advertising his status as the prime buck to Luther Fuller by making a scrape that measured five feet across! This buck was almost completely nocturnal, but Luther was waiting on stand when the deer made his only mistake. *photo by the author.*

When Harold Knight and David Hale talk on their Pro-Grunter, deer listen. These two Kentucky bucks came within arrow range. Hale once called a buck in from 200 yards away: "What's unbelievable is that he never paused, he just kept on coming all the way. I finally arrowed him at 22 steps." The three important calls for hunting are discussed in Chapter 18. *photo courtesy Harold Knight and David Hale.*

Stanley Potts rattles in Illinois superbucks like this record book whitetail; "the week after the rut's peak is my favorite time. Once bucks have a taste of rutting, it's in their blood—they're boiling to come in." *photo courtesy Stanley Potts.*

Alan Altizer with four of the superbucks he's killed with bow and arrow. He took the Tennessee state archery record (second deer from the right) over an old scrape. "It just so happened that the *old* scrape developed into a new scrape. Part of the reason is that it was also a licking branch location." Alan became a believer in scrape hunting. *photo courtesy Alan Altizer.*

Roger Kildow and two of the Oklahoma bow kills that put his name in the Pope and Young book. *photo courtesy Mike Pearce.*

THE TROPHIES

"Socrates," the trophy no hunter could claim. When he was found dead on a fenceline in suburban St. Louis County, the Missouri State Conservation Department officials were certain he'd score high. He did: the Number 1 is going to be hard to beat, but he's also proof that there are a lot of trophy bucks close to home. *photo courtesy Jim Rathert, Missouri Department of Conservation.*

Close!—but Number 3 in the typical category: Larry Gibson's Missouri whitetail shows the symmetry and length of tines that score high in the Boone and Crockett system. *photo courtesy Jim Rathert, Missouri Department of Conservation.*

Chapter 28 relates some of the controversy that surrounded the discovery of The Hole-In-The-Horn Buck, found hanging in a tavern in Ohio in 1983. A fantastic combination of mass and tines, the buck still comes up second to Socrates. *photo courtesy North American Whitetail Magazine.*

Once the undisputed champion typical whitetail deer, the famous Jordan Buck reigned supreme for more than 20 years. This buck's rack has fewer points than the Gibson Buck, but the Jordan Buck's main beams are longer, and start out almost 1½ inches greater in circumference. He beats out Gibson's buck by just 1⅛ points, but the buck that was said to be "unbeatable" wasn't: the Hanson Buck outscored Jordan's great buck by an incredible 7⅛ points. *photo courtesy of the Boone and Crockett Club.*

Duncan Dobie's amazing record of a non-typical rack's development over more than ten years. It shows what deer's genes can do, given enough time and top-notch nutrition. This pen-reared buck, named Desi, also had the benefit of a stress-free life in captivity which may account for the fact that his antlers were larger at age 10½ than they were at 7 years of age. The lesson is that time and nutrition are critical in the development of superbuck antlers. *photos courtesy Duncan Dobie.*

Desi's first forked antlers as a yearling in 1974.

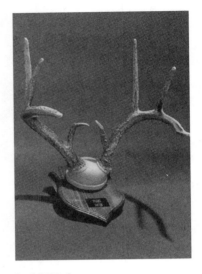

In 1975, he was already showing some mass and length in the G-1 tine.

1976: in three years he shows non-typical antler growth patterns.

In 1977, there's definite palmation.

In 1979, Desi's main beams are still extending forward.

1981: note the larger antler with palmation and the drop tine. The non-typical points, mass, and palmations would have put him in the record book that year.

1982 was a true superbuck antler year: look at those brow tines.

Desi's last set of antlers were mounted with the cape.

The Boone and Crockett Number 1 typical mule deer since 1972 may be a "pretender" to the throne. The Burris Buck holds first place by 9⅞ points, a tremendous margin that, until recently, seemed unlikely to be broken. The hunting world now holds its breath as a buck, unofficially scored at 229⅞ by Boone and Crockett measures an incredible 34 years after being taken in Colorado, seems poised to take over the Number 1 spot. Should the score hold, the new buck would outscore the Burris Buck by 3⅝ points. *photo courtesy the Boone and Crockett Club.*

The Austill Buck, Number 15 Boone and Crockett non-typical mule deer, came to Jim Austill on a snowy day in 1962. It's the third largest non-typical ever taken in Colorado. *photo courtesy Jack Reneau.*

The mind-boggling Mundy Buck was taken by Frank Maestas on the Mundy ranch in New Mexico in 1962, and still holds the Burkett System Number 1 extra-typical record (Number 15 in Boone and Crockett). The outside spread measures over four feet, a spread approaching bull elk measurements. Note there are actually three formal forks on each side of the rack, instead of the usual two mule deer forks. *photo courtesy Bill Mundy.*

A nice mule deer buck in velvet? No, a muley doe with a nice set of 10-point antlers that grew in response to some release of testosterone in her system. *photo courtesy Paul Gilbert.*

A muley sniffs in the urine from a doe he's tending to see if she's approaching estrus, the so-called "Flehmen response" exhibited by both species of deer. *photo courtesy Lee Kline.*

The mule deer superbuck's headquarters in both mountain and desert habitats: the aspen pocket. Since the aspen provides both cover and food, mule deer stick tight in them. *photo by the author.*

A mule deer making a mighty rub high up on a pine tree. Mule deer make many more rubs than whitetails, even though they're not as noticeable. The main purpose seems to be to signal other bucks with the noise. *photo courtesy Lee Kline.*

THE MULE DEER HUNTERS

The late Ted Riggs, perhaps the finest of all the big buck hunters, and one of the mule deer racks he collected on the Arizona Strip area in Idaho. Read about Ted's 5-day hunt for "Bigfoot" in Chapter 45. *photo courtesy Ted Riggs.*

Kirt Darner with a 10 × 9 non-typical mule deer that nets at 273% Boone and Crockett points. Darner once killed a 39-inch spread buck within sight of a busy highway on a hillside that was "so steep and rocky that it discouraged hunters, even though they passed by it on their way to hunt other places. That's exactly where you've got to look for big bucks." The next year he went back to the same spot and took a 38-inch buck. *photo courtesy Rich LaRocco.*

Jay Gates got 185 points with this Colorado muley. "I like to hunt with the wind in my face and the sun at my back," Gates says. "Deer are at a disadvantage staring into the sun's glare." This muley stared at the sun a little too long. *photo courtesy Jay Gates.*

Gordon Blay's mega-muleys: the deer on the left has an outside spread of 35½ inches—but the one on the right has a spread of 37½ inches and scores 239 Boone and Crockett points. *photo courtesy Gordon Blay.*

Frank Hough took this muley with blackpowder arms and scored 223 in the Boone and Crockett books! Frank has hunted mule deer for more than 30 years; he's seen some changes in the critters. "The only time I see big bucks anymore is real early in the morning and just as it is getting dark." *photo courtesy Frank Hough.*

Maury Jones of Jackson Hole Outfitters and "Fred," a 28-inch spread buck that he guided me to—but I didn't take—in the Salt River Range in Wyoming, as described in Chapter 42. High-altitude hunts are strenuous, but that's where the superbucks are. *photo courtesy Maury Jones.*

Ace bowhunter Chuck Adams took this mega-muley in Montana using his favorite "spot and stalk" technique: spot the muley in the morning, then, after he's bedded down, begin a careful upwind stalk. *photo courtesy of Chuck Adams.*

It's Number 24 Typical in the Boone and Crockett books; Kelly Baird recalls the November day when he killed this New Mexico mule deer on a three-day hunter drive. This time you can go along in Chapter 50. *photo courtesy Kelly Baird.*

Do calls work for mule deer? Well, a grunt call worked for Phil Kirkland on the Kansas state typical mule deer that he took with a bow. Read about Phil's amazing decoy-blind in Chapter 43. *photo courtesy Phil Kirkland.*

Lee Frudden (at right) killed this Boone and Crockett-class mule deer in Eagle, Colorado. Frudden likes to hunt muleys late in the season, he says in Chapter 41, because bad weather makes the deer move. On the left is Gary Carracioli. *photo courtesy Lee Frudden.*

Although the buck remained state champion for only two short years, Brunk himself remains a champion hunter. A man who loves whitetails and hunting as much as he does can't be called anything else.

Even though the buck that eventually dethroned Brunk's is spectacular, the story isn't nearly as thrilling. For one thing, the man that took the new Missouri record killed it just because it was a buck. It wasn't anything special to him. And once he'd killed the big deer, he sold the antlers to buy a coondog. For him that may have been a wise choice. But for those of us who long to set our sights on a dream buck like the Phantom, there's no way we'd ever part with the trophy—not while we had breath in our bodies.

Brunk has killed many other bucks since that day in 1969 when he brought the Phantom down. But none holds the place in his heart that the big 13-pointer does. Brunk, a grown farmer now, either owns outright or has permission to hunt on "four or five square miles of land." And while he talks of yet another 190-class buck that he's got spotted, it's unlikely that any other buck could ever equal the thrills and excitement that were the legacy of Missouri's legendary Phantom whitetail.

27

The Number One Non-Typical Whitetail: Socrates

Missouri has long been known as the Show Me State. That's because most Missourians have a natural curiosity about the world around them. And they are naturally reluctant to take anyone's word for anything. If anyone had told the average Missouri deer hunter that the world record non-typical whitetail buck was alive and well in the suburbs of the city of St. Louis on the first day of firearms season in 1981, I know what she would have said. "Show me."

Before the discovery of this deer, the Benson Buck, found in Brady, Texas, in 1892 and scored 286 points, was the hands-down champion non-typical whitetail for almost 90 years. The establishment of a new world record in such a longstanding category was itself hard to believe. When you add the fact that the buck was found in a metropolitan area where over two million people live, it's especially amazing.

The story of Socrates, as the St. Louis buck was named, involves several people. Two archers, Scott Gluckhertz and Rich Askew, were both aware of the big deer's existence. They'd been hunting the trophy steadily throughout that fall of 1981 whenever they were able to get away from their jobs in construction. These two men were responsible for nicknaming the big buck Socrates. During the entire month of October and the first two weeks of November they'd managed to see Socrates on at least five different occasions. But the deer hadn't gotten big by being stupid, and none of their sightings led to a shot. I think all whitetail hunters owe a debt of gratitude to these two for passing up poor shots at the animal. According to Mike Helland, the St. Louis County conservation agent ultimately responsible for recognizing the deer as a possible record, the two archers had opportunities to shoot on several occasions, but either brush was in the way or the shot was too far. So, they both opted to wait for a better moment. Had either one of them shot and his arrow flown true, he would have become an instant celebrity. Then again, he might have only wounded the buck and lost both the animal and his incredible rack forever.

Gluckhertz and Askew weren't in the field on November 15, 1981, the second day of Missouri's firearms season. Bowhunters aren't permitted to hunt with archery equipment during Missouri's gun season without a firearms tag. Agent Helland, however, was on the job patrolling north St. Louis County when he met a successful hunter named Dave Beckman and proceeded to field check his deer. Helland and Beckman soon parted company and the agent went about his duties. He'd just started checking another deer hunter when Beckman returned. "I have something to show you that you aren't going to believe," he said. "So you'd better follow me."

Helland was intrigued, so he followed. After driving a short distance he finally pulled up behind Beckman. Then he got out of his truck and went with him to where a tremendous buck lay dead behind a 10-foot cyclone fence that was topped with barbed wire. Helland has always been interested in trophy heads. Whenever he has the time, he, too, takes to the woods in pursuit of a superbuck. And he knew at once that the big buck was something special. What he didn't know was that the deer would soon be recognized as the new world's record non-typical whitetail.

Helland got permission from the proper authorities to enter the grounds and claim the buck for the state of Missouri. He needed help loading the animal into the back of his pickup, but once he'd accomplished that, he began to try and reconstruct what could have happened to Socrates to cause his death.

First there was the possibility that the buck had been shot by a poacher. Second, since the deer was found within yards of a road and with blood coming from his nose, it was also suspected that the animal may have been hit by a car. If he had been hit a fatal blow, would he still have been able to clear a fence of that magnitude? Helland couldn't be sure.

Finally, the agent theorized that the deer just might have been chased by dogs. When the dogs got too close, it was conceivable that the buck might have run into the fence, either breaking his neck or causing some other massive internal injury. Upon closer inspection, however, Helland could find no evidence such as bite marks to indicate that this last option was feasible.

Later that evening, Helland took the buck's carcass to Rockwoods Reservation, a nearby Department of Conservation area. There he enlisted the aid of the area manager Dave Wissehr to help him try to determine the extent of the animal's injuries. The two of them together were only able to tell that the buck had suffered a slight hemorrhage under the skin of the right shoulder and neck. Since the carcass was rapidly spoiling—the deer had probably been dead for at least 24 hours before Beckman found it—Helland and Wissehr finally called it quits. The head was saved and frozen for a trip to the taxidermist, and, for the time being, the cause of the big buck's death forgotten.

I remember that week the big buck was found very well. For one reason, deer season is always my favorite time of year. For another, my family and I were at a restaurant during this time when a waitress told us that her cousin had found "a buck with 33 points in St. Louis County." She also said that her cousin thought the buck would be a world record. Hunters tend to talk, but a buck with 33 points caught my attention. So when they announced the possibility of a new world record some months later, everything clicked. The waitress was completely wrong on the number of points—the buck has 58 points, 42 scorable ones—but she was right on target about the new world record.

After the required 60-day drying time, Helland and Ken Zehner, a local taxidermist, caped out the head and did a rough scoring job on the massive antlers. The two men had never scored a rack before, yet they came up with 44 scorable points and a total Boone and Crockett score of 333⅝ points—only two eighths of a point off of the eventual final score—not bad for two amateurs.

On January 26, 1982, Randy Herberg, another Conservation Department employee and an official Boone and Crockett scorer, also came up with 44 points. This time, the total score dropped to 325⅞ points, still a phenomenal score. Helland says it was at this moment that he finally realized what he had in his possession.

The official final score was 333⅞ points, 47⅞ points higher than the score of the Benson Buck, the buck that many people had gone on record as saying was "unbeatable." Not only had Socrates's rack beaten the old score, it had annihilated it. The antler mass itself weighs 11¼ pounds. For a rack of this size it is amazingly symmetrical. The greatest spread is 33⅜ inches. The left beam has 23 points while the right one has 19. Drop tines on both sides are stained dark where they came in contact with the ground while the big buck rested his head when bedded. While it was growing, Socrates's rack must have been even larger. One big point on the left side has been totally broken off. The rack is heavily palmated so several minimum circumferences between its various points measure an incredible eight inches.

The buck was large-bodied and weighed 250 pounds, something to be expected in the area of woodlots, rich bottomland and crop fields where the deer was found. What was unusual about the big deer was that his facial features were exceedingly strange. His eyes were deeply sunk back in his head, and a deformity of the lower jaw made it appear as though his chin was receding. His bite was off by several inches so his upper jaw actually overbit the lower jaw. Biologists in the Department of Conservation found a puncture wound in the lower jaw bone. This led to speculation that a canine of some type might have bitten the deer while he was still a youngster. Later on, an infection set in causing all of the animal's lower incisors to fall out. All that remained for the deer to chew with in its lower jaw was spongy bone. It's amazing that he was able to eat well enough to grow the fantastic antlers.

Scientific aging procedures based on cutting a cross section of molar to count the annuli or growth rings confirmed that Socrates was four and a half years old at the time of his death. Since mature bucks usually achieve their top antler growth at ages five and a half to six and a half, it's hard to imagine just what the big Missouri non-typical might have wound up with on his head in another couple of years had he lived.

Naturally, the entire state and especially the Department of Conservation was very proud. Photos of Helland handcuffed to the mount while accompanying it to various functions became commonplace. There was an intense amount of interest generated by people wanting to acquire the antlers. Figures from $20,000 to $50,000 were mentioned casually by antler buyers, so the Department was understandably somewhat nervous and very protective. They'd just acquired a new world's record and they had no intention of losing it.

In a way, this trophy has really become something special for Missourians. All wildlife is the property of the state and therefore ultimately of the people. Rather than having a spectacular animal like Socrates belonging to an individual who might possibly exploit the honor, this trophy remains the property of the state for everyone to enjoy. He is truly of the people, by the people, and for the people—and a reminder to us all that the next world record whitetail could be living in someone's backyard right this very minute.

28

The Number Two
Non-Typical Whitetail:
the Hole-In-The-Horn Buck

There are many similarities between the number one and the number two-ranked Boone and Crockett non-typical whitetails. First, both died natural deaths: neither bullets nor arrows hastened their departure from this world. Second, both heads have tremendous racks with points going up, down, backward and forward—racks that are very similar in overall shape and appearance. Third, both racks score over 320 points. No buck had ever even approached 300 points before Socrates was discovered back in 1981.

The Hole-In-The-Horn Buck, however, had one thing going for it that no other record book buck ever had going for it before: a full-blown public relations campaign. As soon as the head was uncovered in 1983, a massive media blitz began to hype the discovery of the so-called new World Record Non-Typical. There were both reasons to believe that the buck would in fact be the new record and reason to doubt it. Records are elusive things and the Boone and Crockett Record Book scoring procedure used for non-typical racks is even more mysterious.

The Hole-In-The-Horn buck's story is shrouded in mystery, beginning with its origins in the early 1940s. Since all principals involved in the story are dead, details of the buck's discovery are sketchy indeed—right down to the small caliber bullet hole through the massive drop tine off the buck's right antler—although an anonymous tip was relayed to me that this deer was killed during a culling operation organized by officials from a nearby U.S. Army facility.

Dick Idol, research director for the magazine *North American Whitetail*, deserves credit for unearthing the huge rack. In 1977 a fellow hunter first showed photos of the Hole-In-The-Horn to Idol. Idol knew that the buck looked big, but it took him four years until he learned that the rack was located in Kent, Ohio. Then it took him another year to contact officials of the Kent Canadian Club where the head was hanging in order to arrange a visit. In 1983, Idol flew to Kent to see the giant buck firsthand.

At first, Idol said he didn't really believe that the rack would outscore the big Missouri non-typical. Both he and the executive staff of *North American Whitetail* realized the value in owning such a set of magnificent antlers. A deal was struck and soon the big rack was in Dick Idol's home in Seeley Lake, Montana. There, Idol began to measure it: the way he scored it, the antlers were racking up incredible totals, from 338 to 349⅝ points. Any of these scores would be enough to beat the Missouri buck.

Idol then sought expert help. He called Harold Nesbitt, administrative director of the Boone and Crockett Club, for advice. Nesbitt suggested that Idol call in Phillip Wright, chairman of the club's scoring committee, who lived in nearby Missoula. Once Wright started tallying up his totals, it took him three hours to arrive at a score. When he did, it was a whopping 342⅝ points, easily a new world record.

Idol was warned that this score was merely an entry score and subject to the final awards judges' measurement, the official, final score. It was decided to break the story anyway, and the head was quickly termed the New World's Record Non-Typical Whitetail.

Many people were upset, since it was probably the first time that a head was touted as a new world's record before the final judgment was handed down. There was some backlash of sentiments against the Hole-In-The-Horn buck.

As soon as the buck was scored by Wright, *North American Whitetail,* the new owners of the massive rack, published a series of three stories which related both the finding and scoring of the Hole-In-The-Horn Buck, plus a comparison with Socrates. Now in fairness to both Idol and the magazine, the Ohio buck was a tremendous discovery: no one can question that it was indeed a newsworthy event. However, it is certain that they could have sold as many magazines by calling the head a "Possible" or "Probable" New World's Record Non-Typical rather than "The" New World's Record. These three controversial magazine articles did make whitetail aficionados everywhere aware of Idol's incredible find.

The Hole-In-The-Horn Buck was discovered dead along the Erie Railroad right-of-way near Windham, Ohio. Somehow, an Erie engineer named Charlie Flowers gained possession of the buck, and turned it over to the Kent Canadian Club for display. According to Idol's research, some accounts report that the massive buck's antlers had become entangled in the top of a chain link fence which bordered the Rovanna Arsenal in Portage County, Ohio. Other reports say the buck was lying dead on the railroad side of the fence. At this date it's impossible to determine whether the buck met his demise by train or by fence. What is uncanny is that it is possible that the big Missouri non-typical may also have met his death with a chain link fence, since he, too, was discovered next to one.

The cape used to mount the Hole-In-The-Horn was not the one the buck had been born with. Decomposition had already set in when it was found so the only part of the deer that was salvaged was the magnificent rack. Once mounted, the deer hung in the Kent Canadian Club unscored for the next 40 years. When Idol acquired it, he mounted the rack with yet another cape. So the Hole-In-The-Horn Buck seen today does full justice to the majestic animal.

Since there was no deer season in the Ohio of the early 1940s, it's hard to imagine how the antlers acquired the small caliber bullet hole in the big drop tine off of the right antler. It's been theorized that a squirrel hunter, startled at the appearance of the giant buck, fired a round of .22 caliber ammunition by mistake. Even so, from the angle of the bullet hole, it's highly unlikely that the shot contributed to the animal's death, at least not directly. It's much more probable that the buck was shot after it was hanging in the Kent Canadian Club by some careless, drunken party-goer. However, speculation continues that the bullet may have contributed to the buck's eventual death, at least indirectly. Unfortunately, dead men—and dead deer—tell no tales.

For sheer mass, this buck's rack is just awesome. Even after 40 years of drying out, this greatest spread is 34 inches. The main beams measure over 10 inches around at several points. Other points have a circumference of over eight inches. Over 20 points grow out of the rack at a downward angle, and some are as thick as a man's forearm. The two largest drop tines are over 13 inches long.

There were several problems when the final judging took place in 1986. One of these involved the determination of the true main beams. There are an upper pair of points that could be regarded as the true main beams as well as a lower pair of points. The preliminary scoring counted the upper points as belonging to the main beam.

Another thorny problem lies in deciding how long a tine is when palmation is also present. In other words, at what point does the tine actually begin if the main beam is palmated in so many different directions? And finally, in Boone and Crockett scoring, even non-typicals must possess some symmetry. So even though this is definitely a non-typical rack, in order to score it, basic typical points must be matched up, on left and right sides. When looking at a rack like the Hole-In-The-Horn, it's easy to see that some judgements must be made. Wright's original score called this buck a non-typical based on a ten-point frame, for example. The Final Award's Committee used an eight-point frame.

This big buck, like the Missouri buck, has blackened antler tips on the ends of the longer drop tines. This surface has the appearance of black leather, the result of delicate antler velvet that was injured while still growing. Injured velvet won't shed completely. An antler affected like this may be more "spongy" or porous than normal, hardened antler. The Hole-In-The-Horn actually broke off some of this spongy antler material so, as unbelievable as it may seem, as huge as the rack is, some of the original mass is missing.

If Phillip Wright's original score had stood, then the Hole-In-The-Horn would be the world champion. At 342⅜ points, the Ohio buck would have topped the Missouri buck by 8⅜ points.

The former world record non-typical, the Benson Buck of Texas, had stood alone since 1892. When the Missouri buck was found in 1981, people thought it would never be beaten. And only two years later a buck capable of giving the Missouri buck a run for its money was discovered.

The final score wasn't 342⅜ points, however. It was 328⅝ points. The Final Awards Judges measured the rack as a non-typical that was based on an eight-point frame rather than one that was based on a ten-point frame. For this and a few other minor reasons, the buck settled comfortably into second place, 5⅞ points behind the reigning world record non-typical.

Which rack is actually bigger? For sheer mass, I'd have to say the Hole-In-The-Horn. This buck's antlers are said to weigh 11½ pounds while the Missouri buck's antlers weigh something just over 11 pounds. The main question the comparison poses is: does symmetry really have a place in the non-typical category? Just what does "non-typical" mean, anyway?

Since I'm from Missouri—Socrates was found within 25 miles of my home—my own sentiments have to go with our Missouri buck. When I look at the two racks side-by-side, I can't help but wonder what the determination would have been if the Hole-In-The-Horn hype hadn't been quite so—*hyper.* In any case, both animals are fabulous bucks, and either one is worthy of wearing the crown of The Biggest And The Best Rack In The World.

29

The Rompola Buck: Authentic or Sham?

There was an old advertisement that asked, "What becomes a Legend most?" When pondering that particular question, one might be tempted to reply, "Authenticity." For if something isn't authentic, what is it really? A sham, that's what. Authentic or sham? That's the question the hunting world now poses to Michigan's Mitch Rompola, a bowhunter who has managed to stir up a tempest in a teapot.

Rompola's buck: authentic or sham? Wouldn't you like to know? Wouldn't just about everyone like to know? But on the day this edition went to press, only one person in the world knew for certain, and he wasn't providing anyone with any proof.

Sure, Mitch Rompola has his supporters. Lots of them. And he has his detractors, too. Perhaps even more of them. The shame of this entire controversy has to be this: if the Rompola buck *is* real, then this wonderful animal is not getting the recognition it deserves.

What do we know about the Rompola buck? For starters, the world at large learned about this great buck on November 20, 1998, when Mitch Rompola of Traverse City, Michigan, stated that he had used a bow with 70 percent let-off (thus eliminating it from consideration for the Pope and Young record book) to kill the big deer a week earlier in northern Michigan. Rompola further stated that the buck's antlers scored 216⅝ using the Boone and Crockett system. However—and it's a *big* however—Rompola will not allow anyone to X-ray his buck's giant antlers.

Rompola's buck is a 12-pointer. It dressed out at 263 pounds. Its antlers have an inside spread of 38 inches. That's 3½ inches more than the largest spread—the world record Hanson buck boasts a 34½-inch inside spread—now listed in the current edition of the Boone and Crockett record book. That in itself is rather interesting.

Another point is that an observer can count on two fingers the number of typical whitetail trophies with inside spreads greater than 30 inches in the current Boone and Crockett *Records of North American Big Game*. Authentic? Perhaps.

Rompola then announced that he was angry with Boone and Crockett and that he would not enter the deer in the books. He also claimed that four scorers flew into the state to measure the deer secretly, but later dropped that claim. Here's what else Rompola says:

In 1996 he'd spotted the buck and photographed it while only about twenty yards distant from the animal. He told his friends that he'd seen a buck that would give the world record a run for its money, but he didn't elaborate on exactly how big the massive antlers were. "They would have thought I was crazy," he said.

Rompola saw the buck several more times. He photographed it again, too. On November 3, 1998, he was in a tree stand when he finally got a shot at it. His arrow was deflected.

Ten days later, Rompola was watching two bucks sparring near a mock scrape he had made nearby when the two animals looked up the trail and then took off. Sure enough, the big buck walked up soon afterwards. When the deer's head went behind a tree, Rompola shot. The deer ran, but Rompola knew the hit had been a good one. He said he spent the next 15 minutes sitting in the tree stand, shaking so hard that he "knew that if I tried to climb down, I'd fall."

Eventually, he did come out of that tree. He went home for his video camera, returned to the woods, and found the deer 70 yards away.

Eric Sharp, of the *Detroit Free Press*, was, in the beginning, one of Rompola's biggest supporters. But now Sharp has actually written, in reference to Rompola's supposed record, "Put up or shut up."

North American Hunter magazine did a story on Rompola that included a mathematical analysis of each of his record-book claims, including the monster he shot on November 13, 1998. The magazine's editors asked Dr. Steven Wise of James Madison University to calculate the odds of Rompola's claims.

Here are Wise's calculations:

- The odds of anyone taking Commemorative Bucks of Michigan–quality bucks from Grand Traverse County in seven consecutive years are one in 100 trillion, or one in 100,000,000,000,000.

- The odds of taking 11 Commemorative Bucks of Michigan bucks from Grand Traverse in 31 years are one in 7.04 quadrillion, or one in 7,040,000,000,000,000.

- The odds of taking four Boone and Crockett bucks in Grand Traverse County in 17 years are one in 28.2 quintillion, or one in 28,200,000,000,000,000,000.

- The odds of killing nine Pope and Young bucks in Grand Traverse in nine years are 1 in 16.7 quattuordecillion, or 1 in 16,700,000,000,000,000,000,000,000,000,000,000,000,000,000,000, 000.

- And the odds of killing 13 Pope and Young deer in Grand Traverse in 31 years is one in 15.6 octodecillion. Too many zeroes to include here.

"The estimates are actually conservative," wrote Sharp in the September 2, 1999, edition of the *Detroit Free Press*, "because they count only deer that Rompola entered in the records of Commemorative Bucks of Michigan, Pope and Young, or Boone and Crockett. It didn't include a bunch more (Rompola gave me different figures in different interviews) he says he never entered."

If you want to put those numbers in perspective, *North American Hunter* did some research and found that:

- The odds that an airplane will land on you sometime this year are one in 25,000,000.

- The odds that you'll get on a plane with a bomb aboard are one in 100,000,000.

- The odds that you'll be hit by lightning tomorrow are one in 250,000,000.

According to Sharp's column, comparing the number of zeroes following the three latter instances to those in the odds of Rompola's chances of achieving his hunting records results in a startling discovery. Namely, each additional zero multiplies the unlikelihood of the event happening by a factor of 10. And Rompola claimed—to Sharp—to have killed not just 13 record deer in Grand Traverse County but about 20, which would add so many zeroes to the odds that Sharp says, "I'd doubt we could fit them on this page."

On the other hand, here's what we know in Rompola's favor: three respected Michigan scorers actually did measure the buck and came up with an unofficial tally of 215⅜, a full three inches larger than Milo Hanson's buck. Rompola refuses to talk to almost anyone else about any other particulars of this deer.

The deer is not entered with Boone and Crockett, nor with Michigan Commemorative Bucks, which keeps the state's records. The rack has not been X-rayed, other than by Rompola, who states that the X-rays prove that the rack has not been tampered with.

Does anyone else think this last statement is just a little bit strange? The hunter is X-raying his own deer's rack to prove it hasn't been tampered with? Wouldn't the hunter *know* his deer's rack hadn't been tampered with . . . *if* he took an actual living, breathing animal?

None of my whitetail expert friends would go on record for this story. *All*, however, said that they doubted the Rompola buck is a valid trophy. *All* also said that they wished it was the new world record, if only so that the buck would get its due. The comments I received include the following:

"If it's real, why doesn't he have it X-rayed and put the speculation to an end?"

"He's gotten far more publicity like this than he ever could have received had he had the antlers scored properly."

"If he really wanted to hurt one or the other record-keeping organization, the best way to do so would have been to have had the rack X-rayed, prove it's real, then refuse to enter it."

"Why are the ears of the deer in that photograph [of Rompola's buck] so slack-looking? They droop so much, it's like they don't even belong to that deer."

"Why are the antlers so bloody for the first three or four inches? From the burr upward, they are nothing but blood. I've never seen any rack look like this, no matter what the cause."

One critic, Craig Calderone, owner of the Michigan Whitetail Hall of Fame Museum in Grass Lake, has offered to pay $10,000 to a charity of Rompola's choice if Rompola will have the rack X-rayed. In fairness to Rompola, there is bad blood between the two men. Calderone had the top Michigan deer in the mid-1980s. It was disqualified and thrown out of CBM when it was learned that he had two wildlife violations on his record for shining deer after legal hours and shining deer with a gun in his car. Calderone believed Rompola was behind this action and also noted that Rompola's deer became the new state record after his own deer was removed. Then, in 1995, Rompola was convicted of a serious misdemeanor. Pope and Young also learned that he had a 20-year-old felony conviction on his record as well. Both Pope and Young and Boone and Crockett dropped Rompola's memberships in their organizations. Rompola believes Calderone was behind the action by the two national clubs.

Personal animosities aside, anyone who has viewed the Rompola buck's rack has noted how amateurish the taxidermy work is—unusual if this really is the new world record, as Rompola claims. Taxidermists would be vying with each other to mount the new world record—for free! Why would Rompola mount it himself (as seems to be the case) if he had nothing to hide?

Nonetheless, Mitch Rompola, having told the world that he had taken the new world-record typical, soon set out on the show-and-seminar circuit. Rompola endorsed products, marketed T-shirts, hats, and other trinkets with the big buck's image and set about to displace the Hanson buck everywhere but in the record book. His efforts worked so well that Milo Hanson and his partner, Arkansas businessman John Butler, threatened him with a lawsuit, asserting that their earnings from Hanson's record buck have been compromised by "Rompola's unsubstantiated claims."

"Some shows were kind of reluctant to book us," Hanson said. "They said they figured the Rompola buck would be coming down the road pretty soon. And we had just come out with nice prints of our deer, and here they were selling pictures of Rompola's buck." Hanson and Butler called a lawyer. The lawyer cobbled together an agreement, and Rompola signed it. The argument states that Rompola won't claim his deer is a world record and won't try to enter it with Boone and Crockett unless somebody kills one bigger than Hanson's. If that last statement were true, Hanson's deer would no longer be the record and he would have nothing left to complain about.

Rompola still has his supporters, and his detractors, too. Whether you believe him or not, here's one final tantalizing piece to the puzzle that is Mitch Rompola: could this man not only have killed the new world record typical buck—a monster that measures 3½-inches wider than Milo Hanson's giant deer—but also, as he claims, have killed the Missouri world record non-typical when he was a lad of 14? And never tagged it?

A necropsy was performed on the Missouri buck. No broadhead wound—nor any other wound, for that matter—was ever found. Could it, *would it,* have been missed?

Authentic? Or sham?

30

The Future of
Whitetail Superbucks

Today, in the year 2000, all is right with the whitetail world. In many states, the deer have reached the limits of expansion into new habitat and are now in a holding pattern. Populations in some of our heavily-populated eastern states are bound to start a downward shift as habitat is destroyed.

In other areas of the country, deer are still expanding their range. We've learned how adaptable they are as they move into our suburbs, since they've become our next-door neighbors. In many western states, whitetails have moved into mule deer range, often to the detriment of the mule, which must then move on. So the whitetail has a much stronger ecological toehold in the countryside than most of our other wildlife. That's something that won't change drastically, at least not in the near future. So everything *seems* right in the whitetail world. But there's a distant threat to quality whitetail hunting as we now define the sport.

The science of bioengineering has raced ahead of our ethical and moral progress. Genetically-engineered crops are already in production, grown from seeds genetically altered to repel blights and fungi and to improve yields. Cows with altered gene strings are bred to produce more milk; hogs to produce more and even leaner pork. Even human beings are routinely conceived outside the mother's body, while human eggs and embryos are harvested and frozen for use at some later date. The individual genes suspected of producing human birth defects are being identified and targeted for elimination from our DNA. And someday soon, somewhere in the country, it will be possible for a "hunter" to contract for and then shoot a true Boone and Crockett whitetail superbuck.

It is rumored that antler collectors will pay as much as $100,000 for high-ranking heads—not even *world* record heads—so big racks are in demand like never before. A typical Boone and Crockett buck in the 195-plus class is almost as good as a winning lottery ticket. You get money, a replica of the antlers in place on the deer's mounted cape, plus instant fame from outdoor magazines. Even smaller trophies may win the hunter a four-wheel drive vehicle,

$10,000 in cash, or a dream vacation in Hawaii. So much for the thrill of the hunt.

While university programs learn more and more about the genetics, nutrition, and behavior of whitetail superbucks, private-enterprise biologists and wildlife managers lurk just off center stage, waiting to capitalize on what the research scientists discover. No sooner had the universities fertilized an estrous doe with frozen semen from a dead buck than private ranch biologists were duplicating the feat. And as soon as the secrets of antler genetics are completely decoded, be assured that they will be used to make the ranch owners big bucks of a kind far different from the ones with four feet.

Like it or not, we must think about the prospects of man-made superbucks *now*, before it becomes a headline. What will genetically engineered antlers do to the record book as we know it? What is there to keep unscrupulous people from releasing a genetically engineered buck into a hunting area, altering forever the genetic pool of the resident deer? Hunters are currently required to sign a form on their word of honor that states that their hunt was conducted according to the rules of fair chase. Will this be enough when record-book superbucks are for sale for a price?

I must say I doubt it. For every experimenter working in embryo transplantation to save an endangered species, there's a lab technician who's willing to plant tiny embryos in surrogate does for money. It's not too far fetched to fear that if many deer with the same super-buck father were released, the result may be highly inbred populations in some areas of the country. The probability of dangerous or undesirable traits could be genetically increased, until even the wild deer population in that area was affected. And there's scant chance that legislation will restrict armchair biologists from practicing on deer.

Pure research *is* important: the more we know about the whitetail the more we realize there is to learn. Respected university research programs, run by well-qualified scientists, must continue to study every aspect of the animal. Yet, we must ask, could bioengineering eventually degrade or destroy the whitetail as we know him? And what does that do to the hunting experience?

The Boone and Crockett fair chase statement has already been tested in Texas. Many ranches use escape-proof fencing to keep animals within their perimeters. While some of these ranches are immense, often exceeding 100,000 acres in size, the possibility that a trophy animal may have been shot in a fence corner can't be overlooked. "When I was club director, it was our greatest concern," stated W. Harold Nesbitt, formerly with the Boone and Crockett Club. "As long as there was the slightest chance of this happening, we were not about to consider any trophy from a ranch using escape-proof fence." This feeling within the club remains the same to the present day.

New Boone and Crockett entries aren't so plentiful that officials need to suspect every Texas buck someone attempts to list. But Texas isn't the only state with game farms and ranches anymore, either. Every year more and more fenced-in areas are being opened to hunters with lots of money and little time or limited physical ability. Here in my home state of Missouri there's a 1,200-acre ranch where you can shoot a "superbuck" for $5,000 and up. Of course these deer are loose in a compound with wild hogs, blackbucks, javelinas, quail, chukkar, pheasants, and even Rocky Mountain elk. I've never been there myself, so I can only imagine a 1,200-acre enclosure with so many animals running loose inside. Friends who have been there say that each evening, a truck moves slowly through the compound and workers shovel off corn. As they do, animals run forward eagerly to eat it.

There are three forces at work creating game farms like this one. First, game farms exist because of very real problems in public game and land management. Some game farm patrons are afraid to hunt on public or private land because so many unqualified shooters are out there with guns. Secondly, the *only* animal some hunters will take is a superbuck; and they'll take it any way the game farm offers. Thirdly, some state agencies seem bound and determined to limit the quality of deer available by continuing buck-only hunting in unbalanced or overpopulated areas. Hunters who are interested in quality as well as quantity are tempted to look elsewhere. I'd like to see designated "quality hunting blocks" in every state—places where hunting is restricted and as many or even *more* does as bucks are harvested to restore sex balance. With careful attention to habitat, this area would produce some dandy bucks within a few years. Superbuck hunters would willingly pay more for the chance to kill a trophy, and the extra money would make up the difference between over-the-counter license sales lost in the area.

The whitetail has survived in spite of man, but while we're going to have to pay close attention to new developments that affect the wild whitetail, I can't help but believe that he'll survive these changes, too.

Part 4

Mule Deer Superbucks

31

Description of the Mule Deer Superbuck

Like their cousins the whitetails, mule deer belong to the family Cervidae, subfamily Odocoileinae, and the genus *Odocoileus.* But mule deer and blacktail deer belong to the species *"hemionus."* This species numbers between four and six million animals, about one-third the number of whitetails found in North America.

Most of the continent's mule deer belong to the subspecies *hemionus* so the Latin words that mean Rocky Mountain mule deer to biologists are *Odocoileus hemionus hemionus*, genus, species, and subspecies.

Rocky Mountain muleys inhabit most of the range traditionally identified as belonging to muleys in the United States and Canada: windswept ridges and high alpine slopes, black timber, and deep canyons.

But Rocky Mountain muleys aren't the only subspecies of mule deer on the North American continent. The other notable subspecies is *Odocoileus hemionus crooki*, the smaller desert mule deer that thrives in the southwestern United States, northern Mexico, and the northwest portion of Texas.

For the record, there's also the southern mule deer, a subspecies that calls the upper Baja Peninsula (Baja California) and the extreme southwestern corner of California its home. The peninsula mule deer reigns over the lower part of the peninsula and the California mule deer roams over much of the southern reaches of the state from which it gets its name. While these three subspecies of mule deer all have yielded individuals worthy of the title superbuck, generally speaking their antlers are smaller than either Rocky Mountain or desert muleys. At the present time, there are two California mule deer in the Boone and Crockett record book.

Two final mule deer subspecies worth noting include the Tiburon Island mule deer and Cedros Island mule deer. Tiny Tiburon Island lies off the western coast of Sonora, Mexico in the Gulf of California. Cedros Island lies off the western shore of Baja California. These two subspecies aren't hunted any more. A real danger exists that the

Cedros Island mule deer may soon be extinct, a regrettable piece of news for any deer lover.

Taxonomists generally agree on the descriptions of each sub-species of mule deer. While all subspecies have some characteristics in common, differences do occur from one individual to another and from one population to another. Ranges overlap and interbreeding is common. Rocky Mountain muleys and desert muleys often occupy portions of the same range, for example.

Subspecies develop for two basic reasons. First, a group of deer may become isolated from the rest of the population, as was the case with both Tiburon Island and Cedros Island mule deer. Natural selection plays its part, too. Distinct subspecies develop as an adaptation to a particular habitat, like Tiburon Island's deer. It's survival of the fittest. For example, desert muleys adapted physiologically to the hot, arid conditions of the southwest. So this subspecies evolved to a generally smaller deer lighter in color than the Rocky Mountain mule deer. Smaller and lighter bodies absorb less heat and require less sustenance, so desert muleys need less forage and water, prime factors in their ability to withstand the rigors of the desert. Climate, forage, and topography of the land all influence various populations, and eventual evolution of subspecies to some degree.

The mule deer is a fairly recent arrival in North America. It's hypothesized that the ancestors of the mule deer first dispersed over the western portion of the continent about 500,000 years ago. Mule deer range has expanded eastward somewhat, but for the most part the eastern limit of the species remains in the western portions of Kansas, Oklahoma, Texas, Nebraska, South Dakota, and North Dakota. Occasionally, a vagrant mule deer will move a little further eastward to pop out somewhere along the Missouri River bottoms, but one rarely ventures as far as Iowa or Missouri. As agriculture gradually moved westward along the country's fertile riverbottoms, whitetails followed. But mule deer usually expand into prime white-tail areas only when overgrazing and loss of woodlands shifts this habitat back to desert scrubland.

Mule deer aren't named for their stubbornness, but rather for their big ears. That's undoubtedly why Captains Meriwether Lewis and William Clark first referred to them as "mule" deer in the 1804 journals of their search for a northwest passage. A mule deer's ears are big, measuring between 18 and 24 inches. Savvy hunters use their guesstimate of ear-to-ear width to help them decide whether or not a deer is a trophy.

A mule deer superbuck relies a great deal upon his ears to alert him to the presence of danger. Mule deer share habitat with many efficient predators, including cougars and coyotes. So they're always alert to any sound that may mean a stalk is in progress. A muley relies more on both its ears and eyes than his cousin the whitetail according to noted mule deer expert Dr. Valerius Geist of the University of Calgary in Calgary, Alberta, Canada. "Unlike most whitetails, a mule deer will almost instantaneously pinpoint the slightest movement of another deer at 600 yards," Dr. Geist explained. "That makes it very difficult to slip in close to one of them without being detected."

A Rocky Mountain mule deer superbuck's coat turns gray in color during late August, well before the does and fawns get their gray coats. This premature gray coat could be a not-so-subtle advertisement of sexual status. Bucks keep this gray coat during the fall and winter, a period of seven months, and then revert back to reddish-brown for the five months of late spring and summer.

A desert muley's coat is often more washed-out looking than that of the Rocky Mountain muley. Typically, a desert muley's pelage is gray or brown all year long. Hair loss, or molt, is controlled by light. As both summer and winter draw to a close, mule deer of all subspecies look somewhat lighter because of the bleaching effect of the sun.

Deer of both subspecies have a white throat patch, sometimes two *separate* white throat patches. They will always have a white or ivory rump patch that serves an extremely useful purpose: it flares a warning when danger threatens. It's this rump patch that stands out on a mule deer, helping you locate them when they're feeding on rocky slopes. The muley's tail is thin, rope-like, and is usually tipped with black.

A mule deer's cloven hooves are well-suited for climbing. They spread out readily almost grasping rocky cliff-like surfaces encountered in its mountainous habitat. These hooves are well-adapted to the peculiar jump-like gait of the mule deer called "stotting." The stott is a high-bounding gait which also creates noise and ground vibrations that may serve as a warning to other deer. Stotting is a common form of mule deer locomotion, but by no means its fastest gait. But biologists say that the stott gives mule several advantages. First, it permits the deer to make unpredictable changes of direction as it flees. So a predator in pursuit can never anticipate the deer's movements and lunge for the kill. All four hooves hit the ground with each step, so with each step the deer can stott sideways or even backwards as easily as forward. Stotting is also well-adapted to making steep ascents *fast*, and in mule deer country that comes in handy.

As a rule, muleys are larger than their cousins, the whitetails. While they start life weighing between five and eleven pounds at birth, they make up for it quickly. On the average, a mature Rocky Mountain mule deer buck weighs between 200 and 300 pounds on the hoof. Many instances of big mule deer bucks weighing 350 pounds have been recorded. One tremendous mule deer with a live weight of 600 pounds was once reported, but a deer of this size is extremely unusual. Desert muleys are usually smaller in body size than their northern brothers.

Mule deer bucks gain weight during the summer and early autumn while they're growing their spectacular antlers. But once the rut draws near they invariably lose weight, even when there's lots of nutritious food around. This weight loss trend continues into winter and by spring a two-year-old male will have lost about 20 percent of his body weight and a three-year-old about 22 percent. When you're considering a 300-pound buck, that amounts to 66 pounds, no laughing matter when survival is at stake. Bucks lose weight partly because they're more active during the rut. As for whitetails, there also seems to be an inborn mechanism that makes each buck limit his food intake during the critical months of winter. By doing so, he's leaving available forage for does and their unborn young and helping to ensure the survival of the species.

A muley's metatarsal glands are much longer than a whitetail's, about 1⅛ inch longer. The forehead patch is darker in color, often completely black on mature bucks. Some bucks have white muzzles that stand out as they peer through foliage.

Mature Rocky Mountain mule deer measure about 40 inches high at the shoulder. Large, prime specimens will stand several inches higher. A big muley superbuck will be much blockier than a big whitetail, with massive haunches, shoulders, and neck. I was awed by the first real muley superbuck that I killed—he was that much larger than any whitetail I'd ever seen.

Big muleys are at least as long as a big whitetail when measured from the tip of their nose to the tip of their tail. Real superbuck muleys' average length is between 6 and 12 inches greater than the 95 inches recorded for northern whitetails.

You're on the trail of a big'un when you find tracks that are large, round, and make a deep print. Tracks that measure from 3 to 3½ inches long aren't uncommon for a big buck.

ANTLERS

A mule deer superbuck's rack is a thing of beauty and a joy forever to the hunter skilled enough to harvest one. Scientists describe the antlers as "dichotomous," meaning they have forked beams, usually two forks on each antler. The muley's antlers differ sharply from those of the whitetail rack which typically features a number of single tines growing off the main beam. Most typical mule deer are called "four-points," referring to the number of points on only *one* side of the rack, excluding the brow tine. This is also termed a "western count" as opposed to "eastern count" where the hunter counts all points on both sides of the animal's rack. And while mule deer bucks often do have brow tines (also called basal snags), many do not.

How do you decide if a mule deer is of superbuck caliber? Width of the rack is one criterion that's becoming ever more popular as a measure in the West. A 30-inch wide rack is the elusive dream for many of today's hunters, while a few stalwart souls search the rim-rocks for a 36-incher. Both are in pretty short supply these days, so bagging a buck like this takes a good deal of work. To judge the rack's width, look for a couple of inches of daylight between the tips of the ears and the inside curve of the antlers. If the buck looks big in the body as well, you just might be looking at a 30-inch buck.

Extremely wide racks like these are impressive, especially if they have the tremendous antler mass top-caliber muleys are noted for. Such a buck is worthwhile even if he doesn't make the book. But if it's a book buck you're after look for main beams that curve forward in a long, sweeping arc, past the buck's nose if possible. Next, look for long antler tines. Good fork depth, especially on the front fork, will add needed points to the score. If you're determined to bag a record book buck remember that an unequal number of points side to side will count as a deduction. So a 6 × 5 has one point that will subtract from the score. However, for most of us this deduction would be moot; a rack that close to Boone and Crockett standards would be superbuck enough for any hunter.

A super-muley good enough for Boone and Crockett will generally have an inside spread between 22 and 30 inches. Most of the typical heads listed range between 24 and 27 inches. The circumference at the smallest place between the burr and the first point varies on average between 4⅜ inches and 6 inches. Most book bucks are 5 × 5s, five points to a side, that is, a four-point western count. Naturally, the greatest majority of the bucks that qualify for Pope and Young score somewhat lower than the 195 points that it takes to make Boone and Crockett.

Big mule deer bucks require the same three things that it takes to produce a big whitetail: age, nutrition, and good genetics. Like the whitetail, the most spectacular antlers will usually be found on a buck between 4½ and 7½ years of age.

Mule deer rarely cast both antlers at the same time as a whitetail frequently does. Between nine and nineteen additional days are usually required before the second antler drops. Once both antlers are shed, it will take anywhere from two weeks to two months for antler growth to start once more.

As a rule, mule deer populations fluctuate much more than those of the whitetail. But mule deer inhabit areas of the country that are subjected to the worst kinds of weather: extremes of temperature and low precipitation. In much of the west, growing seasons are short and rainfall meagre; forage suffers with a corresponding decrease in fawn production. In fact, forage quality is the main factor governing mule deer population dynamics.

Forage quality also helps determine what antler quality will be like. In the arid southwest, 52 percent of the desert mule deer yearlings grew spike antlers after a droughty summer, a tremendous difference when compared to the 12 percent of spike-antlered yearlings when conditions were good.

Winter mortality is another reason that antler quality deteriorates in a given area. When blizzards dish out their worst, it's not uncommon for entire age classes of muleys to die. One of the worst instances was after the severe winter of 1983–84 in portions of Utah, Wyoming, and Colorado. It took six long years before big bucks were once more being sighted in the hardest-hit areas. In the years between, an average four-point buck (eight- or ten-point eastern count) was considered a trophy in what was formerly high quality ten-point plus big buck range.

Fortunately, few animals have the climate-tolerance range of the mule deer. If there's enough food, water, and escape cover the mule deer will thrive as long as the climate conforms to his very minimal standards. Even in the most severe climates, local populations of mule deer manage to find small pockets with a microclimate to their liking. Often, this microclimate varies only a few degrees in temperature, enough to ensure the deer's survival. Another example of this is seen when groups of mule deer congregate to ride out storms in the lee of a hill where the wind isn't quite so severe.

According to the excellent reference book by the Wildlife Management Institute, *Mule and Black-Tailed Deer of North America*, mule deer can withstand extreme temperatures varying from −76°F below in the winter to 154°F in the summer. They've been known to tolerate wind chills as low as minus 150°F. In a habitat like California's Mojave Desert where rainfall is often non-existent, mule deer do well, getting the water they require from their forage.

Mule deer can tolerate extremely cold temperatures partially because of their coats which are made up of four different types of hair: large guard hairs, internal guard hairs, mane hair that extends down the back, and an incredibly soft and dense wooly underhair. The diameter of a mule deer's guard hairs increases as he gets older. And the longest guard hairs actually act as antennae, helping each deer analyze where he is during periods of low visibility.

The mule deer superbuck is indeed something special. When you see that first one in the wild, you'll be convinced that here is a magnificent trophy worthy of your time and efforts.

32

The Crowning Glory:
The Antlers of a
Mule Deer Superbuck

A mule deer superbuck is an awe-inspiring sight: the heavy, forked antlers sweeping high above his head in an outside spread that could surpass 40 inches. Greenhorns easily mistake them for elk, especially if only part of the rack is visible. Even experienced hunters have been known to discount a tremendous muley's rack as that of an elk, especially if they can only see portions of it. A mega-muley like that is unforgettable.

When a trophy muley moves, you watch. His fluid grace will make chills run up and down your spine. The first time you see one lift his legs and thrust his antlers out before shifting into high, you just might freeze in spite of yourself. For the big mule deer *is* the West; his fantastic antlers represent all that's wild and free in our western states.

A mule deer's rack differs from that of a whitetail in several important ways. First, a muley's rack is generally larger and heavier than that of a whitetail buck of the same age. And a typical muley's rack is made up of two dichotomous, or two-pronged, forks on each antler rather than a series of points growing off of a main beam as the whitetail's do. A muley may or may not have brow tines, but if he does, they're usually much smaller than a whitetail's. And if you were to cross-section a whitetail's brow tine it would be elliptical or oval. The mule deer's is circular.

It is the mule deer antlers' uniform mass together with long, deep forks that contribute the most points to a muley's score in Boone and Crockett or Pope and Young record books. Top rear points that reach 24 inches and higher above the animal's forehead are not uncommon. Because of this rack height, many more deer with spreads of between 22 inches and 28 inches make the book than those that have the magic 30-inch spread common to whitetail trophy classes.

Nonetheless, a mule deer rack with a 30-inch outside spread is a desirable trophy, whether or not he makes the book. A 30-inch spread has become sort of an informal standard by which mule deer bucks are measured. Some hunters feel that deer of this size are getting rarer, as more hunters select them. Jim Carracioli of Salinas, California, a noted mule deer hunter, has taken nearly 30 mule deer with 30-inch spreads during his lifetime. Yet Carracioli took all of them during the 1960s and early 1970s. "I've pulled the trigger on three different bucks that I thought might make 30 inches during the past ten years," he said during a 1985 interview. "But none of them did." And Carracioli's an expert at sizing up big deer.

Field judging a rack's size can be a tricky proposition, since a mule deer's ear size fluctuates so much from one buck to another. A younger, smaller mule deer buck may have an ear-to-ear spread of only 18 inches, while an old, mature buck's ear-to-ear spread could measure 24 inches. If the rack that you're sizing up also has cheaters—points that stick out near the top that gain extra width—it may be darn difficult to judge exactly how wide it is. Cheater points make the rack even more attractive to some hunters since they add width. Cheaters are one reason why the standard measurement for a big muley has evolved from inside spread to outside spread.

If a 30-inch buck is hard to get, think about those hunters with even higher standards of excellence. These are the hunters out looking for a 36-inch buck, an even more elusive trophy.

Kim Mecham, partner in Mecham's Yellow Pine Outfitters of Paradox, Colorado, tells the story of the day her husband, Hal, was guiding a hunter for trophy muleys. "They were hunting in Utah, and there had been a big snow," she said. "Because of the snow, they were able to sneak around pretty well. All of a sudden they walked right up on a tremendous trophy muley. Hal said that the buck's rack was a minimum of 48 inches wide. But even though the hunter took several shots from only 30 yards away—and the buck was lying down—he missed every time. That's what seeing one of those big bucks up close can do to you. And it's the only time I can ever remember Hal saying that he wished he'd been carrying a gun."

A look at the record book, however, suggests that lots of trophy muley bucks are still out there. Boone and Crockett's top mule deer entries in the latest record book (1999) include a remarkable 13 typicals either taken or picked up during the 1990s as well as three non-typicals. The total of 16 amounts to 10 percent of the places included in this analysis, or 83 of the top typicals and 83 of the top non-typicals. Another interesting fact is that due to the difficulty typical mule deer racks were having in making the Boone and Crockett score for this class—which was formerly 195 points—that minimum score was recently lowered to 190.

The non-typical story is the same. A tremendous number of non-typical whitetails were able to make the minimum score for the category of 195, but very few mule deer qualified with more than 240 points, which was the old Boone and Crockett minimum score.

Again, a recent change which lowered that minimum to 230 points for non-typical mule deer appears to be a long overdue move in the right direction toward giving these fabulous animals their just desserts. Even so, there are many pages more of book whitetails than there are of book mule deer. Part of the reason, of course, is due to the above-mentioned difficulty in years past of taking a big mule deer that could qualify for minimums that have been deemed too high. The other reason is that there are so many more whitetails than mule deer available to hunt. Estimates of a continental whitetail herd that approaches 100 million animals—or even exceeds that number—are not uncommon. Compare that with a mule deer census that hovers between 4 million and 5 million animals continent-wide. Since many more people hunt so many more whitetails—and since it is not only easier to do so because most licenses are sold over-the-counter near their homes, but cheaper, too—of course more whitetails than muleys would be represented in the record books.

Mule deer are the easiest of all deer to measure by Boone and Crockett standards. There can be no more than five normal points per antler *including* the brow tine and the main beam tip. A measurable point is any projection at least one inch long, and its length must exceed its width at one inch or more of length. If there are numerous abnormal points, the rack should be scored as a non-typical so that the additional points can be added to the final score rather than be deducted.

To make Boone and Crockett a non-typical mule deer buck would probably need to have ten or more points on each antler. Since a buck must score 230 points to make the book as a non-typical—40 more points than a typical—a rack would need a lot of excess antler material to score high in this category. Even Boone and Crockett officials admit that it's extremely difficult to judge non-typical muleys in the field.

Mule deer are creatures of the wide, open spaces. That makes them very difficult animals to take with bow and arrow. Comparatively speaking, very few typical muley bucks listed in the Pope and Young record book would make the minimum score of 190 required by Boone and Crockett—even though the Pope and Young minimum is significantly lower, and the two systems are virtually identical. Compare that ratio to the numerous the whitetail racks entered in Pope and Young that would qualify for Boone and Crockett with a score of at least 170 points.

The story's the same in the Pope and Young non-typical category: only a few non-typical mule deer bucks that would meet the Boone and Crockett minimum of 230 were taken with bow and arrow, but many whitetails would make the Boone and Crockett minimum of 195. The Pope and Young minimum for non-typical mule deer is 170 points.

In 1989, Pope and Young elected to form a new category of mule deer records: bucks with velvet-covered antlers. Many early-season archery hunts open when bucks are still in velvet, and officials felt it was unfair to require hunters to have the velvet removed for the sake of scoring the trophies. While all subspecies of mule deer are lumped together for both Boone and Crockett and Pope and Young, the other two recordkeeping organizations prefer to separate them. Safari Club International now recognizes mule deer taken south of a line drawn roughly along the 34th parallel in Arizona, New Mexico, and west Texas including the states of Sonora and Chihuahua in Mexico as desert mule deer. The minimum score required of a typical desert mule deer's rack under the SCI system is 150 points. Non-typicals must score 158 points.

The SCI's larger Rocky Mountain mule deer category includes deer taken from all remaining mule deer (not blacktail) range. The minimum score for a typical is 155 points while a non-typical must score 163 points. SCI scores mule deer the same way they score whitetails. The four circumferential measurements are totaled. The remainder of the score for typical antlers is arrived at by adding the length of each main beam, the lengths of all typical points, and the number of typical points on each antler together.

A non-typical's SCI score is the sum of the circumferential measurements of both right and left antlers, plus the lengths of the main beams, and the lengths of all points except the tip of the main beam, plus the number of points. The same restriction applies to the scoring of non-typical SCI mule deer trophies as when scoring whitetail racks.

The Burkett System also separates mule deer trophies into Rocky Mountain and desert mule deer categories. Again, method of collection is also differentiated under the Burkett System into modern arm, primitive arm, archery, handgun, and incidental acquisition categories.

Hunters who take trophies by illegal means will have a rough time entering their trophies in any of the record books. Even a hint of wrongdoing is enough to set officials investigating. There is an excellent communications network between the various organizations but especially between Boone and Crockett and Pope and Young. Since illegally acquired trophies taint all those taken legitimately, it's to everyone's best interest to help these organizations police our ranks.

When illegalities have been proven, Pope and Young has in some cases struck *every* record taken by that hunter from their record book. Boone and Crockett most often limits their action to only the trophy under suspicion. A sport that is often regarded with suspicion by the non-hunting public simply can't afford to recognize people who take advantage of game animals, either for their achievements or for their sportsmanship.

33

The Life Cycle
of a Mule Deer Superbuck

The mule deer doe was heavy with young. Snowmelt had begun early this year, and somehow she sensed that the worst of the storms were over. She and several other does and their fawns from the preceding summer felt the old familiar urge that compelled them to travel. They moved gracefully yet deliberately along the edge of a canyon, like dark gray ghosts, retracing the route they'd taken in autumn when bitter winds and deep snows forced them out of their summer home in a lush basin just below timberline.

Water was already gushing down crevices and trails, merging into the torrent that thundered in the canyon's bottom. Here and there, the earliest harbingers of spring peaked their softly colored petals from receding snowbanks. The doe traveled back with no young of her own. This would be her third summer of life, her second fawning season. Her single buck fawn from the previous year had lived only eight weeks, his life cut short by a quick and hungry cougar.

The route was a tortuous one and the deer took their time. Each day meant there was less snow that they had to deal with. By the time they'd made the 40-mile journey that led to their summer home range, the does were losing patience with one another. Normally, they enjoyed each other's company. But as it got closer to fawning time they grew antagonistic, both to each other and to their own young from the preceding year.

In early May, the split was made. Each animal went its separate way, although in the case of the fawns it meant that their mothers had to chase them off. For the next several weeks, the doe kept to herself feeding on succulent new spring growth. As she gained weight, unknowingly she was preparing for the stresses associated with nursing her new babies. When it finally came time to have her young, she found a secluded spot and there she delivered two healthy fawns, a young doe and a buck.

The tiny fawns each weighed about seven pounds. The doe left them in the clump of stunted Douglas fir that she'd chosen for her labor. Before she left, she made sure that she'd eaten all the evidence that a birth had taken place. Now her young were virtually scent-free, an adaptation to the many predators threatening their survival. Nature ensures that they stay scent-free until they're able to follow their mother around. They void their urine and feces only during their mother's visits, and, amazingly enough, the doe ate whatever the fawns voided. Nothing was left for predators to scent during this early, vulnerable time of the fawns' life.

The doe hid her young well, and they couldn't be seen even six to eight weeks after birth. During that entire time they stayed where she left them, and nursed whenever she appeared. The doe's visits were brief, however: she realized that by being near her young she was putting them at increased risk.

After about eight weeks, the fawns are ready to follow their mother about the steep slopes of their summer home. The alpine flowers bloom and birds sing—it's a wonderful world for a young muley. By now the male, Muley, already weighs more than his sister. As a mule deer buck, Muley will gain weight throughout his life, except for the winter periods when he loses weight because of the rigors of the rut. The doe will gain weight only until she's about 2½ years old. At that point her weight levels off for the rest of her life.

Muley fawns are noisy. They enjoy playing together. Much bleating accompanies their frolicking—needed exercise as well as good practice for the escape maneuvers that will serve them well in later life. Mule deer are affectionate: mutual grooming or licking is common. It's not unusual for a doe to tolerate some nursing by her young well into the rutting season.

When the doe finally leads her two youngsters out onto the slopes, other doe mothers begin to appear with their new fawns, too. These does are the same does that traveled together from the wintering grounds. Doe groups are usually stable groups, headed by a doe mother. A doe and her offspring and her offspring's offspring usually make up a three-generation group of does. More or fewer generations can also be represented. Maternal groups like these usually share a traditional range.

It's summer and the living is easy, even in the forbidding mountains. One day, though, the doe gets a whiff of mountain lion scent. Nervous and upset, she gazes long and hard in every direction. Mule deer rely on their eyes, ears, and nose to warn them of danger. The whole group rarely feeds at once; usually one animal is looking or listening, scouring the surroundings for danger. Muleys form groups as an anti-predator strategy. Five sets of noses, ears, and eyes are far better than one. But even with others nearby, the doe can't relax; the memories associated with the odor of the dreaded lion are too strong. She stamps her foot and gets every other deer's attention.

When she turns to leave, the others follow in single file. They trot up the mountainside, stopping occasionally to watch their backtrail. Then they move over the top. The fawns tag along behind, curious about the smell that makes their mother so spooky. The deer travel until they reach another drainage. All it takes is one whiff of a feared predator like the cougar to send them to another portion of their range, sometimes for good.

The two fawns thrive in the new drainage. By now, they are eating bits and pieces of forbs and shrubs as they continue nursing. In late summer the mountains begin to grow chilly in the evening. There's noticeably less light each day and the animals' coats are beginning to thicken dramatically. They have grown quite a bit larger over the summer and are beginning to act more grown up.

All summer long, the fawns have enjoyed the prime mule deer summer range with their mothers. But the small buck catches glimpses of other deer as well, deer that look like they have branches sprouting out of their skull. These other deer don't usually come near. They hang out higher up the slopes, where the terrain is steeper and the grass isn't as lush. But Muley looks longingly at them, not sure why he feels so drawn to them.

Occasionally, a young buck comes close to the fawn and they sniff about each other. But these meetings usually don't last long enough for Muley to satisfy his curiosity.

In early fall the first snow arrives. The fawns leap and play in the white stuff while the does feel in their bones that the time to move to the wintering grounds is drawing near. Bucks on the slopes above have polished antlers now, and Muley watches as they push and shove at each other. After about two more weeks on the summer range, and after a fairly heavy snow, the does begin to follow the canyon out of the mountains once again. The bucks don't leave at once. They wait until the snow makes the decision for them before bailing out. But ultimately they, too, make the trip down the slope.

As the deer move out of the high country, the fawns become aware of a new smell over the countryside. Sometimes a smoky odor, sometimes a fragrant one, and now they occasionally see strange animals off in the distance. Some of these animals have four legs and others have two. Puzzled, the young buck stares, but his mother pushes him forward. She doesn't want any part of the strangers. A little while later he finds out why.

They'd just finished crossing a gently flowing stream when suddenly an overwhelming smell blew right into his nose. His mother went rigid, then whirled, the fawns following. *"Boing, boing,"* they bounded away using the unusual four-legged springing step, the stott, that serves them so well in rugged country.

"Boom," dust from a boulder that shattered right in front of them got into the young buck's eyes. *"Boom,"* another loud sound and now Muley was panicking inside, but he followed his mother like a good youngster should. He was prepared for the next shot but not the sight of one of the does of the group dropping from sight. He looked

back and saw her tumble down the hill. Seeing her like that made him bound even higher until the deer all disappeared into the rims. The last thing he remembered was a strange sound echoing through the mountains, "I got one!"

Well away from the activity, the doe checked her two fawns and continued on her way, anxious to be gone from the danger. But in another couple of weeks, the bottom fell out of Muley's world. His mother chased him and his sister away. They kept trying to go back to her but she'd lay back her ears and rush them. Once, she even stood on her hind legs and flailed at the young buck. That was what finally convinced him that she meant business. Saddened, he left.

The buck groups had shown up not long after the does and fawns had arrived back at the wintering ground. Several of the bucks were no longer in the group. Muley didn't know it, but they had also met up with hunters. The bucks that had survived should have been nervous but were instead preoccupied with the rut. Muley watched them spar or gently fight with each other. He listened to the sound of their antlers rubbing on trees and brush.

He knew that the bucks were awfully interested in does, but he wasn't quite sure why. There were some intriguing smells out there, but the one time he got close, a bigger buck threatened him with a look, laid back ears, and a horizontal tail that whipped up and down with each step. All he could do was stand there, splay-footed, with his tail pinched in tight between his legs and his back caved inward while the bigger buck approached. He got out of trouble by circling behind the dominant with lowered head, a sign of subordinate behavior.

Muley, lonely without his mother, joined up with some of the other displaced fawns. He looked for his mother, but she was nowhere to be seen. The young deer fed together and watched the strange behavior of the older animals. And when Muley finally did see his mother again, he couldn't wait to run to her.

The winter passed. Snow fell frequently and the deer ate up almost all of their food. That's when someone in the herd got the bright idea of jumping the fence and getting into the haystacks. The feed was good, and there was very little work involved in finding it. But when shots rang out one night it was enough to convince many of the deer it was time to clear out. Luckily, the winter was just about over and the high country beckoned.

In June, the doe got testy again. Once more, she ran off her two youngsters. This time the young buck wasn't quite so upset. He was beginning to expect this kind of behavior from his mother. What was strange, however, was the feeling that he was getting on top of his head. A few times there had actually been pain when he'd playfully rubbed up against a tree.

Two months later, his mother came back to the group with three new babies. Muley was not impressed and although he continued to feed with the does, he sensed something had changed and would never be the same again. He became a bit aloof from the does and ran with another young buck from the group most of the time. When his mother gave him very little attention the remainder of the summer, he knew it was time to move on. Later, he and one of his buddies began feeding away, moving farther all the time. But the farther they got, the farther they wanted to go. The countryside always looked a bit more intriguing from the next ridge over. Without knowing why, nature was aiding and abetting this move, ensuring that the young buck would not breed with his own kin, a move that would weaken the species. Finally, the two young bucks found a basin that looked inviting. What's more, there was a small group of bachelor bucks living there, and it looked like they were eager for company.

Here, for the next couple of months, the bucks lolled in the sun, ate and slept. It was a good life, regardless of all the changes that had taken place. The buck now knew that he also had branches sprouting on his head. And he knew he was growing much larger, too. But right now, all he felt like doing was feeding in the sun with his companions until it was time to travel back down the mountain.

In late August, a peculiar feeling came over the buck. He had the increasing urge to push against trees with his rack just to feel them give. Play-fighting with bucks the same age was lots of fun, too. He sometimes got close to one of the bigger bucks, but he'd always circle to the larger buck's rear, back curved inward, to avoid possible trouble.

Once, however, the very largest buck, after rut-snorting in reply to the sneak-to-the-rear maneuver of the smaller buck, began to graze. So Muley followed his lead and grazed along with him, approaching from the rear and sniffing the larger buck's hocks like a good subordinate should. The dominant buck then turned the tables on Muley and displayed weak behavior, as if he were the subordinate instead of Muley. He'd crouch as he grazed close to the smaller buck. Eventually the big buck gently offered his much larger antlers to Muley, who stepped forward and tentatively placed his rack upon the big boy's.

Both of Muley's antlers proved a match for only one of the dominant's. But that seemed to be all right with the bigger buck. From that day on, the older buck was more tolerant of Muley. He sparred with him and let him come closer than any of the other subordinates. Muley was quite happy to have this new friend and readily followed him off the mountain once the snows began.

This time when the wall of human and horse scent hit the young buck, his reaction was instantaneous. He flared his rump patch, snorted a couple of times, pivoted to his right and fled up the hill. The other bucks followed. By keeping to a distinct gully, the bucks were unseen by the hunters on the next hillside. The young buck learned an escape strategy that worked; he wouldn't forget it in the future.

The next day, the young buck was feeding across a slope dotted with junipers when he noticed a movement on the next ridge. Freezing, he watched intently. Soon he noticed the figure of a human silhouetted for just a moment against the sky. As he looked back at the big dominant, he was surprised to see the buck's knees give in. He watched as the buck almost burrowed under a small bush. Without knowing why, he did the same. And he stayed there the rest of the day. After dark, the two bucks continued safely downhill.

Life went on like this for the youngster. When he was four years old, he got very close to breeding a doe before being run off by a bigger buck. When he was five, he did manage to mate with several does. He followed each around in turn, either rushing her until she would urinate, or practicing a submissive tactic that encouraged the same response. When the doe's urine finally would flow, the buck would bide his time, then snuffle in the ground where it had fallen. He'd perform the lip-curl maneuver, tasting the urine to see if the doe was ready to breed.

It was in his best interest to keep any doe approaching estrus close to him until she'd stand for breeding. But it was in the doe's best interest to visit as many bucks as possible, subconsciously searching for the one with the most dominant genes. Eventually, Muley's perseverance paid off when his first doe permitted him to mount her.

Without even realizing it, Muley had become large enough to intimidate many of the other bucks. This year his antlers began getting gnarled around the base. Each year they'd been getting wider and his rack now measured about 30 inches across. Something else had happened as well. He was rapidly becoming a prime target for the hunters who came up the drainage each autumn. In fact, he narrowly missed disaster when one hunter threw up his gun and fired before the big deer could react. The shot was close enough to crease his shoulder, but not close enough to draw blood.

By the time he was six, Muley was the king of the mountain. He knew exactly what man with his firearm was capable of doing. He'd seen his friend the wise old dominant finally come up against a man that had done the unexpected. The big buck had fallen never to rise again. Muley didn't want the same fate to befall him. But it was becoming harder all the time to avoid it. With a heavy rack that now spanned 34 inches, Muley was rapidly becoming the talk of the area's hunters. One man traveled 1,000 miles when he heard the tale of the big heavy-beamed four-point that lived in the high basin. But his trip was for naught when Muley cleared out as soon as he saw the hunter and his packstring. As the hunter watched him top out on the mountain's crest, he vowed to come back the next year, this time on foot.

Muley kept getting bigger in the body. His face began to take on a grizzled appearance. He never moved without a distinct purpose, saving energy in this way. Other bucks deferred to him now. He had his choice of does, and serviced several distinct groups that lived farther down the slopes. One autumn the winter never came! The does stayed high on the mountain and so did the bucks.

The hunter climbed up after them, with a pack on his back. He managed to get within 400 yards of the big buck before Muley noticed a younger buck making across the canyon intently. When he pinpointed the object of the smaller buck's attention, he snuck away. He found a hiding spot in the next drainage and came out only at night.

It went on like this for two more years. Once the determined hunter managed to shoot at Muley as he ran along a rim, but in his excitement, the man missed. Muley, now a 38-inch buck, kept cool and drifted into some thick firs. That was the last time the hunter saw the buck that year.

The next year Muley's antlers weren't quite so wide. But they were still heavy. Now, several non-typical points had formed. He was the oldest buck on the mountain but no longer the dominant. That was okay with him; he was getting tired. And he knew that with the first chill winds, he could expect to see the hunter again. He kept his eyes peeled, but never saw the one who had dogged his tracks so determinedly.

One day, though, several other men showed up across the canyon. Muley ran as fast as he could through the pine and fir thickets to his hiding spot in the next basin. What he didn't know is that his old nemesis, the big buck hunter, had finally figured out the buck's escape route. He was hiding on the rim where he'd seen the big buck top out so often. So when Muley slipped over the ridge, the hunter was waiting.

It was probably just as well. At the buck's advanced age, his teeth were wearing down. The next year there would have been a marked decrease in the size of his antlers. He would have become easier prey for the mountain lions as well, since he was getting rheumy in his joints. The hunter was happy; after hunting the big buck for several years he finally had a real trophy to hang on his wall. Muley never knew what hit him. What's more, he'd lived a good, long life and had left innumerable sons and daughters throughout the mountains. And these sons and daughters all carried the same genetic code that had enabled Muley to become the king of the hill, good news indeed for the big buck hunters of the world.

34

Mule Deer
Superbuck Behavior

Once upon a time mule deer were looked upon as the whitetail's slightly stupid cousins. Back then, whitetails were regarded as wary, and muleys were gullible by comparison. Whitetails were sneaky: they slithered through coverts. Muleys, on the other hand, were known for blundering right into an opening and then turning around to gawk at the hunter who'd pushed them there. Once upon a time the mule deer, even the mule deer superbuck, were thought of as the whitetail's addled kinfolk. But those days are no more.

Back in the sixties, very few hunters pursued the muley buck. Seasons were liberal with bag limits of two bucks or more. As hunting pressure gradually increased, the muleys changed their ways. The muley *is* a different breed of deer and in some very significant ways not at all like the whitetail. The whitetail is usually a creature of dense cover, a nervous and fidgety animal. Mule deer, on the other hand, live in the wide open spaces. Until recently their behavior reflected the fact that they felt safe when distanced from danger. But with the advent of the flat-shooting modern firearm and new optics, distance is no longer a protection. The new breed of muley has been hunted hard and it has learned a few new tricks, some of them as well as the whitetail learned them. Now they're becoming increasingly adept at holding tight in—you guessed it—the thickest cover they can find.

Mule deer aren't as nervous as whitetails and they are generally much more gregarious with members of their own species. But, like the whitetail, a mule deer must survive many lessons and learn from each if he's to grow into the spectacular animal that is the muley superbuck. In terms of cageyness, the mule deer superbuck has stopped, looked, listened, and learned! In many respects, today you can't tell a whitetail from a muley. Gone—for the most part—are the good old days when a buck would flee up a slope and stop to look back at his pursuer. Gone, too, are those moments when a muley's evasive tactics through the trees were his sole defense. A big mule deer buck will run when pushed, but often right out of sight. He'll gallop through the trees, too, but often while keeping a clump of them between you and him, just like a whitetail. I haven't seen a really big mule deer buck stott in that typical mule deer four-legs-off-the-ground bouncing gait in many a moon. Likely as not, he'll barrel along like a quarter horse, head down and feet barely touching the ground. And a muley is just as liable to hold tight to cover as a whitetail these days. Muleys will hole up in brush, in blowdowns, and even hide under rocks and on ledges. In other words, the mule deer buck has changed his behavior *big time!*

I've hunted in mule deer areas in the desert where bucks were scarce as flying pigs during the hunting season. These same areas, far from any migration routes, were chock full of 30-inch bucks when the rut came along a month later and hunting season was over. So where did the big bucks come from? According to game and fish personnel, they had to be there all the time. They're getting an awful lot like whitetails, wouldn't you say?

Yet in many respects, muleys not only differ from whitetails, they actually have it all over their eastern cousins. It's theorized that their eyes are much better; they rely a lot more on vision than do whitetails. A mule deer's hearing is geared to long-range sensing, too. They'll pick up on small sounds heard a long way off. Scent bothers them as much as it does a whitetail, and when a big buck smells a human, he'll skedaddle—fast.

Speaking of sense, big muleys seem to have a sixth one when it comes to being hunted. Mega-muley hunters tell similar tales of spotting a big, bedded mule deer, one with no apparent idea that anyone's around. After planning a stalk, then creeping out of sight to execute it, finally it's discovered that the object of all this attention is watching *the hunter* well before he's ready to start the final approach. This in spite of the fact that he'd followed all the basic rules: no skylining, keeping the wind in his favor, etc. All agree: a big muley's sixth sense is uncanny.

Trophy mule deer bucks have come a long way in the last 20 years, at least behaviorally. For example, mule deer in general are more gregarious than are whitetails. That's one behavior that could help you harvest one. If you see one mule deer buck, look again. He's probably not alone and you should find even more somewhere near. Mule deer bucks like each other's company. Big bucks often stay hidden, letting smaller bucks act as their more visible eyes and ears. Even during the rut mule deer bucks are far more tolerant of the company of other bucks than are whitetails.

Whitetail bucks will generally share overlapping range with does year round. A big whitetail buck's core area will often be in the densest, thickest cover he can find. But with mule deer, it's the does that keep the best range for themselves and their young. The bucks restrict themselves for much of the year to the highest, steepest portions of the range, areas that often have less palatable food and better views of the surrounding terrain and possible danger, an important big buck concern.

A whitetail is a nervous animal, usually not happy in one place. A muley, on the other hand, is much calmer and he's able to learn quickly. The calm of a muley is thought to be part of an ancient anti-predator strategy, according to Dr. Valerius Geist of the University of Calgary. "Put a mule deer buck in a park where he's not hunted and he tames down very quickly," he said. "Put a whitetail there, and he'll still be nervous. A mule deer can't afford to be nervous and expect to survive. He'd wear himself out with worry with all the predators that lurk on his range. A mule deer buck is a cool, calm customer, much more so than the whitetail."

Dr. Geist doesn't believe that mule deer scrape any great amount, if at all. Hunters like Arizona's Jay Gates disagree. "I've seen lots of scrapes that I suppose have been made by mule deer, yet I've never actually seen one scrape. In any case, if mule deer do scrape it's apparently not for the same reasons that whitetails do—for the advertisement of sexual status and solicitation of does."

Two schools of thought exist as to when is the best time to hunt a trophy muley. One opinion is "the earlier, the better." Early on, the bucks are relaxed; they haven't been disturbed as yet. Early season hunts usually mean a lot of work for high country muleys.

The other school suggests waiting until the bucks become more active during either the rut or the migration. Late season hunts used to be timed to coincide with one event or the other, but usually not both. In seasons past, migrating mule deer were hunted as they moved out of the high country. Many herds' buck-to-doe ratios were a long time recovering from the heavy harvest of bucks. Some hunts still catch a portion of the rut, when bucks are beginning to act less cautiously.

When the mule deer rut does begin, usually in late November, the bucks join the does on their range. The dominant bucks roam around looking for pre-estrous does. When they find one, they repeatedly force her to void her urine, test it to see if she's getting close to estrus, then stick with her until she's ready to copulate.

RUBS

Rubs aren't merely signposts to a mule deer buck as they are to a whitetail. Muleys make many more rubs than whitetails though they may not be as noticeable. Mule deer "horning," as the behavior is called, has a specific purpose. Mule deer rub or horn as an auditory signal to other deer, according to Dr. Geist. "Mule deer horn frequently and noisily, often for very long periods of time," Geist said. "This horning acts like an auditory signal of male dominance. Horning, for mule deer, is almost what bugling is to an elk. A buck stops and listens between bouts of horning to determine whether another buck will reply."

Dr. Geist said that on many occasions he has followed rutting bucks that were horning from a distance of 10 to 50 paces. "Wandering bucks stop every 50 or 200 yards, horn, look, listen, and then move on," he said. "If they hear horning in reply, they'll pinpoint its location, then they often move in to investigate."

Mule deer daily feeding patterns are much more predictable than are whitetails'. Whitetails are often up and about feeding and traveling during the middle of the day. Outside of the rut, mule deer travel to and from feeding areas primarily early in the morning and late in the evening. They will feed around their bedding areas at midday for a time and then lie right back down. If you can find an area where a big muley is feeding, leave him alone. He should be back at the same time, by same way, tomorrow. You can ambush him then. Unless, of course, you spook him. And it's only too easy to spook him.

Mule deer are much more tolerant of the cold than are whitetails. During warm weather you can often find big bucks hiding in the dark timber that grows on north-facing slopes. If the weather's cold or stormy, they might shift to a south-facing slope. Then if the sun comes out and it gets warm, you just might trip them up during the day as they re-bed, shifting positions to take advantage of the shade.

MIGRATION

Other mule deer behavior important to the hunter involves the autumn and spring migration. Whitetails migrate, if conditions require it, but not usually with the same regularity as mule deer. Again, whitetail ranges aren't usually found in the harsh-weather regions of the mountains where mule deer live. And it is weather that causes muley migrations. Traditional mule deer migration routes may vary between one mile to over a hundred miles in length. Muleys will usually abandon their range once snow reaches 18 inches in depth. During mild winters, there may be no migration at all, a point worth considering if you're planning to hunt a migration route late in the season. Always have a contingency plan and place, just in case.

RECRUITMENT

Mule deer productivity—how many young will survive each year—is usually directly associated to the quality of the range. And range quality is linked to precipitation patterns, according to noted mule deer researcher Dr. Richard Mackie of Montana State University in Bozeman. "Mule deer populations can increase or decrease as much as tenfold during a very short time in the most variable type of environment," he said. "The more stable an environment is, the less population numbers will fluctuate."

Droughty conditions affect mule deer survival and recruitment well beyond the summer itself. If forbs and shrubs don't thrive in summer, little palatable forage remains for the winter. When muleys share their range with stock like cattle or horses, population crashes are even more likely. In droughty summers when grass is in short supply, free-ranging cattle will invade traditional mule deer range and devour the available forage, leaving little to sustain resident muleys during the winter. That's why drought conditions can be so devastating to the nation's mule deer.

Because of the tremendous amount of research that's been devoted to whitetail deer, our country's most popular game animal, much more is known about them than about mule deer. Not only do whitetails outnumber mule deer, whitetail hunters outnumber mule deer hunters. Hunters spend much more money on whitetails each year than they do on muleys. And money talks. So when it comes right down to it, the reason we know so much more about the whitetail is an economic one. Likewise in the western states where the mule deer lives, there are other, often more economically important big game animals. Elk are larger so more can be charged for a license. Mountain sheep are scarcer and they have more problems, so more has to be learned about them. And, of course, you can charge more for a sheep license. Mule deer studies are often neglected, or shuffled to the bottom of the bureaucratic pile.

However, there is a ray of hope upon the horizon. Organizations such as the Mule Deer Foundation have created a forum for airing concerned members' views and focusing their combined resources upon desired goals. And one of the group's most urgent goals right now just happens to be learning more about the mule deer. Because as time goes by, more and more hunters are beginning to realize that over the past 25 years we've actually seen the evolution of a new big game animal: today's trophy muley.

Once upon a time only whitetails were thought of as superbucks. But times and mule deer are a-changing. Whitetails, move over. Hunters, take note. There's a new breed of superbuck out there—the mule deer superbuck.

35

Favorite Mule Deer
Superbuck Forage

Like the whitetail, mule deer are opportunists when it comes to eat-ing: they take advantage of what they can find, when they can find it. In the early part of the year they shift from grazing to browsing, then combine the two methods of feeding during the rest of the year.

In spring, both whitetail and mule deer become grazers. They con-sume great quantities of early succulent grasses like bluegrass or junegrass when they first push through the soil. Later on when forbs sprout, deer shift their attention to items like wild onions. As spring wanes, deer concentrate more on browsing upon woody shoots, newly sprouted and chock full of essential nutrients. Browsing deer love certain shrubs and small trees better than others. Plants like the snowberry, rose, or chokecherry are high on their list.

In autumn, mast like berries and acorns are important foods in some parts of the muley's range. When the leaves finally drop from the trees, mule deer once again turn to browse species like rabbit-brush, mountain mahogany, and bitterbrush.

During winter, a mule deer often has no choice whatsoever: he must eat whatever he can find to tide him over until spring. At this time of the year big sagebrush, juniper, and small Douglas firs are all-important in many areas of a mule deer's range.

"A mule deer's food habits follow an annual cycle of availability," explained Dr. Richard Mackie, professor of wildlife biology with Mon-tana State University in Bozeman, Montana. "During the growing season the plants and parts of plants that the mule deer favor most are not only the most palatable, they also are the most nutritious. Springtime finds the muley searching out succulent grasses and forbs. Later, it's new woody growth. It's difficult to say just what kinds of forage deer will favor. Preferences change from region to re-gion. Here in Montana, for example, skunkbrush or fragrant sumac is an important mule deer food in the summer, but over in Utah's Great Basin, deer don't seem to like it.

"To survive, muleys have become selective feeders," Dr. Mackie continued. "They are constantly searching for the highest quality food available at that time. As the weather changes and becomes harsher, food choices become fewer. Mule deer are less selective in winter out of necessity, because there's not much left to eat.

"The rest of the year deer have to be picky. They're basically a small animal with a small gut. They can't eat a whole lot of food like an elk does, surviving simply because of the sheer quantity of food consumed. Mule deer have to eat the very best quality forage they can find. And in much of the mule deer's range, the best quality might not be very good after years of drought. That's when populations can get in trouble."

Dr. Mackie said that the biggest problem with mule deer nutrition isn't always winter weather itself, but the condition of the animals as winter approaches. Sparse rainfall during the summer leaves range plants in poor shape. When plant nutrients are low, deer lose vigor and their chances for survival through the winter diminish.

A harsh Rocky Mountain winter can bring a deer on winter range down fast unless there's enough nutritious feed available. According to the Wildlife Research Institute's book, *Mule and Black-tailed Deer of North America,* having snow on the ground increases the amount of energy a deer must use just to survive. A deer walking in 16 inches of snow uses four to five times as much energy as one walking on bare ground. If the snow is 20 inches deep, the deer must use seven to eight times as much energy. At a temperature of minus 4° F, a 100-pound deer burns 2,000 kilocalories, or *2 million calories* per day just staying alive. Winter forage cannot possibly meet these kinds of nutritional demands all by itself. The deer must be in top shape as bad weather approaches.

Not all deer live in climates that turn bitterly cold in winter. Muleys thrive in an assortment of diverse habitat types, ranging from the chaparral of California and its low, shrubby oak growth, to the northern mountains where fir trees and pines predominate. Mule deer live in aspen pockets and deserts, on the Great Plains and in the Great Basin. With such a tremendous variety of geographic locations interspersed through so many different climate zones, it's hard to definitively pinpoint a superbuck's favorite foods unless it's done region by region and season by season.

ROCKY MOUNTAINS AND INTERMOUNTAIN AREA

Think of mule deer and this is the picture that most hunters get: a sweeping vista of snow-covered peaks looming above alpine meadows and pine-covered slopes. The Rocky Mountain/Intermountain region that the largest muleys call home stretches over 1,500 miles from Arizona to northern Alberta and British Columbia. Mule deer range extends east to west from the tallgrass prairies to the Pacific coastal ranges. Mule deer migrate through much of this region, spending summers in the mountains and winters in foothills and valleys.

Entire papers have been devoted to the foods eaten by mule deer in these mountainous regions. At least 788 kinds of plants have been identified as muleys' forage. Of these, 484 were forbs, 202 were shrubs and trees, 84 were grasses, sedges and rushes, and 18 were lower plants. A list of this size would be overwhelming and self-defeating to hunters.

Favored browse species of the Rocky Mountain muley include snowberry, big sagebrush, rose, chokecherry, bitterbrush, quaking aspen, oregon grape, willow, serviceberry, mountain mahogany, rabbitbrush, and ponderosa pine. Two of the best grasses are bluegrass and wheatgrass. Forbs muleys like are Wright buckwheat, sulfur buckwheat, aster, lupine, phlox, and daisy fleabane. Many of these species are also preferred by the whitetail deer.

Between 99 and 124 million acres of the Rocky Mountain muleys' winter range is composed of a mix of sagebrush and juniper. Serious questions about the nutritional value of both plants have been raised by biologists. First, a diet consisting of more than 30 percent sagebrush could inhibit the fermentation action of bacteria on the rumen contents. The oils contained in juniper can also adversely affect the microorganisms in a deer's rumen. It's estimated that deer can only tolerate a diet consisting of about 20 percent juniper or less. It's easy to see why deer deteriorate during times of heavy snowfalls when the only forage available to them is the juniper and sagebrush that peeks out above the snowcover. Deer can go downhill so quickly that they die six to eight weeks after a prolonged diet consisting of only these two plants. The reason behind the stories of deer dying of starvation with full stomachs can be better understood when the effects of juniper and sagebrush on the muley are taken into account.

CONIFEROUS FOREST

Mule deer habitat intergrades or mixes with that of their cousins the blacktails as it nears the West Coast. The farther west you travel, the more blacktails you encounter. Mule deer in this type of habitat aren't subjected to the extremes of temperature and climate that they are in the Rocky Mountains. Plants like canyon live oak, acorns, salal, grasses and sedges make up the diet of muleys living in these forests. Mule deer also browse on Douglas fir.

Farther north in the coniferous forests of Oregon and Washington, autumn muleys feed on grasses, blackcap, blackberries, bitter cherry, huckleberry, plantain, and big deervetch. This type of habitat melds into that of the Rocky Mountains so there will be an overlap between plant species.

Deer also forage on many coniferous tree species including incense cedar, western red cedar, white fir, grand fir, western hemlock, all kinds of juniper, lodgepole, piñon, and ponderosa pine. Many other types of conifers are also browsed during the year, but these are the primary ones.

DESERT AND CHAPARRAL

One common denominator links mule deer that live in deserts and chaparral: drought conditions. Temperatures are often high and rainfall light. Southern muleys occupy portions of California's chaparral habitat up to about 4,000 feet in elevation; above this height, migratory California mule deer from the Sierra Nevada mountain range spend their winters.

The California chaparral habitat is made up of deep-rooted plants with tough leaves designed by nature to withstand the rigors of temperature and drought. Deer prefer grasses and forbs, but they are usually in short supply. So deer generally resort to less nutritious chaparral browse species like chamise, manzanita, and ceanothus.

Whenever mistletoe, fungi (like mushrooms), and acorns are found, they're eagerly eaten. Mule deer also like Sierra mountain misery, Fremont silk tassel, and interior oak.

California's Mohave Desert area holds sparse populations of both California and southern mule deer subspecies. When the weather is especially dry the animals concentrate near seeps or tanks. Important early autumn foods include the leaves and pods of the honey mesquite. Biologists have also reported mule deer feeding on palo verde, ironwood, catclaw, and mistletoe in late December. Green big galleta is an early January food source.

A narrow belt of Arizona chaparral extends across the state at an elevation between 3,000 and 6,000 feet above sea level. It's been estimated that desert mule deer live in the western portion, in the area around Prescott, Arizona. Major browse species within this type of habitat are desert ceanothus, hairy mountain mahogany, and cliffrose. Other mule deer foods include birchleaf mountain mahogany, juniper, shrub live oak, manzanita, Louisiana wormwood, and hollyleaf buckthorn.

Sonoran Desert habitat is similar to that of California's Mohave Desert. Prominent food species for the desert mule deer who live in this desert include fairy duster browse in early and late autumn; jojoba from late autumn through late winter; Wright buckwheat in mid- and late winter; and mesquite beans, shrub live oak acorns, and catclaw beans in summer. Forbs are also important in autumn and winter, especially bluedicks, filaree, and Louisiana wormwood.

In the Chihuahuan desert of the United States, a small portion of south-central New Mexico and a strip along the Rio Grande River in Texas, four forage species make up the bulk of what the area's mule deer eat: the green leaves of wavyleaf oak, juniper, yucca, and hairy mountain mahogany.

In other areas of Texas the most important mule deer foods year-long were lechuguilla, candelilla, euphorbia, Engelmann prickly pear, acacia, and huayacan. Lechuguilla, with its tough, daggerlike leaves, candelilla, with leafless, waxy green steams, and prickly pear all retain succulence even during droughts. Sotol and yucca are also eaten. Only the flowers offer good-quality food.

PLAINS HABITAT

The Great Plains extend from the Texas panhandle north into the middle of Alberta and Saskatchewan. Their western edge terminates at the Rocky Mountains. The eastern edge peters out about where the old tallgrass prairie began. The Great Plains are complex grass-lands: many areas have a great diversity of plants for deer to feed on, besides just grasses. Small drainages or swales will often contain thickets of snowberry. Along main river systems large cottonwood stands mix with willows, and breaks—small canyons—are common and offer a muley a good spot to hide. Some breaks are famous for mule deer, like the Missouri Breaks or the Cheyenne Breaks. The badlands scattered across the plains provide excellent mule deer habitat wherever they occur.

At one point, overgrazing and over-hunting by the settlers just about wiped out mule deer in the plains states. But they've re-bounded with a vengeance and today are in good supply over most of their former historic range. Within the Great Plains, mule deer for-age upon favored species like snowberry, buffaloberry, chokecherry, skunkbrush sumac, and several species of rose. They'll also eat quaking aspen whenever it's available as well as acorns. Important grasses on the Great Plains include cool season grasses like western wheatgrass, bluebunch wheatgrass, green needlegrass, and needle and thread grass.

On the plains in winter, deer will congregate on south-facing slopes. Cottonwoods, silver sagebrush, rubber rabbitbrush, and snowberry are eaten fairly heavily at this time. Deer will also take advantage of any agricultural crops available during the winter.

Mule deer superbucks feed like any other deer for most of the year. Before the rut the bucks will still be storing up fat; once the rut begins, their behavior is dominated by breeding instincts. Knowing what the *does* will be feeding on during the rut could help determine where the bucks will be using later. Knowing the animals' favorite foods is fitting one more piece in the complex puzzle that is the mule deer superbuck.

36

Where to Find
Mule Deer Superbucks

If you're looking for a mega-muley, some states—and some areas within each state—stand head and shoulders above the rest. So logically, you should start your search there. But remember that lots of other hunters will be doing the same thing; pressure could become intense in certain areas. As I was doing the research for this book, I met two outstanding mule deer superbuck hunters who told me they absolutely refuse to go back to one big buck county in Colorado. The reason? One was shot at, and a shot hit near the other so that neither hunter feels it's worth his life to head back that way again.

When you're confronted with high pressure, consider private hunting land. You can either purchase trespass rights or, with several other hunters, lease ground for the right price. However, the latter option is getting more expensive all the time. Trespass fees may also be high, but they could represent a small price for personal safety. Of course, the more remote any location, the less chance exists for a confrontation with other hunters.

Large ranches often have hunting rights locked up in prime big buck areas and, for a price, are more than happy to let you in to hunt. In some cases, lodging and meals are also available. A letter or phone call to a state's game and fish department may be all that's needed to get you pointed in the right direction.

Hiring an outfitter will usually only work out to everyone's satisfaction if you validate his big buck expertise up front, a proposition that could take a considerable amount of time (sending letters) and money (making phone calls). If you opt for this route, be sure that you inquire of unsuccessful hunters as well as successful ones. Often unsuccessful hunters have a much better insight into an outfitter's overall qualifications. An unsuccessful hunter is not as likely to overlook the bad things that happened on the hunt. But if he's satisfied that he was in a big buck area and that his outfitter had good stock, good gear, and did his level best to produce a big buck, often that's the best endorsement any outfitter could ask for.

A successful hunter will rarely discuss the bad things about a camp. And remember the saying, "even a blind sow will find an acorn once in a while." Be sure to ask more than one hunter from each classification, successful and unsuccessful, for a well-rounded glimpse of what your chances will be in this particular camp.

Public land abounds throughout the western states. Not only are there plenty of national forests, don't forget state forests, wildlife refuges, and Bureau of Land Management (BLM) land. BLM land could often support much more hunting pressure than is currently being given it. And in some western states, there are literally millions of BLM acres waiting to be hunted.

Be sure to write to state game and fish departments every year to inquire about any special hunts they may be conducting. Regulations change continuously. Sometimes old hunts are discontinued; often new ones are added. This type of hunt can offer you a good chance at an undisturbed super-muley.

OUTFITTERS

Over much of the mule deer's turf, an outfitter is almost a necessity, at least for non-residents. In areas within some states, such as Wyoming, an outfitter or registered guide is *required*. Other options available to you include hiring an outfitter to drop you off at a campsite and return later to pack you and your trophy out. This is a more economical variation of the guided trip that, if you choose your area well, can result in a super muley.

You can also trailer your own horses into a big buck state, but remember if they aren't in good shape, the altitude will affect them as badly as it will affect you. And if they're not used to the scent of large predators like bears and cougars, you could be in for some wild chases and wilder rides. Hiring horses to pack you and your gear in is another option. Usually two horses per person are enough for packing into the backcountry.

A mule deer superbuck is a creature that thrives in the most remote places. Often, he'll live in a spot that you'd swear couldn't hold any deer, much less a mega-deer. You'll need enough gear not only to get to these spots but to be able to stay there for a while hunting once you do.

Another item to ponder is the fact that while over 25 percent of the Boone and Crockett whitetails that qualify for the record book were taken during the past eight years, only 10 percent of the qualifying muleys were, despite the lowered minimum scores. That's how tough big muleys come. And always keep in mind whether or not a killer winter has swept through the area that you're planning to hunt. Big bucks *will* be much harder to come by for up to six or seven years after such a winter.

But say you're still determined to get a mega-muley. After all, if something's hard to get it becomes even *more* valuable. Even though big bucks usually prefer the high, wide, and lonesome, some super-buck hunters have taken their best trophies within view of an inter-state highway or town. You just never can tell with muleys. To get you started on the superbuck trail, here are the best states ranked by trophy production, and the best places for superbucks in each:

Colorado. What a state for mega-bucks. Colorado has so many tro-phy-class muleys registered in the books that the state stands head and shoulders above the rest. Out of the top 90 typical heads listed in Boone and Crockett, 35—or just under 40 percent—came from Colorado. Of the top 90 non-typical heads, 19—or about 22 per-cent—came from Colorado. When you add in all the rest of the Boone and Crockett qualifiers, as well as Colorado bucks from the Pope and Young record book, the total goes off the charts. There is reason for concern, though. Even though historically Colorado was *the* place for big mule deer bucks, of these top-placing bucks, only three are bucks of the 1990s. Rather incredibly, both recent typicals scored 204⅞ and were taken by unknown hunters. One came to light in 1990, the other in 1992. The other was a monstrous non-typical that was taken in Mesa County in 1994 and scored 270⅞.

With so many bucks listed as having come from Colorado, there is also an incredible diversity of locations given as the places where these bucks were taken. Here are, in descending order, the counties where your chances of scoring on a trophy muley are best: Mesa (Uncompahgre and Grand Mesa National forests), Garfield (White River and Grand Mesa National forests), Eagle (White River National Forest), Montrose (Uncompahgre and Gunnison National forests), Rio Blanco, Archuleta (San Juan National Forest), Gunnison (Gun-nison National Forest), Routt (Routt National Forest), Delta (Gunni-son and Grand Mesa National forests), Moffat County (Routt Na-tional Forest), Dolores (San Juan National Forest), Grand (Arapaho National Forest), LaPlata County (San Juan National Forest), San Miguel (San Juan and Uncompahgre National forests), Ouray (Un-compahgre National Forest), Chaffee County (White River National Forest), Elbert County on the eastern plains (where big bucks are coming on strong), and the Southern Ute Indian Reservation, which encompasses portions of LaPlata and Archuleta Counties, and Mon-tezuma County (San Juan National Forest).

Other Colorado hotspots include Larimer County, Park County, Summit County, and Saguache County, as well as Boulder and Clark counties. A few bucks have also come from Pitkin and Teller counties.

The Colorado Division of Wildlife, 6060 Broadway, Denver, CO 80216, also administers hundreds of thousands of acres for big- and small-game hunting. This includes the remarkably successful Ranching for Wildlife program by which even less affluent hunters are able to garner points entitling them to someday hunt famous big buck hotspots such as the Forbes Ranch. Colorado also offers early-season plains rifle hunts for mule deer, although tags are very limited and require building up preference points. Some areas may carry antler point restrictions. Although licenses were recently available in unlimited quantities for most Colorado mule deer hunting, that is no longer true. Check well before you plan to hunt the state to be certain you are up-to-date on recent changes and application deadlines.

The Southern Ute Indian Reservation, at one time a top big buck area, also usually holds a late-season trophy hunt on a limited permit basis. Dates and fees vary so check with the Division of Wildlife for all information before you plan the rest of your trip.

If you'd like the name of a Colorado outfitter operating where you'd like to hunt, contact Colorado Outfitters Association, P.O. Box 31438, Aurora, CO 80041.

Utah. Utah can also be heaven on earth for big buck hunters. Although some people persist in believing that Utah is mostly desert, that's not true. Prime mule deer habitat abounds in Utah's 29 counties, 28 of which may boast of having a record book buck come from within their boundaries. Most of Utah's highest-ranking bucks were taken before 1990. Only two were harvested in the 1990s. A huge 205% typical was killed in 1994 in Washington County, while Garfield County yielded up a 293% non-typical in 1993.

There's a lot of public hunting land in Utah, and non-resident licenses for some areas are fairly easy to obtain. As in all western states, non-resident hunters must apply well before the season for details on obtaining Utah's mule deer licenses. Utah has also instituted quality deer management in some of their deer hunting units. When checking into licenses, be sure to inquire about the limited entry areas the state has established in some of the best mule deer habitat in the state. If you're lucky enough to draw a permit, your opportunity for nailing a 30-inch buck on the wall will improve tremendously.

Here in descending order are Utah's top big-buck counties: San Juan County (Manti-LaSal National Forest), Carbon County (Manti-LaSal National Forest), Beaver County, Piute County, Wayne, Sevier, Millard and Juab (the Fishlake National Forest encompasses portions of all these latter counties), Uintah County (Ashley National Forest), Utah County (Uinta and Manti-LaSal National forests), Kane County (Dixie National Forest), Morgan County (Wasatch National Forest), Cache County (Wasatch National Forest), Emery, Garfield, Summit, Weber, Grand, Duchesne, Box Elder, Sanpete, Wasatch, Iron, and Juab.

Remember, a call or letter to the state's Department of Wildlife could help in your search for the right hunting area. Their address is

1594 West N. Temple, Suite 2110, P.O. Box 146301, Salt Lake City, UT 84114-6301; phone 801/538-4700.

There are several Indian Reservations where you might pick up the trail of a big buck. These include the Ute-Ouray Tribe, Fort Duchesne, UT 84026; the Piute and Goshute Branch of Land Operations, Owyhee, NV 89832; and the Navajo Indian Reservation, Window Rock, AZ 86515.

The Utah Guides and Outfitters Association may be written to at P.O. Box 21242, Salt Lake City, UT 84121.

Idaho. Idaho bucks not only placed well in the last edition of the Boone and Crockett record book, the state continues to produce high-scoring bucks in the latest (1999) edition. Most of Idaho's 44 counties have produced record book bucks. Counties producing record-class bucks lie mainly along the eastern border with Wyoming, long a record muley hotspot, and from the drainages of the Boise River, Payette River, Salmon River, and the lower reaches of the Snake River. Thirteen Boone and Crockett deer came from Idaho during the early 1980s, more than from any other state. What's more, Idaho's 1990s record is also solid, with a huge 1997 non-typical that scored 294% coming from Elmore County, the number-eight typical scoring 212% and hailing from Bonneville County in 1996, plus a gem of a buck that scored 207% that was taken in 1991 in, of all places, Gem County.

Counties in which you might want to start your search include Boise County (Boise National Forest), Caribou (Caribou National Forest), Lemhi (Salmon National Forest), Bear Lake County, Adams County (Payette National Forest), Blaine (Challis and Sawtooth National forests), Bonneville County, Elmore County (Boise National Forest), Franklin County (Caribou National Forest), Fremont County (Targhee National Forest), Gem County (Boise National Forest), and Idaho County (Nez Perce, Bitterroot, and Payette National forests).

Other counties worthy of consideration include Owyhee, Ada, Cassia, Power, Shoshone, and Bannock.

Idaho offers a predetermined number of licenses to non-residents on a first-come, first-served basis. There are also some controlled access (limited) licenses available on a drawing basis. Call 208/942-3181 to talk to the Idaho Department of Fish and Game about licensing information. The address is 600 S. Walnut, Box 25, Boise, ID 83707.

The Idaho Outfitters Association's address is P.O. Box 95, Boise, Idaho, 83701.

Wyoming. With its small population, limited system of licensing, and coming off six mild winters (as of autumn 2000), Wyoming is producing some great mule deer heads and lots of them. A big 211⅞ typical was taken in 1995 in Park County. A 209% typical was taken in 1992 in Lincoln County. And another 202% typical was taken in 1992 in Sublette County. Many other Wyoming bucks adorn the pages of Boone and Crockett, many of which were taken during recent years. Wyoming offers all non-resident licenses on a limited basis. Applications must be received early in the year to be considered for one. Call or write to the Wyoming Game and Fish Department, 5400 Bishop Blvd., Cheyenne, WY 82002; phone 307/777-4600.

Wyoming can brag a bit in the big buck department. The current number two typical Boone and Crockett head was taken from the Hoback Canyon area of Teton County, an ideal place for finding an old mossyhorn muley. One thing that's almost guaranteed in Wyoming is the chance for a true quality hunt, especially if you put a little effort into your choice of areas and work just a tad to get off the beaten path. There are lots of places to hunt, too, since Wyoming is composed of a whopping 51 percent public land.

Most of Wyoming's 24 counties are represented on the big buck list. At the top in both quantity and quality is Lincoln County. Lincoln shares a border with both Utah and Idaho. It shares something else, a reputation for growing buster bucks. One big non-typical that scored 244⅞ Boone and Crockett points was taken in 1981 in Lincoln County. Part of the Teton National Forest is available to hunt in Lincoln County, as well as quite a bit of BLM land.

For sheer numbers, Carbon County, along the state's southern border with Colorado, ranks second. Quite a number of record-book muleys come from Carbon County, including several Boone and Crocketts. There is quite a lot of BLM land in Carbon County where hunters can hunt without paying any fee. The hunting is good, but big mule deer bucks can do quite a fine job of staying out of your sight. One top-notch outfitter I'd recommend in Carbon County is Gene Carrico who lives in nearby Rawlins. The name of Gene's outfitting service is Out West Safaris.

Other good superbuck counties include Teton County (Teton and Targhee National forests), Sweetwater County (BLM land), Sublette County (Bridger-Teton National Forest), Natrona (BLM land and a portion of the Medicine Bow National Forest), Johnson County (Big Horn National Forest), Platte County, Fremong County (Shoshone National Forest), Sheridan County (Big Horn National Forest), Converse County (Medicine Bow National Forest), Uinta County (Wasatch National Forest), and Big Horn County (Big Horn National Forest).

The Wyoming Outfitters Association is based in Cheyenne. The phone number is 800/264-0981.

New Mexico. New Mexico is no slouch when it comes to big muleys, with well over 100 listed in the various books. Five national forests, 14 million acres of BLM land, and four different Indian reservations all provide a wonderful diversity of habitat for hunters who want to look for their mega-muley in the desert southwest. Big muleys of both the Rocky Mountain and desert muley subspecies live in New Mexico. Rocky Mountain bucks inhabit the central and northern regions while desert deer live in the southern areas. Not surprisingly, most Boone and Crockett record book deer are the Rocky Mountain subspecies.

New Mexico offers stratified hunts. Several hunts are offered within each area during a season, but most last only from three to seven days. A hunter who is successful in drawing a license may hunt during one season only.

Nine New Mexico counties are represented, but the odds-on winner is Rio Arriba County, just north of Santa Fe. Rio Arriba accounts for most of the record book heads produced in New Mexico. Included among these heads are a number of outstanding trophies taken during the 1990s, which keeps this county high on the list of any hunter desirous of a giant Boone and Crockett typical. These typical racks include a 206% taken in the county in 1996, a 205% taken in 1993, and a 204⅛ taken in 1992. Rio Arriba is a large county and shares a common border with some of Colorado's top big buck-producing areas. Within Rio Arriba County lie the Chama and the Jicarilla Apache Indian Reservation, both trophy hotspots. The Jicarilla is managed just for big bull elk and buck deer. Quite a few of Rio Arriba's Boone and Crockett heads have come from the Jicarilla Reservation.

Public hunting bets in Rio Arriba County would have to include the portion of the Carson National Forest that lies right next to both the Jicarilla and Southern Ute Indian Reservations of Colorado. Another block of Carson National Forest land plus a large tract of the Santa Fe National Forest are also contained within Rio Arriba.

Other good bets for the state's massive muleys include Colfax County (a small portion of Santa Fe National Forest, BLM land), Bernalillo County (Cibola National Forest), Sandova County (Cibola and Santa Fe National forests), Catron County, Los Alamos County (Santa Fe National Forest), San Miguel County (Santa Fe National Forest), Mora County, McKinley County, and Socorro County.

Contact the New Mexico Department of Game and Fish, P.O. Box 25112, Santa Fe, NM 87503; phone 506/827-7911.

Within many of the national forests throughout the West are wilderness areas that allow no vehicular access. Be sure to inquire about these places. They would be the best places to start any big buck hunt.

Anyone interested in possibly obtaining the services of an outfitter should contact the New Mexico Council of Outfitters and Guides, 160 Washington, S.E. #75, Albuquerque, NM 87108. The president of the council is Bill Wright, Hi Valley Outfitters, Inc., P.O. Box 776 A, Tres Piedras, NM 87577.

Write the following tribes for their big buck information: Jicarilla Apache, Box 147, Dulce, NM 87528; Mescalero Apache, Mescalero, NM 88340; Navajo, Window Rock, AZ 86515; and Zuni Reservation, Box 338, Zuni, NM 87327.

Arizona. The desert southwest fields another winner with Arizona. Arizona is home to Rocky Mountain muleys, desert mule deer, and Coues whitetail. Trophy mule deer will generally be found in the state's northernmost counties. Like its neighbor New Mexico, Arizona also has two counties without equal in the big buck roundup, Coconino County and Mohave County. Coconino and Mohave are both large counties, taking up almost the entire north central and northwestern portion of the state. Both contain part of the Grand Canyon National Park, which acts as a refuge for big bucks. Coconino County is also home of the Kaibab National Forest, an unparalleled parcel of buck-producing real estate. Although the Kaibab isn't quite what it used to be in terms of lots of quality heads, it still gives up enough wall-hangers to be seriously considered by any trophy hunter. The Kaibab is a land of steep canyons and rugged plateaus where hunters will be taxed to the limit in their quest for a trophy buck.

Coconino County has produced many record-book trophies in the past, most of them large enough to make Boone and Crockett, including a 206⅝ monster typical taken by a female hunter in 1990. The majority of these big bucks were taken in the North Kaibab National Forest.

Other good bets in Arizona include: Mohave County (Arizona strip country), Pima County (Coronado National Forest), Pima County (Coronado National Forest), Cochise County (Coronado National Forest), Yavapai County (Prescott National Forest), Pinal County (Tonto and Coronado National forests), Santa Cruz County (Coronado National Forest), Greenlee County (Apache-Sitgreaves National Forest), Williams County, and Apache County, where a 203⅞ typical was taken in 1994.

Arizona offers over 32 million acres of federally-operated land, close to 20 million acres of Indian reservations, and 10 million acres of land owned by the state.

Information required to hunt on one of the Indian reservations can be obtained directly from the various tribes by writing to them at the following addresses: White Mountain Apache Tribe, P.O. Box 708, Whiteriver, AZ 85941; San Carlos Tribal Council, P.O. Box O, San Carlos, AZ 85550; Hualapi Wildlife Department, Box 216, Peach Springs, AZ 86434.

Hunter numbers are carefully regulated in Arizona. Write for license requirements and fees to Arizona Game and Fish Department, 2222 W. Greenway Rd., Phoenix, AZ 85068.

Oregon. Oregon, which is more often associated with blacktails than with mule deer, is a star when it comes to big muleys. Well over 100 Oregon trophies are listed in the current record books, including a 201⅞ typical taken in Union County in 1991. Top counties include Grant County, where almost 30 record-book heads have been taken. Portions of both Malheur National Forest and Umatilla National Forest are located in Grant County.

Other good bets include Malheur County, Harney County, Wallowa (Wallowa-Whitman National Forest), Klamath County (Winema National Forest), and Deschutes County (Deschutes National Forest).

Other ranking big muley counties are found primarily in the eastern two-thirds of the state and include Jefferson (Deschutes National Forest), Union (Wallowa-Whitman and Umatilla National forests), Baker County (Wallowa-Whitman National Forest), Clackamas County (Mt. Hood National Forest), Crook County (Ochoco National forest), Lake County (Deschutes and Fremont National Forest), and Umatilla County (Umatilla and Wallowa-Whitman National Forest). The Hart Mountains should also be seriously considered as a top trophy mule-deer destination.

For information write or call the Oregon Department of Fish and Wildlife, 2501 SW 1st Ave., Portland, OR 97207.

Montana. Montana has quite a few heads in the record books, but the heads have been taken in counties scattered across the state, making an analysis difficult. The largest number of Boone and Crockett heads come from the following counties: Ravalli (Lolo National Forest), Lincoln County (Kootenai and Flathead National forests), Petroleum County, Powell County (Deerlodge and Helena National forests), Park County (Gallatin National Forest), and Cascade County (Lewis and Clark National forests).

Curiously, few Montana bucks have made it to the highest echelons of the Boone and Crockett record book.

Surprisingly enough, many of the state's better mule deer have been taken in the state's eastern half where BLM land predominates. But good muleys are taken each year from nearly every Montana county. Mule deer may be found in all of the state's national forests. Some of the more remote regions usually offer the best big buck hunting. It's quite possible that few big bucks are logged in from Montana since it's generally harder to get to than the other popular mule deer states, and the country is pretty darn rough. There are probably quite a few record-breaking buster bucks dying of old age on public land in Montana. Recent Boone and Crockett mule deer have come from the counties of Flathead, Powell, Sanders, and Cascade. Licenses for nonresidents are sold as a combination tag with an elk license on a first-come, first-served basis, except for a small block set aside for the clients of outfitters.

For more information on Montana's hunting seasons and licenses, contact the Montana Department of Fish, Wildlife, and Parks, 1420 E. 6th, P.O. Box 200701, Helena, MT 59620-0701; phone 406/444-3186.

To get a list of Montana's outfitters contact the Montana Outfitters Association, P.O. Box 631, Hot Springs, MT 59845.

The BLM has an excellent map showing its hunting lands, which are located mostly in the eastern prairie portion of the state. Write to request a copy at 3021 Sixth Ave. N, Box 30157, Billings, MT 59103.

Nevada. Nevada is something else when it comes to mule deer. Nowhere else are the deer herds better regulated and maintained than in Nevada. It's hard to draw a license there, but if you do you've got an excellent chance of scoring on a wall-hanger. Nevada is an up and coming Boone and Crockett mule deer state.

All the top-producing big buck counties in Nevada have portions of either the Humboldt National Forest or Toiyabe National Forest within their perimeter except for Washoe County. Washoe as well as most other Nevada counties offer lots of lightly hunted BLM land to the determined trophy hunter. Nevada, in fact, has more BLM land available to public use than any other western state.

The Nevada county that produces the most and the biggest bucks is Elko. Elko County lies in the northeast quadrant of the state, fast against both Utah and Idaho. One of the most popular areas within Elko County for pursuing trophy muleys is in the Ruby Mountains south of Elko in the Humboldt National Forest.

The only other counties with Boone and Crockett bucks listed are Washoe (where a 201% typical was taken in 1991), Eureka, Lincoln, Elko, Humboldt, and Nye.

Backcountry hunts are an obvious choice, but buster bucks can be found as well in the desert if you know where to look. Often, big bucks live to a ripe old age in arid areas simply because many hunters deny the possibility that any animal could exist in such stark surroundings.

Contact the Reno office of the Nevada Department of Wildlife, 1100 Valley Rd., Reno, NV 89512; phone 775/688-1500 for information regarding the state's BLM lands and for license information. They also have a list of guides who can try to lead you to that once-in-a-lifetime trophy.

Kansas. There are enough Kansas mule deer listed in the record books to make this state worthy of mention, although only five are large enough to qualify for Boone and Crockett. Most notable of these is the huge 258% non-typical killed in 1996 in Decatur County. Other Boone and Crockett-represented counties include Sheridan, Rooks, and Cheyenne.

Counties posting Pope and Young heads include Lane County, Gray County, Scott County, Finney County, Morton County, Clark County, Gove County, Trego County, Ness, and Meade Counties.

There is little public land in Kansas. The state Fish and Game Commission administers about 300,000 acres of public ground on its game management areas. The Army Corps of Engineers has huntable lands adjacent to its reservoirs, too, but more than likely, this would probably qualify as whitetail habitat. Federal land includes the Cimarron National Grasslands with 106,000 acres.

For license and season information, contact the Kansas Department of Wildlife and Parks, 900 SW Jackson St., Suite 502, Topeka, KS 66612; phone 785/296-2281.

Washington. Washington state has excellent big buck potential, especially those counties with a long history of producing trophy muleys.

Counties to consider include Chelan County, particularly along Nason Creek. Part of the Wenatchee National Forest is located in Chelan County.

Another good bet is Okanogan County, where the Okanogan National Forest provides good public hunting.

Look as well at Asotin County (Umatilla National Forest), Columbia County (Umatilla National Forest), Pend Oreille (Colville and Kaniksu National forests) and Stevens County (Colville and Kaniksu National forests).

Maps for Washington's national forests may be obtained by requesting them from the U.S. Forest Service.

Information about land managed by the Washington Fish and Wildlife Department and about hunting licenses and fees can be obtained from the department at 600 Capitol Way, N. Olympia, WA 98502-1091; phone 360/902-2200.

Nebraska. Nebraska has a thriving deer herd, located mainly in the western regions of the state. Quite a few trophy muley bucks—including several Boone and Crocketts—have come from Nebraska. Some of the best counties include Chadron, Red Willow, Frontier, Cherry, Sioux, and Lincoln.

Permits are available through drawing only. A pamphlet entitled "Hunting Nebraska's Public Lands" is available from the Game and Park Commission. This pamphlet lists and describes the almost 625,000 acres of both state and federal public hunting areas, locating each on a map. Contact the Nebraska Game and Parks Commission, 2200 N. 33rd St., P.O. Box 30370, Lincoln, NE 68503-0370; phone 402/471-0641.

North Dakota. With few big muleys to its credit, North Dakota can't be regarded as an optimum place to start your superbuck search. If you do opt for a hunt in North Dakota, Billings County, McKenzie County and Slope County are the counties where most of the listed bucks have come from. All are in the west central part of the state, close to the Montana line.

North Dakota's deer licenses are issued through a lottery. Contact the North Dakota Game and Fish Department, 100 N. Bismarck Expressway, Bismarck, ND 58501; phone 701/328-6300 for more information. A brochure is available from the same address that lists and describes the 136 management areas run by the department where hunting is allowed.

Other public hunting ground includes the Little Missouri Grasslands and the Custer National Forest, together totaling over a million acres of prime mule deer habitat. Contact the U.S. Department of Agriculture, Custer National Forest in Montana for more information.

More federal grasslands along the South Dakota border add some prime mule deer habitat. These include Grande River and Cedar River National Grasslands in Lemmon, South Dakota, and Sheyenne National Grasslands with headquarters in Lisbon, North Dakota. The BLM and Army Corps of Engineers have additional land available to hunters.

Alberta. Alberta, Canada, doesn't have a lot of mule deer bucks listed in the record books but that's understandable. After all, both of the record books, while dedicated to North American big game, are administered within the United States. Most of the publicity associated with each organization is also generated within this country.

Most of the top heads come from the plains on the eastern slope of the Rockies. Alberta has a lot of prime mule deer habitat, and undoubtedly many more good bucks are still there. Be sure to check guide laws before you plan any hunting trip.

For information, contact the Department of Environmental Protection, Main Fl., Petroleum Plaza, Edmonton, Alberta T5K 296 Canada; phone 403/427-7381. If you're planning on taking a hunting trip to Canada, be sure to declare your guns with customs before you leave the country. And be sure to have your ownership papers in order, as well as inquire about any export papers you may need to allow you to leave the province and Canada with your guns and without any major hassle.

Saskatchewan. Saskatchewan, another Canadian province and Alberta's eastern neighbor, also lays claim to quite a few top muley heads, most of them qualifying for Boone and Crockett listing. Desirable hunting areas include the areas around Beechy, Cabri, and Leader. For more information, contact the Saskatchewan Environment and Resource Management Dept., 3211 Albert St., Regina, Saskatchewan, S4S 5W6 Canada; phone 306/787-2930.

British Columbia. Another northern neighbor follows Alberta and Saskatchewan. British Columbia continues to hold its own with a fair number of big mule deer bucks. Top areas are located around Princeton and Rossland.

While both Rocky Mountain muleys and blacktails live in British Columbia, Rocky Mountain mule deer are confined mainly to the province's interior. The Columbia blacktail may be found along southern coastal areas and Vancouver Island. The Sitka blacktail subspecies inhabits the northern islands and coast.

Information needed to plan a hunt to British Columbia may be obtained from the Fish and Wildlife Branch in Victoria.

California. The state of the trophy mule deer in the state of California can really make a hunter wonder. On the one hand, there are plenty of deer to hunt, Columbia blacktails, Rocky Mountain mule deer, southern mule deer, and California mule deer. But poor buck-to-doe ratios have been the norm in many places because of strict bucks-only hunting policies. There are a few big mule deer in the state; finding them is your only problem. California is our third largest state—almost 160,000 square miles—but few mule deer bucks taken from this state score high enough to make either Pope and Young or Boone and Crockett. This situation is unlikely to change anytime soon, either, due to increasing numbers of unhunted predators being given sanctuary in the state.

Rocky Mountain muleys inhabit the northeastern reaches of California. Bucks big enough to make Boone and Crockett have come from Modoc County and Mariposa County. In Modoc County the Modoc National Forest is open to public hunting. A Boone and Crockett buck from Mariposa County is difficult for some people to believe, considering how close this county is to large population centers. But Mariposa County butts up to both the large Stanislaus National Forest and the Sierra National Forest, and includes part of Yosemite National Park within its borders. Big buck habitat abounds, and a smart buck would have enough hiding places in Mariposa County to survive to a ripe old age.

Four Pope and Young bucks were taken in Lassen County (Modoc and Lassen National forests); two were taken in Plumas County (Plumas National Forest and a small portion of Lassen National Forest) and two in Siskiyou County (Klamath and Shasta National forests). One each were taken in Madera County (Sierra National Forest), Shasta County (Shasta and Lassen National forests), and Imperial County. The Imperial County buck was undoubtedly a member of either the California or Southern mule deer subspecies.

Although the best California hunting may be found on leases and private land, some of the more remote portions of national forest land could work out for a determined trophy hunter.

The California Department of Fish and Game can answer questions about state lands, license requirements, and fees. Contact them at 1416 Ninth St., Sacramento, CA 95814; phone 916/653-7664.

South Dakota. All of South Dakota's big muleys come from counties lying west of the Missouri River. Haakon County and Lawrence County (Black Hills National Forest) have a history of producing big bucks, as do Butte, Stanley, Meade, Perkins, Harding, and Gregory counties.

Buffalo Gap, Fort Pierre, and Buffalo River National Grasslands provide almost one million acres of additional hunting ground. Contact the Central Plains Forestry Office, Chadron, NE 69337 for maps and other pertinent information. This Nebraska office administers South Dakota's national grasslands.

Some hunting is also allowed on the Indian reservations. The South Dakota Game, Fish, and Parks Department has information on this plus license regulations and fees. Their address is 523 East Capitol, Pierre, SD 57501-3182; phone 605/773-3387.

Texas. Texas has a good-sized herd of desert muleys in its western portion. Rumor has it that quite a few respectable heads are now being produced in this whitetail-oriented state. But as with whitetails, in Texas a good lease is everything. Basically, fee hunting or a lease is the best way to get a big buck in the Lone Star State. Currently, only two Pope and Young-class mule deer have come from Texas, one from Brewster County and one from Culberson County.

Some information is available from Texas Parks and Wildlife, 4200 Smith School Rd., Austin, TX 78744; phone 512/389-4800.

Information on prairie hunting available on almost 120,000 acres of National Grasslands can be obtained from the U.S. Forest Service, 517 Gold Ave., S.W., Albuquerque, NM 87101.

Oklahoma. Oklahoma's potential for trophy mule deer might appear at first glance to be limited, but the state has seen a few good bucks being harvested in the past decade. For more information, contact the Oklahoma Department of Wildlife Conservation, 1801 N.

Lincoln, P.O. Box 53465, Oklahoma City, OK 73105; phone 405/521-2342.

Mexico. Mexico not only has the potential of producing some outstanding trophies; in the last decade, American hunters brave enough to travel into the country have been rewarded for their moxie with some oustanding mule deer. One 204% typical was killed in Sonora in 1986. Some of these mule deer bucks sport amazing outside spread measurements. Many massive Mexican mule deer are taken by rifle hunters, but deductions sometimes keep them from making the Boone and Crockett grade. Mexican muleys generally belong to the smaller desert mule deer subspecies, another factor that can make it more difficult to qualify for Boone and Crockett.

This finishes off the roundup of where to go for mule deer superbucks. It goes without saying that all license information is subject to change, so check for current regulations and fees before planning your hunting trip.

37

Interpreting Mule Deer
Superbuck Sign

A hunter's quest for a trophy muley can be compared to a detective trying to solve a mystery: when the detective finally fits all the clues together correctly, he sees the solution. The hunter gathers all the evidence left by mule deer so that he can feel more secure about his chances of seeing a superbuck. Maybe he'll get a shot, maybe he won't; but all sign must be carefully examined and analyzed to see if it coincides with the presence of a bruiser-sized buck.

The first type of sign that should be looked for isn't sign at all, at least not in the traditional sense. The best mule deer sign of all is an actual sighting by local residents, area game and fish department officials, foresters, BLM employees—anyone who has a handle on the area's game, including sheepherders and ranchers. Local taxidermists can also be invaluable in the search for a trophy buck. Checking these sources before pinpointing a hunting locale can take some of the worry out of choosing an area to hunt.

One of the best sources for finding an area's good bucks is the local game warden or big game biologist. Once, I contacted a biologist stationed 50 miles away from our hunt area because I was in such a hurry for information. In late July we'd been notified that we'd been successful in the Wyoming license drawing. Since some seasons open as early as late August, getting topo maps in time for your trip can be difficult. On this particular occasion my first choice for information—the game warden—was out of town. I didn't want to waste any more time, so I decided to contact the regional biologist in Jackson Hole. Luckily, the biologist was familiar with several outstanding locales for big bucks in our hunt area. And we were easily able to pinpoint one that he felt would offer both Bob and myself an excellent chance at trophy deer. The biologist had seen lots of big bucks in the basin we were to hunt during the summer when his game and fish duties required him to fly the area. That was good enough for me.

The information was correct. I killed a beautiful heavy-horned muley with sweeping antlers. And we saw other good bucks as well, even though Bob wasn't able to connect on another wallhanger. Most game and fish personnel *want* you to be successful. After all, that's part of their job. Everyone wants to feel needed and appreciated. When you politely approach a biologist or game warden, he's probably going to be cooperative. If not, regroup and try someone else. Your attitude is all-important to people who have devoted their lives to wildlife. Don't approach them as a macho expert yourself, but as a hunter seeking *their* expert advice.

When they do give you assistance, be sure you thank them for it. And no matter how unusual some of the advice sounds, *take* it, especially if it is given sincerely. One of our best friends is a game warden. He knocks himself out trying to help non-resident hunters get trophy animals. "Nothing is more frustrating than telling hunters that you've just seen a big buck standing in the next drainage or alongside a road and have them look at you like you're crazy and go the other way," he said. "I have no reason to lie to them. I want them to get a trophy. I just don't understand why they won't even take a look."

This particular game warden knows so much about the animals in his area that it's amazing. A source like him is worth its weight in gold to a big buck hunter who has a limited amount of time for scouting.

Another option available to the mega-muley hunter is Kirt Darner's Hunters' Information Service located in Montrose, Colorado. For a fee, Darner does all the scouting for you. He'll indicate campsites, hillsides on which to concentrate your attention, send you all pertinent maps, let you know where to rent 4WD vehicles, where meat lockers are located, and all the other details so important to the success of your hunt. But before jumping on this option, remember, with a little time and effort you can do the same thing yourself.

Now let's say that you're in the area you've carefully chosen after much calm and dispassionate deliberation. You've checked out all possible sources to decide on a place that has not only produced big animals in the past, but recently, as well. The game warden and local forester have both reported big bucks in the area. You've arranged your vacation so that you can really spend some time looking for Old Mossyhorns, more than two or three days. The terrain looks made-to-order for big muleys. You've pre-scouted at home by circling likely looking spots on your topo map. If time has allowed, you've sent copies of your maps to the game warden or forester so that he can add his own notes, as well. Your own choices include hidden basins or large blocks of land far from any trail or road. You'll make camp well away from the area you plan to hunt, so camp smells and sounds shouldn't affect any nearby deer. But when you finally arrive in the general area, the essential mystery remains to be solved: where is that big buck likely to be? What are the clues, if any, he's left for you? And what do you do next?

A mule deer superbuck leaves clues very comparable to those left by a big whitetail. A mule deer leaves tracks, and a lot of tracks along one corridor will result in a trail. After he eats, grasses and stems will show signs of being nipped or browsed. He rubs his antlers, so some trees will be stripped. He sleeps, so he should leave a bed. Sometimes he'll scrape, too. And of course, he defecates, so there should be droppings.

All of these clues may or may not be evident within the area you've planned to hunt. But before you actually enter an area with big buck potential to look for sign, you might want to hang along the fringes for a day, morning and evening, to see if you spot any deer. A day of scouting like this could keep you from disrupting the whole place and from spooking a big buck that just might be hiding close by. One good, solid sighting of a big muley should be all you need to cement you to an area like glue. Before you ever venture into an area you should be aware of how a big muley may react to your very presence.

According to Phil Kirkland of Hill City, a noted Kansas deer hunter, trophy animals behave in one of two ways. "They either flee or hide," Kirkland explained. "If a big muley exhibits what I call the flight syndrome, he'll just flat leave the area as soon as he spots you," Kirkland said. "If he comes back at all, it won't be for several days. Often, I've followed bucks traveling at a steady trot for over five miles in order to get out of an area where he's been bothered. There's not much chance of actually planning a hunt for one of these bucks. They won't let you get close once they see you or know you're in the area. Your only opportunity lies in surprise. And since a muley's eyesight is unbelievable, you probably won't be able to surprise him.

"If a big muley exhibits the hide syndrome, he'll watch you for a while, then drop to the ground and hide. It's incredible just how easily a buck with a 30-inch spread and antlers 20 inches high can disappear, as if the earth swallowed him whole. If you pay attention to where he lies down, you just might be able to put on a stalk and get him."

Kirkland bowhunts the rolling prairies and woody draws of western Kansas. He's taken eight Pope and Young-class animals, five whitetails and three muleys. His 1988 mule deer grossed 199% Pope and Young points. After deductions it netted 182% points to become the new Kansas state record archery kill. This incredible muley had a 29-inch outside spread, nine points on the left antler and seven on the right.

In western Kansas, much of Kirkland's scouting depends on whether or not he sees a big buck. Often plains bucks can be nomadic, traveling up to 12 or 14 miles overnight. To try to help him determine whether or not a big buck has settled into an area, Kirkland looks for torn-up marijuana plants. "It grows wild everywhere out here," he said, "and the deer love to get in it and rip it apart."

Kirkland also searches for the same things that most big muleys everywhere require: broken terrain that's good for hiding and large blocks of land with no roads or poor access. "To feel secure big bucks want to be able to eat and hide and see all at the same time," he said.

With all this in mind, scan your area with binoculars from a good vantage point before you actually enter it. Never skyline yourself or let your scent blow all over the countryside. Either mistake will quickly clear an area of any savvy big bucks. Be sure to spot carefully both early in the morning and late in the evening, remembering that big bucks are usually more nocturnal than smaller ones. Concentrate on areas that offer a big muley all of his requirements: food, cover, and a good view. Think about the relationship that fish have to structure in a lake or river and relate that knowledge to the big muley. Trophy mule deer are terrain-dependent, hanging close to prominent topographic features for cover.

If you spot a deer—any deer—stay completely quiet. Pick apart the nearby cover for more deer. Muleys love company. If you see does and the rut hasn't started yet, look higher up the mountain for the bucks. Bucks and does usually inhabit different parts of the range with the bucks usually taking the higher, steeper, and rougher sections. If you can't find the bucks, carefully move your position. Glass from another vantage point. They could be just over the ridge on the other side. If you see small bucks, take time to really look the situation over closely. Big bucks love to use smaller bucks as lookouts. Search nearby cover intensively for an ear, an antler, a throat patch, anything that might turn out to be a mega-muley.

If you don't find what you're looking for, and if you feel you must enter your hunt area to look for tangible indicators of a big buck, travel with the wind in your face and travel slowly. Be quiet and try to disturb the area as little as possible. What are you looking for?

TRACKS

Track characteristics vary with terrain. Montrose, Colorado's Gordon Blay says, "It depends on the terrain you're hunting. In rocks like the shell-based pinnacles where I hunt, a big muley will often have shorter, stubbier feet. His hooves get worn down from the constant abrasion. But when you shift your hunting back to flatter land, the big bucks there have longer toes, so a hunter must constantly be thinking and analyzing all the different details that he discovers."

A good deal of mule deer country isn't ideal for finding tracks. It can be hard to locate a crisp, definitive set of tracks when much of the surrounding territory is rimrock. Shifting winds and storms can quickly obliterate tracks throughout much of the muley's range. When you do locate good tracks here's what you should look for: a mix of several different-sized tracks large and small probably indicates a doe family group complete with adults and fawns. An even-sized grouping of tracks can mean that there's a buck group in the vicinity, often made up of several young bachelors. Groups of average-sized tracks interspersed with larger ones may also spell buck group in capital letters. A group like this is often made up of several satellite bucks and one dominant, who wisely lets the smaller bucks act as his lookouts. This could be the buck you're looking for. And a lone set of large tracks, especially ones found as the rut approaches, may mean that the buck of your dreams is nearby.

If you succeed in finding tracks with sharp, distinct edges, they could be fresh. But if you're hunting an arid area tracks remain sharp-looking for several days, or until wind or humidity begins to break them down.

Probably the best tracking conditions exist after a fresh snow or rain. Then tracks often look crisp, like they just came out of a mold. But after a snow, blowing powder sifting into tracks obliterates them. Wind-blown debris like twigs and pine needles can also obscure fresh tracks and add to your difficulty. Thawing and freezing can also make tracks almost totally useless when they're made in snow or mud.

TRAILS

The most heavily traveled trails are those used by doe groups. Bucks will usually travel 10 or 20 yards off the beaten path, often on another, fainter path running parallel to and higher up the slope than the does' trails. In extremely steep country, big bucks will use game trails. During past centuries, animals of the high country have picked out the best routes which are clearly visible to a careful observer. Even the biggest bucks will stick to these trails to get where they're going.

Often, breaks in a rim will offer a big mule deer the only escape route out of an otherwise sheer basin or a bowl. Signs of obvious wear in a rock face combined with a number of trails leading up to it can help you identify one of these hotspots. Locating a cut like this can often help you take your wall-hanger. Some hunters simply cover a spot like this from a distance until a big buck shows up. Others combine constant scrutiny of the cut with a well-planned drive through nearby cover.

TERRAIN

Terrain is very important to a trophy mule deer, and you can count on him to always use it to his best possible advantage. If trails aren't obvious through a particular area, pay attention to strings of boulders and trees dotted across the landscape. A doe will move right through openings, with little or no regard to available cover. A big buck, however, uses swales and coulees as travel routes as he tries to remain hidden from view. He moves from place to place by winding among rocks and bushes; rarely will he venture out in the open for more than a moment. When you're glassing, keep your eyes on strings of natural cover extending from thicket to thicket or from thicket to waterhole. That's the route a big buck will choose. Trophy bucks are also partial to knobs for bedding and feeding, and saddles or dips for travel between basins. Be sure to scope features like these carefully whenever they occur.

All in all, big muleys are such experts at using terrain, you can often find a dozen of them hiding in a draw that you would swear wasn't big enough to hold a rabbit.

RUBS

Muleys, like whitetails, will rub in the same places from year to year, often on the same trees. Like whitetails, large mule deer will often make the largest rubs. Rubs two feet in length and more aren't uncommon. Since big muley bucks and elk often inhabit the same range, you must learn to discriminate between the rubs of each. One way to tell what kind of animal made the rub is by looking for facial hair stuck to the rub. A mule deer's face is gray and black; an elk's is reddish brown.

Gordon Blay, a mule deer outfitter with two Boone and Crockett muleys of his own, says that one sure sign of a big buck is finding buck rubs on the lower limbs of pine trees. "They'll work over a low-hanging branch with their horns for hours," he stated. "Rubs like these are one of the main things I look for when I'm scouting up a trophy buck."

An elk's rub is usually spaced higher on the tree than a mule deer's since elk are so much taller. But a big muley will often attack trees up to nine inches in diameter, an elk-sized rub tree. Trees in the one-inch to three-inch class are much more typical, however.

Favorite rub species include aspen, yellow pine, pinon pine, black pine, and mountain mahogany.

SCRAPES

Most hunters appear to believe that scrape hunting techniques are of little value when applied to mule deer. Researchers report that mule deer don't scrape, but I myself have seen scrapes that must have been made by muleys. Other hunters tell me that not only have they seen scrapes, they've seen muleys make them.

Gordon Blay will hunt scrapes if he happens to find them in an area where he knows there's a monstrous buck. "I firmly believe that mule deer scrapes are made by bucks in the 24- to 26-inch class," Blay explained. "This class of buck is trying desperately to attract the does' attention by advertising their availability. They're big enough to breed, but the oldest bucks won't let them. That leaves them frustrated, so they scrape. Big, trophy bucks probably don't scrape because they know they don't have to. They've already got the does' attention. Does are naturally attracted to the largest set of headgear they can find. That's why they hang around the biggest buck in an area."

BEDS

A mule deer's bed is oval and slightly depressed. When bedding, a muley will paw with a forefoot on the ground, turn part of the way, then kneel and lie down. Once bedded, he'll chew his bolus or cud. He may or may not stretch his head out on the ground. Muleys often bed in the same general area from day to day and it's not uncommon for them to use the same beds. Most often, a big mule deer's bed will be completely hidden from view. I've found mule deer beds under rocks, behind sheer rock faces, and dug deep into earthen banks behind the drooping boughs of mountain mahogany bushes.

Dennis Smith, Rawlins game warden with the Wyoming Game and Fish Department, said, "If you find where a big mule deer's been bedding and he hasn't been disturbed, you can almost count on him returning the next day."

Kirt Darner says that mule deer beds may often be found on the uphill side of rocks and bushy trees. "You have to wait any big buck out that's bedding in one of these spots," he said. "As the sun shifts during the day, he may get up to change position and you might spot him then. But it calls for a lot of patience."

A bunch of smaller beds close together probably indicates a group of does and fawns. Larger beds spaced farther apart could belong to a bunch of bucks. Mule deer situate themselves so that they're never looking directly at each other. Even standing mule deer avert their eyes and refrain from direct eye contact with each other. It's not only social behavior, but it's also an effective anti-predator strategy, since each pair of eyes is concentrating on a different point.

DEER DROPPINGS

Many groups of droppings in one area usually indicate a feeding ground: backtrack from feeding areas to locate bedding areas. Most often, however, many piles of droppings indicate a doe group's feeding area so it's likely that any bedding area you may uncover will hold only does and fawns. Isolated groups of large pellets, on the other hand, could be from a mega-buck.

Pellet freshness can be difficult to determine in the often-arid West; droppings may dry out within a few hours. After a dew, or after freezing and defrosting, deer droppings can get a wet, slick look, falsely promising freshness. Crush the pellets to see if the inside is still soft. If it is, the pellet is less than two days old.

Finding still-steaming pellets is an excellent indication of freshness. Fresh, unfrozen pellets on top of new snow is another sign of recent deposition.

Interpreting sign correctly may not always be as critical to a mule deer hunter as it is to a whitetail hunter. But in the kind of big open country that a mule deer calls home, a superbuck hunter needs all the help, and clues, he can get to help him bag a mega-muley.

38

Mule Deer Superbuck
Travel Patterns

Like all deer, mule deer superbucks have a home range. This home range usually includes a summer range, a winter range and the route traveled between the two. A muley buck's annual range, like a whitetail's, is usually larger than that of a doe. During the summer, bucks take the higher, more forbidding portions of the range leaving lower areas with the most succulent forage to does and fawns.

During normal winters, high country mule deer migrate to their critical winter range. Bucks and does share the habitat on winter range. Muleys who summer in the low country of valleys and river-bottoms may not migrate at all, or if they do, only for short distances. To get from summer to winter range some muleys only need move farther down the mountain. This type of movement is called an altitudinal or elevational migration and is by far the most common migration made by mule deer. Altitudinal migrations can vary from those less than a mile long to those requiring journeys of up to 30 miles to lower elevations where animals can winter. Other, longer migrations occasionally cover a hundred miles and more, along traditional migration routes that have been beaten into the earth by the hooves of mule deer over thousands of years.

With the season's first snowstorms, mule deer begin to get restless. But they usually won't start traveling downslope until snow reaches a depth of about 18 inches or when foraging through encrusted snow becomes difficult, according to studies by wildlife biologists. Some big buck experts dispute this and say that where superbucks are concerned, snow must be chest-deep before they'll move out.

Does almost always migrate before bucks, unless the rut coincides with the journey down. If the rut's going strong, bucks travel with does to their winter range.

In some states, seasons have been manipulated so that hunters are seldom able to hunt migratory herds. In the 1960s, buck kills in some migratory herds were so high that biologists say these herds have yet to achieve the buck-to-doe ratios that existed then. In other states, hunts are scheduled so that late season hunts do overlap with early migratory activity, but are over before the rut starts. When migrations occur during the rut, mule deer superbucks are extremely vulnerable, and that causes wildlife biologists to carefully evaluate late season hunts. When late season hunts are allowed, it is usually because little hunting pressure exists on higher ranges or because populations are building to critical levels. Hunts like these are carefully controlled and monitored.

But say you're on your western mule deer hunt and a big storm moves into your area. It dumps lots of snow. Knowing that muleys do migrate, you decide to capitalize on your good fortune. Where are the true migrating herds of today's western states?

Since the herds are scattered about the west, this can often be difficult to determine. Over the years, construction projects like interstate highways and dams like the Flaming Gorge Reservoir have disrupted some longstanding mule deer migration patterns. For instance, there was once a large herd that crossed the Green River to reach its winter range where Flaming Gorge Reservoir is now located. When the dam was completed, the herd would dutifully swim the reservoir each autumn. But each year fewer and fewer deer swam across until, today, no deer swim Flaming Gorge. What happened to these deer? Where did they go? According to Jim Straley, a retired wildlife biologist formerly with the Wyoming Game and Fish Department, most of them probably died.

"Critical winter range means just that to a migrating herd," said Straley. "If the deer can't get to it, they give up. If forage is insufficient where the deer have to overwinter, as it often is during bad weather, mortality is high. Soon, there are no deer remaining that remember the traditional route because migrations aren't instinctive behavior, they're learned from generation to generation."

Tom Christiansen, wildlife biologist with the Wyoming Game and Fish Department in Green River, says that deer still crossing the river below the dam haven't shifted their route downstream; they're a different group of deer altogether. Some vestigial remnants of the herd that used to migrate across the reservoir do still reside on the Wyoming side, but it is no longer a very productive bunch of animals. "The failure of these deer to do well is probably due to many factors, not only the reservoir, but also highways, mineral exploration, and changing grazing practices. All have impacted these deer."

That's why it's so important that we as hunters head off developers that threaten to cut off a migration route or destroy critical winter range. Winter range is the single most important factor affecting the mule deer's well-being. Unfortunately, most winter ranges are in riverbottoms and valleys, prime locations for houses and malls. When winter range disappears, so will that group of mule deer, and their migration routes. So it becomes imperative to keep up our vigilance when it comes to habitat destruction.

Lloyd Oldenburg, state wildlife manager with the Idaho Fish and Game Department, can also relate instances where entire herds have been disrupted. When one group of deer could no longer cross deer-proof fencing along an interstate highway it was feared they would perish. A decision was made to feed them and now the state puts out food for between 500 to 2,000 animals each winter. Otherwise, these deer would die.

Perhaps the most spectacular example of a migrating herd is that of the deer from the mountains north of Pinedale, Wyoming. For years Jim Straley documented the deer's movements out of the high country and well over 100 airline miles around the southern end of the Wind River Range, to areas as farflung as Big Sandy, LaBarge, and even Lander.

"I can truthfully say that no deer winter north of Pinedale," Straley said. "They move down from the Hoback and Gros Ventre range until not a deer is left up near Jackson. A few over winter in the Snake River Canyon, but the rest move out. As they move down to Pinedale, some drop out to overwinter along the way but most of them keep right on moving."

Straley feels that while the migration was triggered in times past by weather, that's no longer totally true. "I think hunting pressure now forces them out," Straley explained. "When deer begin moving out of the high country they travel nose to tail—huge herds of animals. This migration is a spectacular thing to see, especially in a few places where the corridor that these large herds use is only 20 inches wide."

Straley says that even though the herds migrate out of the higher country in hopes of wintering in milder climate conditions that's not always the case. "Sometimes the low country gets the severe weather and the mountains north of here are fine," he said. "But the mule deer don't move back until it's time to make the trip again in spring regardless of the weather."

Another Wyoming migration occurs a bit farther west. According to trophy mule deer outfitter Maury Jones of Bedford, a third of the deer in the Salt River Range stay there, another third travel 60 miles to Cokeville, and the final third splits up with some moving 50 miles away to Big Piney and others traveling to Evanston, 120 miles away.

Some migrations are almost spur-of-the-moment. Idaho's Oldenburg stated that when the winter of 1988–89 became unusually severe, some deer that didn't migrate previously moved between 60 to 70 miles from Carey to Jerome. "They didn't follow a route," said Oldenburg, "they just moved into the desert."

Deer from Utah, Wyoming, and Colorado travel distances of up to 80 miles to winter in Brown's Park Wildlife Refuge where winters are relatively mild. Brown's Park is situated close to where the three states corner.

Three major migrations are made by Utah's mule deer each autumn. And unlike many other herds, according to authorities these three herds begin to migrate during the first two weeks of October, regardless of the weather.

The Paunsauguant herd travels about 40 linear miles to drop 1500 feet in elevation. They migrate from the highest points of Bryce Canyon National Park and the southern portions of the Paunsanguant Plateau towards the town of Alton. The herd splits up outside of Alton with part of it traveling southwest towards Glendale and into the Hurricane Cliffs area to winter. The other portion of the herd travels east towards the Buckskin Mountains.

The Elk Ridge herd may be found in the San Juan and Elk Ridge Mountains during the summer and early fall. During the first two weeks of October, portions of the herd lying north of a deep canyon called the Notch travel about 25 miles north to Beef Basin, sometimes even as far as the Colorado River. The southern part of the herd will move south to the National Bridges Monument. Some segments travel as far as the Valley of the Gods.

Another Utah mule deer migration occurs when deer in the Boulder Mountains south of Teasdale travel southeast along the Escalante River all the way to the Glen Canyon National Recreation Area.

Minor migrational patterns exist in Arizona, according to Ray Lee, a former big game supervisor with the Game and Fish Department. "We've essentially got two migrating herds," Lee stated, "one on the Kaibab Plateau that drops down off the sides of the plateau in response to snow on the top. Of course these deer don't always move off the plateau; it depends on snow depth and the time of the year.

"Other deer migrate along the New Mexico border in the Blue Primitive Area," he continued. "These deer move down into the canyons from their summer ranges 8,000 or 9,000 feet high in the mountains."

New Mexico sees a general migration as Colorado deer travel out of the mountains along the border and southward into the area bounded roughly by Farmington, Dulce, Chama, and Tres Piedras, according to Bob Jenks, biologist with the New Mexico Game and Fish Department.

Colorado's most well-known migration route takes deer from the White River National Forest about 50 miles south to the Piceance Basin. According to Ron Kufeld, who recently retired from his job as a wildlife research biologist with the Colorado Division of Wildlife, each year many migrating deer are killed by automobiles when they cross Highway 13 between Rifle and Meeker on their way to the Piceance Basin.

"In some cases migrations aren't herd-related but can often be just an individual thing," he said. "We had 18 animals radio-collared in the foothills west of Fort Collins for three years. These animals generally stayed on the same home range where they lived all summer. Except for two deer that would travel 18 miles away each year. Who knows why?"

Kufeld also said there was a definite travel pattern from the top of the Uncompahgre Plateau down off the sides when snow gets deep. But his biggest concern is the one facing many wildlife agencies today, but especially Colorado's because of the state's high influx of new residents.

"We're really having trouble with developments at some ski resorts like those near Vail and Beaver Creek," he lamented. "Developers want to build on winter range or cut off migration routes and they can't understand why animals can't go elsewhere. When you ask them just where they should go they're at a loss for words. They can't relate to the fact that in nearly every case, other winter ranges are carrying as many animals as they can."

In Montana mule deer migrate on the average 10 miles or less, almost all of it up and down movement to different altitudes, according to Glenn Erickson, biologist with the Montana Game and Fish Department. "We do see migrations of animals from 20 to 30 miles as they leave the Bob Marshall and Absaroka Wilderness Areas," he said.

Al Polenz, big game biologist with the Oregon Division of Fish and Wildlife, says some of Oregon's mule deer migrate between 50 and 70 miles but it's more of a general movement and doesn't follow traditional routes. Like many states, Oregon times its mule deer hunting season so that hunters aren't hunting migrating deer. "We have a hard enough time meeting buck-to-doe objectives as it is," Polenz commented.

California, however, times their seasons to pick up the first part of the migration each year. "Our East Tehama deer herd will travel up to 100 miles from their summer range in the high Sierra Nevadas to get to winter range in the Sacramento Valley," said Doug Updike, biologist with the California Department of Fish and Game.

Rolf Johnson of the Washington Department of Wildlife indicated that mule deer migratory behavior there was generally elevational. "We do time our general season to coincide with beginning movements out of the high country during a normal year," he said.

To determine if migration routes exist where you're hunting, ask local residents. Be on the lookout for deer crossing signs along the roads and highways. Road kills can often be an indication that deer are starting their seasonal migration.

If hunting a migration sounds like a good way to get into the big bucks, send away for regulations each year from all western game and fish departments. Seasons are constantly changing, and often you might be able to secure a license for a late season hunt that will give you a chance to see many bucks from which to pick. Some hunters will only hunt mule deer when they're heading them off on the journey to their winter range.

Deer migrations can be unforgettable for those who experience one firsthand. And if you just happen to get in the thick of one, you'll have an excellent opportunity to take a mega-muley.

39

Mule Deer Superbuck Habitat: Mountains and Deserts

Once they've decided to pursue a mule deer superbuck, most hunters ask, "Where should I hunt: in the desert or the mountains?"

Technically, there are nine different types of mule deer habitat. Ordinarily the biggest bucks will be found in one of two broader classifications, the mountain or desert habitats. Learning how to hunt both of them puts you that much closer to a mega-muley.

MOUNTAIN HABITAT

For some hunters, the answer to the question where to hunt the trophy muley of their dreams is pre-ordained. In their minds, muleys are so firmly intertwined with mountains that they can't think of one without imagining the other.

Big buck hunter Kirt Darner says his preference is hunting the austere basins, hidden parks, and craggy cirques of the high mountain ranges. "Mountains really do it for me," he said. "They forever call to me. I'll never get over my love for hunting mule deer in them."

Darner has been so successful in his quest for muley mega-bucks that 14 of his bucks have qualified for Boone and Crockett (although Darner declined to continue having them listed in the records book due to a disagreement regarding one head as to when and how it was taken). Most of Darner's big bucks were mountain muleys.

Mountain muley habitat can be steep or gentle, rocky or covered with vegetation. Whether the cover is hunted hard or hardly hunted, until wild winter weather drives the deer out, nearly all mountain habitats hold mule deer. I've seen bucks picking their way along steep-sided trails that a mountain goat might shun. Muleys hang tight in the sparsest cover, congregate in remote basins, or hole up in aspen thickets.

Big mule deer bucks, like whitetails, have nerves of steel—like the wide, heavy-horned specimen that let two hunters stalk within 20 yards of it. Grant Gretsch was guiding Dave Leedom and Tom

Schmidt out of the Grey's River camp in Wyoming when they spotted a buck feeding far ahead. Now, Jackson Hole Area Outfitter's owner, Maury Jones, promises tough timberline hunts for trophy muleys, and it's not an idle promise. He has some of the best mega-muley hunting anywhere. Grant and Dave decided to try a sneak through the dark timber, while Tom stayed in the open where the muley could watch him. Tom hoped to distract the animal so that he wouldn't realize a stalk was on. Muleys can't count, right?

This one could, it seemed. When Grant and Dave got close, the big buck simply hopped up on top of a huge boulder as easily as a mountain goat. The two stalkers were looking for the deer on the ground—not ten feet above them on a chunk of rock. As the hunters stalked past him, the buck watched without moving a muscle, perched atop the rock with all four hooves bunched together.

Tom could only watch in amazement, but once the hunters were out of his line of fire he fired in the air to alert the stalkers that they'd only outwitted themselves. The buck got away anyway.

"Trophy mule deer are tough because of their uncanny ability to sense a stalk before I even make it," added Kirt Darner. "I've been hundreds of yards away with the sun and wind in my favor and completely quiet only to have a big buck pivot around and look directly at me."

Darner added, "It's hard to find any mountainous terrain too tough or unsuitable for a mega-muley. So be sure to glass *every-where*—with a spotting scope."

My husband and I learned this ourselves on the avalanche slopes of the Wyoming Range. We'd been lured there by tales of spectacular mule deer bucks. In two days, we hadn't seen a buck—or any deer at all, for that matter.

We were hunting along a shelf that jutted over a sheer canyon wall; small trees hung tightly to the steep, near-vertical slopes. "Keep your eyes on those little trees," Garvice Roby, a retired Wyoming Game and Fish biologist, told me during a phone conversation. "They're called 'krummholz' which means 'crooked wood.' Smart old muley bucks use them for hideouts. Krummholz are no taller than a man but their branches spread out and hug the ground. Trophy bucks burrow under the boughs and hide there. During the early part of the season some other trophy hunters reported seeing over 20 big bucks in the 25- to 30-inch antler spread range holed up under the krummholz in the drainages you'll be hunting."

The cluster of krummholz below looked like a good place to start so we stopped to glass them. That's when I noticed "branches" that became antlers once we'd set up our spotting scope. A fine buck was bedded under the little trees, holding tight—300 yards straight down the slope.

"He's heavy and he's high," Bob said as I got into a sitting position. "He's not real wide but he's still a good buck. Are you going to take him?"

With that, the buck turned to look at us. I could see the sweep of his antlers as they jostled the tree branches. He didn't run; he didn't even get up. As far as he could tell, he was safe. Judging from his apparent unconcern, he'd pulled this same trick many times before and it had always worked.

As I settled the crosshairs on the buck's neck I hesitated. It was our first day of hunting after a marrow-chilling ride packing in. Were bigger bucks lurking under other krummholz? Would I regret a hasty decision?

It was the pack ride in that made up my mind. Our outfitter had hauled us in under terrible conditions. Snow higher than the horses' bellies lay upon the summit of Ramshorn Peak. More snow could dump on us at any moment. "A bird in the hand," I thought to myself. . . .

The shot was perfect: the deer slumped over right in his bed. But to get to the deer so we could field dress it we had to travel down a near vertical slope in the failing light.

Bob headed straight down the slope towards the buck while I looked for an easier way. Farther up the drainage the drop wasn't quite so severe, so I started down from there. I'd only gone about 100 yards when the clatter of rolling rocks caught my attention. Less than 150 yards away loped a magnificent four-point muley. His darkened antlers were at least 30 inches wide and extremely high. Dark antlers are a sure way to tell a mountain muley from his lighter-antlered desert muley relatives.

When I yelled for Bob, the buck stopped and turned broadside. All I could do was watch, knowing that Bob couldn't see him to get a shot. Then the big deer turned and bounded from sight. This particular place was loaded with big muleys!

Later on, Bob said he'd found this buck's bed under some krummholz, too. After I'd shot, the big buck spooked from the bed, and a short run later encountered me. Even though Bob didn't get a shot at that buck, our spirits were high that evening when we crawled into our sleeping bags.

I'd like to report that Bob connected on a near-record-book rack, but some things aren't meant to be. We ranged as far as we could— thigh-high snow on all the north and west slopes prevented us from reaching any other drainage—but we saw no other deer. Either the buck I got and the big one I saw were the last two stragglers, or the other bucks beat it out of there after I shot.

Both Kirt Darner and Maury Jones try to locate favored areas called "buck pastures." Since most alpine hunts take place in early fall, the mule deer rut is still several weeks away. Bucks are loners during the rut but they hang out together early in the season: find one and you just might find several.

A good place to look for these bands of bachelor bucks is on a south-facing slope, one that's got intermittent areas of cover, like boulders and scrub vegetation. In September and October mountain nights get chilly, so bucks will naturally congregate in a spot where they can bask in the sun's warming rays. South-facing slopes fill this bill admirably.

We learned this lesson hunting with Maury Jones in the Salt River Range one year. After glassing one basin with binoculars, we decided to break for lunch. While we were eating we set up a spotting scope and started looking a little harder. What we saw was incredible. It seemed like a buck was lurking behind nearly every rock and bush. We counted over 25 bucks in one basin. Some of them were good ones, too: several in the 28- to 30-inch class. Unfortunately, none of our stalks for the bigger bucks panned out, although we did have chances at several 25-inchers from as close as 75 yards.

If you have the opportunity to go after muleys in the mountains, remember that experienced trophy hunters say the biggest mistake neophytes make is hunting too fast. Taking a good mule deer requires both patience and good optical equipment. Find a spot with a good view of the hunt area. Get comfortable, then start scouring the landscape. Begin with binoculars, and take the landforms apart, inch by inch. Start your search high on the drainage and work down. When snow is on the ground concentrate on features near what appear to be the freshest tracks.

Use a spotting scope mounted on a tripod. Begin on low power since it's less tiring to the eyes. Cover the same area once more, even more thoroughly. When you see something that calls out for closer inspection, crank the scope up for a better look. Be especially alert for the sun glinting off anything shiny, or splotches of gray or white that "just don't belong there." Once you've really inspected an area and you feel sure that you have seen no deer, then it's time to move on.

Be sure that any stunted trees with low limbs where deer can conceal themselves are given special attention. Although the term "krummholz" is unique to the northwest corner of Wyoming, these stunted trees occur anywhere near timberline in the Rockies.

Pay close attention to areas next to logs where deer can flatten themselves out to become nearly invisible. Large rocks, like those in avalanche slides, are also excellent hiding places. Look for deer anywhere around boulders, but remember that they'll try to lie with the wind blowing toward them and where they can see activity below them.

Hunting timberline muleys requires glassing in both early and late in the day. Mule deer feed at night and start moving to feeding areas at dusk. Likewise, they head to their bedding areas early in the morning. Be at a good vantage point at both times to determine what deer are inhabiting the area and how best to waylay them. A light snow is a glassing advantage since white snow cover makes the deer stand out from the surroundings.

Mountain breezes often swirl around the terrain, but keep the wind in your face whenever possible. Likewise, never skyline yourself. When you top a ridge, climb right over and don't walk along the edge. Nothing will alert a deer to danger like a strange silhouette.

The most important lesson in mountain muley hunting is probably the hardest to swallow—especially after you've waited an entire year for hunting season or you've travelled thousands of miles to bag a good buck. Once the snows come deep and hard, muleys clear out of the high ranges on traditional migration routes to winter range. When this migration starts, your best plan is to follow them out—and quickly. Dave Lockman, biologist for the Wyoming Game and Fish Department, told us, "Every year the department has to rescue hunters who don't have the sense to get out when the getting is good." Don't be one of those hunters.

DESERT HABITAT

When you think "desert" you know that water is bound to be in short supply. Many dry areas of the West aren't classified as deserts by geologists because they have a slightly greater average annual rainfall. For hunting purposes, however, these lands are included in this discussion of desert habitat.

Besides having little rainfall, deserts and near-deserts have many similarities that are apparent to the hunter. The glare of sunlight coupled with the high plains and desert country's high altitude makes landforms at great distances seem but a stone's throw away. Stark landscapes are the rule, not the exception, here. Mule deer adapt to the cruel, unforgiving terrain that characterizes much of the country's desert habitat.

To understand the psyche of a desert muley, you have to understand his home ground. If you don't know where to look for big bucks in the desert, you may wind up seeing nothing at all. Dennis Smith, Rawlins game warden for the Wyoming Game and Fish Department, explained. "Some parts of the desert act like magnets, drawing big bucks to them for reasons not entirely understood. Watch for locations that combine rimrock, deep washes which can be used for cover and shade, and healthy-looking [tall, deep green] sagebrush for food. Never forget that the more undisturbed an area is, the better it probably will be for big bucks."

As in mountain hunting, once a prime location has been scouted, excellent optics and a good dose of patience are essential. The best times to glass the terrain are early and late in the day. Muleys, even mega-muleys, are creatures of habit. They will generally follow the same daily routine unless scared out or forced to change by weather, declining food sources, or lack of water. Later in the season, the rut takes over as the buck's primary motive for movement out of his area.

Desert muleys are just as cagey as their mountain kin. For example, mule deer bucks will crawl *under* boulders; they will hide *in* crevices and caves; they will hole up *under* earthen banks. Like mountain muleys, they will hold tight no matter how close you get to them—like the buck in the fall of 1987 that brought all these lessons home to us.

The wind coming off the sagebrush flat was hot. As Bob and I worked our way around the stark, silent canyon, blowing sand stung our faces. From a distance the canyon had looked like a sheer rock face. As we'd gotten closer, we could see cracks in the face big enough to hide a buck, and the rubble at the base of these cliffs included huge boulders strewn about everywhere.

Bob eased along 25 yards ahead of me and 30 yards below. He passed a huge boulder on its downslope side. When I started to ease by on the other side of the rock I heard the clatter of hooves as Bob yelled, "Buck!"

It's a muley's nature to follow a canyon rim; once they've been jumped, most bucks will lope around the canyon edge, giving you ample opportunity for a shot. Only the really big ones scramble straight up and over, or dash out of sight before you know what's happening.

Although this particular buck had a decent rack it didn't have the mass that's built into a mega-muley's headset. He darted past Bob and, true to form, around the canyon rim. Although he stopped long enough for a shot, we both let him go.

This buck wasn't a real trophy; he was just a little bit above average. But he had hidden himself *under* the edge of a boulder in a desolate canyon and stayed hidden until first Bob and then I walked within five yards of his hiding place. Even from a few feet away it was impossible to detect the animal. We'd even glassed the area first from over a mile away, but the only way we'd have spotted this buck was if he'd been standing or moving.

Over the years mule deer have discovered that protection from both the elements and hunters can be found in the strangest places. Big bucks choose some of the most desolate-looking habitat. The inhospitable look of these barren wastelands would suggest that no deer could exist there; yet in many desolate canyons deer tracks and droppings are everywhere.

Bob and I have often found where deer have hidden on ledges. One particular ledge bore the impression of a buck's body in the sand on the shelf. He'd had to get out there by crouching like a cougar since it was too cramped to stand. We could tell from his tracks he'd seen us coming, backed off the ledge, urinated, and then fled up a nearly vertical rocky chimney.

The mule deer we spooked from under the boulder had showed a chink in his armor, as many younger bucks under a 25-inch spread do. First, he ran where we could see him, even though escape paths that would have taken him out of our sight a lot more quickly were available: he panicked. Second, he stopped and looked back. A trophy wouldn't have shown curiosity.

A trophy muley's weaknesses are more apparent than those of a whitetail because of the openness of his range. A muley that's been spotted or jumped will often have to run a tremendous distance to get out of the hunter's sight. So the high-powered rifles and optics that make the difference to a mega-muley hunter might not count as much to a trophy whitetail hunter.

When muleys decide to hide they pick almost any kind of cover. Like the dense sagebrush along one particular creek that Bob and I hunted. The whole creekbed was about 50 yards wide, but the creek itself was tiny—only about three feet wide—and it meandered back and forth across the bed as it flowed.

Bob stayed in the creekbed while I walked along the waterway's rim in case a buck dashed up the side. We hadn't walked far when a buck scrambled out of the creek and bounded across the desert. Since the buck was a small four-pointer we let him go.

Later Bob said that the creekbed was full of deer beds that had been hollowed out under the huge sagebrush. Other muley hiding spots we discovered in the desert consisted of depressions that appeared to have been made by the deer themselves. Some beds were between rocks; some completely *under* rocks. Almost all of them were full of old deer droppings. Deer prefer spots like these to avoid sun, snow, rain and wind—and hunters.

On another trip we climbed a rock face that was very nearly vertical in our quest for a desert mega-muley. Small bushes clung tenaciously to the rim of the canyon above. We stalked steadily along with the wind blowing in our faces. We hadn't gone far when we scared another average buck out from under a rock; he jumped up within ten yards of me.

On the next drainage Bob eased across a steep shelf that was dotted with a few tattered aspens. As Bob went into the aspens, a nice muley popped out from almost the exact place that he entered. The buck looked back towards Bob and then snuck along the ledge and popped over the top as I watched in astonishment.

Later that same morning we watched from above as six does and fawns bedded in a shallow ditch. Hunters on the same level as the deer would never have seen them. All of the deer were lying on the shady side of a ditch that couldn't have been more than 18 inches deep. If six does can disappear into such scant cover think what one wary old buck can do!

A deer drive at the Bolten Ranch Club, located just south of Rawlins, Wyoming, taught me even more about muleys. I saw bucks that leaped on rocks and watched the drivers walk right under them. These mule deer should have scurried out of there. Once the drivers had passed, the bucks began feeding again, confident in their ability to go unnoticed by man.

That evening Ken Mauer, another trophy mule deer hunter from Houston, Texas, told us about a good buck he'd spotted a mile behind the ranch house. Since he was leaving the next day, Mauer told us where he'd last seen the big muley.

His information paid off for Bob: the next evening he jumped the big buck and shot as the animal dived over a high earthen bank. When Bob went to look for his buck in the morning, he found signs that the deer had been holed up under the earthen bank behind some mountain mahogany bushes. Tall grass grew down from above, further obscuring the deer's hiding spot. Although he checked the area for several hours he found no blood. So he decided to stillhunt through a nearby stand of aspens.

As soon as he entered the thicket he jumped a deer. Dogging its tracks, Bob jumped the deer twice more, but this tactic was getting him nowhere. So he decided to hunt the edge of the aspens, where a high sagebrush hill melted into the aspen pocket.

By walking quietly along the side of the hill Bob was able to sneak even closer to the deer where it was hiding in the aspens. The fourth time the deer bounded off Bob could tell the animal was really making tracks.

"All of a sudden I could hear a difference in the sound of the hooves," Bob said. "They weren't beating into fallen leaves and striking blowdowns; now they were definitely clattering on rocks.

"I knew the animal was going higher, probably right over the sheer shale face of the mountain on the other side of the aspen pocket. My only chance was to get into position where I could see the rock face, so I ran up the side of the sagebrush hill.

"I'd no sooner gotten into position when I saw this huge buck burst into view above the aspens; he was making a beeline for the top as fast as he could. When I got the scope on him, I fired.

"The deer veered downhill and out of sight immediately. Next, I heard some crashing in the aspens and then nothing but silence."

The one shot from Bob's 30.06 Weatherby Fiberguard had done the trick. The 150-grain Nosler solid base spitzer bullet powered by

59 grains of H4831 went right through the big buck's heart at 200 yards.

Was it a mega-muley? Nothing to make Boone and Crockett, but it was truly a superior mule deer buck with antlers over 28 inches wide and 20 inches high.

The one thing that separates mega-muley hunters from everyone else is sheer persistence. Persistence, and knowing the spots where mega-muleys hole up, whether in mountains or deserts.

OVERLAP AREAS

Certain landforms and types of vegetation carry over from mountains to desert. For example, some of the best mule deer hunting can be found in aspen thickets in either habitat. Aspens are picturesque trees with white trunks and what appear to be eternally-moving leaves that turn golden in the fall. Their beauty makes them the favorite subject of many a calendar photographer, and aspens are also favored by mule deer, for very good reasons.

Aspens thrive throughout most of the West, primarily in elevations between 7,000 and 9,000 feet. Look for their colorful foliage interspersed within a pine/fir forest or hidden deep in the drainages of rolling sagebrush hills. But no matter where you might find them, they'll almost always hold deer.

Aspen thickets not only provide food in the form of snowberry, bitterbrush, serviceberry, mountain mahogany, and aspen leaves and browse, they also provide much-needed cover. In many areas of the mule deer's range, aspens grow in depressions and draws. In the desert limited rainfall means aspen groves are often the only sizeable trees that mule deer can use for cover. But getting the big bucks out of an aspen pocket can be quite a task.

While muleys don't crave heavy cover as much as whitetails do, they still feel more secure when they can hole up in some sheltered nook. Aspen pockets are made to order. One pocket usually includes diverse cover, ranging from impenetrable thickets where moving is nearly impossible, to scattered openings littered with leaves that make desirable bedding areas. Aspen pockets can be hunted in a variety of ways.

If the aspen pocket is fairly small or narrow, one man can drive a pocket. Take advantage of the wind and make it work like another driver, pushing your scent well ahead of you. Shooters should position themselves where they can cover the greatest amount of territory without being in someone else's line of fire. If conditions are right, noise isn't necessary.

If you don't want the wind to push deer out of the pocket way in front of you—say if you are hunting alone—then walk with the wind *in* your face. Under these circumstances, the deer may not move until you're almost on top of them, which gives you the best opportunity for a shot. Big mule deer bucks, like big whitetails, often hold tight allowing hunters to walk right past them. Stay alert.

Another hunting method that works in the aspens is to sit, watch, and wait from a ground stand. Be on your stand well before dawn. Mule deer, especially the biggest bucks, like to travel during hours of low light. Scout any area you plan to cover thoroughly. Learn where game trails are, where they merge, and where they top ridges. Be sure to stay alert to movement: every big buck hunter tells stories about muleys that stand so still that only the flicker of an ear or a tail betrayed their position.

It's a good idea to pace off some standard range distances when you arrive in unfamiliar mule deer country. Distances in the mountains and the desert can be deceiving, especially when the only object available to compare a deer with is a clump of sagebrush. Sometimes what looks like an easy 100-yard shot turns out to be twice that—and no sure thing!

40

Stand Hunting for
Mule Deer Superbucks

Stands are ideal for catching a trophy muley unaware. But the word *stand* doesn't always have the same connotation out West that it does in whitetail country. Whitetail hunters try to get above a deer's line of vision and away from his super sense of smell by using a tree stand whenever it's practical and legal.

The mule deer looks different, acts differently, and lives in surroundings that are often quite different from those of his fidgety cousin. But the one thing that remains the same is the fervent desire of mule deer hunters to get well above their quarry's sight line. And since the muley's eyesight is especially keen, higher stands make even more sense. Two ways to get above a mule deer superbuck's line of sight include vantage points and tree stands. Vantage points are extremely popular with mule deer hunters all over the West, while tree stands have a small but steady following, especially among bowhunters.

VANTAGE POINTS

Muleys are fun to hunt partly because of the sheer scope of the terrain they inhabit. A vantage point perched high in the rocks, where, with a little effort and a spotting scope, an eagle-eyed hunter can keep track of thousands of acres of muley habitat at a time, seems made to order for hunting these gray ghosts.

Mule deer often follow the semblance of a routine, making it somewhat easier to predict their movements. They feed early and then move to their bedding grounds. They may feed again during the day, but usually move less than 100 yards while doing so. As evening draws near, mule deer exit daytime bedding areas and saunter back to feeding grounds. A hunter may have a lot of country to cover, but since undisturbed muleys spend so much time in a relatively small portion of their range, it's not as impossible as it might seem to intercept them.

Points to consider when choosing a vantage point include wind direction, thermals, prevailing wind, and approach. Sun location can be critical: even if you've found the best spot in the world, if you can't see it won't do you much good. Keeping the sun at your back not only illuminates the scene before you, it also helps obscure the vision of any animal that happens to glance your way.

Keep your binoculars or spotting scope trained on both sunny and shaded areas when hunting from a morning stand. Some big bucks may make a beeline for a sunny hillside on an autumn morning, while others linger on shaded slopes. Cold doesn't bother a muley the way it does a whitetail.

Situating your own vantage point so that you can catch a few rays will help temper the morning chill and make it easier for you to stay out longer. There's no law that says a deer hunter has to be uncomfortable.

Thermals must also be considered. Early in the day these vagrant air currents carry your scent downhill and along the ground. As the sun begins to warm the air, thermals gradually shift into their daytime pattern, and your scent will rise with the currents. As evening cools things down, once again thermals become a factor. Lingering scent will plummet towards the ground on evening thermals. Try to position yourself so that while you're there thermals will carry your scent to portions of the muley range generally unoccupied by the animals.

Prevailing wind direction is important, too. While you're scouting make a note of which way grass or bushes are bent. The direction in which their tops are inclined is the way the wind generally blows. Try to locate your vantage point so that the prevailing wind carries your scent away from any deer-use areas.

Check wind direction at various times during the day with either a small squeeze bottle of unscented talc or a frayed piece of dental floss. Changes in wind direction may dictate a shift to a different vantage point. Swirling mountain winds can be quite frustrating. But one whiff of human scent may be all it takes to clear a big buck right out of an area. A high enough vantage point may be all but immune to shifts in the wind.

When considering the wind pay attention to any boulders and bluffs that can double as windbreaks while you're on stand. During much of autumn, and especially when you're above timberline, it won't take much of a breeze to make it downright cold. By taking advantage of natural windbreaks, you can get out of the wind and stay reasonably comfortable. Windbreaks can also keep your spotting scope from being buffeted about.

Use the wind in other ways, as well. Remember that deer don't like strong wind any more than you do. A steady blow should be your cue to shift your attention to areas where deer can get out of the wind. Scope out protected canyons and the leeward side of any nearby mountains or hills. Planning a location for your vantage point can take a lot of time but it can often result in a chance at a super-deer.

Many superbucks are alive today simply because hunters didn't approach their vantage point cautiously enough and gave their presence away. Walk slowly and deliberately to your stand, being especially careful for the last quarter mile. Kirt Darner believes that big mule deer bucks can sense vibrations through their bodies when bedded, and it's not impossible that they also sense ground vibrations through their hooves. If you're clomping along in heavy boots you just might spook a nearby trophy into abandoning the area before you even know he's around.

In the morning you should be at your stand while it's still dark. In the evening you should stay until dark. The biggest bucks are usually the first to drift back to cover in the morning and the last to come out at night.

Never skyline or silhouette yourself coming over ridges. Stick to lines of vegetation or hang close to boulders to obscure your movement and keep animals from spotting you.

There are times when stands that provide only limited viewing opportunity are the ones that produce the biggest bucks. You just might have to ambush a really shy animal in his own bailiwick to get a shot at him. Often that means long hours crouched under dense oakbrush or spent along the edges of waterholes waiting for a glimpse of the humdinger you're after. So even though vantage points that allow you to see great distances are the ones commonly used throughout most of the West, there may come a time when you have to resort to a stand that's literally undercover.

TREE STANDS

Most hunters would no sooner think of hunting for big muleys from a tree stand than they would for the man in the moon. But others, like Colorado's Jay Verzuh, saw a concept with promise and set about adapting it for Pope and Young-class mule deer bucks. Verzuh felt tree stands would be especially well-suited to hunting the thick stands of oak-brush shrub in western Colorado.

"Western hunters are so used to seeing for long distances that they automatically start hunting that way," Verzuh said. "But you can bowhunt mule deer quite successfully from tree stands that have just a limited view."

Verzuh owns and operates Colorado Elite Outfitters, headquartered in Grand Junction. Over the last thirty years he's guided hunters to so many bucks that qualify for Pope and Young, he's simply lost count. His hunters have bagged bucks with racks that score in excess of 170 points. So has Verzuh himself. Many times. "I've had chances at what I know is a new world record Pope and Young buck, too," Verzuh lamented, "but so far I haven't connected."

Verzuh's taken many Pope and Young bucks with his bow and a number of Boone and Crockett muleys with his rifle. So he's an incredibly well-rounded mule deer hunter. He knows a lot about the animals, a fact that explains why he's so much in demand as a mule deer guide.

To get these big bucks, Jay Verzuh has done some serious study of mule deer habits. "Archery hunting is done well before the rut starts," he said. "So I start investigating what the deer are doing early in the summer." Verzuh's techniques aren't earth-shattering, but they require a lot of detailed work. He wants to know why the deer are doing what they're doing as soon as they start doing it.

"Mule deer can be as predictable as any other species," he explained. "But to figure out their movements with any regularity means that I must scout and pattern them almost year-around. I'm always investigating any changes that might have occurred on the land that we lease. Some stands are hotspots year after year. Others might not yield any bucks one year, then produce two or three the next. Minute changes could make the difference between a stand that's a top-producer one year and one that's no good at all the next."

Beginning early in the year, Verzuh makes note of where various deer groups are feeding when he observes them from a distance with binoculars or spotting scope at dawn. "This is when deer are in their primary feeding grounds. I make sure I note what they're eating, how they leave the area, what time they leave, and where I think they're headed to bed. I pay special attention to weather conditions and I always write everything down. Later on, when I'm at home, I look for patterns of predictability. Like where I've seen big bucks feeding and bedding most often, and how the weather affects their use of each."

Verzuh stays put, observing feeding deer until midmorning. Then, he'll start stillhunting through the woods armed only with a camera, note pad, and binoculars. "I'll completely avoid the area I glassed first thing in the morning," he explained. "Now I want to locate primary bedding areas, spots deer bed regularly under certain conditions. At first I won't know why or when a deer is liable to use these primary bedding areas, by the time I'm through I'll have a good idea.

"As I slip through the brush early in the year, it's a good time to practice moving quietly and slowly in preparation for hunting season. I try to see the animal in its bed before it sees me. When I find a group of bucks, I get comfortable and watch them for as long as I'm able. I note the time, weather conditions, and everything else I can, like how big each one is, where their beds are in relation to each other, whether or not I saw other wildlife, whether the location was shady or sunny, and any other pertinent information.

"To make any sense out of a mule deer buck's behavior you have to repeat these daily scouting expeditions," Verzuh stated. "You could return to the same area and find no bucks at all the next time. But if you stumble onto a primary bedding area you will always find bucks there under the right conditions. By writing everything down and continually analyzing it, you'll soon know what those conditions are. Eventually, you'll discover the very best places to hunt bucks at different times and under various weather conditions."

In the evening, Verzuh returns to the same spot he was scouting from at dawn. If the deer were feeding at a primary feeding spot early in the morning, deer should once more be coming out to feed. Verzuh is always sure to note how the deer arrive in the area and then compare that with the way they leave in the morning.

Verzuh follows this same routine exactly for several days, taking note of all deer movements. Then he reverses his scouting schedule so that he's watching the midday location during early morning and late evening hours and stillhunting at midday into the same areas he's been observing from afar early and late. He's always attuned to weather conditions. And before long, he's intimately acquainted with the entire area's potential for holding bucks at any time of day and in almost any type of weather conditions. By studying his notes, he can determine the most productive places to erect tree stands fairly easily.

"As a rule, we'll place treestands along the trail *from* a feeding area or along the trail *to* the feeding area. One thing I've discovered, and the Colorado Division of Wildlife has confirmed it in a study, is that mule deer leave their beds for about an hour at midday to feed. They seldom go farther than 100 yards and then often return to the same bed for the rest of the afternoon."

Wind direction is always of prime importance to Verzuh. "If anything is wrong, back off. You don't want to rile a big buck up. Bedding areas are especially critical to a big buck's feeling of security. It's better to locate stands in the transition area between his bedding and feeding areas."

An important facet of tree stand hunting is the approach. "You must not be detected on your way to the stand," emphasized Verzuh. "Always approach cautiously and quietly. If you've done your homework, you should know everything you need to know about game movement and thermals to get you undetected into your hunting area."

Verzuh scouts whenever he can, all year long. During hunting season, his guides and helpers will glass and scout each day when they're finished with their chores. Each hunter in camp fills out daily hunt reports as well. These detail what they saw and when and where they saw it. Once the reports are complete, the entire camp discusses them twice each day, at midday and again after supper. Only then is the next hunting day planned.

Of course, when you're hunting mule deer there are always variables that can't be predicted with any degree of accuracy, things like the effect of the rut, hunting pressure on neighboring tracts of land, or the presence of predators. All these factors could negatively influence deer movements in your area. But by continually observing and monitoring and then adapting your hunting strategy to encompass the changes you've noted, there's no reason why tree stands can't work as well for you as they do for Colorado Elite's Jay Verzuh in his bid for trophy mule deer.

41

Stalking the Mule Deer Superbuck

Some hunters call it stillhunting; others call it stalking. No matter: either technique can turn a super-muley hunt upside down, from passive to active. When you wait on a stand, you do just that: wait. You sit and hope that a buck will show up. But stalkers take an active part: they either try to force the buck to move and divulge his presence, or they actually go out and locate a buck, then move in for the kill.

A successful stillhunter moves like a wraith; he uses the wind to carry his scent away from any area he plans to stillhunt through. He'll always hunt into the wind or across the wind. He avoids skylining himself at all times. His movements are slow and deliberate; a good stillhunter will make no hasty motion. He'll walk silently and avoid brushing up against any undergrowth that could give him away.

Noisy clothing is out for the dedicated stillhunter. Cotton, wool, or fleece garments are chosen for their quiet properties. If blaze orange is required, use garments constructed of soft fabrics, never plastic or plastic-coated materials. Quiet isn't the only consideration here. Plastic fabrics are far more reflective than natural fibers. Blaze orange garments made of cotton, wool, or fleece won't tip your hand as quickly as the mirror-bright surface of a plastic one will.

When stillhunting, stop every few steps to look and listen. Moving more than 100 yards in an hour is moving too fast. Take advantage of snow or rain; both these conditions help muffle the sound of your movements. Wind can help too, by rustling vegetation it can help camouflage the sounds of your passing.

Always stick to the shadow side of rocks and vegetation when slipping through cover. Movement isn't as obvious when it's partially obscured by shadows. Study all openings carefully but avoid walking through them. Instead, move quietly along the cover near the edges.

Combine stand hunting with stillhunting for the best of all possible worlds. Get up early and use your spotting scope from a good vantage point. Make a note of areas with thick cover located near feeding grounds. If these areas are along travel routes to and from feeding grounds, so much the better. When activity dies down in mid-morning, slip up to these pre-selected areas and stillhunt through them. Late in the afternoon, slip back out of the area and return to a spot where you can use your optics. Spot until dark and plan the next day's hunt while you do.

Many top hunters rely heavily on stillhunting and Kirt Darner of Montrose, Colorado, is one of them. Darner has elevated stillhunting through the heaviest brush he can find to an art form. He doesn't move fast; in fact, he doesn't cover very much ground at all if there's a chance that a big buck might be hiding there. Of course, Kirt wouldn't waste his time on a patch of cover if he wasn't reasonably sure that it was the kind of stuff a big buck would like.

When Darner was still a youngster he accidentally discovered one of the best mega-muley tactics there is. He calls it the "fishhook pattern" and it's a tried and true method of driving big bucks to yourself while stillhunting.

Here's how it works: find a patch of cover and slip into it being careful to keep the wind in your favor. Move very slowly, watching all around as you do. Move straight ahead but, every now and then, make a 90-degree turn to either your left or your right and travel 50 or 100 yards. Then turn again and sneak back parallel to your original route, only now you'll be headed in the opposite direction. When just stillhunting through, you probably won't be able to spook a big, smart buck out of his hideout. But he will react in one of two ways: either by holding tight or circling around behind you.

A buck that holds tight will let you pass, then stand up and follow your trail for a while to see where you're headed. A buck that circles you will then usually sneak right back to the spot where he started from. In either case, these bucks will both be much more visible than they were the first time you went by simply because now they're standing or moving. And since they're intent on where they last saw you, they won't usually notice when you sneak up behind them.

PERSEVERANCE

Perseverance is another trait that trophy muley stillhunters should have in good supply. One of the West's top mule deer hunters, Bob Adamson of Franklin, Idaho, took his best mule deer because he just wouldn't give up.

"I knew the buck was in the area," Adamson said, "but I was sure having a tough time locating him. The weather had turned cold and wet. My camper was quite a distance from where I suspected the big buck was hanging out. So each day I'd have to walk at least two or three miles just to get to the spot where I *thought* the buck might be. After two whole days, I was beginning to wonder. My boots had given out so my feet were soaked through. And by the end of the third day, my feet were really beginning to hurt. Not only were they wet, it was now so cold that they'd turned numb.

"It was late afternoon when I came to the area where I knew the buck had been earlier in the year," Adamson continued. "As I was slipping through the area, I saw some brush moving about 100 yards away. Carefully, I snuck closer until I could see it was a fantastic buck. The deer was ripping up some brush, but his whole front half was hidden in some quakies and I couldn't get a shot. I waited for a while, but I finally began to wonder if he'd come out at all before it was dark. I took a chance on a spine shot and dropped him. I had my buck.

"After I field dressed the deer, I walked back to the camper. When I took off my boots and socks, an entire layer of skin came off, too. Talk about painful. And I still had to skin, cape, and quarter the deer and then backpack it out the next day."

Adamson's giant buck was a dream deer. It had massive 4 × 5 antlers and a 34½-inch spread and is the best buck he's taken. If he hadn't stuck out miserable conditions, that buck would probably have died of old age.

Montana's Chuck Adams is America's top bowhunter. He advocates the "spot and stalk" technique for trophy mule deer. Another archer who swears by the spot and stalk method is John Cole of Oregon. Cole has taken many Pope and Young muleys, as well as trophy mule deer with his rifle, too. He also guides hunters in his spare time. One of his clients took a Boone and Crockett buck that scored 196⅛ points.

"Personally, I've switched completely to bowhunting," he stated. "I really enjoy the challenge of stalking close to big mule deer. My favorite time for hunting trophy bucks is during late August and early September when the buck groups are just starting to break up."

Cole hunts high desert areas. He gets out before dawn and as it gets light tries to find a good deer in his spotting scope. Once he does, he waits until the buck beds down and gives erratic morning thermals time to change to their predictable daytime pattern. Then he attempts to stalk close enough to the buck for a shot.

"I use all the ground cover I can and approach from downwind," Cole explained. "It's fairly easy to get within 75 or 100 yards of nearly any deer. But it's darn difficult to close that gap to the 40 yards I need for a sure shot.

"Often, I'll wait until the sun gets to the bedded deer. When it gets too hot, they'll get up and move. With any luck, they'll either move in my direction or bed someplace where I can approach a little closer without them seeing me.

"Over the years I've noticed that the very best bucks will bed with three or four other bucks in a place where it's impossible to make a stalk. Not only do they make the terrain work for them, they're facing in every direction and watching and listening to everything.

"Once I managed to get close to a buck that would have scored somewhere in the neighborhood of 205 or 207 Boone and Crockett points," Cole said. "He was bedded with four other bucks and as the sun got hotter, one of the smaller bucks got up and headed right for me. Even this 'little' buck was a good one. I figured he'd have gone about 190. I decided to try for him, and as he walked my way, I shot. Unfortunately, a branch deflected the arrow.

"If you blow a stalk for one of these big bucks he'll move right out of the vicinity. It may take three or four days until you can locate him again.

"There's a world of difference between what you can get away with on a young buck and what you can do with an old buck," Cole continued. "For one thing, the older a deer gets, the more of a sixth sense he'll acquire. For example, when you start your stalk you'll usually lose sight of the buck for a short time. You might be out of sight of the animal for 10, 20, or 30 minutes while trying to ease closer. Everything might be perfect for the stalk and yet when you get into position where you should be able to see him, he's gone. Invariably, if you turn around and look behind you, he'll be watching *you* from about 200 yards out."

Another hunter who both specializes in giant mule deer bucks and prefers stillhunting is Lee Frudden of Fort Collins, Colorado. Lee and I both hunted mega-muleys on what was once the Bolten Ranch south of Rawlins, Wyoming, a real big buck hotspot. Lee took one big deer on the Bolten that scored 193, falling short of Boone and Crockett by only two points. He took another super deer in Colorado's Eagle County, a Boone and Crockett that scored 197⅞ points, and his hunting buddy took a big Boone and Crockett non-typical at the same spot and on the same day. Lee also took a heavy-horned 9 × 11 on the Jicarilla Apache Indian Reservation. This buck had a 35-inch outside spread. Other notable Frudden bucks include a 30-inch wide 5 × 5, a 34-inch wide 4 × 6, and one other super-heavy, super-high buck.

"When I took the buck that scored 193 on the Bolten I'd been creeping along through some heavy brush and clumps of quakies that lies just behind the main ranch house," Frudden said. "I wasn't seeing very many deer up to that point even though we'd gotten an eight-inch snow that should have made it easier to pick them out from the background.

"There's a big rim at the end of the basin and I was creeping right beneath this rim, watching my feet. When I looked up, there was a big buck standing not 20 yards away from me. I had on a camo coat and gray wool pants, the only blaze orange was on my cap. And for some reason, he didn't know what I was. The wind wasn't blowing his way so smell wasn't going to give me away. I waited and he waited. Finally I raised my gun, but I decided not to shoot because I'd seen another buck that I thought might be bigger two nights before the season started.

"With that, the buck walked out of sight. As he left, I realized that he was a lot better than I originally thought he was. So I followed him and caught up with him and three does. As soon as I walked up, they all ran off. My only chance was in getting up a little higher so that I could see where he was running. I ran to a little knob, sat down in the snow, and shot when the buck was about 150 yards away. That was it; the buck dropped."

Frudden likes to hunt as late in the season as possible. Not only is a later hunt closer to the rut, but opening weekend hunters have gone home. The weather's generally nastier, too, and bad weather will make deer move.

"When I'm hunting big bucks I cover lots of country," he said. "I'm not much for sitting around and looking. I'll get into an area and hit all the pockets, the thicker the better, because that's what a big buck likes."

Stillhunting and stalking are a couple of techniques that could turn your deer hunting world upside down, too. When you take your time and pay attention to details, either strategy could help you become an active player in the super-muley game.

42

Glassing for
Mule Deer Superbucks

Even in your wildest dreams it's tough to imagine the stark beauty of the West's timberline high country. Think of cliffs as sheer as glass with room-sized boulders strewn like gravel at their bases. Think of peaks that reach into azure skies where eagles soar on the wind.

Now, add some autumn mountain weather. A few Indian summer days to taunt and tantalize, when aspens gleam like burnished gold and the smell of Ponderosa pine lays heavy in the canyons. Throw in some darker days, when monster storms dump squalls of rain and tons of snow on the ride back to a sodden camp.

That's just a hint of what's waiting once you decide to hunt timberline trophy mule deer. The country is rough and it requires a hunter just as unyielding, one that's hell-bent on bagging a buster muley. When you go for high country bucks, you start your search in the most unforgiving terrain around. Even if you pace yourself, an average altitude of 9,500 feet in Colorado and Wyoming takes a toll.

If the altitude doesn't get you, the unpredictable behavior of a trophy buck just might. Often you won't even get the *chance* to pull the trigger. If it's challenges you're after, then a real timberline mule deer hunt will fill the bill.

My husband, Bob, and I have been hunting timberline muleys for almost 35 years now. We've hunted on our own, out of drop camps, and with a number of outfitters, and we've killed nice bucks everywhere we've gone. One year I hunted with Maury Jones, a top trophy mule deer outfitter who hunts out of Bedford, Wyoming. Then I realized the difference between hunting big muley bucks and hunting *mega*-muley bucks—those in the 28-inch plus category. And it was during this hunt when the vital importance of having the best optics you can afford really became clear to me.

Jonesy's hunt area includes portions of the Little Greys River drainage east of Alpine Junction, Wyoming, home to some of the biggest bucks in North America. Our first morning there, we were awakened at 3:00 A.M. Within the hour we were riding our horses up steep mountains in the dark, around switchbacks and across icy hogback ridges.

Our goal was to reach two small timberline basins by dawn. Before the season, Jonesy had located two 30-inch bucks and a 38-incher in these basins. The plan was for Bob and me to each bag one. Jones put us in place; after sitting in the blowing snow for three hours, we still hadn't seen a deer.

"I don't know where they could have gone," Jonesy muttered to himself. "They were working this basin just like clockwork."

It wasn't until later that Jonesy discovered that another group of hunters had backpacked in before us and set up camp nearby. Wild muleys aren't nearly as adaptable to human presence as whitetails are. A big mule deer buck won't flag his tail goodbye; he'll simply swap ends and clear out, often for good. A mule deer's home range is immense; he could go a half mile or a half-*dozen* miles. So one secret to getting a big buck is to disturb its area as little as possible. This means that when you're after a mega-muley, you're going to have to learn to depend on your optics so you aren't kicking up every corner of a big buck's home range.

Today's optics are better than ever before and more affordable, too. If you're spending a lot of money to go with a top-notch outfitter, why skimp on optical quality—an item that could mean the difference between getting a mule deer superbuck and not? Even if you hunt on your own, just to get into megabuck country is time-consuming and often somewhat dangerous. Why go to all that trouble and risk and then have your optics let you down?

Buy the best that you can afford, both in binoculars and spotting scope. While you're at it, don't forget that you're going to be lugging your purchase either around your neck or in your daypack or backpack: size is also a serious consideration.

A few years ago we both bought Swarovski's 10 × 40 SLCs. What can I say other than that they are the answer to a big-buck hunter's prayers? And Swarovski has improved on these binoculars, although I don't see how that could be possible. Lightweight for their capabilities, crystal clear, and with more light-gathering ability than I ever would have believed, these are the Mercedes-Benz of optics. Plus, they are tough as nails. I am hard on gear, but I've never managed to do anything to these binoculars other than nick the exterior housing.

Another great set of binoculars is Nikon's Venturer LX 10 × 40. Although this binocular is slightly heavier than Swarovski's SLCs, I also think it may produce a somewhat brighter image. Again, it must be magic—or coatings—as I am baffled as to how any optical equipment could be better than the SLCs I've used and loved for so many years. But when I let others peer through these Nikons, the one comment that I've gotten used to hearing is that "They're too bright." As if such a thing were possible.

Cabela's has broken into the optical market as well with their Alaska Guide series. I've got a pair of their 10 × 40s, and in every way that matters, they're as good as the Swarovski SLCs. Remarkable statement, but true. And also just half the price. I feel confident that some fine optical company is private labeling these binoculars for Cabela's, but I haven't been able to ferret that information out of my contacts at the store.

Kirt Darner doesn't waste time with mini-binoculars. He prefers larger-sized military-type binoculars because they give him the ultimate in light-gathering capability. For a long time he used a pair of military 7 × 50s. With seven-power magnification and an objective lens of 50mm for optimum light-gathering capability, Darner felt he was getting the ultimate in mega-muley spotting equipment. Recently, he switched to a new set of 7 × 50s made by Swarovsky. The reason? "They were quite a bit lighter than my old pair," said Darner, "and in the mountains, weight counts!"

Binoculars aren't the only bit of optical equipment that you should seriously consider taking along on any trophy mule deer hunt. Be sure to leave room in your backpack or duffle for a good spotting scope. Don't buy one that's so large that you get sick of lugging it around with you. I bought a spotting scope a few years back that does everything but tell you how wide the buck's rack is. But I never haul it along because it weighs over three pounds, too much for any kind of rough-country hunting. Not only does it weigh too much, it measures 17.5 inches long. It's hard to find the room to even carry it along.

Far better is the Bushnell Spacemaster spotting scope that Bob bought 30 years ago and took along for 15 years. It was usurped only by Leupold's new spotter. I use Nikon's fantastic 15 × 45 spotting scope with its handy snap-on cover that protects the optics under even the worst conditions.

But there are lots of excellent spotting scopes in the marketplace today. Many of them are also armor-coated. And while 45 power comes in handy, 20 power is usually sufficient to tell if a buck is worth pursuing.

Still another bit of optical equipment that will make your quest for a mega-muley a little easier is a rangefinder. Leupold markets a fine variable scope, the Vari-X III that has the easiest, most efficient rangefinder built into its reticle that I've seen yet. Not only that, one Vari-X III is available in 2.5 × 8, a fine choice of powers on a tube that is much more compact than a 3 × 9. This scope costs quite a bit, but its superior resolution and rangefinding capability are worth it. And it's also available in a matte finish as well as one that's glossy blued, important to some trophy hunters who try to reduce telltale glare as much as possible.

As it turned out, our hunt with Maury Jones had a second chapter. The rest of the first day was a washout with snow, fog and drifting clouds hindering us until evening. The following day, however, was a buck hunter's dream. At dawn we were once again on top of the world, glassing with our binoculars so that we didn't disturb the area. As morning faded it became downright hot, the complete opposite of the day before. But we didn't see a thing until we finally dragged out the spotting scopes. Our binoculars alone weren't powerful enough to penetrate the deep shadows where all the bucks in the area were currently bedding.

I'd heard of "buck pastures," but the whole concept of an area so favored by bucks that they congregate there in droves seemed a little unlikely to me. As we lay there glassing the basin in front of us, however, it became apparent that we'd found one.

The slope in front of us was alive with bucks—over 30 of them— most bedded in the shade of boulders. It takes a lot of patience and a steady hand to be a successful big buck spotter. Anything that looks even remotely like a *piece* of a buck has to be analyzed. Throat patch, rump patch, portion of antler—all have to be stared at until the sun shifts or the shadow moves a bit. Only then can you be sure that your eyes haven't been playing tricks on you. And you'd be surprised how often a piece of a deer actually *becomes* a deer.

Anyway, we spotted bucks for nearly two hours. Several sparred playfully in a grassy opening. Other bucks ringed them, looking like an audience at a heavyweight fight. Unfortunately, none was worth pursuing.

One animal, however, did seem a cut above the rest so we thought we'd try for a closer look. Getting to him didn't look as if it would be too difficult, but getting back out in the dark might be a little tricky.

We hurried down the ridge, knocking an occasional piece of shale bouncing into the canyon below. The way got steadily rougher until we were following little more than a goat trail, worn into the rock over eons of time. Finally we dropped into a grassy swale.

It had taken us 30 minutes to negotiate the slope, but now the buck was lying less than 75 yards away.

"He's just a youngster," Jonesy whispered. "Only about 25 inches wide."

Some youngster, I thought. A 25-incher is a darn good buck in many areas. But the minerals around the Little Greys help grow them bragging-size. We watched the deer for a while, but when the sun dipped below the peaks behind us and a chill wind blew over us, we knew it was time to head back.

When hunting in the mountains, you face a double dose of risk. It's usually harder to keep your balance and footing when traveling downhill over steep terrain than going up. But climbing back up is no piece of cake when breathing the thin air that accompanies 10,000-foot heights. It took us well over an hour to reach the summit. Once we did, we headed for the horses in the rapidly fading twilight.

We'd only gone about a half mile when Jonesy stopped us. "Deer," he said, adjusting his binoculars. "Two does and a dandy buck, about 29 inches wide with matching drop tines on each side that really give his rack character."

It was Bob's turn for first shot, so I followed the men across the meadow. When they neared the spot where the deer had last been seen, they began their stalk. I stayed back, guarding the most obvious escape route, a depression that led to the ridge where we'd spent the day glassing.

They didn't return until dark. The buck had escaped, slipping off in a completely different direction than expected. He'd stopped momentarily for a look back when he was over 200 yards away, but it wasn't long enough for Bob to safely shoot. In fading light, with two does milling about, positively identifying the buck was imperative.

We didn't finally climb into our sleeping bags until 11:30 P.M. Scaling those mountains on 3½ hours of sleep has to be experienced to be believed.

The hunt took its toll on a couple of our fellow hunters as well. After two days of timberline, they demanded easier hunting. "I just want to be in a place where if I fall down, I won't die," commented one. These hunters were young and in good shape, but the rigors of timberline weren't for them.

The next morning Bob decided to hunt another area on his own, giving me the opportunity for first shot if Jonesy and I should happen upon a trophy. So, Jonesy and I headed out alone at 4:00 A.M., right on schedule. I was tired but excited. Maybe this would be the day.

This time up we located two deer in the buck pasture that really looked good. One was lying sprawled out over a half mile away. But even from this distance his rack looked awesome. The other one was even farther, feeding in some thick mountain mahogany. Since the first buck looked like he'd be easier to approach, we decided to go after him.

We snuck around the basin's rim to get the sun at our backs. That way, although a doe was standing next to the big buck's bed, the sun blinded her to our presence.

We went as far as we dared without spooking the two deer, which we'd named Fred and Ethel. Even with the sun in her eyes, the bouncing rocks we knocked loose on our approach were making Ethel nervous. Fred couldn't have cared less. He was stretched out on the ground, jaw agape, only his antlers propping up his dignity.

We got as close as we could. Then I moved into a stand of small firs to scope Fred out once more. Jonesy figured him at just under 30 inches with heavy, high main beams. And it looked like he had several brow tines on each side. In any case, he was good enough for me.

"How far is it?" I asked.

"Too far," Jonesy replied.

"It only looks like 300 yards," I stubbornly insisted. (Since I didn't yet have my Leupold Vari-X III with the rangefinder, I could only guess at the distance.)

"It's at least 400," Jonesy said.

"It looks like 300," I nagged. "And if it is, I can hit him. I can get in a prone position and use this log as a rifle rest." (I practice from 300 yards.)

"I can get you closer," Jonesy countered.

"How?" I said. I looked around and there was no way that I could see to get any closer. I argued but I lost.

"Follow me," Jonesy said. I bowed to Jonesy's superior mule deer knowledge and the two of us started down the cliff behind us, hoping to flank the sleeping buck.

I should have pretended to follow and shot instead, risking Jonesy's wrath, because the snow that had blown in on that first day had really done a number on Jonesy's "route" to the buck. We had to travel several hundred yards down an icy rock face and then across a snow-covered boulder field at the bottom. The route was still icy since it faced north and was rarely exposed to the sun. Finally, we eased behind the slope where the sleeping buck lay. Now only a vertical climb separated me from my trophy.

It had taken us over two hours to get here, yet I was exhilarated, both by the danger we'd successfully negotiated and the chance that was near. My heart was pounding as I snuck over the ridge. But instead of a tremendous buck, there was only an empty bed. When I walked closer I could see deer tracks that were wider than my hand and almost as long.

We could only guess that the constantly shifting thermals had carried our scent to the buck. The length of time it took for the stalk probably worked against us as well. Deer will leave an area when it's no longer to their liking. With evening approaching, the air was getting chilly. The buck may simply have decided to move on.

In any case, Jonesy and I found ourselves in the buck pasture. So we crept about, looking for any sign of Fred. Although we searched until dark, we couldn't locate him. So once again we rode out with the moon high in the sky.

The next morning—since we were obviously such gluttons for punishment—Jonesy led us back to where we'd last seen the buck. We made a silent drive through some nearby dark timber on the chance that we might jump the big deer.

While Bob and I snuck through the thickest timber, Jonesy popped into a small patch of woods near the bottom of the slope. Sure enough, Fred and Ethel came scurrying out the other side. Neither Bob nor I saw them and Jonesy didn't have a gun. So Fred escaped once more.

After seeing Fred, it was hard to settle for a lesser buck, especially since we had many other bucks in the 24-inch to 26-inch class at home. So, at the end of our five days we wished Jonesy well and gratefully headed for a motel, a real bed, and a real night's sleep.

Jonesy's outfit, like that of many high country outfitters, is first-rate. Food, guides, stock and tack are all excellent. But after a hard timberline hunt, you'll *deserve* a rest.

The snows came early to Wyoming in 1986. Soon, only one deer hunter remained in camp, and he was being guided by someone else. Since Jonesy still had his own deer tag to fill, he headed back to—where else?—the buck pasture.

This time instead of approaching the big basin from the back as we always did, Jonesy took the frontal route. The snow was knee-deep by October 5th but Jonesy climbed to where he could get a look at the buck pasture. He spotted until 4:00 P.M. (see what I mean about patience?) without seeing a buck worth pursuing. So he began to climb up where we'd discovered Fred's empty bed less than two weeks before.

"It was steep so I was using both hands to climb," Jonesy said. "About halfway up, I cut my hand on a sharp rock that jutted from the cliff's face. When I stopped to check it I caught a glimpse of a deer's rump to my left out of the corner of my eye. Slowly, I took the gun off my shoulder, cranked the scope to 9×, and spotted the rump patch . . . and a big rack. I aimed and waited. When the animal turned, I let him have it with my .243.

"Getting down to where the buck had slid after dying was another major exercise. But as soon as I got close to the animal, I recognized him. It was Fred."

The big buck's rack measured well over 28 inches wide. But the main beams were the kind that every mega-muley hunter dreams of—high, heavy, and with three brow tines to a side.

Timberline mule deer hunting in the high country defies the imagination. But if it's trophy bucks you're after, imagine yourself there—then do something about it. I can almost guarantee you won't be sorry.

43

Scents, Calls, and Rattling

Calls, rattling horns, and scents have developed into outstanding aids for the whitetail hunter. Often they've been directly responsible for some hunters' superbucks. By using calls and scents you can switch your role from passive to active hunter with tangible results.

Since mule deer are usually hunted at greater physical distances, aids such as calls, designed to draw furtive animals into the open, haven't been needed. Mule deer hunters are aware, however, of the phenomenal success achieved by some whitetail hunters while using calls and scents. Although the jury is still out, preliminary findings indicate that there just might be something to calls, rattling, and scents for the muley superbuck.

CALLS

Phil Kirkland of Hill City, Kansas, is one top mule deer hunter who has become a believer in calls for big bucks. Kirkland took the Kansas state record archery muley in 1988 while using a long-distance grunt call that he'd purchased from Russell Hull of G&H Trophy Products. Kirkland's interest in the call stemmed from a conversation that he'd had with Russell Hull three years before. At that time Hull told him that he'd been able to call a few mule deer bucks in close enough to take good photos. Although Kirkland still wasn't convinced that it would work in a hunting situation, he was willing to give it a try, particularly since he often hunted big bucks by spot and stalk methods. He was hoping that the call just might give him an edge.

"I'd been trying to take a good mule deer with my bow for quite some time," Kirkland said. "So I took the call out with me the next time I went hunting. I tried a stalk on a nice mule deer that would have scored about 155 points. When I couldn't get close enough for a shot, I remembered the call. I blew on it once, and the deer moved in to within 20 yards of me. I shot and missed. But now I knew that the call would work on muleys just like Russell said it would."

The next morning Kirkland saw a buck that would score right at 140 points in one of the fields he was hunting. "There wasn't any cover in that field, so I held a big Russian thistle (tumbleweed) in front of me to help break up my silhouette as I snuck closer. When I felt I'd gotten as close as I could, I made a grunt on the call. The buck looked at me. I grunted again, and he walked up to within 15 feet. But the buck was a little suspicious. He'd drop his head, then lift it real quick, trying to get me to move. After he'd done this several times, I finally got a chance for a shot. The arrow struck home and the buck was mine."

Kirkland practiced with the grunt call until the following season. He used it to call in bucks to the camera. During this time he not only became familiar with what the call could do, he gained a lot of insight into the behavior of mule deer.

"I've hunted both whitetail and muleys and have taken Pope and Young-class animals of each species, and personally, I think the whitetail is easier to hunt," Kirkland explained. "First, there are more big whitetails in Kansas than there are big mule deer. Second, if you do your homework, you can find a whitetail's bedding ground, feeding area, and the trails that he uses. You can usually find a good spot for a tree stand where you can waylay him on his trails. At least you have a starting point.

"But a mule deer's different. You've got to do a lot of looking and walking just to find a big mule deer. Then you've got to get close enough to him to get a shot. Usually, he'll stay in the open, in a place where there aren't any trees to hide your movements. An archer has to be prepared to hunt him from the ground, an animal with the most unbelievable eyesight and hearing there is. And that can be tough."

Kirkland remembers vividly the morning he got his record muley. "It was a calm, crisp morning, the kind of morning when a deer call works best," he said. "I'd already decided to head to my whitetail spot. But while I was driving there a pretty good mule deer buck crossed the road in front of me. It just so happened that Russell and I had seen a tremendous buck at the same spot a few days earlier. I had permission to hunt there, so I changed my mind and decided to hunt mule deer instead."

Kirkland leaves very little to chance. He moves into his hunt area in the dark, using the grunt call to mask the sounds he makes as he travels. "Deer have their own way of communicating," he said. "Often, I'll hear them grunt in reply, responding to the 'deer' that's making the call."

To combat human scent, he uses Cover-Up, a masking odor based on the pleasing scent of vanilla. Cover-Up is also made by Russell Hull. He wears complete camouflage, and even covers his arrow fletchings with camo fabric sleeves. He always uses face paint and wears gloves. "Seeing a white face or hands is enough to scare any good buck off," he explained.

Kirkland even paints his brass sight pins so that they don't shine. "A big muley is tuned in to everything he sees, even from a mile off," Kirkland stated.

The area where the two men had seen the big buck was basically a fallow field. Many western Kansas fields like this have been set aside in the Conservation Reserve Program. Lush stands of Sudan grass, known locally as "cane," thwart erosion and aid wildlife by providing cover. Large globs of tumbleweed, or Russian thistle, add an eerie touch to the landscape.

"These cane and thistle fields are central pivot areas for deer," Kirkland explained. "Deer move through them to get to their bedding locations in the thicker stuff.

"As far as timing, I figured it would be right on the money. Over the years, I've figured out that the rut in western Kansas starts about the 3rd of November. It was now November 6th. I just had a feeling that the bucks would really be running the does that morning."

The call wasn't the only ace up Kirkland's sleeve that morning. "Russell and I had noticed how the biggest bucks can't tolerate the presence of a little buck when there's a hot doe around," he said. "So we decided to build a decoy of a smaller buck, something we could use with the call to lure bucks closer. Russell cut a plywood pattern, used some hinges so it could be folded, mounted a set of antlers on it, and then added some taxidermy eyes. Soon our decoy looked like a small buck. He made both a frontal view and a side view, and attached them to a sharp stake that I could stick in the ground and hide behind."

Canefields are ideal for obscuring sounds of movement when stalking close to deer. Cane is noisy, crackling even in faint breezes, so the deer are immune to the sounds you make as you move through it. Once Kirkland got to his chosen spot, he was soon able to pick out two good mule deer bucks in a little coulee, plus four more small bucks and fifteen does. He also saw a good eight-point whitetail and a doe in the cane patch. The field was crawling with deer, but Kirkland wanted a good buck. He patiently watched as the best mule deer buck chased a hot doe, then gradually started to head in his direction.

"Suddenly, the doe ran by about 35 yards away," Kirkland related. "I knew the big buck was behind her, so I came to full draw. When the buck ran into view moments later, he glanced over at me. But since I was behind the decoy he wasn't the least bit suspicious. As he ran past, I shot, and the arrow penetrated well into his left shoulder. With that he turned and ran away, and in that cane it sounded like a stampede."

Kirkland let the deer alone for a couple of hours before even trying to track it. In late autumn cane is red, so he knew a blood trail would be difficult to follow in the field. And while he had a few anxious moments, he soon found his buck not far from the place where he shot it.

The buck was everything Phil had hoped for and then some. It grossed 199⅞ points and netted 182⅞ points after deductions.

Good woodsmanship was the hand that Phil Kirkland played to get his big muley. But he held two trump cards: the grunt call and the decoy.

"Most people call too much," he explained. "I really believe they like to hear themselves make noise. But it's very easy to overcall deer.

"My calling technique isn't difficult but it does require a little bit of common sense," he continued. "I've listened a lot to the sounds that deer make. And the one thing that I've noticed is that everything in nature has its own rhythm. When a buck is walking along, often he'll grunt with every step he takes. That's the type of thing I try to duplicate when I'm imitating a buck: the rhythm.

"And after I make a bad call, I shut up. Don't continue making unnatural sounds. Wait a minute and try again. Another thing I've found is that, if you call and the deer starts coming towards you, don't call again unless he changes direction. He'll spot you if you move at all when he's headed your way. Only call enough to get him coming, then stop."

Bob Adamson, a big buck expert from Franklin, Idaho once called in a big 26-inch muley for a friend. "But it was an accident," he said. "I took this fellow out coyote hunting and this nice buck came in to within 100 yards of us. For the last 50 yards he was running, looking all around, trying to find out where the sound was coming from."

Murry Burnham of Marble Falls, Texas, has also had success calling in mule deer. Burnham uses his own D4 deer call and makes a bleat or bellow on it. "I make a terrible noise on it," he said. "But I've found that calling works as well or better on mule deer as it does on whitetails. I've had a lot of luck calling deer all through the fall when I've been bowhunting in Colorado. In fact, one time I called up a big 16-point buck out of the dark timber to within 25 yards of my brother during the middle of the day."

Burnham is convinced that, because mule deer are more family-oriented, they're more likely to respond. "Most of the deer that respond are does," he said, "but every now and then a buck will come in, too. They stick closer together because there's so much trouble with predators where they live.

"The secret to using a call successfully for mule deer is in not spooking the animals. Slip along quietly and be careful where your scent is blowing.

"A big, smart mule deer is as hard a trophy to collect as any that I know of," Burnham concluded. "The hunter is going to need all the help he can get."

RATTLING

Although many hunters have seen young bucks spar, only a very few have seen truly big bucks in a dominance fight. So while mule deer bucks butt antlers quite frequently, apparently the art of rattling has few proponents among western hunters.

Dr. Valerius Geist writes that mule deer bucks use the sound of antlers rubbing on wood as an auditory signal to determine if other bucks are in the neighborhood. I wasn't able to determine if any modern hunters rub antlers on wood in an attempt to attract bucks, even though if Dr. Geist is correct, it could succeed in doing exactly that.

One hunter who has experimented with antler rattling of a sort for mule deer bucks is Frank Hough of McCammon, Idaho. Hough has taken many big bucks, including one typical Boone and Crockett buck that scored 197⅜ points. He's also taken a big non-typical that netted 223 points with his muzzleloader. Plus he's taken four other typicals that score over 190.

"Rattling will work when the rut's in progress," Hough said. "But a mule deer won't usually come in aggressively like a whitetail will. The way I use antlers is I get across a canyon from where I think the bucks will be. I hide in the brush and hit the horns together. Bucks on the other side of the canyon will get curious and come out into openings to see what's going on. Then I'm able to look them over to see if any of them are worth going after. So far I've had quite a few bucks come out, but I've never seen one big enough to take."

SCENTS

The only mule deer hunters I could find that used any kind of scent while mule deer hunting were Phil Kirkland, who believes in Cover-Up, a masking scent, and Bill Nation of Rawlins, Wyoming, who opts for estrous-cow elk scent.

All commercial scents that I'm aware of are geared towards whitetail deer. Whether or not estrous doe urine from a whitetail is comparable to that of a mule deer is open to debate. However some outstanding mule deer hunters believe that big muley bucks key in on estrous cow elk, so there's no reason to believe they would reject whitetail scents.

By far the largest segment of advice from hunters on scents was simply to be sure no mule deer superbuck got *your* scent.

The jury is still out on calls, rattling, and scents for mule deer. But calling and rattling techniques are sound, and have produced at least some super muley bucks. It will take a few more years—and many more experiences—before anyone knows for sure whether calling and rattling will ever produce favorable results consistently in the realm of the mule deer superbuck. Until then, knowing that other hunters have used them successfully will give you an extra option when you're up against the buck of a lifetime.

Part 5

Mule Deer Superbuck Hunters and the Stories Behind the Trophies

44

Kirt Darner

When you think of trophy muleys, one name immediately comes to mind: Kirt Darner. Kirt has taken an incredible total of 12 super mule deer bucks that have qualified at one time for Boone and Crockett, plus two others that, since his dispute with the organization, he has not even submitted to be officially scored. Some of his bucks include typicals that measure 197⅞, 199⅜, 203⅜, and two that score 209 Boone and Crockett points (minimum currently 195) and a big non-typical that measures 273⅜ points (minimum currently 240).

Darner is an outstanding big-buck hunter, but one that has found himself surrounded by controversy. Some of the allegations remain unproven. One was serious enough to cause Boone and Crockett to question the origins of one of Darner's largest heads and, eventually, to inspire Darner to withdraw willingly all of his heads from the organization's record book, an action Darner doesn't regret. There isn't enough space here to go into all the particulars, but suffice it to say that Boone and Crockett believed that one of Darner's bucks had been taken years before by someone else. The head had been stolen, and when suspicion was centered on Darner, he reacted as he felt he must.

Nevertheless, that still leaves the man with 12 other big mule deer heads upon which no aspersions have been cast, including a 216⅞ typical taken in Sonora, Mexico, and a 196 Colorado typical.

"You have to remember, I've been dedicated to hunting for trophy bucks probably longer than anyone else," he said. "Back in the 1960s . . . I had a real advantage. There were more big bucks then, or at least fewer hunters determined to take trophies, so the competition wasn't nearly as great. Tags and licenses weren't as expensive either, so I'd hunt in as many different states as I could.

"And in the 1960s, which were banner mule deer years, you used to be able to take more than one buck in Colorado each year," Darner explained. "Since the overwhelming majority of trophy muleys come from Colorado, I could turn down as many as twenty different 30-inch bucks. Now you would be lucky to see two 30-inch bucks in the same amount of hunting time."

Darner had an additional advantage: his work for the Forest Service allowed him the luxury of scouting tremendous blocks of country on company time. At times he's been able to scout as many as 300 days a year, gathering detail that's been crucial to his success.

Darner is a rifle hunter. He's killed most of his bucks with an old Remington Model 700 in 7mm Remington Magnum that he bought back in 1962. He's mounted a 3×9 Redfield Illuminator scope on it. One reason Darner relies on a rifle for big muleys is that, unlike whitetails, he feels it's almost impossible to bag a muley buck of Boone and Crockett caliber with a bow. "The only real advantage a sportsman has when pursuing record-book muleys is in the long-range capabilities of the modern firearm," Darner flatly stated.

"Some people will manage to take a big buck through a stroke of luck," he said. "But more often than not, in order to connect you have to hunt harder and more intelligently than the next guy. You must also be able to read and interpret buck sign better, and shoot better, too. In other words, to consistently be successful requires that you possess greater skill levels than the other hunters."

Darner takes pride in outsmarting big mule deer bucks. "These animals are very wary and intelligent," he commented. "It's hard to take a 30-inch buck and it's much, much harder to get a Boone and Crockett. Today's deer is a different breed of muley. The dumb ones have all been killed. The genes that made a buck jump up and run when a hunter got close are all but gone. The bucks left to breed are the ones that will lie low, hold tight, and then sneak off.

"Today's trophy muleys will rarely break and run," he said. "They're hard to see when they're bedded down or when they're moving about since they are so naturally camouflaged. When they do get up and move, they move slowly, so they very rarely get into danger. A slow, deliberate movement, the kind a trophy buck makes, is hard to see. You *won't* see it, either, unless you take the time to look for it. Since so many hunters are in such a big hurry, few of them ever see trophy bucks. To take trophies, first you must see them. And to see them you have to slow your hunting down.

"A trophy buck's best defense is his radar," Darner continued. "It can be absolutely uncanny. You've got the wind in your favor and you're watching a big buck feed contentedly 200 yards away. All of a sudden he'll whip right around and stare at you. I don't know how these bucks do it, but it's happened often enough that I know it isn't just coincidence. They just seem to *sense* danger."

Darner is a big advocate of glassing. "You need to use your eyes and a good pair of binoculars," he advised. "For 20 years I used a pair of military 7 × 50s. Now I've gone to some Swarovsky 7 × 50s because they're lighter. There are lots of good binoculars available today. Look for something waterproof and shockproof. If you're going to be serious about hunting big mule deer bucks, you need something that can take the punishment."

Darner glasses for hours on end. "I'll watch muleys whenever possible, even when it's not deer season, to learn as much as I can about the way they act in different situations," he stated. "Big bucks are very cautious. They won't be up and about as long as smaller deer will be when it's daylight. Some big bucks are loners; others will often hang out with a bachelor band except during the peak of the rut in November and December when they'll be with does. When you do locate a smaller buck, take your time and glass all around him—especially in any nearby cover. Often a big buck will let a smaller buck act as a lookout while he hangs back out of sight where it's safe.

"Above timberline, big muleys are extremely hard to hunt. Up there, a trophy buck can see for a long way because there's nothing to obscure his vision. And believe me, a buck that's up that high is constantly searching for danger.

"I believe a mule deer buck's vision is as good as a bighorn sheep's," Darner emphasized. "Their sense of smell is great, and their hearing is keen, too. They move their ears constantly, searching for any unusual sounds. As amazing as it may seem, it appears as though they can actually differentiate the sound of a person walking on the ground even over the sound of a fairly strong wind through the quakies. I think it's extremely possible that, when they're bedded down, big muleys can sense ground vibrations through their belly and chest."

Darner prides himself on finding big bucks in unlikely places. Like the tremendous bucks he took two years running within sight of a busy highway. "With my binoculars I could watch hunters wearing blaze orange driving along the highway," he said. "None of them knew that a big 39-inch buck was watching them, too. Not only did I kill that deer, I came back the next year and took a 38-inch non-typical in the same spot. I guess the hillside was so steep and rocky that it discouraged hunters, even though they passed by it on their way to hunt other places. But that's exactly where you've got to look for big bucks, places so inaccessible or so difficult to hunt that other hunters overlook them."

When so many people long to take one 30-inch buck, Darner has taken several that crack the *40-inch* barrier. He's quick to point out that the 40 inches doesn't refer to inside spread, the standard measurement. The figure used for his widest-racked bucks refers to their greatest point-to-point *outside* spread. These are still phenomenal bucks. One measures 42 inches and another measures 43 inches. The 43-incher would make the book if Darner would allow the velvet to be scraped off for scoring purposes, a requirement of the scoring committee. But he prefers that the buck stay like it was when he killed it, velvet intact, which makes a stupendous set of headgear look even more awe-inspiring.

When Darner glasses, he's careful to keep the sun at his back whenever possible. He doesn't look at big areas of countryside all at once. Rather, he takes each piece apart, little by little. "Big bucks like to lay on the uphill side of a bushy tree," he said. "Or in the shadow of a boulder. If something looks out of place, like a stick that looks like an antler or a white spot where one shouldn't be, keep watching. It might turn into part of a big buck."

Darner looks for trails even though the ones that big bucks use usually don't show much wear. Little knobs or points are really given the once over since big bucks prefer bedding on them. Like white-tails, muleys often cross from one drainage to another at a saddle. If you can locate a low point like this before a jumpy buck busts out of cover, you just might get a shot.

Other than verifying their presence by actually sighting big bucks, Darner looks for other clues like big tracks. "A big buck will usually leave a large, blocky track somewhere in the neighborhood of 3½ inches long," he said. "I carry my ruler with me. A live round of 7mm Remington Mag ammunition is 3¼ inches long. If it fits inside the track, I figure it's a trophy buck."

Sometimes Darner travels as much as 900 miles in one weekend to scout an area. He'll verbally scout an area as well, by talking to game managers, foresters, sheepherders, literally anyone who spends time out in the countryside.

He feels the best time to scout is from July 1 to September 10. The next best time is right before the season starts. Whenever possible, Darner advises hunters to arrive in their hunt area several days in advance to look it over carefully. And Darner, like Gene Wensel, likes to hire an airplane to fly over an area so he can tell how the land lies.

A good guide or outfitter could help a hunter get a big buck in less time than he might on his own, but according to Darner, finding one that knows his business is fairly difficult. And it can also be quite expensive. "I look at it like this," Darner commented. "I've spent hundreds of thousands of dollars during the past 38 years for li-censes, horses, vehicles, ammunition, groceries, and everything else that it took for me to take eight bucks that qualify for Boone and Crockett. I once calculated that it rounds out to $12,500 per buck. To consistently take big mule deer requires both time and money, whether you do it yourself or hire an expert."

One option Darner does suggest is that, after you either verbally or physically scout an area, you consider hiring an outfitter to take you to a prearranged drop camp of your own choosing. "Not only is this less expensive, it can often be a very successful tactic if you've picked your area well," he said.

Another option for the trophy mule deer buff is to use Darner's own Hunters Information Service which is located in Montrose, Colorado. "I'll actually pinpoint campsites and hunt locations right down to what hillside to watch," he said. "My service provides maps, names of places that rent 4WD's or horses, and even locates lockers where wild game can be processed. For an additional fee, lease hunting is available on property that I've hand-selected for its big buck potential."

One tactic that Darner's found to be extremely effective is the one he calls the "fishhook." "To properly execute this maneuver, follow behind someone as they walk through dense cover where a big buck might be holed up," Darner explained. "Big bucks usually won't bolt out ahead of you. They'll stand up after the first hunter walks past and then circle to the rear. With any luck, they'll run into you as you're following behind.

"There's another variation that's effective when you're hunting alone," he continued. "As you're slipping through the cover, every now and then turn sharply to the right or left and go straight ahead for 50 to 100 yards. Then sneak back parallel to your original route. By doing this, you can often intercept deer as they come slinking back behind where they *think* you are!"

Since Darner has been judging mule deer trophies for quite some time, he has excellent advice on how to determine just how good a buck's rack is.

"First, before you even go hunting, find as many mounted mule deer bucks as you can," he said. "Look them over and measure them. Judge how wide the ears are in relation to the rack's width.

"Correctly estimating the tip to tip distance between a buck's ears is critical to a trophy hunter's success," Darner said. "The total ear width of most muley bucks is between 18 to 24 inches. To determine whether the buck that you're looking at is an 18-incher or 24-incher, look at his nose. The ears of a dainty buck, one that has a slender neck, will often measure no more than 18 inches. And a big Roman-nosed buck with a well-muscled neck will usually have much wider ears. So if it's a big old buck with a few inches of daylight between the ends of his ears and the inside curve of the antler on each side, then quite possibly you're looking at a 30-inch plus buck.

"Since length of the main beams is so important try to get a side view of the buck. Long main beams will appear to extend forward to intersect an invisible line running straight up from the tip of the nose. To make the book 27 inches of main beam length seems to be the magic number, even though a few 25-inchers have done so.

"Next thing to consider is tine length," Darner continued. "A record-class buck will have antler tines that are quite a bit longer than his ears. Look for deep forks. Bucks that are strong in the front forks will usually score better than those strong in the back forks. One hint to remember is that the points on most record-class mule deer bucks all seem to be about equal in height.

"When you're attempting to judge a buck try not to judge him from one angle only. For one thing, bucks look wider than they are when you see them from the rear or as they're angling away from you. That's because a muley will often hold his ears back to listen behind him as he leaves. With his ears flat back, his rack will appear wider.

"If a buck does stampede away, take your time when you shoot," Darner said. "And don't shoot all your shells. Save one or two. Because even though most of the time they are extremely wary, even now muleys will occasionally pause to look back before they top out that last ridge. Be ready when they do."

Darner's most exciting buck ever was a big typical that he killed in New Mexico in 1968. "In August I spotted this buck while on a scouting trip," he said. "He was still in velvet and was being very careful as he fed along a hillside with several other bucks. I watched him from across the canyon, hoping that he'd still be there when the season opened.

"In September I went back to the same location but didn't see him. I did see what I thought were his tracks. There was snow on the ground in October when I went back again. During this trip I eventually located him in a spot farther up the canyon than the place where I'd originally spotted him.

"When deer season finally arrived, I was ready. But on the first day I didn't see hide nor hair of him. On the second day, I was hunting in the canyon the buck had been in before when I finally saw him and another big buck feeding on the opposite side. I motioned to my partner, who had been hunting on the canyon's rim, that I'd seen a big buck and was going to head out after it.

"Unfortunately, by this time it was late in the day. Soon, it was getting dark so I had to get out of there. The next day the same thing happened. By the time I located the buck and started my stalk, it was too late. Luckily, the next day I got in there earlier and broke the pattern. When I finally spooked the buck, he ran right at me. I shot him at 15 yards.

"He was a tremendous deer, too," Darner enthused. "The typical rack eventually scored 209 Boone and Crockett points. And even though I took the head and antlers with me, the field-dressed carcass weighed 302 pounds. This buck was the New Mexico state record typical muley at the time and it still ranks as number two even after 20 years."

45

Ted Riggs

In a small Nevada town near the country he loved to hunt once lived the man who just might have been the best mule deer hunter the world has ever seen. Ted Riggs, who died not so very long ago, was that man. As recently as 1988, Riggs located two giant bucks, killed one of them himself, and then guided a friend to the other one. Riggs' big non-typical had a 36-inch outside spread and 21 total points, 11 on one side and 10 on the other. The one his friend took had a massive 8 × 7 rack that was 31 inches wide. This was done at a time when many trophy hunters were decrying the decrease in the number of big mule deer out West.

Ted Riggs took three big muleys that have been listed in Boone and Crockett after he started seriously pursuing trophy animals in 1945. One big typical is no longer listed; when minimum scores were raised to 195 points, it no longer qualified. But two of his non-typicals still make the book; one scores 240⅜ points and the other 249⅞ points.

Holding three record book entries was in itself an achievement, but Riggs never pursued a buck simply because he had the type of antlers that are needed to garner a high Boone and Crockett score. He liked big, wide racks, and that's what he went after. Over the years he took 15 big heads that measure over 36 inches in width, and countless others between 30 inches and 36 inches wide.

His achievement is even more impressive when you learn just how Riggs got his big bucks. He went to a spot that looked like it should hold a big deer, usually in the Arizona Strip country that he knew like the back of his hand, and started walking, searching for a monster-sized track. When he found a track, he stayed with it, sometimes for days, as he tracked the buck across arid, merciless country until he caught the animal making a mistake.

Riggs took his biggest buck, a tremendous 29-pointer with a 43½-inch outside spread, by dogging its tracks for six days, morning to night. During that time he never saw another person. Without pressing the animal, he relentlessly followed until he got a shot. "My secret is that I stick with it," said Riggs at the time. "When I find a big buck, I don't let up on him. That's my favorite tactic."

The Arizona Strip where Riggs pursued his monster muleys lies north of the Grand Canyon of the Colorado, from Lake Powell to Lake Mead all the way to the Nevada–Utah border. Lying on the west side of the Kaibab Plateau, the desolate Strip was rarely hunted when Riggs began seeking big mule deer there many years ago. Riggs' grandfather was the area's first forest ranger back in the 1880s when the Kaibab National Forest was established. His roots lay deep in the land that he loved. Riggs Spring and other area landmarks were named for his family.

With a background steeped in both the love of the land and the lore of the outdoors, it surprised no one when Riggs became a government hunter and trapper for the U.S. Fish and Wildlife Service. In no time, he became the scourge of the area's mountain lions and coyotes.

Riggs also hunted big bucks in Utah and Nevada. He was a trophy mule deer guide for 28 years, too, during the mule deer heydays of the 1950s and 1960s. Many of the hunters he guided have monster muleys today because of his expertise. For years he gave away to friends any big deer head he had taken that they wanted. That was before he realized that the animals were getting scarcer and he'd better start holding on to his trophies.

Riggs didn't take every deer he set out after. A few of them gave him a run for his money. He remembered one in particular, a spectacular heavy-horned buck that he called "Bigfoot."

"You could tell Bigfoot from the rest of the deer by the size of his track and his one crooked foot," Riggs recalled. "When Bigfoot rubbed on a tree he'd pick out a big juniper, get under it and rub on branches higher than my shoulders. As he'd stand there scratching his horns, he'd leave a good track. I could lay my pocketknife widthwise in Bigfoot's track, and that knife was 3½ inches long. That's a big track.

"One day I really got stubborn and wouldn't let him rest," Riggs continued. "I trailed that buck from daylight to dusk, to two or three different waterholes and all over the countryside. When I finally gave up at dark, the rancher I'd told my story to, a guy that knew all the landmarks of where I'd been hunting, said that I'd walked 27 miles tailing that buck on that one day alone. And even though I'd caught several glimpses of Bigfoot, he was smart. He'd mingle with the cattle so I couldn't get a shot.

"Bigfoot was a tough old deer. Every time I saw him he knew he was in danger so he never gave me a good chance for a shot. When he was really spooky he'd cross a flat ahead of me, then hide in the brush on the other side. As soon as I'd show my face, I'd see the flash of an antler as the deer whirled and ran into the scrub. When I'd get to the place I'd last seen him, there would be a bunch of tracks made while he milled around waiting for me to catch up."

Riggs tried for five years to take Bigfoot, but the buck had other notions. The hunter never tagged this particular muley, an animal that Riggs estimated had at least a 38-inch spread and tremendous 6 × 6 palmated antlers. Riggs came up against other monster muleys that managed to outsmart him as well, perhaps six in his lifetime.

Through the years Riggs became accustomed to the types of places where a big buck was likely to hole up. Being able to read the land and deciphering what it possibly held was very important. And while he said his main secret was perseverance, outstanding skills in the art of tracking also played a big part in his success. Riggs claimed that a big mule deer will leave a hoofprint like a beef calf: big and wide and blocky. The deer of the Arizona Strip are humdingers in weight, too, with some of Riggs' animals pushing 300 pounds after field dressing. A heavy-bodied animal like that makes deep tracks, too, another trait that Riggs looked for.

"The worst problem I have when I'm on the trail of a smart old buck is when he gets running with a bunch of cattle," Riggs confided. "It's hard to separate a big buck's hoofprint from those of the calves."

For years Riggs would often try to waylay a buck he was trailing by attempting to anticipate his moves and then trying to cut him off. But usually the buck did something unexpected. If Riggs would miss in his shortcut attempt, he'd have to backtrack and pick up the trail all over again. So he went back to sticking with a track, no matter how long it might take. "I lost too much time the other way," he said.

Through the years Riggs got so proficient in interpreting tracks that not only could he tell exactly how far ahead of him a buck was, he usually knew what he was doing. "You have to learn that quickly," he confided. "Never walk so close to him that you spook him out of his bed. He'll be gone so fast that you'd never get a shot."

Riggs hunted in all the different vegetational types and topography that the Arizona Strip can offer, from Ponderosa and piñon pine to oak and juniper. Some really dry areas were full of cactus and joshua trees.

"Big bucks will hide in many kinds of vegetation," he said. "But they seem to prefer areas where juniper, piñon pine, and oaks all come together.

"As for beds, a big buck's can be hard to spot. I've seen them bed between two ledges or under boulders. When they rest they'll pick out a spot where they can see, hear, and smell in all directions at once.

"Years ago I'd track a buck to his bedding or feeding area so I could make him jump up and run off," Riggs explained. "Without fail he'd stop and turn around a couple of hundred yards away, and that would be my chance for a shot. If you jump a big buck out of its bed today, he won't stop running for miles."

Riggs had his best big buck luck right after dawn because he thought they were most active then. He also believed a mule deer can be patterned somewhat during certain weather conditions. "If it's cold or if there's a light rain, mule deer—even big bucks—will feed all day," he said. "I've managed to get up within 10 feet of bucks when I'm stalking them in rain. I've gotten so close to a few does that I've slapped them right on their rumps and surprised the heck out of them."

Riggs also believed that he had good luck tracking because he tried to make as little noise as possible. "Over the years I've learned how to walk through the brush without making noise," Riggs stated. "I never step on sticks, try not to rustle leaves, and take care not to brush up against bushes."

Unlike other hunters who specialize in big muleys, Riggs didn't rely on optics for spotting his trophies. "I'll keep an eye out for what I can see, but I'll also go by what I *assume* should be in an area," he said. "I don't use either a spotting scope or binoculars very much. I just head out walking. I know that often big bucks are back in the same areas where I've taken trophies before. By the time I've circled the country looking for tracks, I know what's around that's worth hunting."

When Riggs killed his biggest buck, the one with the 43½-inch spread, he said he didn't realize just how big it was until after he'd shot it. "When I walked up to it and saw what a tremendous deer it was, that's when I came down with buck ague."

Riggs said even after all the time he spent after the critters, it wasn't always that easy to tell a truly big mule deer from one that's just good. For example, his 21-year-old grandson Terrence was along while he was hunting for his 1988 buck. After spotting a deer that Riggs eventually got, Terrence took a series of photos of the deer from about 50 yards away. "He kept saying, 'Why don't you shoot him, Grandpa? He's bigger than any deer I've ever seen,' " said Riggs. "Jokingly, I told him you had to pass up little bucks like him to get a big one.

"But the more I looked at the deer, the more I realized that it *was* a big buck, with many more points than I'd thought at first. By the time I decided to shoot him, the deer had been bothered enough and was running away. For some reason, he paused at the edge of a clump of trees about 250 yards away and that's when I shot him.

"When Terrence asked why I waited so long before I shot, I told him that I had to let him get out to where I could hit him," Riggs laughed.

Riggs knew better than probably anyone else the quality of deer the areas near the Arizona Strip are capable of producing. In 1940, he found a lion-killed buck that had between 30 and 40 points, and an outside width of 47½ inches. That's just a half-inch less than four feet, a tremendous spread for a muley and a good spread for an elk.

Riggs also picked up a pair of horns from a couple of bucks that died locked together. These two big muleys each had a 36-inch plus spread.

Riggs passed up many big bucks that any other hunter would be ecstatic about because they didn't meet his demanding specifications. Just eleven years ago, not long before he died, he spotted a buck in Nevada that he figured had a 36- to 40-inch outside spread. He watched as the deer got too close to a camp full of people for its comfort, backed off, and then, in a leisurely gait, walked down into a nearby canyon. The deer didn't want any part of the people that it had heard in the camp, but it wasn't in any big hurry to get away either. Riggs let the buck go because the animal's antlers were "willowy," not massive like the kind he preferred.

Ted also called coyotes, and he had many interesting experiences with the mule deer that come in to his dying rabbit call. "A buck will come in all bristled up to see what's going on and then just sneak away afterwards," he said. "A doe that comes to the call will be all bristled up, too, but she'll want to fight you, not sneak off."

Ted Riggs took his impressive array of trophies the hard way: by picking up their tracks and then walking them into the ground. He took plenty of mega-muleys in the past due to his love for the sport and dogged determination. Ted continued to track and take monster bucks well into his seventies, and because of his extreme dedication to his hunting, his spirit remains an inspiration for hunters of all ages.

46

Jay Gates

When it comes to trophy deer, Jay Gates could write a book. In fact, he's determined to *rewrite* at least one book—the Boone and Crockett Club's *Records of North American Big Game.* Gates has made an impressive start with a Boone and Crockett Coues deer which scored 110% points and a Columbia blacktail scoring 132% points. But Gates isn't about to rest on these laurels.

Gates has entered in these pages an incredible 14 bucks of the various deer species. That's right. You didn't read that incorrectly: 14 Boone and Crockett bucks. These bucks aren't "squeakers," either. They roar into the pages. His trophies include two Boone and Crockett mule deer—including a hog that nets 197; five Boone and Crockett Columbia blacktailed bucks—including bucks that netted 145 and 146, both monstrously huge for Columbias (he would have had eight blacktailed bucks in the book but the minimum score was raised); and seven Boone and Crockett Coues whitetails, generally regarded as the most difficult of all deer to bag. One of those Coues scores an unbelievable 154 Boone and Crockett points, which is a fine score for a standard whitetail but mind-boggling for a Coues. And while Jay's whitetails have come close to making the Boone and Crockett grade, broken tines on bucks that net 168 and 169 Boone and Crockett points make this species an 'almost but not quite' for the hunter. This is one situation Gates is trying to remedy. And no one is betting against him.

Jay Gates may be the finest all-around deer hunter in the world. Consider these statistics, if you're still harboring doubts: 17 mule deer bucks that score 175 Boone and Crockett points or above; nine whitetails scoring 145 Boone and Crockett points or above; eight Columbia blacktails scoring 120 points or above, all of which at one time qualified for listing in Boone and Crockett; six Sitka blacktails of 85 points or above, including one that scores 108 Boone and Crockett; and 13 Coues whitetails that score over 100 points.

Another statistic to consider is this: Jay Gates has succeeded in bagging nine different Grand Slams of Deer. A Deer Grand Slam consists of one buck of each of the following species—Rocky Mountain mule deer, whitetail, Coues (desert) whitetail, and blacktail. In 1984, when Boone and Crockett split the blacktail division into two categories—Columbia and Sitka—Gates never faltered. He simply added the Sitka to his list. Jay ups the ante by taking his slams *in the same year!*

Gates doesn't stop there, either. Each year he manages to bag excellent specimens of several other major deer subspecies *in addition* to the species listed in the book. Just any deer won't do. He tries for and gets the best that he possibly can.

What force drives Gates, a family man and retired beer distributor, into logging close to 30,000 miles each year while locating and taking trophy animals with such enviable consistency?

When I posed this question to him, Gates replied, "Deer are the most fascinating of all the big-game animals I've hunted. Trophy deer present a challenge that few other animals do. And only a couple of other guys have *ever* taken a Grand Slam of Deer in one year. I like to think that the record I'm setting will last a long time."

Jay Gates is a man driven to succeed at the task of taking a record-class deer of each Boone and Crockett listed species. This hasn't been accomplished since Herb Klein and Elgin Gates (no relation) did it back in the '50s and '60s when trophies were easier to get and the Sitka blacktail wasn't included.

To what does Jay owe his success? In a nutshell, he credits the 3 P's—patience, persistence, and physical fitness. His entire life revolves around the fall hunting season. He literally lives, thinks, and dreams deer hunting. Few waking moments are spent without thinking about his obsession—trophy deer. You can't be consumed with the desire for trophy deer like Jay Gates is and not have some excellent advice for the rest of us would-be record breakers.

Jay Gates has deer hunting down to a science. And he calls the method he uses to take excellent heads his Ten Steps To Trophy Deer. Here they are:

STEP 1: HUNT WHERE THE BIG BUCKS ARE

Big bucks have to be available in an area before it qualifies as a possible Gates hunting ground. So he spends hours reading hunting magazines and Boone and Crockett records to identify locations where "book" deer are taken.

Gates talks to outfitters, taxidermists, and sporting goods stores. He haunts big buck contests and hunting clubs. He calls game wardens, biologists, and forest managers to get the latest deer hunting scoop.

Unlike most hunters, after selecting an area, he usually won't lay eyes on it until the first day of his hunt when he "pre-scouts" the area.

Gates pre-scouts from roads and trails to see if the area looks worthwhile. If the sign looks good, he'll hunt hard the next day; if not, he moves to a new area. He won't waste time. If it means covering 5,000 acres in one day to find good sign, that's what he does.

Pre-scouting pays off in other ways, too. Once a friend picked him up at a California airport and drove him to base camp before a blacktail hunt the next day. That evening, Jay and his buddy did a little pre-scouting near camp. Sure enough, they located and killed two excellent bucks while searching for fresh sign. "And I nearly broke my neck," Jay commented, "stalking in those darn slick cowboy boots I travel in and didn't change. But it was worth it—and by far the easiest hunt I've *ever* had."

STEP 2: HAVE THE RIGHT EQUIPMENT

Gates is painstaking when selecting gear. High price alone doesn't mean the best, he says. He evaluates each piece of equipment carefully; after the season, he decides whether or not it performed according to his expectations. If it didn't, he'll replace it.

STEP 3: KNOW YOUR RIFLE

Gates uses two custom-built guns with Remington 700 actions in .270 Winchester caliber. Each is outfitted with a Brown Precision fiberglass stock. Gates calls them his "plastic guns" and he wouldn't shoot with anything else. The possibility of wood stocks warping in wet weather is a prime consideration.

"When I pull the trigger on a record-class Sitka 6,000 miles from home, a 'flier' because of warpage is the last thing I want," he says.

Both guns have glass bedded actions and free-floating 20½-inch barrels. They each weigh in right at 6½ pounds, including scope.

Gates has further weatherproofed his guns by outfitting them with Shilen stainless steel barrels that are electroless nickel-plated and then completely camouflaged. The guns are expensive but worth it, he says.

He reloads for peak performance and when he's faced with a ballistics problem, he consults the experts. For example, his old load of 59 grains of H4831 behind a 130-grain Sierra spitzer boattail bullet resulted in a 1¼-inch three-shot group at 100 yards. On his gunsmith's advice, he switched to 57½ grains of H4831 pushing a 130-grain Sierra flat base and loaded in only new or once-fired brass. His groups improved dramatically—to ½ inch.

Gates is a fanatic about sighting in, too. From May until August he shoots at least 20 rounds each week. His guns shoot 1½ inches high at 100 yards. This puts the load right on at 200 yards.

STEP 4: MENTAL PREPARATION

Physical preparation is easy in Gates' opinion; mental preparation is tough—especially when you're faced with a grueling 120-day season.

Mental preparation is what keeps him hunting. "I tell myself that no matter how tough the hunt, or how hard the pack in, or how miserable the weather, I'm going to stick it out and follow my hunt plan," Gates says. "And then once I'm in whatever hell hole I've chosen, I hunt every daylight minute of every day I've alloted. Weather means nothing; sometimes the worst weather makes for the best hunt."

STEP 5: PHYSICAL PREPARATION

The words "physical preparation" seem a feeble way to describe the reality of Gates' regimen. Ninety-nine percent of all his hunting is walk-in—by himself. So it's up to him to pack his bucks out from rough country.

To get in shape, he runs 18 to 20 miles each week from January until May. During that time he also does aerobics and lifts weights twice each week.

Then, from June until September he runs three times a week in the mountains. Each run is at least three miles long. The other four days he totes from 40 to 90 pounds on his back through the same mountains for five miles. As September nears, the weight increases. This is in addition to weight-lifting and special leg exercises. "If you're not in shape," Gates says, "by the end of a season like mine you're either dead or wish you were."

STEP 6: DESIRE

"Desire is the result of mental preparation. You must be dedicated to success. Desire is the fuel that fans the flame. Any hunter can luck into a good buck once or maybe twice in his life. But to score consistently under the most adverse conditions comes from desire," Gates says.

"Desire is what kept me dogging the tracks of a record muley this year in Nevada," he noted. "I jumped the deer but decided not to shoot at a running animal in heavy brush. I let him go, deciding instead to track him. Another guy and I tracked him for 10 hours until his tracks merged with those of another buck. The buck I let go was a monster—between 195 and 200 points—and would have made the book. So I kept on his trail. When the trail split, I went after the biggest tracks. That was a mistake. I had one chance for a shot through some thick cedars and took it. I saw heavy antlers and gray hair and then I realized I'd shot the wrong deer. He was a cactus buck with 17 points on one side and 14 on the other—a trophy, but not when compared with the one that got away."

STEP 7: KNOWLEDGE

Each species of deer is different according to Gates; you can't hunt them all the same way. Each must be studied to learn feeding, bedding, rutting and living habits.

"To hunt muleys, Sitka, and Columbian blacktail, climb high early in the morning and glass. Do the same thing late in the afternoon," Gates says.

"Coues whitetail blend in so well that you need the sun shining on them to pick them out from the landscape. Watch southeastern slopes early and northwestern slopes late and kick out draws during the middle of the day.

"For all of these species," Gates adds, "the biggest bucks are usually loners. I often find them on the highest points, often in rimrock or mountain mahogany. Big bucks all seem to prefer the same kind of terrain.

"When whitetail hunting, I glass ridges and coulees to find bedding and feeding grounds or travel lanes. And I try to find a buck's 'rutting area,' " Gates continued. "In the West where I hunt, nearly every big buck usually has what I call a 'rutting area.' " When pressured, either by other bucks or hunters, he'll have a secluded spot to herd receptive does, a spot far from bedding or feeding areas—sometimes five or six miles away.

"To find the rutting area I glass river bottoms early and late to discover a buck's travel pattern. What I learn determines where I place my stand."

STEP 8: DEVELOP GLASSING AND STILLHUNTING SKILLS

Practice makes perfect: this is where patience and persistence pay off. Stealth is not an inbred trait; it must be attained. The knowledge of how to use wind, sun, and terrain to your advantage comes from years of practice.

"I like to hunt with the wind in my face and the sun at my back," Gates says. "Deer are at a disadvantage staring into the sun's glare. I move slowly and quietly and try to use natural cover to camouflage my movements."

Interestingly, Gates killed his second best Coues buck while he was stillhunting. The wind was blowing on the back of his neck. "My scent was blowing right towards him. I jumped him *three* times before I finally killed him. You just never can tell with deer."

Likewise the skill needed to pinpoint movement and home in on it instantaneously with binoculars isn't acquired overnight, but proficiency will eventually be rewarded.

"Binoculars and a spotting scope are two 'must haves' that I'm never without," he emphasized. "I always travel with a walking stick that doubles as a rest for my optics when I'm glassing. And I never skimp on the time I spend glassing. It can take anywhere from 15 minutes to an hour and a half *each time I stop,* depending on the terrain."

STEP 9: JUDGMENT

Judgment is important for two reasons: first, you have to know *when* to shoot. "What I want is a standing shot or a shot while a deer is in its bed," Gates says. "But in the middle of the day I may jump a deer and have to make a split second decision—to shoot or not. Sometimes you know the shot is bad and don't risk it. Other times you take the chance and it pays off. And then there are those other times you prefer to forget."

Gates' knowledge of deer also helps him decide when to shoot. He knows he'd better shoot when a buck puts his ears back and flicks his tail. That's a sure sign that the deer will be off and running—pronto.

Judgment includes estimating distances. "Once I located a dandy nine-point whitetail with a 22- or 23-inch spread," he related. "I flipped down my bipod and settled it squarely so it wouldn't wobble. Then I squeezed off a shot aimed right behind the buck's shoulder. The buck didn't even flinch. I shot three more times. Finally, on the fourth shot, the buck looked in my direction when snow flew under his belly. I reloaded and sighted over the buck's back and shot again. Down he went. When I paced it off, what I'd guessed to be a little over 200 yards was 400 yards. No matter how often you estimate range, you can always make a mistake. Fortunately, I still got the buck."

Judgment is also important for another reason. "Once you pull that trigger it's all over," Gates says. "And you'd better be happy with what you've decided to shoot. Determine beforehand just what kind of a buck you're after and how to identify a buck of that caliber out in the wilds."

Although Gates is looking for record-book deer, he'll take what he considers a trophy regardless of book standards of excellence. A deer with a spread wider than his ears is always a good trophy in his opinion.

Other criteria Gates uses in judging trophy quality bucks include muleys that go 4 × 4 or better with deep forks and long main beams; 4 × 4 blacktails with heavy beams; 3 × 3 Coues (excluding brow tines) with long, curving main beams; and whitetails with ten long points.

Gates says he considers any 4 × 4 Sitka a trophy because to date he's only seen one in the field.

STEP 10: INSTINCT

Gates believes instinct is a skill like any other. It may be born in you or developed over the years. Sometimes, it might be a combination of both. "It's not luck when you take an animal in a remote aspen patch. You're not guessing when you kick out a draw and just *know* a buck's hiding there. But it is a funny feeling when a big old mossy-horns makes a run for it and you sense where he's going to jump up. Even if you're born with *déjà vu*, it takes hard work and good practical experience to make it work for you."

Now, when Jay Gates looks at the Boone and Crockett records he gets a feeling of *déjà vu*. He knows he's been there before. If things work out, he'll be there again and again and again—until he realizes his dream of having a record-book deer grand slam of all five listed species. When that happens he'll literally have rewritten the book, and his ten steps to trophy hunting success will be the reason why.

47

Gordon Blay

Gordon Blay may be the best mule deer outfitter operating in the West. Part of his success is undoubtedly due to the fact that he's one of the country's best mule deer hunters as well. From his home outside of Montrose, Blay operated Western Colorado Outfitters for many years after he quit his job as a construction engineer in Pennsylvania back in 1974. He now runs an outfitting business out of his Horsefly Ranch, and the mule deer are still the animals he most enjoys to hunt. Ever since Blay got into the business, he's been acquiring a reputation as the outfitter to see if you sincerely want a trophy muley. Gordon has taken two Boone and Crockett bucks, three other great muleys that each have an outside spread greater than 35 inches, and several other bucks in the 30-inch plus class. Blay's Boone and Crockett typical mule deer buck is a big 4 × 4 with two sets of eyeguards, an outside spread of 39⅞ inches, and a net score of 197 points. His non-typical entry is a tremendous 13 × 12 with a 35½-inch spread and a net score of 264⅜ points.

Not only has Blay taken these two Boone and Crockett bucks, he's guided two other hunters who have taken Boone and Crockett bucks as well. In the 25 years he's been outfitting, he estimates that he personally has guided 100 hunters to mule deer with 30-inch or better spreads. During that same time he figures that his guides have come close to matching his accomplishment, taking another 50 trophy-class bucks for their combined clients. Blay is so successful because he concentrates his efforts on prime areas where big bucks live.

Blay was raised in northern California where he was weaned on blacktail hunting by a father who would have rather hunted than anything else. "When I was still a kid, Dad would take me out hunting with him," Blay reminisced. "I really enjoyed it and I was really impressed with his skill. He'd tell my Mom that he'd be back in 30 minutes with a buck, and he would be. I always wanted to be as good a hunter as he is. Dad, in fact, killed what I believe is the largest non-typical blacktail ever taken, one that scores 239 points, only a few points less than the score required for any non-typical Boone and Crockett mule deer. Unfortunately, Boone and Crockett has no non-typical classification for blacktail deer, so it looks as though his accomplishment will never be officially recognized."

Blay is hooked on muleys, calling a buck of trophy caliber "the most spooky, awesome animal in the world." He's hunted muleys in every state where the animals roam, with the exception of Texas. While many other hunters are lamenting the loss of big muley bucks throughout the West, Blay maintains there are as many as there ever were, at least in the area he hunts. "You have to look in the right places to find them," he said. "And you have to know how to hunt them to kill them."

Blay's favorite trophy buck terrain is located high in the rock pinnacle country of the Gunnison National Forest. "It's a rugged area with lots of big boulders strewn about right above timberline at an elevation of about 11,000 feet," he said. "Big muleys like to lie around those pinnacles, especially those that are close to fingers of dark timber. It's rough country, but it's just right for the way I hunt."

When he's after a superbuck, Blay always hunts from the top of the mountain down, never from the bottom up. "When I'm trying to get close to a buck, I never use a trail," he explained. "A big muley watches trails; it's the obvious way for danger to approach. I'd rather go around the mountain, climb up from behind, and go over the top there. Through the years, I've noticed that big bucks won't look up in high country. A trophy muley lives on top, he knows the area backward and forward. He travels through it in the dark and he really believes that nothing can get above him without his seeing it first. He's only worried about what might approach him from below.

"I got one of my hunters a great 37-inch buck this way," Blay said. "We just never gave up on one buck that continually bedded in the same spot right at the very top of the mountain. We had to approach him five times before we finally killed him. It was difficult trying to find a route up where he couldn't see us coming. Finally, though, I did, and my hunter shot the buck in his bed from 150 yards away.

"The toughest part about hunting these smart old deer is convincing my hunters that if they're just patient, they'll get a chance at a big one. A trophy buck will pick the worst spot to bed in, one that's almost impossible to see and one that's hard to approach. My hunters get discouraged when I bring them back to the same location time after time and there's no buck around. But I know those big bucks. Every one of them will stay near the place he knows best. And eventually we're going to catch him there."

Blay doesn't waste time scouting new territory. He spends his hours riding and looking over the same country that's been productive in the past. "The places I hunt must have a history of big bucks," he explained. "I go there in mid-August to see what kind of bucks are hanging around there. I want to get there while their antlers are still in velvet. Velvet antlers keep the deer out in the open. Their horns are tender and they don't want to bang them into trees and branches, so they'll stay where you can see them. If you spot a big buck feeding while he's still in the velvet, you can bet that he's within 300 or 400 yards of his bed."

Once the bucks start rubbing in early September, Blay scouts areas where he's seen good rubs before. He looks for new rubs near old rubs, even those made on top of old rubs. When he finds them, he'll get off his horse and walk the whole area looking for deer beds. Blay only looks for beds when he's reasonably sure that the bucks are out feeding and not in them. "I never want to catch a buck in his bed while I'm scouting," he explained. "That just makes him move to another area and my job becomes that much more difficult."

A big buck will often shift his bed between four and five locations. Usually, all the beds are fairly close to each other. During the months of August and September, if left undisturbed, a trophy buck probably won't travel any farther than ¾ mile from his bedding area.

When Blay was just starting out as an outfitter, trophy bucks managed to evade him by using smaller bucks as their lookouts. "Whenever you see a buck in his bed, look around for those smaller 'lookout' bucks before you make your stalk," he advised. "I don't know how many big bucks those lookouts cost me over the years before I finally figured out what they were doing. A lookout might not even be where an old buck can see him. But he'll be close enough to hear the smaller buck running off. And when he hears the smaller buck go, he'll disappear, too."

Gordon has studied big bucks exhaustively, noting little details that other hunters might overlook. For instance: "You can tell whether a set of tracks belongs to a doe or a buck by the way the animal travels and where it goes," he stated to illustrate just how well he understands trophy muleys. "Say there are ten trees scattered through an opening. A doe will just walk right on through, not worrying about whether or not she can be seen. A buck will weave his way through the trees, trying his best to stay invisible as he moves along. A big buck will use every part of the terrain to his advantage. He'll move through the low points, stay behind knolls, and won't walk along ridgelines. He makes the lay of the land work for him."

According to Blay, a big buck can often be patterned in his preference for a particular escape route. Placing an unseen hunter on the escape route and then forcing the buck into using it can often be his downfall. But every now and then, you'll find a buck that behaves unpredictably. You want him to go up, and he goes down. You want him to run north, and he runs south.

Through the years Blay's observed mule deer during all the seasons and under all types of situations. "I say a mule deer is spooky because a big buck won't feed for even a minute without lifting his head to look around and see what's going on. When several of them are together, it seems like one is always looking around."

Blay does a lot of stillhunting for trophy muleys, too. "It's a productive technique, but you have to know a big buck is in the area to make it worthwhile," he said. "Always stalk into the wind and look over every significant change in the terrain as soon as you come to it, before you make another move. You *must* see a big buck first; if he sees you first it's *adiós*. So if you come to a dropoff, look into it with your eyes only. After you cover what you can from where you are, ease up a little farther and look some more. You must know what's in any basin that you approach before you show yourself. If you have to squat down to get a better view, then do it. Look for the parts of a deer, the eyes, ears, tail, or antler, not the entire deer.

"If you happen to step on a twig and it cracks, it's not the end of the world," he continued. "Just don't move *after* you hear it crack. Stay perfectly still because that buck will be listening hard, trying to hear whatever it was that cracked that twig. If you stay still, he'll eventually go back to feeding. It's simply amazing how far a mule deer can hear. I've seen them lift their heads at the snap of a twig 500 yards away."

Gordon prefers the very first hunting season for trophy muleys. "I want to be the first hunter that big buck sees," he said. "I want the moment of surprise on my side. When you're hunting super-sized bucks, you need every advantage you can get.

"For example, one thing I've noticed is that big monstrous bucks are up and about around 2:00 P.M. Oddly enough I've killed more at that time than at any other. I believe that they think they're safe then, that humans are all sleeping or something.

"And if you're ever in hunting camp for a snowstorm that lasts for two days, get out on the third day between the hours of 1:00 and 3:30 P.M. I positively guarantee that big bucks will be moving.

"Finally, when there's between 8 and 18 inches of snow on the ground, a high country muley buck will be moving constantly. With his gray coat, he should be fairly easy to spot. An old monarch won't move out of the high country until there's 3½ or 4 feet of snow on the ground to push him out. If I have any doubts as to whether he's still there, I look for the does. If they're still around, then you can bet the big bucks are still there."

Blay has tried just about everything on big muleys to see what will work on the animals. "I've tried a bleat call and had some success, only it's been mainly does that have come in," he said. "Small bucks might come in out of curiosity, but it's been my experience that a big buck won't.

"I've tried rattling but not very successfully, even when I tried it during the rut. I watched one big monster as I rattled the horns together and he was completely disinterested; I couldn't even get him to move. I figure a buck that's seven years of age or older doesn't want to fight. He's already fought enough in his lifetime and really doesn't have anything left to prove."

The one buck that will always be special to Gordon is his big non-typical. "I saw the buck early in the morning on opening day in 1975," he reminisced. "As soon as I saw it, I knew it was a record-class head and sent a couple of my hunters out after it. They weren't gone long, and when they returned, they said the big buck had given them the slip.

"I figured the animal was probably still in the area, so I decided to take them back to check it out personally," Blay continued. "Sure enough, we soon spotted the buck, only now he'd joined up with four other bucks. And one of those was another Boone and Crockett record-class deer, a big typical. We took out after the bucks and tracked them on horseback for a little over two miles before the deer dropped over the edge of a steep cliff and into a deep canyon. My clients got spooked when they saw how rugged the country was getting. They said they'd had enough and they didn't want to follow.

"I told them that bucks like that come along only once in a lifetime, but they still didn't care to go after them. So I asked them if it would be all right if I went after the deer. They told me that was fine with them. Then I said they could either wait for me or go back to camp. They said they'd go back to camp. With that, I took off into the canyon after the bucks."

Gordon followed the bucks for five hours with only an occasional glimpse as they moved ahead of him. The sight of the big non-typical as he topped distant ridges acted as a strong incentive to keep him on their trail. Finally, he got his chance for a shot. It was a long one at that, about 350 yards. But he made it count. When he shot, the buck went down. But then he quickly scrambled back up on his feet and took off running. Gordon waited until it stopped again, fired twice, and the buck fell.

"After my buck was down, the big typical stopped and looked as if he was saying, 'What's going on?' I field dressed the deer and I let my horse drag it back to camp. I walked ahead and managed to beat the horse there by about 15 minutes. All the hunters were waiting, wanting to know what happened, so I told them that I never caught up with the buck. You can imagine their surprise when my horse turned up a short time later, dragging that tremendous deer."

Gordon took another hunter after the big typical the following year, but even though the fellow got a couple of shots off at the buck, he never managed to hit it.

"I respect the mule deer more than I can say," Blay concluded. "Taking a truly big deer one on one is without a doubt one of the biggest thrills there is."

48

Frank Hough

Frank Hough of McCammon, Idaho, grew up in mule deer country. He's been hunting muleys since he was 12 years old and concentrating on super-muleys for most of the years since. Hough mixes business with pleasure: he runs a taxidermy shop where he has the chance to see some of the biggest deer taken in the mega-muley country of southeastern Idaho.

Hough's credentials easily qualify him as a superbuck hunter worthy of note. He's taken a 197⅞-point Boone and Crockett typical, four other typicals that score more than 190 but fall short of the Boone and Crockett 195 minimum, and a 223-point non-typical buck that he took with his muzzleloader. One of his bucks is 39 inches wide, and the 223-point non-typical will rank in the top five mule deer ever taken with a muzzleloader.

"I don't zero in on a single antler characteristic like width when I hunt mule deer," Hough explained. "In fact, even though many guys are crazy about width, I prefer a big non-typical that will score well typically or a big typical that's real symmetrical and scores 190 or better."

Hough has many other trophy mule deer that he's taken over the years. "I love to look at them," he said. "When I do, I remember everything about the hunt where I took each and I get real sentimental. The memories mean a lot to me."

According to Hough, mule deer haven't changed their tactics very much over the years, but hunters have. "I hear a lot about how the mule deer used to stand around out in the open, but around here they've always lived in brushy country," he said. "Big mule deer are real adaptable, and when I say that I think of the first superbuck that I ever took.

"I'd just started bowhunting when I first ran into this buck. Bow season started in late summer, and the farmers had been seeing a tremendous buck out in their hayfields. Of course, I ran into him. When I saw those big 39-inch antlers I was so stunned at his size that I couldn't even draw my bow. The deer took off and ran into a canyon. I figure he'd been living in a series of canyons that ran up between the farmers' fields. At night, he wouldn't have far to go to feed.

"Anyway, later that year during rifle season I was riding my horse back from the high country. I was only about a quarter of a mile from the road when I stopped for a while to rest my horse. It just so happened that the place I decided to rest was only about ten yards away from the spot where that same big buck was bedded. His bed was behind a serviceberry bush, and when I stopped, he jumped up and ran off. I watched as he ran across several canyons and into one last one, and then didn't come out. I knew he still had to be in there so I hurried home and got my friend, Fred Bischoff. I told him what had happened and persuaded him to come back with me and help jump the buck out of there.

"Pheasant season was still on so Fred said he'd like to bring his shotgun," Hough continued. "When we got back to the canyon that I figured the buck must still be in, I looked it over. It was about 1,000 yards long altogether, and the first thing we did was walk along parallel to each other for the entire length of the canyon. We didn't jump the buck, but I had seen a cock pheasant fly up and land in a thicket of rosebushes.

"I yelled to Fred that I'd seen a pheasant and I'd direct him to the bird. Sure enough, he walked right up on the bird, flushed it, and shot it. The bird fell in another bunch of thick undergrowth. I saw exactly where the pheasant had dropped so again, I directed him to the bird. Fred saw it and reached out to grab it while he was cussing the rosebushes for sticking him. At that moment he looked and there was that buck, lying down not two feet away from Fred. But as soon as Fred saw the deer, the buck jumped up and ran down into the bottom of the canyon.

"I was in a panic, couldn't see the deer because he was running in all that thick stuff. But there was a big coulee that cut down into the canyon from a ridge at the top, and suddenly the buck charged right into it. I looked and saw that there was one opening that the buck would have to run through before he'd be out of sight at the top of the gulch. This spot was only 20 yards wide and the coulee was 300 yards away, but I knew the buck would have to run through it, so I got ready. I didn't have to wait very long, and when he thundered into the opening, I fired and killed him with the very first shot."

The one change Hough does believe that big muleys have incorporated into their behavior patterns recently is that they've become nearly completely nocturnal. "The only time I'll see big bucks any more is real early in the morning and just as it's getting dark at night," he commented.

"Of course, part of the reason for this behavior is that there's so much hunter competition for bucks. Everyone's out and moving through the foothills. Many hunters have started using eastern tactics for deer and they're extremely effective. Drives through big thickets push out lots of deer, and some hunters will shoot anything, so many of our small bucks never get a chance to grow up."

When Frank scouts, he looks for big rubs. "They tell me there's a good buck around," he said. "I like rubs that are at least six inches in diameter.

"But over the years I've sort of lost faith in trying to tell a big buck solely by his tracks. Some bucks with the nicest antlers aren't big-bodied so you can't always go by the size of his feet. In fact, the best non-typical mule deer taken in Bannock County dressed out at only 150 pounds."

Hough also believes that bucks become superbucks by utilizing retreats. "Once that first shot is fired, or the buck is moved by hunters, he heads for his retreat and stays there until the snow flies or the rut starts," he stated. "He'll do whatever he can to keep any-one from seeing him again."

Frank believes in rattling but doesn't try to get bucks to come in to the noise. Rather, he uses it to make bucks show themselves cross-canyon. "They'll come out into an opening to see what's going on and give you an opportunity to size up their antlers."

He's somewhat ambivalent about scents for mule deer hunters. "I can see how scents might help out a whitetail hunter from back East," he commented. "Back there you can get to your stand without sweating and giving off lots of body odor. But here you usually have to really travel to get to where you're going to hunt. In these moun-tains that means plenty of exertion, so by the time you get where you're going you're sure to smell. Out here, the wind is so variable that it's really your worst enemy. If it's blowing right, the buck won't scent you no matter what; but if it's blowing in his direction, I'm not sure that the best scent in the world would help you out. I've often thought that a really big buck would be able to smell you right through any scent anyway."

Sometimes Frank uses whitetail tactics to take his big mule deer. And sometimes he even carries these tactics a little bit further. "I'll stillhunt if there's a real big area that looks like it might be holding a good buck," Hough said. "I just move real slow and watch the wind and where I put my feet.

"If it's not wet, sometimes I use a tactic that's a little crazy. I get on a game trail, get down on my belly and crawl along on my elbows. As I inch along, I glass for deer legs and do whatever I must do so that the deer in these thickets don't see me. I'll try whatever I believe no one else in the area has tried in order to get close to these big deer. And yes, I took one real good mule deer like that. All I saw were his legs. So I lay there and watched, and every now and then I'd get a glimpse of his rack. But it took almost a half hour of waiting before I got a shot."

One thing Hough feels makes mule deer superbuck hunting such a gamble is the ever-present danger of severe weather. "We can have four or five good winters in a row," he said, "and the bucks are really beginning to look good. Then a killer winter moves in, and that's it. Nearly entire age classes die, and big bucks become scarce for years afterward." This happened as recently as 1993–94, which prevented Hough from hunting Idaho muleys for many seasons. "When they're hurting, there's no sense in taking one of the few bucks that are still alive," he said.

With so many top trophies to his credit, Frank Hough has no intention of slowing his search for the animal that still gives him a thrill. "You never know just what you're going to come up against when you head out after a big buck," he said. "They can be so smart that it's often hard for someone else to believe. I do all right, I guess, but if I had a dollar for every time one of those big deer outwitted me, I'd be a rich man today."

49

The Number One Typical Mule Deer: the Burris Buck

People are forever guessing when the number one typical whitetail buck will finally topple from its place at the head of the Boone and Crockett Record Book. But there's very little guessing going on about when there will be a new number one in the mule deer category. For one thing, the distance between the number one and number two typical whitetail heads is a paltry 1½ points. In fact, the distance between the top *five* typical whitetail racks is only 4⅛ points.

When we look at mule deer, however, Doug Burris, Jr.'s number one buck has been ranked at the top for 17 years, and it doesn't look as if there's much chance of any other buck outdistancing it. The Burris buck is out ahead of the number two typical muley by 8⅝ points, quite a healthy margin.

The Burris buck is a spectacular trophy. It's got width—a 30⅞-inch inside spread; long main beams—the right one measures 30⅛ inches while the left one measures 28⅝ inches; a decent amount of mass, and 11 nice, long points. The rack's symmetry and depth of forks, both front and rear, add up to several good reasons why it's still number one after all these years.

The head is all the more remarkable when you realize that Burris took the big deer when he was hunting Colorado, the most heavily hunted mule deer state, and on public ground in Dolores County in the San Juan National Forest.

Burris knew the area he hunted was a good place to find a big buck because in 1969 he took a big, heavy-horned 18-pointer. He was positive that the buck would score high in the book. But to his surprise and disappointment, the buck didn't even garner enough points to make the minimum score.

In 1972, Colorado's firearms deer season opened in late October. The weather had had plenty of time to turn nasty and miserable, and that's precisely what it did. On opening morning a steady drizzle succeeded in soaking Burris and his three hunting buddies. The four men were camped close to their hunting area. Each morning, they'd climb into a Jeep and head up a mountain two-track. When they reached the top, they'd climb out and work the sides of the hills and the thick draws, hoping to jump a buster muley out of the cover.

That first day was a bust: none of the hunters was successful. On the second day, right at noon, Burris saw a big-bodied deer moving through some heavy oak brush about 200 yards ahead. He assumed that the deer was a buck because of its size. But by the time he was able to stalk closer through the thick brush, the deer had disappeared. At one point, Burris got a glimpse of trophy-sized antlers, all that he needed to increase his excitement to record-book proportions.

That evening, at least two hunters were happy. When he got back to camp, Burris discovered both his buddies had killed nice five-pointers during the rainy, overcast day. He hoped that the next day his luck would change, too. When he awakened the following morning, that didn't appear to be the case: the sky was still leaden with clouds that hung low on the horizon. Burris wasn't discouraged. He stuffed his pockets full of jerky and dried fruit and headed out even though the day was going to be cold and nasty like the two preceding it. Bucks would be out and about in this kind of weather, and he wasn't going to be caught hanging around camp all day.

Burris dropped off his only remaining hunting companion and then drove the Jeep close to the spot where he'd seen the big deer the day before. A mountain loomed directly in front of his position and, as he looked it over, he realized that a breeze tumbled right down that mountain and hit him in the face. With the wind working to his advantage, he began stillhunting right into it, easing even farther back into rough country.

He was about three-quarters of the way to the mountain's top when he spotted two bucks. They were feeding in a clearing 1,000 yards away from where he'd stopped to observe. Burris was amazed, because even at that tremendous distance he was clearly able to distinguish their racks *without* binoculars. These must be big bucks, he said to himself. With that he took out his binoculars for a closer look and confirmed what he'd thought: both deer were definitely in the trophy class. He immediately made up his mind to stalk them.

He'd only moved about 200 yards in their direction when he spooked a doe out of the heavy cover in front of him. Even though she bounded off towards the bucks, Burris wasn't worried. He watched closely anyway, just in case, but sure enough, the two trophies kept feeding up the slope, away from where he was standing.

Forty-five minutes later, the stalk was still in full progress. But now, the drizzle was turning into a rain; Burris hoped that the bucks were still close to the spot where he'd last spotted them. During this portion of the stalk, the deer had finally fed out of sight and into a thick patch of brush. Burris was pretty sure that they'd be nearby, but he had no way of telling exactly *where.* However, he could clearly see an opening at the top of the canyon where they'd last been feeding. If they moved out into it, he'd be able to see them. Below was the clearing in which he'd initially spotted them. The rain kept up a steady, muffled beat but if the deer spooked anyway, Burris thought he'd be able to pick up the clatter of their hooves upon the canyon's rocky sides and spot them that way.

Another 30 minutes passed. By this time Burris was in the high state of suspense known only too well by trophy hunters. Would the bucks still be there? By now he calculated that less than 200 yards separated him from the bucks. The brush was well over his head now, probably ten feet high. As Burris slipped through the thick stuff, a doe suddenly spurted out ahead of him. As luck would have it, she crashed right towards the bucks.

Burris immediately reacted. He decided that he'd run to an opening directly in front of him on the slim chance that the bucks might run through it. Seconds later, his instinct paid off and three deer burst through the clearing. Two of them were the bucks he'd been stalking. A third deer, lagging behind the other two, was even bigger. Burris had the extra split-second he needed in which to shoot.

Burris fired: the 125-grain Nosler bullet which he'd handloaded specifically for his Sako .264 caught the big buck right in the chest. The animal stumbled, fell, and lay still. There was no doubt in the man's mind. The big buck was undoubtedly the finest mule deer that he'd ever seen. Not only that, the animal's huge body was another matter for concern. He had no idea how long it would take him to get it out of there since he'd killed it far away from where his 4WD would be able to go.

Burris hiked back to the Jeep and drove back to camp. Since two of his buddies had already taken their bucks, he guessed that they would still be in camp. Burris told them to climb in the Jeep and get ready to do some work. Once they got back to the deer, all three of them got busy dressing it, quartering it, and packing it out to the vehicle. By the time they got back to camp, Jack, the last hunter, was also there, with good news as well, since he'd killed a heavy-antlered five-point buck.

Burris knew that his buck was a good trophy so he took it to a taxidermist in San Antonio for mounting. The preliminary score revealed that the buck would probably rank in the top ten muleys of all time. But although Burris was happy, he didn't think much more about it until one night several months later when the phone rang at 1:00 A.M.

It was Ed Schlier, the taxidermist, and he blurted out the news that Burris's buck could very well be the best typical mule deer *ever* taken. His total score of 226 would put it at the top of the Boone and Crockett heap, nine points out in front of the next best head. With a carrot like this in front of him, Burris was only too glad to send the head off to Boone and Crockett headquarters.

In February of 1974, Burris was invited to the Fifteenth North American Big Game Awards of the Boone and Crockett Club, which were to be held in Atlanta. At first he declined, however, because of business commitments. But Boone and Crockett officials weren't going to give up on him that easily. Burris got the distinct impression that if he missed this program, he'd be missing something very special indeed.

That was certainly the case when, at the banquet, Burris was presented with the award for not only the largest typical mule deer buck ever taken, but also the Sagamore Hill Award, which is given only to hunters whose Boone and Crockett trophies are of the very highest distinction.

50

The Number Twenty-four Typical Mule Deer: the Baird Buck

The record-book hunter has a special experience: the thrill of killing a Boone and Crockett deer. The intensity of the moment when he first realizes just how large his buck's antlers are becomes emblazoned in his memory forever. From that day forward, the memory is his and his alone, a cherished point in time that will remain his own private preserve until the day he dies. In that moment, the buck becomes a part of him, fused in time, so that the memory will always be vivid and the thrill will always be new. Such is the case with Kelly Baird of New Mexico. When he killed his tremendous buck in November of 1984, he was making a memory that would last for a lifetime.

Kelly was hunting in the Carson National Forest in northern New Mexico. The Carson National Forest is located in Rio Arriba, Colorado, an area renowned for its big bucks located along the western edge of the Jicarilla Apache Indian Reservation, another trophy mule deer stronghold. Kelly's father, Lavall Baird, was intimately acquainted with the country since he and a few of his friends had been hunting near the same site for 20 years. Kelly, along with a few relatives of Bruce Sullivan, another charter member of the group, had been introduced to the awesome canyons and rim territory some time earlier. The younger hunters had already become quite proficient in the skills required to connect on mule deer bucks.

But things were looking bleak the evening before New Mexico's 1984 season opener. A light rain had fallen for much of the evening. By morning it had stopped, however, and hopes were high at a predawn breakfast where Kelly, Eric Smith, and Mike and Danny Sullivan firmed up their hunting plans for the day. Kelly and Mike had decided to stillhunt along the edge of a rugged canyon. Kelly planned to slip along the topmost rim of the steep cut, while Mike was going to work around a lower bench. Plans called for the two to stalk silently three miles down the canyon, then they would swing around and work their way back to another large drainage where Danny and

Eric would be waiting on their stands. By choosing this strategy, it was quite possible that all the hunters would have opportunities for deer.

The morning was strangely beautiful as the sun poked through the clouds in the east. Fog blanketed the topmost rims of the canyon, and a feeling of distant times was upon the place as Kelly picked his way quietly among the rimrock. Broken shards of Indian pottery at his feet reminded him of other, more primitive hunters, men who had walked these same canyons, pursuing the same animal so many years before. As he walked, the shadowy gray figures of mule deer appeared and dissolved once more as they slipped through the junipers, like specters in the mist. But try as he might, Kelly couldn't see any antlers on the animals.

At 7:00 A.M. Kelly had already covered about a mile when he noticed some deer drop off a point directly in front of him. Slowly, he worked around the head of a small side canyon. Ahead was a heavy game trail that dropped off the rim and into thick junipers below. While Kelly watched for Mike, who was working the brush somewhere below him, he walked out onto a sandstone rim that gave him a view of yet another canyon.

"About 250 yards below me I could see a deer standing in the dark shadows of a large juniper," he said. "We saw each other at the same instant. I could see massive antlers towering above the deer's head as he stared up at me, his attention riveted to the spot where I stood. Other deer were moving past him and out into the sagebrush. I stayed completely motionless, almost afraid to move, as I watched the tremendous buck begin to move around the base of the hill."

Kelly shifted his location then, moving to another rock so that he could see better. As the big buck stopped and looked back again, Kelly lay down and brought his rifle up. His heart was pounding furiously as he found the buck in his crosshairs. The big muley stood there, broadside, as Kelly slipped the safety forward and squeezed the trigger. The .22-250 cracked once and echoed through the canyons. As he watched, the big buck fell to the ground, slammed there by the 55-grain bullet from his gun.

Anxiously, Kelly chambered another round as the big buck staggered to his feet. As his trophy trotted into the sagebrush that would carry him across the canyon's floor, Kelly fired another shot. "I couldn't tell whether I'd hit him or missed him," he said, "so I loaded and fired again. That made him stop, so I quickly chambered another round."

Kelly tried to find the buck in his binoculars at that point but only succeeded in losing sight of the animal completely. But when the buck began trotting again, putting even more distance between the hunter and himself, Kelly once more managed to pick him up. "I watched as he crossed an arroyo, his dark antlers outlined against the light sand background, looking even bigger than they had before," Kelly remembered. "As he scrambled up the other side of the wash, I fired again. Then I fired one last shot as he disappeared into a stand of trees at least 500 yards away. I watched the hillside above the trees for quite some time through my binoculars. But while I saw several does, there was no sign at all of my buck."

Mike had heard the shooting and was coming over to see what was going on. Kelly picked up his brass and went down the hill to meet him. They went directly to the big juniper where he'd first seen the buck standing in the shadows. The only sign of a hit was a few flecks of blood scattered among the buck's tracks as they headed across the canyon. Doggedly, the two kept on his trail. When they reached the line of trees where Kelly's trophy had disappeared, Mike circled the thicket while Kelly sat on the bank of the arroyo, gun at the ready. He had a good view of the entire hillside, so if Mike jumped the buck up, he'd be able to spot him for sure.

After long minutes spent waiting, Kelly began to worry. Mike hadn't jumped or found any sign of the buck. It was finally too much for him to take; he jumped up and stalked into the trees.

"I hadn't gone more than 50 yards when I spotted a set of antlers sticking above a small tree. My heart leaped into my throat as I crept around the tree to see my trophy lying there, not 10 yards ahead of me, dead."

Kelly's first shot had hit the buck in the top of his back, between his shoulders. Although it didn't break any bones, it managed to do a lot of damage. Two more of Kelly's bullets had entered his chest cavity and never exited. A fourth hit him low in the chest. Even after taking all this punishment, the only indication there was that he'd hit the big buck was after the first shot. After caping and field dressing the trophy, Mike and Kelly continued on their way to complete their drive and rendezvous with Danny and Eric.

The hunt was a smashing success; Mike got a three-point on the run during the walk back, and Danny had scored on a nice four-point early in the morning.

After the 60-day drying-out period was up, Kelly's wallhanger scored 208%, making it the top-ranking buck taken in the 1980s. It ranks number 24 overall, tied with two other impressive bucks, one of which was taken in Montrose County, Colorado, in 1974 by Mike Thomas, and another, owned by John McClendon, which was found in Coconimo County, Arizona. It has an inside spread of 28% inches. There are five points on the buck's right antler and seven points on his left. Main beam length is almost equal left and right with measurements of 27% inches and 27% inches. The circumference of the bases at the smallest point between burr and first point is exactly the same for each antler at 5% inches.

Kelly Baird's success while hunting on his own illustrates only too well that you never can tell when you'll meet up with a superbuck. Where you choose to hunt is important. So is how you plan your strategy. But what it all boils down to is a test of nerves and skill between you and the buck, and you have to be up to the challenge because you might not ever get a second chance. Kelly Baird has taken other supercaliber mule deer, and one other that scores 175 points. But no matter where he goes or what he does for the remainder of his years, he'll always remember that November morning when he—and a giant buck—made a memory for a lifetime!

51

The Number One Burkett System Extra-Typical: the Mundy Buck

This trophy is simply incredible. For one thing, it is the number one Burkett system extra-typical buck in the world. And while the Burkett system has never attained the cachet of any of the other scoring systems, when it comes to sheer, unadulterated antler mass, Burkett is the way to go. The Burkett system is especially kind to non-typical bucks like Bill Mundy's immense specimen. Under Burkett, however, this great buck is known as an *Extra-Typical*. But no matter what it may be called, this buck is a champion. The Burkett system, as stated in an earlier chapter, measures non-typical antler mass through metric displacement of water. Using this system, the Mundy Buck takes first prize. Even when scored the traditional Boone and Crockett non-typical muley way, Mundy's buck still garners 288⅜ points, enough to keep it number 33 in the world 38 years after it was killed in 1962. If we were able to disregard the 51⅜ inches of non-typical Boone and Crockett points, the big deer would score an unbelievable 237⅜ points as a typical, beating the current world record Burris Buck by 11⅜ inches. If these two facts aren't reason enough to include it in this short summary of some of the best heads ever taken, how about Kirt Darner's statement: "This is my favorite mule deer; the rack's got beautiful balance." If it's Darner's favorite, a man who has some real monster bucks and who has seen—on the hoof and in private collections—many more, it must be *some* deer.

Unlike most big muleys which have two formal forks per side, the Mundy Buck gains mass with three formal forks per side. And the big animal's greatest claim to fame—an outside spread of 49¾ inches—approaches that of many very respectable bull elk. The inside spread is 26⅜ inches, the right main beam length is 30⅜ inches, and the left main beam is 31⅜ inches long. The head has 23 total points. Twenty-two of them are storable, with twelve on the left side and ten on the right.

The Mundy Buck was taken on the Mundy Ranch, a 16,000-acre working ranch just south of Chama, New Mexico. According to the best of owner Bill Mundy's recollection, as of 1988 there were between 16 and 18 different Boone and Crockett bucks taken off his Chama spread, although only two were actually scored and submitted to the club. Since that time, Bill Mundy says quite a few additional Boone and Crockett bucks have been taken, but declines to name a specific number. "I'm an old man now," he said. "My memory isn't what it used to be." Suffice it to say that close to 20 total bucks listed up until year 2000 in either typical or non-typical categories were killed near Chama. One of them is the magnificent Joe Garcia non-typical buck, second in 1964 and still sixth with 306⅞ Boone and Crockett points, now owned by a collector, Homer Sage. Since some bucks may not have been entered because of an owner or hunter's aversion to publicity, Mundy could very well be right when he states, "There have been more Boone and Crockett bucks taken off my ranch than from any comparable area in the United States."

Mundy was not only a rancher, but also an outfitter. His love of the land and of the hunt have been passed down to his son Jim, who carries on the family's ranching and outfitting traditions on the very land that produced the fabulous buck that bears the family name. Trophy mule deer hunts remain a real attraction on the Mundy's Chama spread. But even though this, the largest buck to come off the place, is called the Mundy Buck, no Mundy actually killed it.

Back in November of 1962, when the big buck was taken, Mundy's son was 14 years old. Mundy had the boy working in sheep camp on top of the mountain before the mule deer season opened. His son kept telling him that every day, without fail, he'd see the biggest mule deer that he'd ever seen feeding around the sheep camp. "The boy wanted me to kill the buck," Mundy said, "but I was too busy trying to fix up a new ranch that we'd just bought."

Part of the renovation at this new ranch included the building of several earth dams for the formation of tanks or ponds. Mundy had hired a local man, Frank Maestas, to operate the equipment needed to build these dams. "I was so impressed by the job that Frank was doing that I told him that he could hunt on my ranch for free," Mundy recalled. "And while I was at it, I thought I'd really make it worth his while. I said, 'Son, I know where you can kill the biggest buck in the world.'

"Now, Frank looked at me like I was crazy or something. But I knew what I was doing, all right. I drew a map showing him exactly where the big buck was hanging out and told him to go on up there. The only stipulation that I made was that if he killed the deer, I had to own the head. Frank said that was no problem and soon he was on his way.

"He went right to where my son had reported seeing the buck, and sure enough, the very first deer he spotted was *the* buck. When he saw him it was 3:30 P.M. and the deer was over 200 yards away. Frank took his time and fired one shot from his 30.06 rifle. The shot was good, and he was back in camp an hour and a half after he'd left us. And was he ever excited."

Mundy was as good as his word. Frank Maestas took the biggest buck in the world—at least according to the Burkett System—and Bill Mundy then proceeded to pay him $100 to buy the antlers back. To this day, Mundy retains ownership of the big buck's mount. "It's a tremendous boost for my outfitting business," he said. A head like the spectacular Mundy Buck would be a tremendous boost for *any* outfitting business.

52

The New World-Record Typical Mule Deer?

Were this revision of *Hunting Superbucks* to have come out even a few months later, it might have contained news of the truly spectacular variety. As it is, however, we can only surmise that a new world-record typical mule deer is waiting in the wings for its coronation at the Boone and Crockett Awards not six months distant.

The buck was not taken by any well-known hunter nor was it taken in the last month or even year. In fact, the story of this buck is one of the most compelling in the long and honored history of hunting.

The buck in question was taken by Lee Spurgeon, a hunter who once lived in Des Moines, Iowa. Lee is a friend of Kirt Darner's dad, Don Darner, and both men hunted to put meat on the table for their families during the Depression. As luck would have it, both men saw their futures in the West and both moved there. The Darners and the Spurgeons landed in Albuquerque, New Mexico, where they shared many family hunting and fishing outings.

Lee called Kirt and extended to him the chance to go on an October 1963 mule deer hunt to LaPlata County in Colorado. Kirt could not make it, so Lee went on his own. Later, Kirt stopped by Lee's house to see how the hunt had gone. Lee told him: "The weather was horrible, but I found this buck in a blinding snowstorm." As Kirt told it, "I knew Lee was happy as punch that it was snowing so hard, because it just made the hunt that much harder." As Lee told Kirt the story, he stated that he'd taken a 5×5 typical and he was sure hoping it would be good to eat!

When Kirt finally got a look at Lee's buck, all thoughts of eating fled his mind. The big typical was the finest buck Kirt had ever seen. "I told him we should measure it, but Lee wasn't too keen on that," Kirt recalled.

The story would have ended like that, but for Kirt Darner's continued fascination with Lee Spurgeon's huge deer. "After I left New Mexico, I'd visit Lee and his family only occasionally," Darner said. "The Meat Buck,' for that's what I jokingly called him, decorated the wall of Lee's reloading shop. I was always amazed to see that buck again and see its magnificent rack. I nagged Lee about measuring it, but his reply was always the same: 'I don't care about that stuff!' This went on for 30 years."

Several years ago, Lee suffered a debilitating stroke. His left side was paralyzed; his speech became slurred. His children had to make one of the worst decisions a family has to make. They placed Lee in a nursing home. But Lee didn't improve; his conditioned worsened. One day, as Kirt sat by Lee's bedside, the older man told him to stop by Lee's home on the way home. "Stop by and see Jane," Lee Spurgeon said. Jane was Lee's daughter.

Kirt did so. When Jane came to the door, she began to cry. "Daddy wants you to have his buck," she said. "You've always liked it so much. And he wants you to have his 7mm Ackley rifle, too." Kirt knew that was the gun Lee Spurgeon had used to harvest his monster typical.

Last spring, Lee Spurgeon passed away. He did not live to know how high his wonderful mule deer scored, nor would he have cared to know. But the Spurgeon buck is, at this point in time, on the fast track to gaining one of the most coveted titles in all of huntingdom: Number One Typical Mule Deer Trophy under the Boone and Crockett scoring system. The Doug Burris buck has reigned supreme for almost 30 years. Many hunters thought it would never be surpassed. But it has been, or it should be, by a modest and unassuming hunter who just wanted a nice meat buck!

The Spurgeon buck is a typical 5 × 5 with a spread of 29⅞ inches. The rack is as close to perfect as it can be with just 3⅞ points of total deductions. Seeing is believing, too. View a photo of this magnificent animal and realize that you are in the presence of greatness.

Lee Spurgeon's buck, if certified by the Boone and Crockett panel of judges, will roar into the record book with a score of 229⅞. That's 3⅞ more than the Burris buck scores. The buck that couldn't be toppled very well might be. And while Kirt Darner has had his own battles with the Boone and Crockett organization—battles that we won't dwell upon here—he isn't about to deny to this great buck its rightful place at the top of the record book listings. It's the least he can do for mule deer and mule deer hunters. And even though Lee Spurgeon didn't know how immense his wonderful mule deer's rack really was, it's the least Kirt Darner can do for a man who was, in many ways, a second father and mentor to him.

Lee Spurgeon, while alive, was an unassuming man. He hunted for the pleasure of it, for the very joy of the chase. It is right and fitting that the new world record would be bequeathed to the hunting world by such a man: a man who put more stock in the thrill of the hunt than in attaining the top spot in the most prestigious trophy record book in the world.

May every hunter who loves to hunt learn a lesson from Lee Spurgeon!

53

The Future of Mule Deer Superbucks

In the year 2000, with mule deer numbers increasing slightly and whitetails still expanding their range, North American hunters enjoy the best of both worlds. This wasn't always the case.

Both species of deer suffered tremendous reverses from unlimited hunting and habitat destruction between the turn of the century and the 1930s. These thirty years saw the formation of state wildlife agencies created specifically to deal with the resources of fish, birds, and animals. By this time, stringent measures were required to save the few mule deer that were left in this country. Herds were so depleted that no hunting at all was allowed for several years in some states. But with regulations in place, populations began to grow once again and peaked in the late 1950s and early 1960s. Because of this success, game managers thought they knew all they needed to know about the mule deer.

The late 1950s and early 1960s became known as the golden age of mule deer hunting. Long seasons and generous limits were the rule. Two buck tags were common, and does were heavily hunted, too. During these years many hunters fondly remember tagging two 30-inch muleys each season. The supply of trophies seemed endless. Late season hunts scheduled to coincide with the peak of the rut or migrations took tremendous tolls on the animals.

Then in the early '70s, the bottom suddenly dropped out. Mule deer populations crashed in states all over the West and no one knew why. It was back to square one for wildlife managers. Problems with winter range, habitat destruction, nutrition, predation, and disease were all suggested as possible causes of the decline. All these reasons were soon discarded. But by the late 1970s, herds were on the rebound once more, with only occasional setbacks from severe winter weather since then.

A great deal is known about the muley's fidgety cousin, the whitetail, but not nearly so much is known about the mule deer. Wildlife agencies based in western states have only so many dollars to spend and they have a multitude of big game animals to spend it on. Only rarely is the mule deer given the emphasis that it deserves. For example, both elk and sheep licenses command top dollar from sportsmen, consequently these animals and their needs get the most management attention. Muleys, the mainstay of most fish and game departments, usually take a back seat to the flashier big game species.

Another problem facing the animals is people—wild muleys aren't as tolerant of people as whitetails are, and people are constantly encroaching on their range. This trait could be the biggest management problem facing today's western wildlife professional. Mule deer are especially vulnerable on winter range when they are more visible and more accessible. ATV and snowmobile harassment stirs the animals up and makes them burn the body fat that's been stored to help them endure the rigors of the season.

Encroachment by the Forest Service is another problem facing mule deer management. The Forest Service sees as its primary goal the delivery of timber from national forests. To achieve this end, they're steadily building more roads into areas where no roads existed before. Hunters follow these roads to penetrate the wilderness where muleys used to live untroubled by human encroachment. ATVs, mountain bikes, motorbikes, even 4WDs make it easy for out-of-shape hunters to travel great distances into the heart of trophy buck country on brand new roads. A network like this leaves the animals few sanctuaries over great portions of their range. Instead of opening more areas up to vehicular traffic, the Forest Service should be closing more down, making more wilderness areas to protect animals from armchair athletes, hunters who would never go as far if they had to walk or ride a horse. Not only would areas like this offer the chance for a quality hunt, far from the madding crowd, but more animals might then grow to trophy size.

Muleys also lose out in many areas where grazing rights are leased to ranchers who pay a pittance for BLM leases, then overgraze the ground, leaving it ill-suited for wildlife. Much of this land is arid, desert country where ecological scars remain for a long time. Flora damaged by long term grazing abuse take years to recover. Taxpayers subsidize these grazing rights so the ranchers can make a profit. Then, when states have to fork over supplemental feed for wildlife in the winter, the sportsman foots the bill. Supplemental feeding is needed because of poor range management. In other words, we pay twice. Much of this overgrazed land is critical winter range, the most crucial portion of a mule deer's annual habitat.

Even the federal interstate highway system has been a culprit in the subtle yet relentless attack on mule deer habitat. Small yet vital portions of many herds have disappeared forever because construction projects like highways and dams block traditional migration routes to winter range. The herds die off gradually, as every year there are fewer deer to try to make the migration. Finally, no deer remain from that migrating group. The memory of the migration dies with them, and people forget the animals ever lived.

Public lands are under constant pressure by businesses looking for new ways to exploit them. Mineral and oil exploration are just two of the ways that could lead to even more degradation of mule deer habitat. Public lands should remain in the public domain and never shift to special interest groups. If public resources become crucial to the nation's well-being, then leases and contracts must be negotiated to mitigate damage to wildlife. All land developed must be reclaimed and returned to wildlife production in a condition equal to or better than that existing before development. And only small areas should be released to development at a time.

As with the whitetail, many wildlife agencies put too small a premium on a mule deer license. In some cases non-residents are charged 10 or 20 times the amount a resident is charged. Most out-of-town sportsmen don't mind paying a lot more for the privilege of hunting out West; but they do resent the small value placed on mule deer by many resident hunters who only have to part with a few dollars for a license. More resident license money just might equal more resident respect for the animal in many cases.

In the past, judges have been too lenient with many wildlife offenders, a situation that, thankfully, has begun to change. Poachers should be—and recently have been—paying very dearly for indiscriminate use of our wildlife. Most muleys roam public land. So they really *are* our muleys.

Populations once manipulated for quantity are now sometimes being managed for quality. Although some state agencies remain gung-ho in their determination to provide every sportsman and woman with the opportunity to take a spike or fork-horned buck, others are instituting programs designed to improve the chances of big bucks to grow to an age where they might attain the spectacular antlers for which so many hunters long. All mule deer are noble animals; now, hunters who want to pursue a wallhanger have areas where their chances are better than they were just a decade ago.

Counties and regions where big bucks were once commonplace are trending back to becoming quality hunting areas. Management plans formulated by each state are fast providing both quality and quantity hunting in units that can support each.

Crises continue to assail the mule deer on all fronts. But not all the news is bad. Hunters everywhere are taking a long look at the mule deer and they like what they see. Organizations are springing up dedicated to ensuring that the animals get a fair shake. Hunters who have decried some of the abuses the animals have had to endure are now acting in their defense. The Mule Deer Foundation, in particular, has put their time and money where their ideals are. This group is making a significant difference, not only in the way the animals are managed, but also the way sportsmen and women perceive them.

The mule deer should never have to take a back seat to any big game species. The wild and free, beautiful and bold mule deer super-buck has grabbed the imaginations of hunters in a way few animals have ever done. He's glorious in his own right and worthy of our admiration and respect. Over the years he's proven that he's a survivor, too. With luck, and a little help from his friends, he should be an important part of the American way of life forever.

Epilogue

54

Superbuck Taxidermy

If all goes as planned, you'll read this book and know exactly how to go after and bag your very own superbuck. It may be a whitetail or it may be a mule deer; what kind of deer doesn't matter as much as the mere fact that you actually *got* one. And whether or not your superbuck qualifies for either the Boone and Crockett or Pope and Young record books isn't of earth-shattering importance either. For the beauty of trophies—especially in the matter of superbucks—is in the eyes of the hunter. My husband and I have taken several muleys that fell quite a bit short of the Boone and Crockett mark, measuring between just 165 and 188 points. But they're still awe-inspiring to both me and my friends. The mounts gaze out serenely from their place of honor on my wall. Every time I look at them I'm immediately transported back through time to the place where each was taken. I can still see limestone cliffs or rimrock canyons; smell the fragrance of ponderous Douglas firs or the pungent scent of sage. The alpenglow has set fire to the snow and the skies are streaked with red and gold; a circling hawk's keening cry echoes across the plains. These memories and these bucks mean as much to me as they would if the bucks actually made the book.

The same is true of a couple of whitetails that I was privileged enough to shoot as well. My top-ranking whitetail scores only 165⅞ gross Boone and Crockett points, but I enjoy reminiscing about the thrill of the hunt where I took him. And that's really what it's all about. As long as your trophy is a handsome buck; if you outwitted him through perseverance and hard work; and, if he represents your personal best, then he qualifies as a superbuck, at least in my opinion.

Let's say that you've made your decision and pulled the trigger or loosed the arrow that's found its way deep into the body of your superbuck. He drops over and moves no more. You stand there dealing with a hunter's plethora of conflicting emotions. You're glad your search is over, glad you shot when you did—and yet you regret the fact that this graceful and beautiful animal had to die. These feelings are entirely normal. Without them, surely you've lost something of the essence of the hunting experience. Slowly, you move forward, still not quite believing your good fortune.

Stop right there! Don't let over-eagerness or over-confidence rob you of the trophy of a lifetime. Be especially cautious if you have a long history of one-shot kills. After I killed at least 15 animals with one shot, I then lost a fine whitetail buck because I was so *sure* he was dead. My guide and I watched as the buck flipped over with all four feet in the air, just like a cartoon character. We walked forward, talking excitedly, and were unprepared when the buck suddenly bolted forward on his knees to disappear in a patch of oak brush. The big whitetail was hit hard, and was bleeding from both his side and his nose, indicative of a solid lung shot. I now believe that the bullet only struck one of his lungs, leaving him sufficient air to recover and eventually disappear completely. We tracked him for over three hours and jumped him once more. I would have stayed with him longer, but we were hunting in desert-type terrain and the blood trail just petered out. Believe me, losing that buck was a bitter pill to swallow.

So if you've just shot the buck of *your* life, be sure that you have another shell in your gun's chamber or another arrow nocked on your string. Put your scope or sights on him and wait several minutes without moving in case he jumps up again. After a short period of time, make a mental note of the place where you last saw him and then move forward towards that spot purposefully and slowly, until finally you see him lying on the ground. Stand there for a moment and watch for signs of life such as breathing, twitching, or sparkle in the eyes. Don't *wait* for a superbuck to die; he might be merely stunned, and you risk losing him if you just watch. If there's any doubt, shoot again, making sure that you aim for the vitals in the rib cage and that neither entrance nor exit wound will ruin the animal's cape for eventual mounting.

If your buck manages to slip away wounded, take heart. First, make sure that you know exactly where you were standing when you made your shot. Then, pick out landmarks where the animal was last seen when hit. Mark both locations with a brightly-colored fluorescent ribbon, an item that's light, compactible, and should always be carried when in pursuit of any game animal.

Once you've found the spot where the animal was standing, look for blood, hair, tracks or skid marks. Stand there and slowly rotate your head, looking first near and then far, for signs of either the carcass or antlers sticking up at an odd angle.

If you see the animal, rejoice and then proceed cautiously. Always make the final approach from an uphill position if possible. Momentum can make dying superbucks formidable foes with the force of their weight behind dagger-sharp tines and slashing hooves. Again, dispatch the buck with another shot if he's still alive. While you have a big buck down but not quite dead is no time to be worrying about either meat loss or the cost of ammunition.

If the buck manages to evade you, track him as long as it's humanly possible to do so. Only a lost blood trail, or the secure knowledge that the wound is superficial, should deter you from the path.

Once your buck is dead, sit down and admire him for a while. You worked long and hard for him, didn't you? Congratulate yourself inwardly! You've earned it. And while you're doing this, you can accomplish something else: let your nerves relax and stop the shakes. While you sit there, try to decide what you're going to have done with the animal. Will you mount it life size, an expensive option that's becoming more common all the time for trophy animals? Or will you opt for a head and shoulder mount only, a more economical decision yet one that will still show off quite adequately the beauty of the animal. Another alternative is the European mount, where the skull plate is cleaned and bleached with the antlers still attached and then mounted on a plaque.

Never cut the throat of a trophy animal. Dr. Jan Roth of Craig, Colorado's outstanding Rimrock Taxidermy Shop, explains why. "Bleeding a big game animal is just not important," he said. "To be effective, the throat should be cut while the animal is still alive so that the heart can pump blood out of the veins and arteries. Bleeding a dead animal serves absolutely no purpose except to ruin the cape for mounting. Hunters who insist on cutting a big buck's throat should at least use a vertical cut instead of a horizontal one. Vertical cuts are easier to repair."

Roth adds that horizontal cuts may make a cape unuseable, or at the very least, add quite a bit of work and cost to the finished mount.

When you start the job of field dressing your superbuck take a good look at the animal. Remember that on a life-size mount, every single cut is important. If you're able to get the entire animal to the taxidermist, then make only one incision in the abdomen for field dressing and try to make it as short as possible. You may get bloody as you work to get the entrails out, but it can be done.

Skinning out an entire animal calls for a steady knife hand and a goodly supply of patience and is best left to the experts.

CAPING IN THE FIELD

Luckily, most hunters still prefer the standard shoulder mount. While it doesn't look like much of the cape is involved for this mount, appearances can be deceiving. "Don't start the cut any further forward than behind the forelegs on a buck that's a candidate for a shoulder mount," stated Roth. "The hide covering the brisket or chest must be intact. If you can't bring the buck into the shop in one piece to be caped by a taxidermist, then make sure that the cape's got as much of the animal's armpit or arm pocket as possible. Make your cut up the back of the front leg all the way to the point where long hair meets short hair. Then make a diagonal slit forward to the brisket and skin the rest of the way to the ears."

Caping out an entire head and neck is a delicate task that's better left to skilled taxidermists or guides. One slip of the knife could ruin the hide for mounting. My husband and I have had many trophy-quality animals mounted, even those we've taken in the backcountry, by skinning out the shoulders and neck tube-style. Cut up to the back and then around the entire body from a point starting behind the front legs. Once you get the shoulder portion of the skin separated from the rear body portion, use your knife gently to skin and slip it forward to the animal's ears in one piece. The tube-like sheath of skin from the shoulder to the head is *not* cut up the back of the neck. When you reach the ears, simply cut through the neck and spine with a stout knife, hatchet, or saw, being extremely careful not to cut the hide at the same time. If you have trouble cutting through the vertebrae in the neck, twist the head in one direction until the neck cracks. An animal partially caped like this lets the taxidermist complete the caning to his own specifications. A deer head with antlers intact is heavier to pack out than just the cape, but the finished result might make the extra effort worthwhile.

"Hunters of trophy bucks should always try to remember that a taxidermist will never complain about getting too much of the hide," said Roth, "but he can very easily wind up with too little."

A cape with the head still intact should be all right for at least two days during all but the warmest weather. If you're with a guide or outfitter, they'll usually have the experience to cape it out completely.

If you feel you must cape the animal, visit your taxidermy shop before you head out hunting. The taxidermist will be able to tell you how he'd prefer you to cape out the animal.

As for the rest of the animal, be sure to prop the body cavity open so that the meat can cool. Hoist or position the carcass in such a way so that accumulated blood can drain out. Black pepper sprinkled over the carcass will help keep flies off the meat until it's dried and is no longer attractive to insects. Cheesecloth game bags are ideal for packing out quarters or boned meat and they keep bugs off as well.

BUTCHERING

Consider boning your buck. It doesn't take as long as you would think and it will considerably lighten your load, an important consideration for walk-in or backpack hunters. But remember to leave the sex organs attached to one of the quarters if it's required by law in the state where you're hunting.

Consider butchering your buck yourself. This takes much less time than you might imagine, and one of the benefits is that you can regulate the cleanliness of the conditions in your own kitchen. Not only that, you're sure of getting your own meat back, especially if you've gone to great pains to take good care of it in the field. Another bonus is that you can wrap packages in whatever size you like, considering things like family barbecues well ahead of time. If you like roasts, then wrap roasts. If the meat is shot up where the roasts would ordinarily be, as the butcher you have the option of cutting out steaks instead.

When preparing meat for the freezer, de-bone or instruct the butcher to de-bone whenever possible. Bone dust and marrow will make any venison taste gamier. If you get dirt and hair on the meat, wash it off before wrapping. And finally, cut off all fat, veins, and anything white for the best-tasting venison. If the meat is too bloody for your liking, soak it in cold water for ten or fifteen minutes, drain, and then wrap. Soak again right before cooking. Properly prepared venison, even that of a big, rank buck, is excellent table fare.

CHOOSING A TAXIDERMIST

If you've planned well, then before you even set out on the trail of superbuck you've already consulted with several taxidermists to look at their work and discuss possible mounts. Be choosy about where you have your buck mounted. Look over their work closely. There's no substitute for real wildlife artistry, even if you are tempted to go with a fly-by-night taxidermist who may be able to get your mount back a little bit sooner by cutting corners.

Never pick a taxidermist that pickles or quick-tans his capes. Tanning is a tried and true method that, when done right, will last well over 100 years. Quick-tan practitioners can turn a complete mounting job over in between four to six weeks, but you'll be the loser in the long run. True tanning takes a long time to break down fibers in the hide and make them soft and pliable. Improperly treated, these fibers will cause an untanned skin to contract and expand in response to heat or moisture. So your mount will probably crack and split. Tanning also dissolves the glues and oils in the skin, another reason why untanned skins crack so readily. If you decide on a quick-tanned mount, you'll be lucky if it lasts five years.

Whenever possible, request that the taxidermist let you view the work on your mount while it's in process. That way, if something bothers you, you can let him know right away. Checking up on your superbuck could save you regret later on.

If the taxidermist does his job right, every time you look at the buck of your dreams hanging on your wall, you'll remember the moment you finally had him in your sights. Your hunt might have occurred in bitter cold weather, been physically grueling and mentally exhausting, but if your mount's done right, the only thing that you'll remember is the glory of taking *your* superbuck the way it's supposed to be done, one on one. Who could ask for anything more?

Appendix I

Maps for Hunting
Mule Deer Superbucks

Anyone who has hunted muleys or elk in the vast wilderness of the American West can well appreciate the task confronting a superbuck hunter. It's like looking for a needle in a haystack, an immense one at that, with deserts and plains, sagebrush steppes and subalpine forests. Mule deer inhabit some of the most awesome country in the world. Merely setting out after them raises your adventure quota a cut above that of most eastern hunters.

Back country hunting for big mule deer bucks can be exciting and inspiring. One trip could turn into the hunt of a lifetime and you're addicted forever. If you're drawn to the western grandeur that waits for you on a mule deer hunt, don't delay any longer. With proper planning, good companions, and the right maps, you can surmount any problems.

Lots of books have already been written on how to plan and pack gear for a hunt. No one can help you choose your companions. But maps are something else again. No one should ever have to say that he or she didn't go after their muley superbuck because they didn't know where to go, or worse, how to get there.

There are so many hunting places available to a dedicated hunter that choosing will be the hardest part. Almost every big mule deer area in the country includes at least some public land. Public land means maps, lots of maps of all different kinds. These maps are one of the best outdoor bargains available. For no more than a few dollars you can literally see your hunting area before you step out of your home. You can envision streams and cliffs, roads and forests. And you can actually plan where you want to make your camp or sit that first morning afield. What are these different kinds of maps and where can you get them?

U.S. GEOLOGICAL SURVEY TOPOGRAPHIC MAPS

Surveyors began mapping this country in Colonial times. With crude tools and methods of measure, they set about platting America's hills, rivers, and valleys, a job which they continue today with sophisticated photogrammetric devices used from airplanes. I'm always amazed when I compare a map to the area I'm hunting and realize just how accurate it is.

U.S.G.S. topographic maps may be printed one of two ways: on a 7.5 minute scale or on a 15 minute scale. A 7.5 minute map is drawn to a larger scale than a 15 minute map is, usually so that 1 inch on the map represents 24,000 inches or .38 mile. Put another way, 2.64 actual inches on a 7.5 minute topographic map equals one mile. This translates into about 8.5 miles of latitude (height of your map) and 6.8 miles of longitude (width) shown on your map. Usually you'll need between one and four topo maps to thoroughly cover a potential hunting area.

A 15 minute map drawn on the same size paper would show four times as much territory as a 7.5 minute map, so the scale would be much smaller.

A topographic map, or as it's more commonly known, topo map, is a three-dimensional map. Not only does the map show length and breadth of various geographic features, it also indicates relief, or the difference in altitude between the high and low parts of the land. It also shows you an area's topography, defined as the relief and form or shape of the land. Cartographers do this through the use of contour lines.

A contour line is drawn so that it passes through all the points having exactly the same altitude. You could, in theory, walk along a contour line. Say you start out walking around the side of a basin, never walking any higher up the basin, never walking any lower down the basin. When you arrive back at your starting point, your path has curved around hillsides, bent upstream where valleys enter the basin, and swung outward around spurs. You've made a contour. Every contour must be a closed line, just like the shoreline of an island. Some won't close on your particular map, however; but they do close on the neighboring map.

The distance between each contour line on your topo map represents a contour interval. This contour interval is fixed at the bottom of each topo map that you buy. Where land is level, the contour interval is small, say 10 feet. But in typical mule deer territory, it's not uncommon for contour intervals to jump up to 40 feet. And when you see a lot of 40 feet contour intervals spaced so close together that they look dark, you know immediately that you're looking at a very steep mountainside or a cliff.

Topo maps are usually colored green for forests and white for grasslands. Lakes, rivers, springs, even wet-weather springs and creeks are indicated. Every significant man-made or natural object is shown. You'll be able to see if there are foot trails or 4WD trails, old cabins or corrals. As you walk into a place, you can trace your progress on your map and that way ensure that you won't get lost.

Magnetic declination is also shown, the amount off true north your compass will be when you're in your hunting area.

To order topo maps, first request the index sheet that's available free of charge from the U.S. Geological Survey Map Center in Denver. You can reach them at U.S.G.S., Map Sales, Box 25286, Federal Center, Denver, CO 80225.

The index shows every topo map in a state by name. When you decide which ones you need, you order them from the above address. The cost in 2000 is $4.00 per map plus $5.00 for postage and handling for any order that totals less than $10.00. When you receive your maps, there will be a free symbol sheet included. But remember to order U.S.G.S. topo maps at least eight weeks *before* you need them to be sure you get them in time for your trip. Or, you might consider visiting the United States Geological Survey's web site so that you can save time by ordering them online. The web site's address is http://www.usgs.gov/.

FOREST SERVICE MAPS

The U.S. Forest Service controls large blocks of land in today's West. They need maps as badly as we do, and the maps they'll supply are good ones. First of all there's the free travel map. These are black and white maps of a particular ranger district that give you an overview of the area at a glance. Forest Service land is indicated as are buildings, roads, primary drainages and significant landforms.

For more detailed information—and details are what a good hunter wants—buy the recreation map for the national forest you plan to hunt. These maps are four-color maps that fold out like highway maps. They indicate all of the recreation sites in the forest, things like campgrounds, picnic grounds, wilderness areas, etc. All national forest land is indicated, as is Bureau of Land Management (BLM) land, state land, and national monuments or parks. Trails, roads, drainages, and landforms are shown but no relief is shown. These maps are invaluable since they are broken up into sections which are often one square mile in size. If you're hiking or packing in a good distance, it's fairly easy to keep track of your progress. When combined with a topo map, you've got an excellent tool to help you take that big muley.

Here alphabetically listed are the names, addresses, and phone numbers of the national forests in each state where you'll be most likely to find the best mule deer bucks. If you can't find the national forest you're looking for under the state where you plan to hunt, look for it under the neighboring states. Some national forests (NF) do overlap between states. Should you wish to order

your maps online, here is the U.S. Forest service web site: http://
www.fs.fed.us/links/maps/shtml.

Arizona

Apache-Sitgreaves NF, Box 640, Springerville, AZ 85938

Coconino NF, 2323 E. Greenlaw Lane, Flagstaff, AZ 86004

Coronado NF, 300 W. Congress, Tucson, AZ 85701

Kaibab NF, 800 South 6th St., Williams, AZ 86046-2681

Prescott NF, 344 S. Cortez, Prescott, AZ 86303-1762

Tonto NF, 2324 E. McDowell Rd., P.O. Box 5348, Phoenix, AZ 85010

California

Angeles NF, 701 N. Santa Anita Ave., Arcadia, CA 91006

Cleveland NF, 10845 Rancho Bernardo Rd., Suite 200, San Diego,
CA 92127-2107

Eldorado NF, 100 Forni Rd., Placerville, CA 95667

Inyo NF, 873 N. Main St., Bishop, CA 93514

Klamath NF, 1312 Fairlane Rd., Yreka, CA 96097-6131

Lassen NF, 55 S. Sacramento St., Susanville, CA 96130

Los Padres NF, 6755 Hollister Ave., Ste. 150, Goleta, CA 93117

Mendocino NF, 825 N. Humboldt Ave., Willows, CA 95988

Modoc NF, 800 W. 12th St., Alturas, CA 96101

Plumas NF, 159 Lawrence St., Box 11500, Quincy, CA 94971-6025

San Bernardino NF, 1824 S. Commercenter Circle, San Bernardino,
CA 92408-3430

Sequoia NF, 900 W. Grand Ave., Porterville, CA 93257

Shasta-Trinity NF, 2400 Washington Ave., Redding, CA 96001

Sierra NF, 1600 Tollhouse Rd., Clovis, CA 93611-0532

Six Rivers NF, 1330 Bayshore Way, Eureka, CA 95501-3834

Stanislaus NF, 19777 Greenley Rd., Sonora, CA 95370

Tahoe NF, 631 Coyote St., Nevada City, CA 95959-6003

Colorado

Arapaho and Roosevelt NF, 240 W. Prospect St., Fort Collins, CO
80526

Grand Mesa NF, Uncompahgre NF, and Gunnison NF, 2250 Highway
50, Delta, CO 81416

Pike and San Isabel NF, 1920 Valley Dr., Pueblo, CO 81008

Rio Grande NF, 1803 W. Highway 160, Monte Vista, CO 81144

San Juan NF, 15 Burnett Ct., Durango, CO 81301-3647

White River NF, 900 Grand Ave., Box 948, Glenwood Springs, CO 81602-0948

Idaho

Caribou NF, 250 S. 4th Ave., Suite 172, Federal Bldg., Pocatello, ID 83201

Clearwater NF, 12730 Highway 12, Orofino, ID 83544

Idaho Panhandle NF, 3815 Schreiber Way, Coeur d'Alene, ID 83815-8363

Nez Perce NF, Route 2, Box 475, Grangeville, ID 83530

Payette NF, 800 W. Lakeside Ave., Box 1026, McCall, ID 83638

Salmon-Challis NF, RR 2, Box 600, Salmon, ID 83467

Sawtooth NF, 2647 Kimberly Rd., E., Twin Falls, ID 83301-7976

Targhee NF, 420 N. Bridge St., P.O. Box 208, St. Anthony, ID 83445

Montana

Beaverhead-Deerlodge NF, 420 Barrett St., Dillon, MT 59725-3572

Bitterroot NF, 1801 N. 1st St., Hamilton, MT 59840

Custer NF, 1310 Main St., P.O. Box 50760, Billings, MT 59103

Flathead NF, Box 147, 1935 3rd Ave. E., Kalispell, MT 59901

Gallatin NF, 10 E. Babcock Ave., Box 130, Bozeman, MT 59771

Helena NF, 2880 Skyway Dr., Helena, MT 59626

Kootenai NF, 506 Highway 2 W., Libby, MT 59923

Lewis and Clark NF, Box 869, 1101 15th St., N., Great Falls, MT 59403

Lola NF, Bldg. 24, Ft Missoula, Missoula, MT 59801

New Mexico

Carson NF, 208 Cruz Alta Rd., Taos, NM 87571

Cibola NF, 2113 Osuna Rd. NE, Suite A, Albuquerque, NM 87113-1001

Gila NF, 3005 E. Camino Del Bosque, Silver City, NM 88061

Lincoln NF, Federal Bldg., 11th and New York, Alamogordo, NM 88310

Santa Fe NF, 1474 Rodeo Rd., Santa Fe, NM 87504

Nebraska

Nebraska NF, 125 N. Main St., Chadron, NE 69337

Nevada

Humboldt-Toiyabe NF, 1200 Franklin Way, Sparks, NV 89431

North Dakota

Dakota Prairie Grasslands, 240 W. Century, Bismarck, ND 58501

Oregon

Deschutes NF, 1645 Highway 20 East, Bend, OR 97701

Fremont NF, HC 10, Box 337, 1300 S. G St., Lakeview, OR 97630

Malheur NF, 431 Patterson Bridge Rd., P.O. Box 909, John Day, OR 97845

Mt. Hood NF, 16400 Champion Way, Sandy, OR 97030

Ochoco NF, Box 490, Federal Bldg., Prineville, OR 97754

Rogue River NF, Federal Bldg., 333 W. 8th St., Box 520, Medford, OR 97501

Siskiyou NF, 200 NE Greenfield Rd., Box 440, Grants Pass, OR 97528-0242

Umatilla NF, 2517 SW Hailey Ave., Pendleton, OR 97801

Umpqua NF, Box 1008, Roseburg, OR 97470

Wallowa-Whitman NF, Box 907, Baker, OR 97814

Willamette NF, 211 E. 7th Ave., Box 10607, Eugene, OR 97440-2607

Winema NF, 2819 Dahlia, Klamath Falls, OR 97601

South Dakota

Black Hills NF, Hwy 385 N., RR 2, Box 200, Custer, SD 57730-9501

Utah

Ashley NF, 355 N. Vernal Ave., Vernal, UT 84078

Dixie NF, 82 N. 100 E. St., P.O. Box 580, Cedar City, UT 84720

Fishlake NF, 115 E. 900 N., Richfield, UT, 84701

Manti-LaSal NF, 599 W. Price River Dr., Price, UT 84501

Uinta NF, 88 W. 100 N., Provo, UT 84601

Wasatch-Cache NF, 8236 Federal Bldg., 125 S. State St., Salt Lake City, UT 84138

Washington

Colville NF, 765 S. Main, Colville, WA 99114

Gifford Pinchot NF, 10600 NE 51st Circle, Vancouver, WA 98682

Mt. Baker-Snoqualmie NF, 21905 64th Ave. W. Mountlake Terrace, WA 98043

Okanogan NF, 1240 S. Second, Okanogan, WA 98840

Olympic NF, 1835 Black Lake Blvd. SW, Olympia, WA 98512-5623

Wenatchee NF, 215 Melody Lane, Wenatchee, WA 98801

Wyoming

Bridger-Teton NF, 340 N. Cache, Box 1888, Jackson, WY 83001

Bighorn NF, 2013 Eastside 2nd St., Sheridan, WY 82801

Medicine Bow-Routt NF, 2468 Jackson St., Laramie, WY 82070-6535

Shoshone NF, 808 Meadow Lane, Cody, WY 82414-4516

BUREAU OF LAND MANAGEMENT MAPS

The Bureau of Land Management (BLM) offers several maps that are useful to hunters. The BLM state map covers all of the BLM land in a particular state. BLM land is blocked out so that you can tell at a glance which areas are open to public hunting. These maps don't show as much detail as do some of the other BLM maps available. At the end of 2000, they cost $4.00 each, plus postage, and are available from BLM offices, which will be listed later in this chapter.

One of the handiest maps for hunters that I know of is the BLM's Surface Management Map. The scale is usually smaller than on U.S.G.S. topo maps, often 1:100,000, but many other details are the same. Plus you have the added benefit of being able to tell at a glance whether you're on public land, what kind of public land it is, or whether it's private land. These maps are great if you want to secure permission to hunt from a neighboring landowner. BLM Surface Management Maps show contours and elevations (usually in meters), highways, roads, trails, other manmade structures, all water features, and include all geographic names. At the end of 2000, they cost $4.00 each, plus postage.

The last BLM map available is called a Resource Area Map. This map usually covers a certain county and shows BLM land, private land, and forest service ground in different blocks of covers. Significant landforms and manmade structures are also shown. These maps aren't available from all offices so you'll have to check around before buying. At the end of 2000, they cost $4.00 each, plus postage.

Here is the list of BLM offices where you can buy maps in each state.

Arizona

Arizona BLM State Office, 222 N. Central Ave., Phoenix, AZ 85004-2203

Arizona Strip Field Office, 345 E. Riverside Dr., St. George, UT 84790-9000

Kingman Field Office, 2475 Beverly Ave., Kingman, AZ 86401-3629

Lake Havasu Field Office, 2610 Sweetwater Ave., Lake Havasu City, AZ 86406-9071

Phoenix Field Office, 2015 W. Deer Valley Rd., Phoenix AZ 85027

Safford Field Office, 711 14th Ave., Safford, AZ 85546-3321

Tucson Field Office, 12661 E. Broadway, Tucson, AZ 85748-7208

Yuma Field Office, 2555 E. Gila Ridge Rd., Yuma, AZ 85365-2240

California

Alturas Field Office, 708 W. 12th St., Alturas, CA 96101-3102

Arcata Field Office, 1695 Heindon Rd., Arcata, CA 95521

Bakersfield Field Office, 3801 Pegasus Dr., Bakersfield, CA 93308

Barstow Field Office, 2607 Barstow Rd., Barstow, CA 92311

Bishop Field Office, 785 N. Main St., Suite E, Bishop, CA 93514

E. Centro Field Office, 1661 S. 4th St., El Centro, CA 92243

Folsom Field Office, 63 Natoma St., Folsom, CA 95630

Lytle Creek Field Office, c/o U.S. Forest Service, 1209 Lytle Creek Rd., Lytle Creek, CA 92358

Needles Field Office, 101 West Spikes Rd., Needles, CA 92363

Palm Springs Field Office, 690 Garnet Ave., N. Palm Springs, CA 92258

Paso Robles Field Office, 715 24th St., Suite L, Paso Robles, CA 93446

Redding Field Office, 355 Hemsted Dr., Redding, CA 96002

Ridgecrest District Office, 300 S. Richmond Rd., Ridgecrest, CA 93555

Shasta Lake Field Office, 14225 Holiday Rd., Redding, CA 96003

Surprise Field Office, P.O. Box 460, 602 Cressler St., Cedarville, CA 96104

Susanville Field Office, 2950 Riverside Dr., Susanville, CA 96130

Ukiah Field Office, 2550 N. State St., Ukiah, CA 95482

Colorado

Northwest Center & Grand Junction Field Office, 2815 H Rd., Grand Junction, CO 81506

Glenwood Springs Field Office, 50629 Hwys 6 & 24, P.O. Box 1009, Glenwood Springs, CO 81602

Gunnison Field Office, 216 N. Colorado St., Gunnison, CO 81230

Kremmling Field Office, 1116 Park Ave., P.O. Box 68, Kremmling, CO 80459

LaJara Field Office, 15571 County Rd. 75, LaJara, CO 81140

Little Snake Field Office, 455 Emerson St., Craig, CO 81625

San Juan Field Office, 15 Burnett Ct., Durango, CO 81301

Saquache Field Office, 46525 Highway 114, Saquache, CO 81149

Uncompahgre Field Office, 2505 S. Townsend Ave., Montrose, CO 81401

White River Field Office, 73544 Highway 64, Meeker, CO 81641

Idaho

Burley Field Office, 15 E. 200 S, Burley, ID 83318

Challis Field Office, HC 63, Box 1670, Challis, ID 83226

Coeur d'Alene Field Office, 1808 N. 3rd St., Coeur d'Alene, ID 83814

Cottonwood Field Office, House 1, Butte Dr., RR 3 Box 181, Cottonwood, ID 83522

Four Rivers Field Office, 3948 Development Ave., Boise, ID 83705

Idaho Falls Field Office, 1405 Hollipark Dr., Idaho Falls, ID 83401

Idaho BLM State Office, 1387 S. Vinnell Way, Boise ID 83709

Jarbridge Field Office, 2620 Kimberly Rd., Twin Falls, ID 83301

Malad Field Office, 138 S. Main St., Malad City, ID 83252

Owyhee Field Office, 3948 Development Ave., Boise, ID 83705

Pocatello Field Office, 1111 N. 8th Ave., Pocatello, ID 83201

Salmon Field Office, 50 Highway S, Salmon, ID 83467

Shoshone Field Office, 400 W. F St., P.O. Box 2-B, Shoshone, ID 83352

Montana

Billings Field Office, 5001 Southgate Dr., Billings, MT 59101

Butte Field Office, 106 N. Parkmont, P.O. Box 338, Butte, MT 59702-3388

Dillon Field Office, 1005 Selway Dr., Dillon, MT 59725-9431

Lewistown Field Office, P.O. Box 1160, Lewistown, MT 59457-1160

Malta Field Office, 501 S. 2nd St. E, HC 65 Box 5000, Malta, MT 59538-0047

Miles City Field Office, 111 Garryowen Road, Miles City, MT 59301-0940

Missoula Field Office, 3255 Fort Missoula Road, Missoula, MT 59804-7293

Montana BLM State Office, P.O. Box 36800, Billings, MT 59107-6800

New Mexico

Albuquerque Field Office, 435 Montano Rd. NE, Albuquerque, NM 87107-4935

Carlsbad Field Office, 620 E. Greene St., Carlsbad, NM 88220-6292

Farmington Field Office, 1235 La Plata Highway, Suite A, Farmington, NM 87401-8731

Las Cruces Field Office, 1800 Marquess, P.O. Box 1420, Las Cruces, NM 88005-3371

New Mexico BLM State Office, P.O. Box 27115, 1474 Rodeo Rd., Santa Fe, NM 87502-0115

Roswell Field Office, 2909 W. Second St., Roswell, NM 88201-2019

Socorro Field Office, 198 Neel Ave. NW, Socorro, NM 87801-4648

Taos Field Office, 226 Cruz Alta Rd., Taos, NM 87571-5983

Nevada

Battle Mountain Field Office, 50 Bastian Rd., Battle Mountain, NV 89820-1420

Carson City Field Office, 1535 Hot Springs Rd., Suite 300, Carson City, NV 89701

Elko Field Office, 5665 Morgan Mill Road, Carson City, NV 89701

Ely Field Office, 775 N. Industrial Way, HC33 Box 33500, Ely, NV 89301-9408

Las Vegas Field Office, 4765 W. Vegas Dr., Las Vegas, NV 89108

Winnemucca Field Office, 5100 E. Winnemucca Blvd., Winnemucca, NV 89445

North Dakota

North Dakota Field Office, 2933 3rd Ave. West, Dickinson, ND 58601-2619

Oklahoma

Tulsa Field Office, 7906 E. 33rd St., Suite 101, Tulsa, OK 74145-1352

Oregon

Burns BLM District Office, HC 74-12533 Highway 20 W, Hines, OR 97738

Coos Bay District Office, 1300 Airport Lane, North Bend, OR 97459-2000

Eugene District Office, 2890 Chad Dr., P.O. Box 10226, Eugene, OR 97440

Lakeview District Office, 1300 S. G St., HC 10, Box 337, Lakeview, OR 97630

Medford District Office, 3040 Biddle Rd., Medford, OR 97504

Oregon BLM State Office, 1515 S.W. 5th Avenue, P.O. Box 2965, Portland, OR 97208

Prineville District Office, P.O. Box 550, Prineville, OR 97754

Roseburg District Office, 777 NW Garden Valley Blvd., Roseburg, OR 97630

Salem District Office, 1717 Fabry Rd. SE, Salem, OR 97306

Spokane District Office, 1103 N. Fancher, Spokane, WA 99212-1275

Vale District Office, 100 Oregon St., Vale, OR 97918-9630

South Dakota

South Dakota Field Office, 310 Roundup St., Belle Fourche, SD 57717-1698

Texas

Amarillo Field Office, 801 South Fillmore St., Suite 500, Amarillo, TX 79101-3545

Utah

Cedar City Field Office, 176 East D. L. Sargent Dr., Box 724, Cedar City, UT 84720

Fillmore Field Office, 35 East 500 North, Fillmore, UT 84631

GSENM (Grand Staircase-Escalante National Monument) Field Office, 180 W. 300 N, Kanab, UT 84741

Kanab Field Office, 318 N. 1st E., Kanab, UT 84741

Moab Field Office, 82 E. Dogwood, P.O. Box 768, Richfield, UT 84701

Monticello Field Office, 435 N. Main St., P.O. Box 7, Monticello, UT 84535

Richfield Field Office, 150 E. 900 N., P.O. Box 768, Richfield, UT 84701

St. George Field Office, 345 E. Riverside Dr., St. George, UT 84720

Utah BLM State Office, P.O. Box 45155, 324 S. State St., Salt Lake City, UT 84145-0155

Vernal Field Office, 170 S. 500 E. Vernal, UT 84078

Wyoming

Buffalo Field Office, 1425 Fort St., Buffalo, WY 82834-2436

Casper Field Office, 2987 Prospector Dr., Casper, WY 82604-2968

Cody Field Office, 1002 Blackburn, P.O. Box 518, Cody, WY 82414-8464

Kemmerer Field Office, 312 Highway 189 North, Kemmerer, WY 83101-9711

Lander Field Office, 1335 Main, P.O. Box 589, Lander, WY 82520-0589

Newcastle Field Office, 1101 Washington Blvd., Newcastle, WY 82701-2972

Pinedale Field Office, 432 E Mill St., P.O. Box 768, Pinedale, WY 82941-0768

Rawlins Field Office, 1300 N. Third St., P.O. Box 2407, Rawlins, WY 82301-2407

Wyoming BLM State Office, 5353 Yellowstone, P.O. Box 1828, Cheyenne, WY 82003

Appendix II

Scoring Charts

Records of
North American
Big Game

250 Station Drive
Missoula, MT 59801
(406) 542-1888

BOONE AND CROCKETT CLUB®
OFFICIAL SCORING SYSTEM FOR NORTH AMERICAN BIG GAME TROPHIES

MINIMUM SCORES		
	AWARDS	ALL-TIME
whitetail	160	170
Coues'	100	110

TYPICAL
WHITETAIL AND COUES' DEER

KIND OF DEER (check one)
☐ whitetail
☐ Coues'

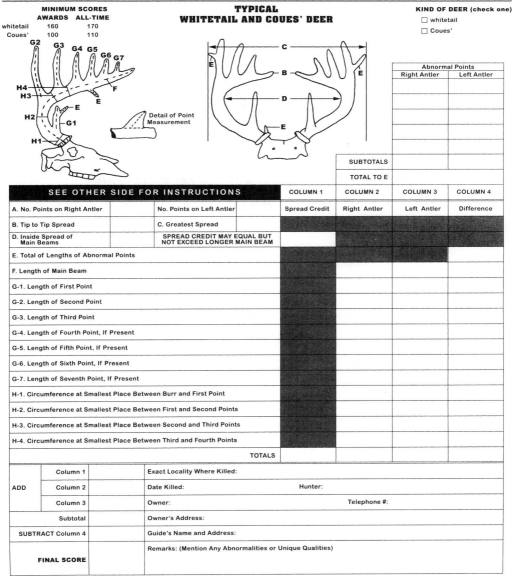

Detail of Point Measurement

Abnormal Points	
Right Antler	Left Antler

SUBTOTALS	
TOTAL TO E	

SEE OTHER SIDE FOR INSTRUCTIONS				COLUMN 1	COLUMN 2	COLUMN 3	COLUMN 4
A. No. Points on Right Antler		No. Points on Left Antler		Spread Credit	Right Antler	Left Antler	Difference
B. Tip to Tip Spread		C. Greatest Spread					
D. Inside Spread of Main Beams		SPREAD CREDIT MAY EQUAL BUT NOT EXCEED LONGER MAIN BEAM					
E. Total of Lengths of Abnormal Points							
F. Length of Main Beam							
G-1. Length of First Point							
G-2. Length of Second Point							
G-3. Length of Third Point							
G-4. Length of Fourth Point, If Present							
G-5. Length of Fifth Point, If Present							
G-6. Length of Sixth Point, If Present							
G-7. Length of Seventh Point, If Present							
H-1. Circumference at Smallest Place Between Burr and First Point							
H-2. Circumference at Smallest Place Between First and Second Points							
H-3. Circumference at Smallest Place Between Second and Third Points							
H-4. Circumference at Smallest Place Between Third and Fourth Points							
TOTALS							

ADD	Column 1		Exact Locality Where Killed:
	Column 2		Date Killed: Hunter:
	Column 3		Owner: Telephone #:
	Subtotal		Owner's Address:
SUBTRACT Column 4			Guide's Name and Address:
FINAL SCORE			Remarks: (Mention Any Abnormalities or Unique Qualities)

I, _____, certify that I have measured this trophy on _____
          PRINT NAME   MM/DD/YYYYY

at _____
        STREET ADDRESS   CITY   STATE/PROVINCE

and that these measurements and data are, to the best of my knowledge and belief, made in accordance with the instructions given.

Witness: _____ Signature: _____ I.D. Number [ ][ ][ ][ ]
                                              B&C OFFICIAL MEASURER

INSTRUCTIONS FOR MEASURING TYPICAL WHITETAIL AND COUES' DEER

All measurements must be made with a 1/4-inch wide flexible steel tape to the nearest one-eighth of an inch. (Note: A flexible steel cable can be used to measure points and main beams only.) Enter fractional figures in eighths, without reduction. Official measurements cannot be taken until the antlers have air dried for at least 60 days after the animal was killed.

A. Number of Points on Each Antler: To be counted a point, the projection must be at least one inch long, with the length exceeding width at one inch or more of length. All points are measured from tip of point to nearest edge of beam as illustrated. Beam tip is counted as a point but not measured as a point.

B. Tip to Tip Spread is measured between tips of main beams.

C. Greatest Spread is measured between perpendiculars at a right angle to the center line of the skull at widest part, whether across main beams or points.

D. Inside Spread of Main Beams is measured at a right angle to the center line of the skull at widest point between main beams. Enter this measurement again as the Spread Credit if it is less than or equal to the length of the longer main beam; if greater, enter longer main beam length for Spread Credit.

E. Total of Lengths of all Abnormal Points: Abnormal Points are those non-typical in location (such as points originating from a point or from bottom or sides of main beam) or extra points beyond the normal pattern of points. Measure in usual manner and enter in appropriate blanks.

F. Length of Main Beam is measured from the center of the lowest outside edge of burr over the outer side to the most distant point of the main beam. The point of beginning is that point on the burr where the center line along the outer side of the beam intersects the burr, then following generally the line of the illustration.

G-1-2-3-4-5-6-7. Length of Normal Points: Normal points project from the top of the main beam. They are measured from nearest edge of main beam over outer curve to tip. Lay the tape along the outer curve of the beam so that the top edge of the tape coincides with the top edge of the beam on both sides of the point to determine the baseline for point measurements. Record point lengths in appropriate blanks.

H-1-2-3-4. Circumferences are taken as detailed in illustration for each measurement. If brow point is missing, take H-1 and H-2 at smallest place between burr and G-2. If G-4 is missing, take H-4 halfway between G-3 and tip of main beam.

ENTRY AFFIDAVIT FOR ALL HUNTER-TAKEN TROPHIES

For the purpose of entry into the Boone and Crockett Club's® records, North American big game harvested by the use of the following methods or under the following conditions are ineligible:

   I.   Spotting or herding game from the air, followed by landing in its vicinity for the purpose of pursuit and shooting;
   II. Herding or chasing with the aid of any motorized equipment;
   III. Use of electronic communication devices, artificial lighting, or electronic light intensifying devices;
   IV. Confined by artificial barriers, including escape-proof fenced enclosures;
   V.   Transplanted for the purpose of commercial shooting;
   VI. By the use of traps or pharmaceuticals;
   VII. While swimming, helpless in deep snow, or helpless in any other natural or artificial medium;
   VIII. On another hunter's license;
   IX. Not in full compliance with the game laws or regulations of the federal government or of any state, province, territory, or tribal council on reservations or tribal lands;

I certify that the trophy scored on this chart was not taken in violation of the conditions listed above. In signing this statement, I understand that if the information provided on this entry is found to be misrepresented or fraudulent in any respect, it will not be accepted into the Awards Program and 1) all of my prior entries are subject to deletion from future editions of **Records of North American Big Game** 2) future entries may not be accepted.

FAIR CHASE, as defined by the Boone and Crockett Club®, is the ethical, sportsmanlike and lawful pursuit and taking of any free-ranging wild, native North American big game animal in a manner that does not give the hunter an improper advantage over such game animals.

The Boone and Crockett Club® may exclude the entry of any animal that it deems to have been taken in an unethical manner or under conditions deemed inappropriate by the Club.

Date: _____ Signature of Hunter: _____
                                             (SIGNATURE MUST BE WITNESSED BY AN OFFICIAL MEASURER OR A NOTARY PUBLIC.)

Date: _____ Signature of Notary or Official Measurer: _____

250 Station Drive
Missoula, MT 59801
(406) 542-1888

BOONE AND CROCKETT CLUB®
OFFICIAL SCORING SYSTEM FOR NORTH AMERICAN BIG GAME TROPHIES

NON-TYPICAL
WHITETAIL AND COUES' DEER

MINIMUM SCORES

	AWARDS	ALL-TIME
whitetail	185	195
Coues'	105	120

KIND OF DEER (check one)
☐ whitetail
☐ Coues'

Abnormal Points	
Right Antler	Left Antler

Detail of Point Measurement

SUBTOTALS	
E. TOTAL	

SEE OTHER SIDE FOR INSTRUCTIONS				COLUMN 1	COLUMN 2	COLUMN 3	COLUMN 4
A. No. Points on Right Antler		No. Points on Left Antler		Spread Credit	Right Antler	Left Antler	Difference
B. Tip to Tip Spread		C. Greatest Spread					
D. Inside Spread of Main Beams		SPREAD CREDIT MAY EQUAL BUT NOT EXCEED LONGER MAIN BEAM					
F. Length of Main Beam							
G-1. Length of First Point							
G-2. Length of Second Point							
G-3. Length of Third Point							
G-4. Length of Fourth Point, If Present							
G-5. Length of Fifth Point, If Present							
G-6. Length of Sixth Point, If Present							
G-7. Length of Seventh Point, If Present							
H-1. Circumference at Smallest Place Between Burr and First Point							
H-2. Circumference at Smallest Place Between First and Second Points							
H-3. Circumference at Smallest Place Between Second and Third Points							
H-4. Circumference at Smallest Place Between Third and Fourth Points							
			TOTALS				

ADD	Column 1		Exact Locality Where Killed:
	Column 2		Date Killed: Hunter:
	Column 3		Owner: Telephone #:
	Subtotal		Owner's Address:
SUBTRACT Column 4			Guide's Name and Address:
	Subtotal		Remarks: (Mention Any Abnormalities or Unique Qualities)
	ADD Line E Total		
	FINAL SCORE		

COPYRIGHT © 2000 BY BOONE AND CROCKETT CLUB®

I, _____ , certify that I have measured this trophy on _____
PRINT NAME   MM/DD/YYYYY

at _____
STREET ADDRESS   CITY   STATE/PROVINCE

and that these measurements and data are, to the best of my knowledge and belief, made in accordance with the instructions given.

Witness: _____ Signature: _____ I.D. Number | | | |
                                              B&C OFFICIAL MEASURER

INSTRUCTIONS FOR MEASURING NON-TYPICAL WHITETAIL AND COUES' DEER

All measurements must be made with a 1/4-inch wide flexible steel tape to the nearest one-eighth of an inch. (Note: A flexible steel cable can be used to measure points and main beams only.) Enter fractional figures in eighths, without reduction. Official measurements cannot be taken until the antlers have air dried for at least 60 days after the animal was killed.

- **A. Number of Points on Each Antler:** To be counted a point, the projection must be at least one inch long, with the length exceeding width at one inch or more of length. All points are measured from tip of point to nearest edge of beam as illustrated. Beam tip is counted as a point but not measured as a point.
- **B. Tip to Tip Spread** is measured between tips of main beams.
- **C. Greatest Spread** is measured between perpendiculars at a right angle to the center line of the skull at widest part, whether across main beams or points.
- **D. Inside Spread of Main Beams** is measured at a right angle to the center line of the skull at widest point between main beams. Enter this measurement again as the Spread Credit if it is less than or equal to the length of the longer main beam; if greater, enter longer main beam length for Spread Credit.
- **E. Total of Lengths of all Abnormal Points:** Abnormal Points are those non-typical in location (such as points originating from a point or from bottom or sides of main beam) or extra points beyond the normal pattern of points. Measure in usual manner and enter in appropriate blanks.
- **F. Length of Main Beam** is measured from the center of the lowest outside edge of burr over the outer side to the most distant point of the main beam. The point of beginning is that point on the burr where the center line along the outer side of the beam intersects the burr, then following generally the line of the illustration.
- **G-1-2-3-4-5-6-7. Length of Normal Points:** Normal points project from the top of the main beam. They are measured from nearest edge of main beam over outer curve to tip. Lay the tape along the outer curve of the beam so that the top edge of the tape coincides with the top edge of the beam on both sides of the point to determine the baseline for point measurement. Record point lengths in appropriate blanks.
- **H-1-2-3-4. Circumferences** are taken as detailed in illustration for each measurement. If brow point is missing, take H-1 and H-2 at smallest place between burr and G-2. If G-4 is missing, take H-4 halfway between G-3 and tip of main beam.

ENTRY AFFIDAVIT FOR ALL HUNTER-TAKEN TROPHIES

For the purpose of entry into the Boone and Crockett Club's® records, North American big game harvested by the use of the following methods or under the following conditions are ineligible:

- I. Spotting or herding game from the air, followed by landing in its vicinity for the purpose of pursuit and shooting;
- II. Herding or chasing with the aid of any motorized equipment;
- III. Use of electronic communication devices, artificial lighting, or electronic light intensifying devices;
- IV. Confined by artificial barriers, including escape-proof fenced enclosures;
- V. Transplanted for the purpose of commercial shooting;
- VI. By the use of traps or pharmaceuticals;
- VII. While swimming, helpless in deep snow, or helpless in any other natural or artificial medium;
- VIII. On another hunter's license;
- IX. Not in full compliance with the game laws or regulations of the federal government or of any state, province, territory, or tribal council on reservations or tribal lands;

I certify that the trophy scored on this chart was not taken in violation of the conditions listed above. In signing this statement, I understand that if the information provided on this entry is found to be misrepresented or fraudulent in any respect, it will not be accepted into the Awards Program and 1) all of my prior entries are subject to deletion from future editions of **Records of North American Big Game** 2) future entries may not be accepted.

FAIR CHASE, as defined by the Boone and Crockett Club®, is the ethical, sportsmanlike and lawful pursuit and taking of any free-ranging wild, native North American big game animal in a manner that does not give the hunter an improper advantage over such game animals.

The Boone and Crockett Club® may exclude the entry of any animal that it deems to have been taken in an unethical manner or under conditions deemed inappropriate by the Club.

Date: _____ Signature of Hunter: _____
                                              (SIGNATURE MUST BE WITNESSED BY AN OFFICIAL MEASURER OR A NOTARY PUBLIC.)

Date: _____ Signature of Notary or Official Measurer: _____

250 Station Drive
Missoula, MT 59801
(406) 542-1888

BOONE AND CROCKETT CLUB®
OFFICIAL SCORING SYSTEM FOR NORTH AMERICAN BIG GAME TROPHIES

	MINIMUM SCORES	
	AWARDS	ALL-TIME
mule deer	180	190
Columbia blacktail	125	135
Sitka blacktail	100	108

TYPICAL
MULE DEER AND BLACKTAIL DEER

KIND OF DEER (check one)
☐ mule deer
☐ Columbia blacktail
☐ Sitka blacktail

Detail of Point
Measurement

Abnormal Points	
Right Antler	Left Antler
SUBTOTALS	
TOTAL TO E	

SEE OTHER SIDE FOR INSTRUCTIONS		COLUMN 1	COLUMN 2	COLUMN 3	COLUMN 4
A. No. Points on Right Antler	No. Points on Left Antler	Spread Credit	Right Antler	Left Antler	Difference
B. Tip to Tip Spread	C. Greatest Spread				
D. Inside Spread of Main Beams	SPREAD CREDIT MAY EQUAL BUT NOT EXCEED LONGER MAIN BEAM				
E. Total of Lengths of Abnormal Points					
F. Length of Main Beam					
G-1. Length of First Point, If Present					
G-2. Length of Second Point					
G-3. Length of Third Point, If Present					
G-4. Length of Fourth Point, If Present					
H-1. Circumference at Smallest Place Between Burr and First Point					
H-2. Circumference at Smallest Place Between First and Second Points					
H-3. Circumference at Smallest Place Between Main Beam and Third Point					
H-4. Circumference at Smallest Place Between Second and Fourth Points					
TOTALS					

ADD	Column 1		Exact Locality Where Killed:	
	Column 2		Date Killed:	Hunter:
	Column 3		Owner:	Telephone #:
	Subtotal		Owner's Address:	
SUBTRACT Column 4			Guide's Name and Address:	
FINAL SCORE			Remarks: (Mention Any Abnormalities or Unique Qualities)	

I, _____, certify that I have measured this trophy on _____
PRINT NAME   MM/DD/YYYYY

at _____
STREET ADDRESS   CITY   STATE/PROVINCE

and that these measurements and data are, to the best of my knowledge and belief, made in accordance with the instructions given.

Witness: _____ Signature: _____ I.D. Number ☐ ☐ ☐
                                                        B&C OFFICIAL MEASURER

INSTRUCTIONS FOR MEASURING TYPICAL MULE AND BLACKTAIL DEER

All measurements must be made with a 1/4-inch wide flexible steel tape to the nearest one-eighth of an inch. (Note: A flexible steel cable can be used to measure points and main beams only.) Enter fractional figures in eighths, without reduction. Official measurements cannot be taken until the antlers have air dried for at least 60 days after the animal was killed.

- **A. Number of Points on Each Antler:** To be counted a point, the projection must be at least one inch long, with length exceeding width at one inch or more of length. All points are measured from tip of point to nearest edge of beam. Beam tip is counted as a point but not measured as a point.
- **B. Tip to Tip Spread** is measured between tips of main beams.
- **C. Greatest Spread** is measured between perpendiculars at a right angle to the center line of the skull at widest part, whether across main beams or points.
- **D. Inside Spread of Main Beams** is measured at a right angle to the center line of the skull at widest point between main beams. Enter this measurement again as the Spread Credit **if** it is less than or equal to the length of the longer main beam; if greater, enter longer main beam length for Spread Credit.
- **E. Total of Lengths of all Abnormal Points:** Abnormal Points are those non-typical in location such as points originating from a point (exception: G-3 originates from G-2 in perfectly normal fashion) or from bottom or sides of main beam, or any points beyond the normal pattern of five (including beam tip) per antler. Measure each abnormal point in usual manner and enter in appropriate blanks.
- **F. Length of Main Beam** is measured from the center of the lowest outside edge of burr over the outer side to the most distant point of the Main Beam. The point of beginning is that point on the burr where the center line along the outer side of the beam intersects the burr, then following generally the line of the illustration.
- **G-1-2-3-4. Length of Normal Points:** Normal points are the brow tines and the upper and lower forks as shown in the illustration. They are measured from nearest edge of main beam over outer curve to tip. Lay the tape along the outer curve of the beam so that the top edge of the tape coincides with the top edge of the beam on both sides of point to determine the baseline for point measurement. Record point lengths in appropriate blanks.
- **H-1-2-3-4. Circumferences** are taken as detailed in illustration for each measurement. If brow point is missing, take H-1 and H-2 at smallest place between burr and G-2. If G-3 is missing, take H-3 halfway between the base and tip of G-2. If G-4 is missing, take H-4 halfway between G-2 and tip of main beam.

ENTRY AFFIDAVIT FOR ALL HUNTER-TAKEN TROPHIES

For the purpose of entry into the Boone and Crockett Club's® records, North American big game harvested by the use of the following methods or under the following conditions are ineligible:

- I. Spotting or herding game from the air, followed by landing in its vicinity for the purpose of pursuit and shooting;
- II. Herding or chasing with the aid of any motorized equipment;
- III. Use of electronic communication devices, artificial lighting, or electronic light intensifying devices;
- IV. Confined by artificial barriers, including escape-proof fenced enclosures;
- V. Transplanted for the purpose of commercial shooting;
- VI. By the use of traps or pharmaceuticals;
- VII. While swimming, helpless in deep snow, or helpless in any other natural or artificial medium;
- VIII. On another hunter's license;
- IX. Not in full compliance with the game laws or regulations of the federal government or of any state, province, territory, or tribal council on reservations or tribal lands;

I certify that the trophy scored on this chart was not taken in violation of the conditions listed above. In signing this statement, I understand that if the information provided on this entry is found to be misrepresented or fraudulent in any respect, it will not be accepted into the Awards Program and 1) all of my prior entries are subject to deletion from future editions of **Records of North American Big Game** 2) future entries may not be accepted.

FAIR CHASE, as defined by the Boone and Crockett Club®, is the ethical, sportsmanlike and lawful pursuit and taking of any free-ranging wild, native North American big game animal in a manner that does not give the hunter an improper advantage over such game animals.

The Boone and Crockett Club® may exclude the entry of any animal that it deems to have been taken in an unethical manner or under conditions deemed inappropriate by the Club.

Date: _____ Signature of Hunter: _____
                                            (SIGNATURE MUST BE WITNESSED BY AN OFFICIAL MEASURER OR A NOTARY PUBLIC.)

Date: _____ Signature of Notary or Official Measurer: _____

250 Station Drive
Missoula, MT 59801
(406) 542-1888

BOONE AND CROCKETT CLUB®
OFFICIAL SCORING SYSTEM FOR NORTH AMERICAN BIG GAME TROPHIES

MINIMUM SCORES

AWARDS	ALL-TIME
215	230

NON-TYPICAL MULE DEER

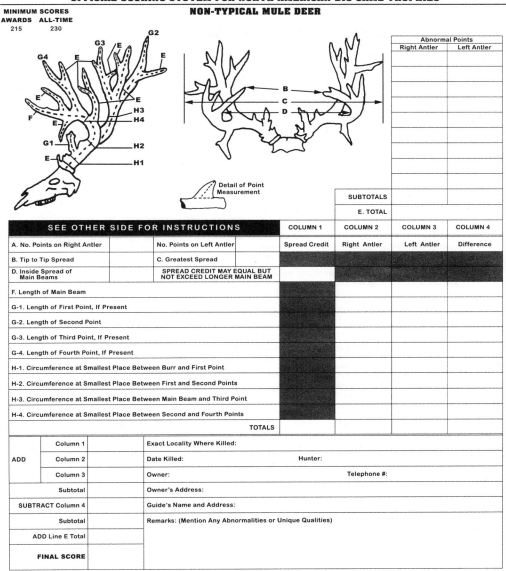

Detail of Point Measurement

Abnormal Points	
Right Antler	Left Antler
SUBTOTALS	
E. TOTAL	

SEE OTHER SIDE FOR INSTRUCTIONS			COLUMN 1	COLUMN 2	COLUMN 3	COLUMN 4
A. No. Points on Right Antler		No. Points on Left Antler	Spread Credit	Right Antler	Left Antler	Difference
B. Tip to Tip Spread		C. Greatest Spread				
D. Inside Spread of Main Beams		SPREAD CREDIT MAY EQUAL BUT NOT EXCEED LONGER MAIN BEAM				
F. Length of Main Beam						
G-1. Length of First Point, If Present						
G-2. Length of Second Point						
G-3. Length of Third Point, If Present						
G-4. Length of Fourth Point, If Present						
H-1. Circumference at Smallest Place Between Burr and First Point						
H-2. Circumference at Smallest Place Between First and Second Points						
H-3. Circumference at Smallest Place Between Main Beam and Third Point						
H-4. Circumference at Smallest Place Between Second and Fourth Points						
		TOTALS				

ADD	Column 1		Exact Locality Where Killed:	
	Column 2		Date Killed:	Hunter:
	Column 3		Owner:	Telephone #:
	Subtotal		Owner's Address:	
SUBTRACT Column 4			Guide's Name and Address:	
	Subtotal		Remarks: (Mention Any Abnormalities or Unique Qualities)	
	ADD Line E Total			
	FINAL SCORE			

I, _____ , certify that I have measured this trophy on _____
PRINT NAME   MM/DD/YYYYY

at _____
STREET ADDRESS   CITY   STATE/PROVINCE

and that these measurements and data are, to the best of my knowledge and belief, made in accordance with the instructions given.

Witness: _____ Signature: _____ I.D. Number [ ][ ][ ][ ]
                                                            B&C OFFICIAL MEASURER

INSTRUCTIONS FOR MEASURING NON-TYPICAL MULE DEER

All measurements must be made with a 1/4-inch wide flexible steel tape to the nearest one-eighth of an inch. (Note: A flexible steel cable can be used to measure points and main beams only.) Enter fractional figures in eighths, without reduction. Official measurements cannot be taken until the antlers have air dried for at least 60 days after the animal was killed.

A. Number of Points on Each Antler: To be counted a point, the projection must be at least one inch long, with length exceeding width at one inch or more of length. All points are measured from tip of point to nearest edge of beam as illustrated. Beam tip is counted as a point but not measured as a point.

B. Tip to Tip Spread is measured between tips of main beams.

C. Greatest Spread is measured between perpendiculars at a right angle to the center line of the skull at widest part, whether across main beams or points.

D. Inside Spread of Main Beams is measured at a right angle to the center line of the skull at widest point between main beams. Enter this measurement again as the Spread Credit if it is less than or equal to the length of the longer main beam; if greater, enter longer main beam length for Spread Credit.

E. Total of Lengths of all Abnormal Points: Abnormal Points are those non-typical in location such as points originating from a point (exception: G-3 originates from G-2 in perfectly normal fashion) or from bottom or sides of main beam, or any points beyond the normal pattern of five (including beam tip) per antler. Measure each abnormal point in usual manner and enter in appropriate blanks.

F. Length of Main Beam is measured from the center of the lowest outside edge of burr over the outer side to the most distant point of the main beam. The point of beginning is that point on the burr where the center line along the outer side of the beam intersects the burr, then following generally the line of the illustration.

G-1-2-3-4. Length of Normal Points: Normal points are the brow tines and the upper and lower forks as shown in the illustration. They are measured from nearest edge of main beam over outer curve to tip. Lay the tape along the outer curve of the beam so that the top edge of the tape coincides with the top edge of the beam on both sides of point to determine the baseline for point measurement. Record point lengths in appropriate blanks.

H-1-2-3-4. Circumferences are taken as detailed in illustration for each measurement. If brow point is missing, take H-1 and H-2 at smallest place between burr and G-2. If G-3 is missing, take H-3 halfway between the base and tip of G-2. If G-4 is missing, take H-4 halfway between G-2 and tip of main beam.

ENTRY AFFIDAVIT FOR ALL HUNTER-TAKEN TROPHIES

For the purpose of entry into the Boone and Crockett Club's® records, North American big game harvested by the use of the following methods or under the following conditions are ineligible:

I. Spotting or herding game from the air, followed by landing in its vicinity for the purpose of pursuit and shooting;
II. Herding or chasing with the aid of any motorized equipment;
III. Use of electronic communication devices, artificial lighting, or electronic light intensifying devices;
IV. Confined by artificial barriers, including escape-proof fenced enclosures;
V. Transplanted for the purpose of commercial shooting;
VI. By the use of traps or pharmaceuticals;
VII. While swimming, helpless in deep snow, or helpless in any other natural or artificial medium;
VIII. On another hunter's license;
IX. Not in full compliance with the game laws or regulations of the federal government or of any state, province, territory, or tribal council on reservations or tribal lands;

I certify that the trophy scored on this chart was not taken in violation of the conditions listed above. In signing this statement, I understand that if the information provided on this entry is found to be misrepresented or fraudulent in any respect, it will not be accepted into the Awards Program and 1) all of my prior entries are subject to deletion from future editions of **Records of North American Big Game** 2) future entries may not be accepted.

FAIR CHASE, as defined by the Boone and Crockett Club®, is the ethical, sportsmanlike and lawful pursuit and taking of any free-ranging wild, native North American big game animal in a manner that does not give the hunter an improper advantage over such game animals.

The Boone and Crockett Club® may exclude the entry of any animal that it deems to have been taken in an unethical manner or under conditions deemed inappropriate by the Club.

Date: _____ Signature of Hunter: _____
                                          (SIGNATURE MUST BE WITNESSED BY AN OFFICIAL MEASURER OR A NOTARY PUBLIC.)

Date: _____ Signature of Notary or Official Measurer: _____

All score sheets reprinted courtesy of the Boone and Crockett Club,
250 Station Dr., Missoula, MT 59801, 406/542-1888,
www.boone-crockett.org.

Bibliography

Most of the facts and figures in this book come from different books and scientific writings. I've prepared a list of literature which I consulted in the preparation of my manuscript for anyone wishing to continue on their own research into whitetail and mule deer.

Atkeson, T.D., R.L. Marchinton, and K.V. Miller. 1988. *"The American Midland Naturalist* Vol. 120, No. 1 (January), pp. 194–200.

Brown, R. 1983. Antler Development in Cervidae: In *Proceedings of the First International Symposium of the Caesar Kleberg Wildlife Research Institute.* Texas A&I University, Kingsville, TX.

Darner, Kirt. 1983. *How to Find Giant Bucks.* Walsworth Publishing, Marceline, MO.

Gates, Jay M. III. 1988. *Bucks I Have Taken (And Bucks That Got Away).* Deer Hunter Enterprises, Kingman, AZ.

Halls, Lowell K. 1984. *White-tailed Deer, Ecology and Management.* A Wildlife Management Institute Book. Stackpole Books, Harrisburg, PA.

Hull, Russell. 1984. *Trophy Bowhunting—The Supreme Challenge.* G&R Trophy Products, Hill City, KS.

Kline, Lee. 1987. *Bowhunting Big Game Records of North America.* Third Edition. Pope and Young Club, Placerville, CA.

Kufeld, Roland C., O.C. Wallmo, and Charles Feddema. 1973. "Foods of the Rocky Mountain Mule Deer." USDA Forest Service Research Paper RM-111.

Marchinton, R.L., K.L. Johansen, and K.V. Miller. 1988. Behavioral Components of White-tailed Deer Scent Marking: Social and Seasonal Effects. Paper presented at Chemical Signals in Vertebrates V Conference. Oxford, England.

Marchinton, R.L., J.R. Fudge, J.C. Fortson, K.V. Miller, and D. Dobie. 1987. Genetic Stock and Environment as Factors in Production of Record Class Antlers. Presented at the *XVIII Congress of International Union of Game Biologists.* Krakow, Poland. (In Press.)

McGuire, Bob. 1983. *Advanced Whitetail Hunting Techniques.* B.H. P. Books, Johnson City, TN.

Miller, Karl V., O.E. Rhodes, Jr., T.R. Litchfield, M.H. Smith, and R.L. Marchinton. 1987. Reproductive Characteristics of Yearling and Adult Male White-tailed Deer. *Proceedings of 41st Annual Conference Southeastern Association Fish and Wildlife Agencies.* Mobile, AL. (In Press.)

Nesbitt, W.H., and Jack Reneau. 1999. *Records of North American Big Game,* 11th Edition. The Boone and Crockett Club, Dumfries, VA.

Nesbitt, W.H., and Jack Reneau. 1987. *Records of North American Whitetail Deer.* The Boone and Crockett Club, Dumfries, VA.

Reneau, Jack, and Susan Reneau. 1983. *Colorado's Biggest Bucks and Bulls.* Colorado Big Game Trophy Records, Inc., Colorado Springs, CO.

Richardson, L.W., H.A. Jacobson, R.J. Muncy, and C.J. Perkins. 1981. *Acoustics of White-tailed Deer.* Journal of Mammology Vol 64 pp. 245–252.

Thornberry, Russell. 1982. *Trophy Deer of Alberta.* Greenhorn Publications Ltd., Rocky Mountain House, Alberta, Canada.

Wallmo, Olof C. 1981. *Mule and Black-tailed Deer of North America.* A Wildlife Management Institute Book. University of Nebraska Press, Lincoln and London.

Wensel, Gene. 1988. *One Man's Whitetail.* Gene Wensel, Hamilton, MT.

———. 1981. *Hunting Rutting Whitetails.* Gene Wensel, Hamilton, MT.

Zumbo, Jim. 1981. *Hunting America's Mule Deer.* Winchester Press, Piscataway, NJ.

Index